Quod scriptura, non iubet vetat

The Latin translates, "What is not commanded in scripture, is forbidden:'

On the Cover: Baptists rejoice to hold in common with other evangelicals the main principles of the orthodox Christian faith. However, there are points of difference and these differences are significant. In fact, because these differences arise out of God's revealed will, they are of vital importance. Hence, the barriers of separation between Baptists and others can hardly be considered a trifling matter. To suppose that Baptists are kept apart solely by their views on Baptism or the Lord's Supper is a regrettable misunderstanding. Baptists hold views which distinguish them from Catholics, Congregationalists, Episcopalians, Lutherans, Methodists, Pentecostals, and Presbyterians, and the differences are so great as not only to justify, but to demand, the separate denominational existence of Baptists. Some people think Baptists ought not teach and emphasize their differences but as E.J. Forrester stated in 1893, "Any denomination that has views which justify its separate existence, is bound to promulgate those views. If those views are of sufficient importance to justify a separate existence, they are important enough to create a duty for their promulgation ... the very same reasons which justify the separate existence of any denomination make it the duty of that denomination to teach the distinctive doctrines upon which its separate existence rests." If Baptists have a right to a separate denominational life, it is their duty to propagate their distinctive principles, without which their separate life cannot be justified or maintained.

Many among today's professing Baptists have an agenda to revise the Baptist distinctives and redefine what it means to be a Baptist. Others don't understand why it even matters. The books being reproduced in the *Baptist Distinctives Series* are republished in order that Baptists from the past may state, explain and defend the primary Baptist distinctives as they understood them. It is hoped that this Series will provide a more thorough historical perspective on what it means to be distinctively Baptist.

The Lord Jesus Christ asked, *"And why call ye me, Lord, Lord, and do not the things which I say?"* (Luke 6:46). The immediate context surrounding this question explains what it means to be a true disciple of Christ. Addressing the same issue, Christ's question is meant to show that a confession of discipleship to the Lord Jesus Christ is inconsistent and untrue if it is not accompanied with a corresponding submission to His authoritative commands. Christ's question teaches us that a true recognition of His authority as Lord inevitably includes a submission to the authority of His Word. Hence, with this question Christ has made it forever impossible to separate His authority as King from the authority of His Word. These two principles—the authority of Christ as King and the authority of His Word—are the two most fundamental Baptist distinctives. The first gives rise to the second and out of these two all the other Baptist distinctives emanate. As F.M. Iams wrote in 1894, "Loyalty to Christ as King, manifesting itself in a constant and unswerving obedience to His will as revealed in His written Word, is the real source of all the Baptist distinctives:' In the search for the *primary* Baptist distinctive many have settled on the Lordship of Christ as the most basic distinctive. Strangely, in doing this, some have attempted to separate Christ's Lordship from the authority of Scripture, as if you could embrace Christ's authority without submitting to what He commanded. However, while Christ's Lordship and Kingly authority can be isolated and considered essentially for discussion's sake, we see from Christ's own words in Luke 6:46 that His Lordship is really inseparable from His Word and, with regard to real Christian discipleship, there can be no practical submission to the one without a practical submission to the other.

In the symbol above the Kingly Crown and the Open Bible represent the inseparable truths of Christ's Kingly and Biblical authority. The Crown and Bible graphics are supplemented by three Bible verses (Ecclesiastes 8:4, Matthew 28:18-20, and Luke 6:46) that reiterate and reinforce the inextricable connection between the authority of Christ as King and the authority of His Word. The truths symbolized by these components are further emphasized by the Latin quotation - *quod scriptura, non iubet vetat*— i.e., "What is not commanded in scripture, is forbidden:' This Latin quote has been considered historically as a summary statement of the regulative principle of Scripture. Together these various symbolic components converge to exhibit the two most foundational Baptist Distinctives out of which all the other Baptist Distinctives arise. Consequently, we have chosen this composite symbol as a logo to represent the primary truths set forth in the *Baptist Distinctives Series*.

PÆDOBAPTISM
EXAMINED

ABRAHAM BOOTH
1734-1806

PÆDOBAPTISM EXAMINED

ON THE

PRINCIPLES, CONCESSIONS, AND REASONINGS

OF THE

MOST LEARNED PÆDOBAPTISTS.

WITH

REPLIES

TO THE

ARGUMENTS and OBJECTIONS

OF

DR. WILLIAMS AND MR. PETER EDWARDS.

BY ABRAHAM BOOTH

With a Biographical Sketch of the Author by John Franklin Jones

IN THREE VOLUMES.

VOLUME 1

Printed for Ebenezer palmer,
18 Paternoster-Row,
LONDON
MDCCCXXIX

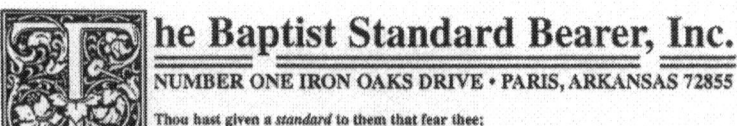

The Baptist Standard Bearer, Inc.
NUMBER ONE IRON OAKS DRIVE • PARIS, ARKANSAS 72855

Thou hast given a *standard* to them that fear thee;
that it may be displayed because of the truth.
-- Psalm 60:4

Reprinted 2006

by

THE BAPTIST STANDARD BEARER, INC.
No. 1 Iron Oaks Drive
Paris, Arkansas 72855
(479) 963-3831

THE WALDENSIAN EMBLEM
lux lucet in tenebris
"The Light Shineth in the Darkness"

ISBN# 1579783732

ADVERTISEMENT

TO THIS

THIRD EDITION.

The Treatise of the late Reverend Abraham Booth, entitled "Pædobaptism Examined," &c. having become very scarce, and being regarded by us, as a standard work on that subject, we feel great pleasure in seeing this new and complete Edition presented to the Public.

While we are aware that the character of the learned, pious, and venerated Author, and the admitted sterling and intrinsic worth of these publications, render any recommendation from us quite superfluous, we must acknowledge our obligations to John Satchell, Esq. for the compilation of a complete Index to the whole, and also for the great attention that gentleman has paid to the Work, while passing through the press;

ADVERTISEMENT.

and to Mr. EBENEZER PALMER, the publisher, who has spared no expense in rendering this Edition worthy the patronage of the public.

(Signed)   JOHN RIPPON, D.D. London.

ISAIAH BIRT, Hackney.

WILLIAM STEADMAN, D. D. President of the Baptist Academy, Bradford, Yorkshire.

WILLIAM NEWMAN, D.D. London.

JOSEPH KINGHORN, Norwich.

JOSEPH IVIMEY, London.

THOMAS GRIFFIN, London.

GEORGE PRITCHARD, London.

F. A. COX, LL.D. Hackney.

ISAAC MANN, A.M. London.

MICAH THOMAS, President of the Baptist Academy, Abergavenny.

T. C. EDMONDS, A.M. Cambridge.

THOMAS MORGAN, Birmingham.

RICHARD PENGILLY, Newcastle-upon-Tyne.

W. H. MURCH, Theological Tutor of the Baptist Academy, Stepney.

JOHN DYER, Secretary to the Baptist Missionary Society.

SAMUEL SAUNDERS, Liverpool.

BENJAMIN GODWIN, Classical Tutor of the Baptist Academy, Bradford, Yorkshire.

EDWARD STEANE, Camberwell.

THOMAS PRICE, London.

JAMES EDWARDS, Shipley.

LONDON,
November 26, 1828.

PREFACE.

Having observed, for a course of years, that many of the most learned and eminent Pædobaptists, when theological subjects are under discussion, frequently argue on such principles, admit of such facts, interpret various texts of scripture in such a manner, and make such concessions, as are greatly in favour of the Baptists; I extracted a number of passages from their publications, and made many references to others, which I thought might be fairly pleaded against infant sprinkling.* On reviewing these quotations and *memoranda*, I concluded, merely for my own private use, to employ some leisure hours in transcribing and arranging them, under different heads of the Pædobaptist controversy.

When I had made a considerable progress in the work of transcription and arrangement, Mr. Henry's Treatise on Baptism fell into my hands.† Prepossessed

---

* N.B. As the terms *infant sprinkling,* wherever they occur in this Treatise, are used merely by way of distinction, and not of contempt; so the expressions, Pædo-*baptism,* and infant *baptism,* are used in compliance with general custom; not because the author thinks an infant is *baptized,* on whom water has been solemnly poured or sprinkled.

† The Monthly Reviewers, after pronouncing this " the most popular defence of infant baptism and of the mode of sprinkling that hath appeared," very justly add; "Some reflections, however, which he casts on their [the Baptists] mode of baptism (which, perhaps, the editor might as well have omitted,)—are *scarcely consistent with that candour and liberality* which might have been expected from the author, and which, had he been now living, he would probably have discovered." Monthly Review, for April 1784, p. 313. My reader may see in what an illiberal manner Mr. Henry has reflected on the baptismal immersion, and some animadversions upon it, Vol. I. Chap. IV. Reflect. VII. p. 231, this edition.

of a high regard for the character of that worthy author, I perused the treatise with care. Not convinced, however, by any thing contained in it, that the sprinkling of infants is an appointment of Christ; and being fully persuaded that Mr. Henry had employed his learning and zeal in defence of an unscriptural ceremony; I determined to prosecute the subject with greater application, and to publish the result of my enquiries and thoughts concerning it. Such was the occasion of this publication.

The method of arguing here adopted, is far from being either novel or unfair: it has been used by the spirit of infallibility against Pagans;* by Christians againsts the Jews;† by the Reformed against Roman Catholics; and by Protestant Dissenters against our English Conformists.‡ It is, in a particular manner, employed and pursued by the author of Popery confuted by Papists; a book, indeed, which I had not seen, till the far greater part of these pages was composed. The following words of that anonymous writer may be justly applied, *mutatis mutandis*, to the present subject. " I will call the church of Rome for a witness to our cause; and if she do not plainly confess the antiquity of our tenets, and the novelty of her own; if she herself do not proclaim the universality of our faith; if she do not

---

* Acts xvii. 28; Titus i. 12.

† So Witsius, for instance, in his Judæus Christianizans, p. 276—402; and Hoornbeekius, Contra Judæos, l. ii. c. i.; l. iv. c. ii.

‡ A remarkable instance of this kind, is mentioned by Mr. Peirce, who having informed us, that Bp. Hoadly and Mr. Ollyfe wrote against Dr. Calamy, in defence of their own Conformity, adds; " It happened, as is very usual with our adversaries, that these two defended conformity upon different principles. Dr. Calamy, therefore, in his answer, set their arguments one against another, and so handsomely defended our cause—that the Dissenters looked upon themselves obliged, not only to the doctor for his defence, but to his antagonists, who gave him the occasion of writing." Vindicat. of Dissent. part i. p. 282.

confess that we are both in the more certain and safe way in the Protestant church, I will neither refuse the name"*— of an *Anabaptist*, nor any part of that censure which is due to such a character.

Though I do not approve of every sentiment contained in the following quotations produced on behalf of the Baptists, yet, as the generality of those Pædobaptists, from whose writings the extracts were made, must be considered as persons of learning and eminence in the several communions to which they belonged; and as no small number of them were famous professors in Protestant universities, their declarations, in the *argumentum ad hominem*, cannot but have the utmost weight. Nor can their testimonies, concerning the signification of Greek terms, or the practice of the church in former ages, be hastily rejected, without incurring the imputation of gross ignorance, of enormous pride, or of shameful precipitancy. Considering the quotations adduced, and the characters of those writers from whom they were taken, it is presumed, that the leading ideas of another paragraph, in Popery confuted by Papists, may be here applied. " If these witnesses had been ignorant and unlearned men, or excommunicate persons in their own church — there might be some plea why their testimonies should not be admitted. But when the points in question are articles of their own creed; when they are witnessed by popes, by councils, by cardinals, by bishops, by learned doctors and schoolmen in their own church, on our behalf, and against their own tenets; I see no cause why I should not demand judgment in defence of our church, and trial of our cause. It is the law of God and man, ' I will judge thee out of thine own mouth.' "† Thus also Mr. Claude, when confuting the Roman Catholics; " I will make their authors that are not suspected by them

---

* Popery confuted by Papists, sect. viii. p. 43.
† Ut supra, sect. x. p. 152.

to speak, whose passages I will faithfully translate, which they may see in the originals if they will take the pains."* To which I may add the following words of another Pædobaptist, which are considered by him as a kind of axiom. "The confessions of enemies, and circumstances favourable to any body of men, collected from the writings of their adversaries, are deserving of particular regard." † *Testimonium Adversarii contra se Validissimum.*

The reader will find, that our auxiliaries in this dispute are both numerous and respectable; for while a multitude of Pædobaptists reluctantly concede this, that, and the other, in support of immersion upon a profession of faith, those who may be justly esteemed impartial judges of the evidence produced on both sides of this debate, very cheerfully award the cause to us. Yes, those disinterested Friends, the people called Quakers, without so much as one exception occurring to observation, pour in their attestations on our behalf, and treat infant sprinkling as a merely human invention.

Though I am not conscious of having misrepresented the meaning of any Pædobaptist, whose testimony is produced, yet, as the quotations are very numerous, and as many of them are translated from the Latin, it is possible that mistakes may be discovered, by those readers who accurately compare my quotations with the writers from whom they were taken. Such mistakes, it is hoped, however, will be found comparatively few, and of trifling importance. I am persuaded,

---

* Defence of Reformation, part ii. p. 127.

† Dr. Priestley's Letters to Dr. Horsley, p. 137. " What," says the learned Chamier, " can be a more convincing proof, than that which arises from the confession of an adversary?" Panstrat. tom. iv. l. viii. c. ix. § 4. Conformably to which, Mr. Travis, when speaking of a particular fact, says : It " is proved by the best testimony possible, the acknowledgment of an adversary." Letters to Mr. Gibbon, lett. iii. edit. 2nd.

therefore, that the judicious and candid will impute them to inadvertency, or ignorance, rather than to a disingenuous intention.

A learned foreigner has justly observed, that while all Christians deservedly acknowledge the Bible as a divine revelation, it has fallen out, that every one desires to find in that sacred volume whatever in his own imagination seems divine; and that men are so wonderfully happy in this respect, as hardly ever to complain of being disappointed, or of having lost their labour, in searching the sacred records for what they wanted; but all, in the language of self-gratulation, repeat the old ευρηκα of Archimedes, *I have found it! I have found it!**—"It is but too frequently," says Mr. Placette, "that we see truth clashing with our temporal interests, with the secret bias of our hearts, with our most violent passions, and with other things which we make the ordinary measures of our conduct. Whenever this happens, we ought to despise these vain interests, to stifle these inclinations, to repress these criminal motions, and in all our proceedings to stick close to the unalterable rule of truth. But we cannot bring ourselves to such a resolution: on the quite contrary, we endeavour to ply and bend this rule; and instead of conforming ourselves to it, would have it conform to ourselves. Not being able to change it, because it is really constant and perpetual, our next attempt is to change our own judgment about it. We try to persuade ourselves out of its directions; and, with much pains and labour, we come at length to succeed in our design. No man can, indeed, be ignorant of that mighty sway which the heart bears over the understanding. According to the order of nature, and the intention of its divine Author, it is the understanding that ought to guide the heart, and to be set up as its faithful lamp and light; but in common experience we see the reverse of this.

---

* Werenfelsii Opuscula, p. 376, 377.

The heart draws aside the understanding that way to which itself inclines; and if it fail to do this immediately, and by absolute command, it carries its point by time and stratagem.—It hinders the intellective power from attending to such reasons as are disagreeable to itself, and keeps it perpetually busied about the opposite arguments.—It makes us look on the former with a secret desire, that they may prove false; and on the latter, with a most unjust wish that we may find them true: and then, no wonder if it be successful in its arts, and if it effectually lead us into error."*

Very important is that declaration of our Lord; "If any man will do his will, he shall know of the doctrine, whether it be of God, or whether I speak of myself:" with which the following direction of Bp. Taylor agrees: "If a man enquires after truth earnestly, as after things of great concernment; if he prays to God to assist, and uses those means which are in his hand, and are his best for the finding it; if he be indifferent to any proposition, and loves it not for any consideration, but because he thinks it true; if he will quit any interest rather than lose a truth; if he dares own what he hath found and believed; and if he loves it so much the more, by how much he believes it more conducing to piety and the honour of God; he hath done what a good and wise man should do: he needs not regard what any man threatens, nor fear God's anger when a man of another sect threatens him with damnation. For he that heartily endeavours to please God, and searches what his will is, that he may obey it, certainly loves God; and nothing that loves God can perish."†—Such is the rule of our duty in this respect; but as we are far from being insensible of our liability to be influenced by prejudices and corrupt affections in our enquiries after the mind of God

---

* Christian Casuist, b. ii. chap. xxiii.

† Ductor Dubitant. p. 755. See Mr. Locke's Conduct of the Understanding, sect. xi.

respecting the ordinance of baptism, it is no small satisfaction to find, that our most learned and eminent opposers have said so much in favour of immersion, upon a profession of faith, as the appointment of Jesus Christ. For, as Dr. Owen observes, "Truth and good company will give a modest man confidence."*

In proportion as I have become acquainted with the Popish controversy, and with that between our English Episcopalians and Protestant Dissenters, the more have I been convinced, that there is a remarkable similarity between the arguments used by Roman Catholics in defence of Popery; by our Conformists, in support of their Establishment; and by Pædobaptists in general, in favour of infant sprinkling. It gives me, therefore, peculiar pleasure to find, that the general principles on which I oppose Pædobaptism, are the very same with those upon which the Reformed have always proceeded, in confuting the Papal system, and upon which Protestant Dissenters argue against the constitution, government, and unscriptural rites of the English church. By these considerations, I am the more confirmed in my disapprobation of infant sprinkling. Agreeable to which are the following words of Dr. Calamy, when speaking of the persecuted Nonconformists, and of their leading principles: "They were the more confirmed in their adherence to these principles, by finding the most eminent divines of the church forced to make use of the very same in their noble defence of the Reformation against the Romanists; and, indeed, it seemed to them remarkable, that those which were reckoned by the clergy the most successful weapons against the Dissenters, should be the same that are used by the Papists against the Protestant Reformation."†

In the course of my reflections on the language and

---

* Vindication against Sherlock, p. 41.
† Nonconformist's Memorial, Introduct. p. 53.

arguments of some Pædobaptists, the reader will meet with a few strokes of pleasantry. It is presumed, however, that he will have no reason to complain of *ill temper*, or of a want of benevolence to any from whom I conscientiously differ. For though it appears, from several quotations, that the harshest things have been said of the Baptists by some of their opposers;* and though it must be acknowleged the Baptists have sometimes retorted in an unbecoming manner; yet, as every one must confess, that "the wrath of man worketh not the righteousness of God," so it may be observed of the cause that is here pleaded,

Non tali auxilio, nec defensoribus istis.

Some persons, to avoid the labour of thinking, and to keep their consciences easy in a compliance with prevailing custom, pronounce baptism *a controverted point;* and then infer, that all disputes about the mode and subjects of the ordinance, are not only stale and unimportant, but unworthy the character of any who profess a warm regard for the interests of moral virtue, or for the person, the atonement, and the grace of Jesus Christ. That baptism has been the subject of much controversy must be allowed; but then I will say, with Bp. Hurd; "Show me the question in religion, or even in common morals, about which learned men have not disagreed; nay, show me a single text of scripture, though ever so plain and precise, which the perverseness or ingenuity of interpreters has not drawn into different, and often contrary meanings. What then shall we conclude? that there is no truth in religion, no certainty in morals, no authority in sacred scripture? If such conclusions as these be carried to their utmost length, in what else can

---

* Dr. Featley acknowledges that, when writing against the Baptists, "he could hardly dip his pen in any other liquor than the juice of gall." In Crossby's Hist. Bap. vol. i. Pref. p. 5. See Backus's Church Hist. of New Eng. vol. ii. p. 323, 324.

they terminate, but absolute universal scepticism?"* I may add, in the words of Dr. Waterland, "As long as religion [or any particular branch of it,] is held in any value or esteem, and meets with opposers, it must occasion warm disputes. Who would wish that it should not? What remedy is there for it, while men are men, which is not infinitely worse than the disease? A total contempt of religion, [or an universal and absolute indifference for any particular article in it,] might end all disputes about it; nothing else will."†

It must, indeed, be acknowledged, that positive rites, forms of worship, and ecclesiastical order, are not of equal importance with doctrines that immediately respect the object of our worship, as rational creatures; the ground of our hope, as criminals deserving to perish; or the source of our blessedness, as intended for an immortal existence. Nor is the most punctual performance of a ritual service, detached from faith in Christ and benevolence to man, worthy of being compared with truly devotional principles and virtuous tempers, though attended with much ignorance relating to the positive parts of divine worship. But is this a sufficient reason for treating the law of baptism as of little or no importance — as if it were obsolete, or as if our great Legislator had no meaning when he enacted it? That mutilation of the sacred supper, which is practised in the Romish communion, has been sharply opposed and loudly condemned by all denominations of Protestants: and is it not lawful, is it not matter of duty, to oppose and condemn such an outrage on divine authority and primitive example? Are we not required to *contend earnestly*, but with virtuous dispositions, *for* every branch of *that faith which was once delivered to the saints?* If, therefore, infants be solemnly sprinkled by divine right, it must be the indispensable duty of Pædobaptists to

---

* Introduct. to Study of Prophecies, serm. viii.
† Importance of Doct. of Trinity, p. 206.

contend for it; but if, on the contrary, infant sprinkling be a human invention, the Baptists are equally bound to oppose it, as deserving to be banished from the worship of God, where it has long usurped the place of a divine institution. If Christ be the only Lord and Lawgiver in his own kingdom, then certainly it is far from being a matter of indifference whether the laws which he enacted be regarded or not: for, with equal reason, might any one question, whether our Saviour should be *believed*, in what he declares; as whether he should be *obeyed*, in what he commands. Under the fair pretext of charity, forbearance, and catholicism, we might, with Melancthon and other adiaphorists in the sixteenth century, consider the doctrine of justification by faith alone, the number of the sacraments, the jurisdiction claimed by the pope, extreme unction, the observation of Popish festivals, and several superstitious rites, as things *indifferent*: * or, with others, we might assert the innocence of mental error in matters of doctrine and of worship; and so, by unavoidable consequence, render the Bible itself of little worth.

It has been often asserted, both by ancients and moderns, that the followers of Christ should never seek for peace at the expense of truth, nor of religious duty. Thus, for example, Hilary, bishop of Poictiers: "The name of *peace* is, indeed, very specious, and the mere appearance of *unity* has something splendid in it; but who knows not, that the church and the gospel acknowledge no other peace than that which comes from Jesus Christ, that which he gave to his apostles before the glory of his passion, and that which he left in trust with them by his eternal command, when he was about to leave them?"†——Dr. Owen: "We are not engaged in an enquiry merely after

---

* See Mosheim's Eccles. Hist. cent. xvi. sect. iii. part. ii. § 28. Venemæ Hist. Eccles. secul. xvi. § 156.

† In Claude's Defence of Reformation, part iii. p. 3.

peace, but after peace with *truth*. Yea, to lay aside the consideration of truth, in a disquisition after peace and agreement, in and about spiritual things, is to exclude a regard unto God and his authority, and to provide only for ourselves.... The rule of unity, as it is supposed to comprise all church communion, falls under many restrictions. For herein the special commands of Christ, and institutions of the gospel committed unto our care and observance, falling under consideration, our practice is precisely limited unto those commands, and by the nature of those institutions.... We are not obliged to accommodate any of the ways or truths of Christ unto the sins and ignorance of men."*—— J. A. Turrettin: " There ought to be no charity without truth; no charity that is an injury to truth; no charity which causes us to offend against the truth.... For this ought not to be called *charity*, but a confederation and a conspiracy of error. ' We wish,' says Jerome, ' for peace; and we not only wish, but also pray for it: but it is the peace of Christ, true peace, peace in which no war is involved.' Otherwise, as Nazianzen teaches, ' war is more eligible than that peace which separates us from God.' "†—— Mr. Henry: " The method of our prayer must be, first for truth, and then for peace; for such is the method of the wisdom that is from above; it *is first pure, then peaceable*."‡ With this both prophets and apostles agree; for their language is, *Love the truth, and peace—Speaking the truth in love.* §

The folly and impiety of pleading for charity and peace, at the expense of divine truth and of religious duty, are well represented and properly chastised by a Pædobaptist author, in the following manner: " A considerable succedaneum for the Christian unity, is the Catholic charity; which is like the charity commended

---

* Discourse on Evangelical Love and Peace, p. 17, 24, 233.
† Oratio de Theologo Veritatis et Pacis Studioso.
‡ Exposit. on Rom. xv. 5.
§ Zech. viii. 19; Eph. iv. 15.

by Paul, in only this one instance, that it *groweth exceedingly*.—Among the stricter sort, it goes under the name of *forbearance*. We shall be much mistaken if we think that, by this soft and agreeable word, is chiefly meant the tenderness and compassion inculcated by the precepts of Jesus Christ and his apostles. It strictly means an agreement to differ quietly about the doctrines and commandments of the gospel, without interruption of visible fellowship. They distinguish carefully between *fundamentals*, or things necessary to be believed and practised; and *circumstantials*, or things that are indifferent. Now, whatever foundation there may be for such a distinction in human systems of religion, it certainly looks very ill-becoming in the churches of Christ, to question how far HE is to be believed and obeyed. Our modern churches.... have nearly agreed to hold all those things indifferent which would be inconvenient and disreputable; and to have communion together, in observing somewhat like the customs of their forefathers. Many of the plainest sayings of Jesus Christ and the apostles are treated with high contempt, by the advocates of this forbearance.—The common people are persuaded to believe, that all the ancient institutions of Christianity were merely local and temporary, excepting such as the learned have agreed to be suitable to these times; or, which have been customarily observed by their predecessors. But it would well become the doctors in divinity to show, by what authority any injunction of God can be revoked, besides *his own;* or, how any man's conscience can be lawfully released by custom, example, or human authority, from observing such things as were instituted by the apostles of Christ in his name.... This corrupt forbearance had no allowed place in the primitive churches. The apostle, in the Epistle to the Ephesians, required of them, to adorn their vocation ' with all lowliness and meekness, with long-suffering, forbearing one another, IN LOVE.' But had they dispensed with the laws of Christ, for convenience and ease, it had been forbearing one another in hatred; for those laws were expressions of his love; the most fervent love that was ever shown among men, directed by infallible wisdom. Whosoever, therefore, would obliterate them, or any how attempt to change them, must either suppose himself wiser than Jesus Christ, or a greater friend to mankind. He must be moved, either by an enormous self-conceit, or by the spirit of malevolence.... The more thinking part of religious men, observing what great mischiefs have arisen from contentions about truth,—have found it most desirable to let truth alone, and to concern themselves chiefly about living profitably in civil society. To be of some religion, is but decent; and the interests of human life require that it be popular and compliant. If men have different notions of Jesus Christ, his divinity, his sacrifice, his kingdom, and the customs of his religion, even from what the apostles seemed to have; charity demands that we think well of their religious characters, notwithstanding this. It is unbecoming the modesty of wise men to be confident on any side; and *contending earnestly* for opinions, injures the peace of the Christian church. Thus kind and humble is modern charity! Instead of rejoicing in or with *the truth*, it rejoiceth in contemplating the admirable piety that may be produced from so many different, yea, opposite principles.... The Christians of old time were taught, not to dispute about the institutions of their LORD, but to observe them thankfully; and hereby they expressed their affection to him and to each other. If that affection be granted to be more important than the tokens of it, it would be unjust to infer that the latter have no obligation; which would imply, that Christ and the apostles meant nothing by their precepts. The Methodists have not, indeed, gone so far as their spiritual Brethren [the Quakers] have done, in rejecting all external ceremonies; but they are taught to believe, that all concern about the ancient order and customs of the Christians is mere party-spirit, and injurious to the devout exercises of the heart. Thus the modern charity vaunts itself, in answering better purposes than could be accomplished by keeping the words of Christ. It produces a more extensive and generous communion, and animates the devotion of men, without perplexing them by uncertain doctrines or rigorous self-denial.... Although it supposes some revelation from God, and some honour due to Jesus Christ, it claims a right to dispense with both—to choose what, in his doctrine and religion, is fit to be believed and observed."*

While, however, we think it our duty with a resolute perseverance to maintain the purity and importance of baptism, as a divine institution; we are far from considering ourselves as the only disciples of Christ, or our own communities as the only Christian churches. Nor is an idea of that kind justly inferable from our denying communion at the Lord's table to Pædobaptists.† Respecting this particular, Dr. Owen says; "There is no necessity that any should deny all them to be true churches, from whom they may have just reason to withdraw their communion.... When we judge of our own communion with them, it is not upon this question, Whether they are true churches, or not? as though the determination of our practice did depend solely thereon. For as we are not called to judge of the being of their constitution, as to the substance of it, unless they are openly judged in the scripture, as in the case of idolatry and persecution persisted in; so a determination of the truth of their constitution, or that they are true churches, will not presently resolve us in our duty, as to communion with them.... It is most unwarrantable rashness

---

* Strictures upon Modern Simony, p. 48—55. Luther, in his vehement manner, says; " Maledicta sit charitas quæ servatur cum jactura doctrinæ fidei, cui omnia cedere debent, charitas, apostolus, angelus e cœlo." Comment. in Epist. ad Galat.

† See my Apology for the Baptists.

and presumption, yea, an evident fruit of ignorance, or want of love, or secular private interest, when, upon lesser differences, men judge churches to be no true churches, and their ministers to be no true ministers."* The same excellent author says; " There is nothing more clear and certain, than that our Lord Christ.... never joined with [the Jews] in the observance of their own traditions and pharisaical impositions, but warned all his disciples to avoid them and refuse them; whose example we desire to follow: for, concerning all such observances in the church, he pronounced that sentence, 'Every plant that my heavenly Father hath not planted shall be rooted up.'"†

It is against what the author considers as an error in sentiment, and a corruption of worship, that the following Examination of Pædobaptism makes its appearance: *errors*, not *persons*, are here opposed. He thinks, with Mr. Leigh, that we should "distinguish between loving of men's persons and their errors;"‡ and, with Bp. Burnet, that "whatever moderation or charity we may owe to men's persons, we owe none at all to their errors, and to that frame which is built on and supported by them."§ Nay, as Dr. Waterland in another case observes, "While we are of a contrary judgment, it cannot but be guilty practice and conduct in us, and very great too, to smother our sentiments, or not to bear our testimony in such a way as Christ has appointed, against all notorious corruptions, either of faith, or worship, or doctrine."‖

Should this Examination of Pædobaptism have the honour of being regarded as deserving an answer, and

---

* Discourse on Evangelical Love and Church-Peace, p. 82, 83, 84. See Plain Reasons for Dissenting from the Church of England, part i. reason i.; and Stapferi Theolog. Polem. tom. i. p. 518.

† Enquiry into Orig. and Nature of Churches, p. 253.

‡ Treatise on Relig. and Learning, b. i. chap vii.

§ In Mr. Robinson's Plan of Lectures, Motto.

‖ Importance of Doct. of Trinity, p. 135.

should any of our opposers write against me, it will not avail to refute some particular parts of the work, detached from the general principles on which I proceed. No; the *data*, the *principal grounds* of reasoning, which are adopted from Pædobaptists themselves, must be constantly kept in view, or nothing to the honour of infant sprinkling will be effected. For as the grand principles on which my argumentation proceeds, and whence my general conclusions are drawn, are those of Protestants when contending with Papists, and those of Nonconformists when disputing with English Episcopalians; it will be incumbent on such opposer to show, either that the principles themselves are false, or that my reasoning upon them is inconclusive. Now, as I do not perceive how any Protestant can give up those principles, without virtually admitting the superstitions of Popery; nor how they can be deserted by any Dissenter, without implicitly renouncing his Nonconformity; so I conclude, that the whole force of any opponent must be employed in endeavouring to prove, that I have reasoned inconsequentially from those principles. That this might be easily proved, I am not at present convinced; and whether any of our Pædobaptist Brethren will consider this publication as of sufficient importance to excite such an attempt, is to me uncertain.

To the conclusions inferred from those very numerous concessions which our opposers have made, (and my reader will find that many of the greatest eminence among them have been the most free in making concessions,) it may, perhaps, be objected: " Notwithstanding all their concessions, they continued in the profession and practice of infant baptism." Granted; but then it should be considered, that this objection is quite futile; because I professedly argue against Pædobaptism, on the principles, reasonings, and concessions of *Pædobaptists*. Besides, though such an exception to my conclusions expresses a fact, yet it pays the consistency of the authors concerned but a poor compliment. In this light similar concessions from Roman Catholics have always been viewed by Protestants; of which the reader will meet with various instances in the course of this work.*

Being fully persuaded, that I appear in defence of a divine institution and of apostolic practice, I earnestly commend this publication to the blessing of that sublime Being, who " worketh all things after the counsel of his will." Sincerely praying, that evangelical truth and experimental religion, that purity of worship and the practice of holiness, may flourish among all denominations of Christians, I conclude in the following words of Lord Bacon: " Read, not to contradict or confute, nor to believe and take for granted, nor to find talk and discourse, but to weigh and consider."†

A. BOOTH.

Goodman's Fields,
Aug. 8, 1787.

---

* See particularly Vol. I. p. 268, 269, this edition.
† In Dr. Edwards's Discourse concerning Truth and Error, p. 456.

ERRATA.

Vol. I.	p. 28. l. 24, *for* supercription,	*read* superscription.
	48, l. 22, — ἑαυτου,	— ἑαυτον.
Vol. II.	p. 25, l. 7, — childisly,	— childishly.
	105, l. 18, — μαθητευειν,	— μαθητευειν.
	142, l. 2, — parishoners,	— parishioners.
	431, l. 29, — destitue,	— destitute.
Vol. III.	p. 156, l. 30, — σοματα,	— σωματα.
	175, l. 5, — fortels,	— foretells.
	189, l. 5, — πνευηατι,	— πνευματι.
	236, l. 10, — proxility,	— prolixity.
	246, l. 24, — essense,	— essence.
	331, l. 34, — ominious,	— ominous.

GENERAL CONTENTS.

VOL. I.

PÆDOBAPTISM EXAMINED.

PART I.

The Mode of Administration.

Page

CHAPTER I.—Concerning the Nature, Obligation, and Importance of Positive Institutions in Religion - - - 1—39
CHAP. II.—Concerning the Signification of the Terms, Baptize and Baptism - - - - - - - - 40—131
CHAP. III.—The Design of Baptism; or, the Facts and Blessings represented by it, both in regard to our Lord and his Disciples - - - - - - - - 132—170
CHAP. IV.—The Practice of John the Baptist, of the Apostles, and of the Church in succeeding Ages, in regard to the Manner of administering the Ordinance of Baptism - 171—238
CHAP. V.—The present Practice of the Greek and Oriental Churches, in regard to the Mode of Administration - 239—244
CHAP. VI.—The Design of Baptism more fully expressed by Immersion, than by Pouring or Sprinkling - - - 245—252
CHAP. VII.—The Reasons, Rise, and Prevalence of Pouring or of Sprinkling, instead of Immersion - - - - 253—300

PART II.

The proper Subjects.

CHAPTER I.—No Express Precept nor Plain Example for Pædobaptism, in the New Testament - - - - 303—367
CHAP. II.—No Evidence of Pædobaptism, before the latter End of the Second, or the Beginning of the Third Century - 368—411
CHAP. III.—The high Opinion of the Fathers concerning the Utility of Baptism, and the Grounds on which they proceeded in administering that Ordinance to Infants, when Pædobaptism became a prevailing Practice - - - - - - 412

VOL. II.

Page

CHAP. IV.—Concerning the Modern Grounds of Pædobaptism; namely, Jewish Proselyte Baptism—External Covenant Relation—Jewish Circumcision—Particular Passages of Scripture—and Apostolic Tradition.
SECTION 1.—Jewish Proselyte Baptism - - - - 1—33

GENERAL CONTENTS.

                    Page
SECT. 2.—External Covenant Relation - - - - - 33—68
SECT. 3.—Jewish Circumcision - - - - - - 68—97
SECT. 4.—Particular Passages of Scripture: viz.
 § 1.—Matt. xxviii. 19 - - - - - - - 97—134
 § 2.—Gen. xvii. 7 - - - - - - - 134—152
 § 3.—Ezek. xvi. 20, 21 - - - - - - 153—157
 § 4.—Matt. xix. 14 - - - - - - - 157—164
 § 5.—John iii. 5 - - - - - - - 164—170
 § 6.—Acts ii. 39 - - - - - - - 170—177
 § 7.—Acts xvi. 15, 33; 1 Cor. i. 16 - - - - 177—185
 § 8.—Rom. xi. 16 - - - - - - - 186—189
 § 9.—1 Cor. vii. 14 - - - - - - 189—231
SECT. 5.—Apostolic Tradition, and the Impracticability of pointing out the Time when Pædobaptism commenced - - 231—251
CHAP. V.—Infant Baptism and Infant Communion introduced about the same Time, and supported by similar Arguments - - - - - - - - - 252—279
General Remarks - - - - - - - 279—342

PART III.

REPLY TO DR. WILLIAMS.

CHAP. I.—Concerning the Title of Dr. Williams's Book, his Professions, and his Conduct, relative to this Controversy, 353—395
CHAP. II.—On the little Regard Dr. Williams pays to Quotations produced from Pædobaptists; and on his Disposition to extort Concessions from the Baptists - - - - - 396—406
CHAP. III.—On Dr. W.'s Pretence, that his Book includes a full Reply to my Pædobaptism Examined - - - - 407—454

VOL. III.

                    Page
CHAPTER IV.—Concerning Positive Institutions and Analogical Reasoning - - - - - - - - 1—119
CHAP. V.—On the Meaning of the Words Baptize and Baptism, as represented by Dr. W. - - - - - - 120—236
CHAP. VI.—The General Principles on which Dr. W. founds the Right of Infants to Baptism - - - - - 237—325
CHAP. VII.—Infant Communion and Infant Baptism compared - - - - - - - - - 326—344
CHAP. VIII.—On the Utility and Importance of Baptism, as represented by Dr. W. - - - - - - - 345—366

PART IV.

REPLY TO MR. PETER EDWARDS.

MR. DORE'S PREFACE - - - - - - - 369—388
THE REPLY - - - - - - - - 389—460

PART I.

PÆDOBAPTISM EXAMINED,
&c.

THE MODE OF ADMINISTRATION.

PÆDOBAPTISM EXAMINED,

&c.

CHAPTER I.

Concerning the Nature, Obligation, and Importance of Positive Institutions in Religion.

Dr. Doddridge.—" Those are called positive institutions or precepts, which are not founded upon any reasons known to those to whom they are given, or discoverable by them, but which are observed merely because some superior has commanded them." Lectures, Definit. lxxi. p. 238.

2. Bp. Taylor.—" All institutions sacramental, and positive laws, depend not upon the nature of the things themselves, according to the extension or diminution of which our obedience might be measured; but they depend wholly on the will of the Lawgiver, and the will of the Supreme, being actually limited to this specification, this manner, this matter, this institution: whatsoever comes besides, it hath no foundation in the will of the Legislator, and therefore can have no warrant or authority. That it be obeyed, or not obeyed, is all the question and all the variety. If it can be obeyed, it must; if it cannot, it must be let alone.... Whatsoever depends upon a divine law or institution, whatsoever God wills, whatsoever is appointed instrumental to the signification of a mystery, or to the collation of a grace or a power, he that does any thing of his own head, either must be a despiser of God's will, or must suppose himself the author of a grace, or else to do nothing at

all in what he does; because all his obedience and all the blessing of his obedience depend upon the will of God, which ought always to be obeyed when it can: and when it cannot, nothing can supply it, because the reason of it cannot be understood.... All positive precepts, that depend upon the mere will of the lawgiver, admit no degrees, nor suppletory and commutation; because in such laws we see nothing beyond the words of the law, and the first meaning, and the named instance: and therefore it is that *in individuo* which God points at; it is that in which he will make the trial of our obedience; it is that in which he will so perfectly be obeyed, that he will not be disputed with or enquired of, *why* and *how*, but just according to the measures there set down; *so, and no more and no less, and no otherwise*. For when the will of the lawgiver is *all the reason*, the first instance of the law is *all the measure*, and there can be no product but what is just set down. No parity of reason can infer any thing else; because there is no reason but the will of God, to which nothing can be equal, because his will can be but one." Ductor Dub. b. ii. chap. iii. § 14, 18.

3. Mr. Reeves.—" The distinction of obligations between moral and positive duties is to be understood with great caution. For though the goodness of a law be a great motive and inducement to obedience, yet the formal reason of obligation does not arise from the goodness of a law, but from the authority and will of the legislator. God commands a thing which was before indifferent; therefore that thing is as much a law as if it was never so good in its own nature: he forbade the eating of a tree in the midst of the garden, which without that prohibition had been indifferent. But Adam, and in him all his posterity, was condemned for the breach of a law purely positive.... When God therefore says, that he 'will have mercy and not sacrifice,' it is not to be understood as if God would have

any of his laws broken; but, as our Saviour explains it, 'These ought ye to have done, and not to leave the other undone.' I ask then, what are natural laws? Why, what we conclude merely from the light of nature that God has commanded or forbidden, either to be believed or done. What then are *positive* laws? Why, what we know to be the will of God by his *express word* only. In both cases then we see, that it is the will of God, and not the goodness of the thing, or the manner of the discovery, which induces the obligation." Apologies, vol. ii. p. 217, 218, edit. 1709.

4. Dr. Fiddes.—"The distinction between positive law and moral law is founded in this difference: the subject matter of positive law is something to which we are antecedently under no obligation, and which only obliges by virtue of its being enacted, and perhaps to a certain limited period. The subject matter of a moral law is, on the other hand, something antecedently, in the visible reason of it, obligatory to us, and the obligation thereof will always continue unchangeably the same.... By a positive command, I understand an *express* declaration made by competent authority, whether concerning things to be done, or to be omitted." Theolog. Pract. b. i. chap. vi. p. 50; b. ii. part i. chap. i. p. 105.

5. Dr. Owen.—"Positive institutions are the free effects of the will of God, depending originally and *solely* on revelation, and which therefore have been various and actually changed." Discourse concerning the Holy Spirit, b. i. chap. iii. § 3.

6. Buddeus.—"The obligation by which men are bound rightly to use positive appointments, is to be derived from the moral law itself; by which it is manifest, that men are obliged to do all those things by which their eternal felicity may be promoted.... God had the wisest reasons, why he would have an appointment administered in this or the other manner. It is not

lawful, therefore, for men to alter any thing, or to mutilate the appointment. Thus the sacraments are to be used, not according to our own pleasure, but in the manner appointed by God." Institut. Theol. Moral. pars i. c. v. § 18; pars ii. c. ii. § 50. Lips. 1727.

7. Bp. Butler.—" Moral precepts are precepts, the reasons of which we see; positive precepts are precepts, the reasons of which we do not see. Moral duties arise out of the nature of the case itself, prior to external command; positive duties do not arise out of the nature of the case, but from external command; nor would they be duties at all, were it not for such command, received from Him whose creatures and subjects we are. But the manner in which the nature of the case, or the fact of the relation is made known, this doth not denominate any duty either positive or moral.... The reason of positive institutions, in general, is very obvious; though we should not see the reason why such particular ones are pitched upon, rather than others. Whoever, therefore, instead of cavilling at words, will attend to the thing itself, may clearly see, that positive institutions in general, as distinguished from this or that particular one, have the nature of moral commands, since the reasons of them appear. Thus, for instance, the external worship of God is a moral duty, though no particular mode of it be so. Care then is to be·taken, when a comparison is made between positive and moral duties, that they be compared no farther than as they are different; no farther than as the former are positive, or arise out of mere external command, the reasons of which we are not acquainted with; and as the latter are moral, or arise out of the apparent reason of the case, without such external command. Unless this caution be observed, we shall run into endless confusion. Now this being premised, suppose two standing precepts enjoined by the same authority; that in certain conjunctures it is impossible to obey both; that the

former is moral, *i. e.* a precept of which we see the reasons, and that they hold in the particular case before us; but that the latter is positive, *i. e.* a precept of which we do not see the reasons: it is indisputable that our obligations are to obey the former, because there is an apparent reason for this preference, and none against it. . . . As it is one of the peculiar weaknesses of human nature, when, upon a comparison of two things, one is found to be of greater importance than the other, to consider this other as of scarce any importance at all; it is highly necessary that we remind ourselves how great presumption it is, to make light of positive institutions of divine appointment; that our obligations to obey all God's commands whatever, are absolute and indispensable; and that commands merely positive, admitted to be from him, lay us under a *moral* obligation to obey them; an obligation moral in the strictest and most proper sense." Analogy of Religion, part ii. chap. i.

8. Dr. J. G. King.—" Positive duties, having no obligation in the reason of things, can have no foundation but in the *express words* of the institutor, from which alone they derive their authority." Rites and Ceremonies of the Greek Church in Russia, p. 12.

9. Mr. Jonathan Edwards.—" Those laws whose obligation arises from the nature of things, and from the general state and nature of mankind, as well as from God's positive revealed will, are called *moral* laws. Others, whose obligation depends merely upon God's positive and arbitrary institution, are not moral: such as the ceremonial laws, and the precepts of the gospel about the two sacraments.". . . . Positive " precepts are the greatest and most proper trial of obedience; because in them the mere authority and will of the legislator is the sole ground of the obligation, and nothing in the nature of the things themselves; and therefore they are the greatest trial of any person's respect to that authority and will." Sermons, p. 232.

Hartford, 1780. Sermons on Imp. Sub. p. 79. Edinb. 1785.

10. Bp. Burnet.—" Sacraments are positive precepts, which are to be measured ONLY by the institution, in which there is not room left for us to carry them any farther." Exposit. Thirty-nine Articles, Art. xxvii. p. 279, edit. 5.

11. Mr. Steele.—"Sacraments depend merely upon their institution : hence doth their being result, and upon this their matter and signification do depend. The institution, with the element, makes the sacrament; and so the *only* rule and balance for them must needs be their institution." Morning Exercise against Popery, Serm. xxii. p. 764, 765.

12. Stapferus.—" Visible signs are the matter of sacraments.... Signs are either natural or arbitrary. Sacred ceremonies are of the latter kind. But whatever an arbitrary sign be, it is such by institution." Institut. Theolog. Polem. tom. i. cap. iii. § 1623, 1624.

13. Dr. Goodman.—The term *institution* " implies a setting up *de novo*, or the appointing that to become a duty which was not knowable, or at least not known to be so, before it became so appointed. For this word, *institution*, is that which we use to express a positive command by, in opposition to that which is moral in the strictest sense, and of natural obligation. Now it is very evident, that all things of this nature ought to be appointed *very plainly and expressly*, or else they can carry no obligation with them; for seeing the whole reason of their becoming matter of law or duty, lies in the will of the legislator, if that be not *plainly* discovered, they cannot be said to be instituted, and so there can be no obligation to observe them; because where ' there is no law, there can be no transgression ;' and a law is no law, in effect, which is not sufficiently promulgated." Preserv. against Popery, title viii. p. 7.

14. Dr. Sherlock.—" What is matter of institution depends wholly upon the divine will and pleasure; and though all men will grant, that God and Christ have always great reason for their institution, yet it is not the reason, but the authority which makes the institution. Though we do not understand the reasons of the institution, if we see the command we must obey; and though we could fancy a great many reasons why there should be such an institution, if no such institution appears, we are free, and ought not to believe there is such an institution, because we think there are reasons to be assigned why it should be." Preserv. against Pop. title ix. p. 419.

15. Anonymous.—" We deny that there are any accidental parts of instituted worship; for if instituted, (*i. e.* commanded by Christ,) it cannot be accidental, (*i. e.* left to our liberty, as what may or may not be done without sin.) If accidental, it may be a part of somewhat else, but of the instituted worship of Christ it cannot be.... Circumstances of worship (as such) undetermined by the Lord, to be appointed by men, we deny.... These circumstances are such as, without which the worship of God is perfect, or it is not. If the *first*, we need them not; they are vain, fruitless, having without them a perfect worship. If the *second*, the worship God hath commanded, as it comes out of his hands, without human additaments, is imperfect: but this is little less than blasphemy.... To assert, it is lawful to conform to any part of instituted worship, without warrant from the scripture, reflects sadly upon the wisdom and faithfulness of Christ. For, either he was not wise enough to foresee that such a part of worship was or would be requisite; or had not faithfulness enough to reveal it: though the scripture compares him to Moses for faithfulness, who revealed the whole will of God, to the making of a pin in the tabernacle.... We had thought, that the perfection of scripture had consisted

in this, that the *whole* of that obedience that God requires of us, had therein been *stated* and *enjoined;* for which end we conceive it was at first commanded to be written, and hitherto by the wonderful gracious providence of the Lord continued to us. The accidentals of worship are either *part* of that obedience we owe to God, or they are not. If not, how came they to be such parts of worship, as without them we are interdicted to perform it? or, indeed, whence is it, that we are tendering them up to God, when all our worship is nothing else but the solemn tender of that obedience that we owe to him? If they are, then there is some part of our obedience that is not prescribed in the scripture: then is the scripture imperfect, and that with respect to the main end for which it was given forth, viz. to indoctrinate and direct us in the whole of that obedience that God requires of us." Jerubbaal, chap. ii. p. 154, 155, 156.

16. Chamierus.—"This is a most certain principle, that the sacraments are nothing, except from their institution; and this institution must be divine. Whatever, therefore, was invented by man, does not belong to a sacrament. . . . The use of the sacraments depends upon their institution. . . . Nothing belongs to the institution of the Lord's supper, that is not *essential* to it. . . . If the whole essence of the sacrament be of divine institution, certainly, that being violated, the sacrament itself cannot stand." Panstrat. tom. iv. l. v. c. xvi. § 23; l. vii. c. iii. § 1; c. xv. § 7; l. viii. c. ii. § 3.

17. Gerhardus.—"Seeing that a sacrament depends entirely on the appointment of God, when we do not what God has appointed, it certainly will not be a sacrament." Loci Theolog. tom. iv. De Sacram. § 52. Francof. 1657.

18. Dr. Clagett.—" To conclude, that in matters depending upon the pleasure of God, he hath done that which seemeth best to our reason, is to suppose that

in these things we know what is best, no less than God doth; that we have weighed all the conveniences and inconveniences of either side; the advantages and disadvantages of every thing that lies before us; the arguments for, and the objections against this or that, with the same exactness, wherein they are comprehended in his infinite understanding.... When once the institutions of God are revealed and testified to us, we must not only conclude that they are wise and good, because they are his; but we ought also to take notice of those footsteps of divine wisdom and goodness, which are discernible in them: and the more that a wise man considers and understands their ends and usefulness, the more worthy of their Author he will find them to be. But their congruity to our reason is not the *proof* of their divine institution; since there are very many things, which to our finite understandings would appear as useful and as reasonable, but which yet God hath not instituted.... Even where the appointments of God are evident, that wisdom and goodness which I can discover in them, is not the proper ground of my assurance that he hath established them; for that is no other than *the evidence of the institution.* Nor can that discovery alone give me the least assurance, that in making such provision he hath not been wanting to our needs; for the reason of that assurance is this, that it is *He*, it is God, I say, *that hath made such provision for us.* When it once appears what God hath instituted in order to our salvation, and no more, we are to conclude that this is enough in its kind, because it is all that God hath done. But for that other kind of arguing, that God hath been wanting to us in his institutions, if he has not instituted [this or that,] and therefore he *has* instituted it, I leave to those whose conclusions need it; very much desiring them to consider, *what a cause that must be* which drives them to such bold reasonings as these are." Preserv. against Pop. title vii. p. 93.

19. Dr. Grosvenor.*—" The diminutive things that have been said by some, of the positive appointments in religion, and the extravagant things that have been said by others, are two extremes which true reasoning leads nobody into, on either hand. It is as contrary to the nature of things to make *nothing* of them, as to make them *the whole* of religion. To know exactly the regard that is due to them, is to find out the rank and order they are placed in by Him who has appointed them.... I shall lay together what I have to say on this subject, under the following propositions.

" Proposition I. Some things are absolutely necessary to salvation, and in their own nature. We call those things absolutely necessary, without which there can be no salvation at all. Thus, a mind suited to the happiness intended by the word *salvation*, is absolutely necessary; or holiness, ' without which no man shall see the Lord.' All the titles in the world to heaven, can never give the pleasure of heaven, without a suitableness to its enjoyments. Fitness here is as the eye to the delights of colours and prospects; the ear, to the pleasures of harmony; and as the palate, to those of taste and relish; that is, a capacity of enjoyment. As there must be an animal nature for animal pleasures, and a rational nature for rational ones; so there must be the divine and heavenly nature, for those that are divine and heavenly. No man would care to live even with a God whom he did not love.

" Prop. II. No merely positive appointments are necessary in this sense, *i. e.*, absolutely and in their own nature. If there never had been a sacrament in the world, I might have been happy without it: you cannot say so of love to God and likeness to him....

" Prop. III. A disposition to obey divine orders, wherever they are discerned, either positive or moral, is

---

* Anonymous, indeed, but supposed to be Dr. Benj. Grosvenor.

part of that 'holiness, without which no man shall see the Lord.' I may be saved without a sacrament; but I cannot be saved without a disposition to obey God's authority wherever I see it. A sacrament is a positive rite, and not to be compared with moral virtue: but is not a disposition to obey God's order, moral virtue and Christian grace? Or can there be any moral virtue, or Christian grace, without a disposition to obey the authority of Christ, wherever I discern it? Surely, obedience to God's command is a moral excellence, though the instances of that obedience may lie in positive rites. The command to Abraham, to sacrifice his son, was a positive order, and a very strange one too; seemingly opposite to some moral orders given out before: and yet his disposition to obey, when he was sure of a divine warrant in the case, has set him as the head of all the believing world; as the hero of faith, the father of the faithful, and the friend of God. The command of sprinkling the blood of the passover upon the doorposts of the Israelites, was an external positive rite: if there had not been a disposition to obey that order, it would have cost some lives; as it had like to have done to Moses, the neglect of circumcising his child, as good a man as he was in other respects. Was not the forbidden fruit a positive instance? an external thing? Setting aside the divine prohibition, there was nothing immoral in eating of that, any more than of any other tree; but disobedience is an immorality, let the instance be what it will.

"Prop. IV. The sincerity and truth of such a disposition, is best known by its being uniform and universal. (Psalm cxix. 6; Col. iv. 3.) The Author of our religion has told us, and added his example to his word, that 'thus it becomes us to fulfil all righteousness,' and so ordered himself to be baptized. Baptism was a positive rite, an external thing; and yet he calls it *righteousness*. Such righteousness as became Him who was the Holy One of God; became Him who had intrinsically no need of any outward ceremony; whose inward purity was perfectly divine: and if it became Him to fulfil such a sort of righteousness, it can hardly become any who pretend to be his followers to neglect it.

" Prop. V. As a competent evidence is supposed needful, for any external rite being of divine appointment; so again, a wilful ignorance of that evidence, or not discerning it, through criminal causes, will not excuse from guilt. The criminal causes of not seeing the evidence for such appointments, are, in this case, as in many other cases, non-enquiry, laziness, prejudice, lust, pride, and passion. That an ignorance owing to these causes, cannot be pleaded for a neglect of any of God's appointments, is so much the general sense of all casuists, that I shall only add here, THAT IT IS AT EVERY MAN'S PERIL, HOW HE COMES NOT TO KNOW THE WILL OF GOD, AS WELL AS NOT TO DO IT. We must look to it, how we came not to see the appointment, and must answer that to God and our own conscience. It is not enough to say, *Lord, I did not know it was appointed;* when the answer may justly be, *You never enquired into the matter: you never allowed yourself to think of it: or if you did, you resolved in your mind that you would not be convinced. You made the most of every cavil, but never minded the solution to any of your objections.*

" Prop. VI. The duty and necessity of any external rites, and particularly of sacraments, have their measures and degrees. And here I apprehend, the measures of the duty and necessity of sacraments to be,—The *authority* enjoining. When we see the broad seal of heaven, where there is the divine warrant, ' Thus saith the Lord;' it is worse than trifling, to cavil and say, *It is but an external rite.*—The *degree* of evidence of their being so appointed. Where the evidence is not so clear, the obligation is weakened in proportion; but where the terms are plainly binding, and strongly commanding, there the obligation is not to be evaded. When positive appointments and moral duties cannot be both performed; when the one or the other must be omitted, the preference is given to the moral and spiritual duty.—The *stress* God lays upon them for the time they are to continue. Sprinkling the blood of the passover upon the posts of the doors, was not at all necessary in itself to preservation from the destroying angel; but God laid that stress upon it. The oracle, or the mercy-seat, was a mere positive appointment. God could have met Moses any where else; but God laying that stress upon it, measures the degree of the necessity of observing that order: 'There will I meet thee, and commune with thee,' Exod. xxv. 22. Moses might have reasoned with himself, *God is every where, and can meet me any where, if he pleases, and if he does not please, he will not do it here;* and so have missed the honour of communion with his Maker; broke the divine order; lost the benefit of the oracle; and offended God, by the neglect.—The *reason* and *end* of them. If there should be any reasons of these injunctions that we do not know, it is sufficient that they are known to God. Our obedience is always a *reasonable service* whether we know God's reasons for the injunction or not. His command is always reason enough for us....

"Prop. VII. He that commands the outward positive rite, commands the inward and moral temper at the same time. He does not say, *Do this*, without concerning himself *how* it is done; whether in a manner suitable to an end appointed or not.... There is no such command of his, as enjoins the outward act without the inward temper and disposition.

"Prop. VIII. Positive appointments for such uses and ends as these, are of a quite different nature from arbitrary impositions, with which they are too often confounded. The idea of *arbitrary* I think, implies a weakness incompatible to the divine nature; whose perfection it is, to do nothing but for some wise reason, and for some good end....

"Prop. IX. Though no positive appointments are absolutely necessary, yet the contempt of them, and of the divine authority discerned in them, cannot consist with holiness. This contempt may be shown—by contemptuous language....a careless attendance....a total neglect....and by prostituting them to persons that do contemn them, and to purposes that are unworthy....

"To conclude: External rites are nothing without the inward temper and virtue of mind; the inward temper is but pretended to, in many cases, without the external rites, and is acquired, promoted, and evidenced by the use of them. If 'I give all my goods to the poor, and have not charity;' there is the external act, without the inward moral temper, and so it is all *nothing*. If, on the other hand, I say, I have the inward temper of charity, and give nothing to the poor, but say to my brother, 'Be thou warmed; be thou clothed:' how dwelleth the love of God in that man? Therefore what God hath joined together, let no man put asunder. Whatever comparative excellence there may be in the two different instances of obedience, they are both instances of obedience; and the direction of our regard is summed up in that text, (Matt. xxiii. 23,) 'These ought ye to have done, and not to have left the other undone.'" Moral Obligation to the Positive Appointments in Religion, passim. Lond. 1732.

20. Bp. Hoadly.—"I. The partaking of the Lord's supper is not a duty of itself, or a duty apparent to us from the nature of things; but a duty made such to Christians, by the positive institution of Jesus Christ.

"II. All positive duties, or duties made such by institution alone, depend entirely upon the will and declaration of the person who institutes or ordains them, with respect to the real design and end of them; and consequently to the due manner of performing them. For, there being no other foundation for them with regard to *us* but the will of the institutors, this will must of necessity be our sole direction, both as to our understanding their true intent, and practising them accordingly: because we can have no other direction in this sort of duties, unless we will have recourse to mere invention; which makes them *our own* institutions, and not the institutions of those who first appointed them.

"III. It is plain, therefore, that the nature, the design, and the due manner of partaking of the Lord's supper, must of necessity depend upon what Jesus Christ, who instituted it, hath declared about it.

"IV. It cannot be doubted, that he himself sufficiently declared to his first and immediate followers the whole of what he designed should be understood by it, or implied in it. For this being a positive institution depending entirely upon his will, and not designed to contain any thing in it, but what he himself should please to affix to it, it must follow, that he declared his mind about it *fully* and *plainly*: because otherwise, he must be supposed to institute a duty, of which no one could have any notion without his institution; and at the same time not to instruct his followers sufficiently what that duty was to be.

"V. It is of small importance, therefore, to Christians to know what the many writers upon this subject, since the time of the evangelists and apostles, have affirmed. Much less can it be the duty of Christians to be guided by what any persons, by their own authority, or from their own imaginations, may teach concerning this duty. This reason is plain: because in the matter of an instituted duty, (or a duty made so by the positive will of any person,) no one can be a judge, but the institutor himself, of what he designed should be contained in it; and because, supposing him not to have spoken his mind plainly about it, it is impossible that any other person (to whom the institutor himself never revealed his design) should make up that defect. All that is added, therefore, to Christ's institution, as a necessary part of it, ought to be esteemed only as the invention of those who add it: and the more there is added (let it be done with never so much solemnity, and never so great pretences to authority,) the less there is remaining of the simplicity of the institution, as Christ himself left it....

"VI. The passages in the New Testament, which relate to this duty, and they *alone*, are the original accounts of the nature and end of this institution; and the only authentic declarations, upon which we of later ages can safely depend." Works, vol. iii. p. 845, 846, 847. See also Heidegg. Corp. Theol. loc. ix. § 40; loc. xxv. § 2. Mr. Alsop's Antisozzo, p. 468. Dr. Ridgley's Bod. Div. quest. xci. xcii. p. 491, 492. Glasg. edit. Puffendorff's Law of Nat. and Nations, b. i. c. vi. § 18. Mr. Reynolds on Angelical Worlds, p. 11, 12, 15.

REFLECTIONS.

Reflect. I. By this learned and respectable body of Pædobaptists we are taught, that positive institutions originate entirely in the sovereign will of God, No. 1—20;—that positive laws must be plain and express, No. 4, 8, 12, 13, 20;—that the obligation to observe them arises, not from the goodness of the things themselves, but from the authority of God, No. 2, 3;—that they are determined by divine institution, as to their matter, manner, and signification, No. 2, 16, 20;—that they admit of no commutation, mutilation, or alteration, by human authority, No. 2, 6;—that they depend entirely on divine institution, and are to be regulated by it, No. 10, 11, 16;—that we ought not to conclude that God has appointed such a rite, for such a purpose, because we imagine ourselves to stand in need of it, and that there are sufficient reasons for it, No. 14, 18;—that our obligation to observe them does not result from our seeing the reasons of them, but from the command of God; and that his positive command is enforced by the moral law, No. 6, 7, 14;—that there are no accidental parts of a positive institution, No. 15;—that it is unlawful to conform to any part of a religious rite, without a divine warrant, No. 15;—that it is at our peril to continue ignorant of the will of God, relating to his positive appointments, No 19;—that it is great presumption to make light of them, No. 7, 19;—that a disposition to obey God in his positive institutes, is part of that holiness without which none shall see the Lord, No. 19;—and, that external rites are of little worth, detached from virtuous tempers, No. 19. Such are the declared sentiments of these respectable authors concerning positive institutions.

Reflect. II. As it seems to be the unanimous and well attested opinion of these learned Pædobaptists, that positive institutions derive their whole being from the sovereign pleasure of God; so his revealed will must have given them their existence under every dispensation of true religion. Consequently, we cannot know any thing about their precise nature, their true design, the proper subjects of them, or the right mode of their administration, farther than the scriptures teach: for "they are to be measured *only* by the institution, in which there is not room left for us to carry them any farther." See No. 10, 20. It follows, therefore, from the nature of the case, that positive ordinances must be entirely under the direction of positive precepts, or of examples in scripture, that are warranted by the Holy Spirit. For, as Dr. Goodwin observes, "There is this difference between doctrinal truths and institutions, that one truth may be, by reason, better fetched out of another, and more safely and easily than institutions: for one truth begets another, and truth is infinite in the consequences of it; but so institutions are not. And the reason of the difference is this; because they depend upon a promise, and upon the power and will of God, immediately to concur with them, and set them up. They are things that are singled out by the will of God, to a spiritual end, with a spiritual efficacy. We may be assured what is an institution of God, by examples which we meet with in the scriptures: for one way by which Christ was pleased to convey his institutions to us, is by way of examples in the New Testament; without the which, being intended as a rule for us, we acknowledge that a complete rule for all things could not be made forth.... If an example be written as a rule, then it will bind, because there is no supposition of error."*

Remarkably strong to our purpose, is the language of Dr. Sherlock, who speaks as follows: "I would not be thought wholly to reject a plain and evident consequence from scripture; but yet I will *never admit* of a mere consequence to prove an institution, which must be delivered in *plain* terms, as all laws ought to be: and where I have no other proof, but some scripture-consequences, I shall not think it equivalent to a scripture-proof. If the consequence be plain and obvious, and such as every man sees, I shall not question it: but remote, and dubious, and disputed consequences, if we have no better evidence, to be sure are a very ill foundation for articles of faith, [or ordinances of worship.] Let our Protestant then tell such disputants, that for the institution of sacraments, and for articles of faith, he expects *plain positive proofs:* that, as much as the Protestant faith is charged with uncertainty, we desire a little more certainty for our faith, than mere inferences from scripture, and those none of the plainest neither."†
—With Dr. Sherlock, Peter Martyr agrees, when he

---

* Works, vol. iv. Government of the Church of Christ, chap. iv. p. 21, 22.

† Preserv. against Pop. vol. ii. Appendix, p. 23.

says, " It is necessary that we should have a *clear* testimony from the holy scriptures, concerning sacraments."*

It seems, indeed, to be the general practice of all Protestants, when contending with Roman Catholics about their claims of prerogative and their numerous rites, to proceed on this principle: nothing short of an *explicit* grant, a *positive* command, or a *plain* example in the New Testament, can prove their divine origin. Is the debate concerning Papal *supremacy*, or *infallibility?* No reasonings from remote principles, no conclusions from far-fetched consequences, are allowed. The honours in dispute being such as depend entirely on the sovereign pleasure and special donation of God, an *explicit* divine grant of these prerogatives is loudly demanded.—Are five of their seven sacraments; the ceremonies performed by them, when administering baptism and the Lord's supper; their withholding the cup from the people, and other things of a similar kind, the subjects in debate? Protestants hardly ever fail to require a *direct* proof,— a *positive* precept, or a *plain* example, from the New Testament. All arguments drawn from ancient Jewish rites; all that are formed on general principles, or moral considerations; and all endeavours to produce inferential proof, are justly discarded as incompetent—as having nothing to do with the subject. For the subject being no other than the *ritual* part of that worship which God requires under the New Testament; a divine institution of the rites in question, a plain positive order, or an apostolic example, may well be required, before they have a place in our creed, or become a part of our solemn service. If, therefore, the New Testament say nothing about the institution or the practice of such rites, we have nothing to do with them, nor any thing to believe concerning them.—On the same principle Protestant dissenters proceed, when defending Nonconformity; using many of the same arguments

---

* Apud Chamierum, Panstrat. tom. iv. l. i. c. xi. § 8.

against their Episcopalian opponents, which those Episcopalians employ when vindicating their own secession from the church of Rome. The demand of Nonconformists upon their Episcopalian brethren is; *Produce your warrant* (for this, that, and the other,) *from our only rule of faith and practice—a divine precept, or an apostolic example, relating to the point in dispute.* So important is this principle, respecting every thing of a positive nature in Christianity, that I can hardly imagine any sensible Protestant would ever think of writing against the Popish system; or any conscientious Dissenter of justifying his Nonconformity, without availing himself of it in many cases. Nay, so obvious and so important is this principle, so congenial to that grand maxim, THE BIBLE ONLY IS THE RELIGION OF PROTESTANTS; that we might well wonder if a judicious author omitted it, when handling the doctrine of positive rites; except it appeared, that he laboured to establish some hypothesis, to which this principle is inimical.

Nor does it appear from the records of the Old Testament, that when Jehovah appointed any branch of ritual worship, he left either the subjects of it, or the mode of administration, to be inferred by the people, from the *relation* in which they stood to himself, or from general *moral* precepts, or from any branch of his *moral* worship; nor yet from any other well known *positive* rite: but he gave them special directions relating to the very case; and those directions they were bound to regard, whether they appeared in a pleasing or a painful, in a decent or a disgusting light. For as nothing but the divine will can oblige the conscience, and as that will cannot be known unless revealed; so, when made known, whether in reference to moral or positive duties, it must oblige. We are bound, therefore, to regard the divine laws, not so much on account of what they are in themselves, however excellent; as because they are *the will of* HIM whose claim of obedience is prior to every other consideration. See No. 2, 3. Consequently, seeing baptism is as really and entirely a positive institution, as any that were given to the chosen tribes; we cannot with safety infer, either the mode, or the subject of it, from any thing short of a *precept*, or a *precedent*, recorded in scripture, and relating to that very ordinance.

That the laws of positive worship under the Old Testament were particular, clear, and decisive, will not be denied; and that our Lord has furnished the gospel church with as complete a rubric of solemn service in the New Testament, as that recorded by Moses in the Pentateuch, our Pædobaptist brethren assert. Thus Dr. Owen, for instance: "All things concerning the worship of God in the whole church or house now under the gospel, are no less perfectly and completely ordered and ordained by the Lord Jesus Christ, than they were by Moses under the law."* Dr. Isaac Chauncy: "Christ hath been more faithful than Moses, and therefore hath not left his churches without sufficient rules to walk by."† Dr. Ridgley: "It is a great dishonour to Christ, the king and head of his church, to suppose that he has left it without a rule to direct them, in what respects the communion of saints; as much as it would be to assert that he has left it without a rule of faith. If God was so particular in giving directions concerning every part of that worship that was to be performed in the church before Christ's coming, so that they were not, on pain of his highest displeasure, to deviate from it; certainly we must not think that our Saviour has neglected to give those laws by which the gospel church is to be governed."‡ Mr. Polhill: "Christ was as faithful in the house of God as Moses; his provision was as perfect for rituals, as that of Moses' was."§

---

* On Heb. ii. 2, 3, vol. ii. p. 26.
† Preface to Dr. Owen's True Nature of a Gospel Church.
‡ Body of Divinity, quest. lxi—lxiv.
§ Discourse on Schism, p. 66.

Reflect. III. It seems natural hence to infer, that our sovereign Lord must have revealed his will concerning the ordinance of *baptism*, in a manner proportional to its obligation and importance. For, as an appointment of Christ, it originated in his will, and from a revelation of that will the whole of its obligation results. In proportion, therefore, as we annex the idea of obscurity to what he says about the mode and the subject of it, we either sink the idea of obligation to regard it, or impeach the wisdom, the goodness, or the equity of our divine Legislator; for we neither have, nor can have any acquaintance with a positive institution, farther than it is revealed; and a *natural* incapacity will always excuse the non-performance of what would otherwise be an indispensable duty. We are therefore obliged to conclude, that our Lord has *clearly* revealed his pleasure, with reference to both his positive appointments, in that code of law and rule of religious worship, which are contained in the New Testament. See No. 20.

On this point let us hear Mr. Payne, when contending with the learned and artful Bossuet, bishop of Meaux. " Surely," says the Protestant Pædobaptist, " so wise a lawgiver as our blessed Saviour, would not give a law to all Christians that was not *easy* to be understood by them; it cannot be said without great reflection upon his infinite wisdom, that his laws are so obscure and dark, as they are delivered by himself, and as they are necessary to be observed by us, that we cannot know the meaning of them without a farther explication.... God's laws may be very fairly explained away, if they are left wholly to the mercy of men to explain them."*
Agreeable to this is the language of Mr. Arch. Hall, when he says, " The appointments of the Deity concerning his worship, are not to be gathered from the uncertain tradition of the elders, the authority of men,

---

* Preserv. against Popery, title vii. p. 147.

or the dictates of our own reason: no; they stand engrossed in the volume of *his Book*, which is the ONLY rule to direct us how we may glorify and enjoy him."* J. A. Turrettinus tells us, " That whatever of importance the scripture delivers concerning the sacraments, may be included in a few pages, nay, perhaps, in a few lines; and that so as a little child may understand it."† Once more: Chemnitius assures us, that a positive rite "should have an express divine command.... Whatever is maintained to be necessary in the church of Christ, should have a command in the divine word, and scriptural examples."‡ Nay, even Bellarmine declares, that " in things which depend on the will of God, nothing ought to be affirmed, unless God hath revealed it in the holy scriptures."§—Clear, however, as the positive laws of Christ are, Dr. Waterland has well observed from Le Clerc, that if men be " governed by their passions, and conceited of their prejudices, the most evident things in the world are obscure; and, that there is no law so clear, but a wrangler may raise a thousand difficulties about it." ||—It is, I think, worthy of remark, that though Protestant authors in general, consider the meaning of the law of Christ relating to his *last supper*, as being evident beyond all reasonable doubt; and though they severely censure the Roman Catholics for insinuating the contrary, yet, with regard to the law of *baptism*, they frequently represent its meaning, as ambiguous and embarrassed; nay, as favouring opposite practices: so that whether an infant, or one professing faith, be sprinkled, or immersed, the whole design of the law may be fulfilled, and a divine blessing on the administration expected. But whether this be consistent or scriptural, is left with the reader.

---

* Gospel Worship, vol. i. p. 30. † Cogitat & Dissertat. tom. i. p. 18, 19 ‡ Examen Concil. Trident. p. 204, 285.
§ In Preserv. against Popery, title viii. p. 83.
|| Importance of Doct. of Trinity, p. 461, edit. 2nd.

Reflect. IV. That no *addition* should be made by human authority to the positive appointments of Jesus Christ; and that it is not lawful, under any pretence, either to corrupt or depart from the *primitive institution* of those appointments; are things generally maintained and strongly urged against the Papists, by Protestants of all descriptions. The following quotations may serve as a specimen of their language and sentiments, in reference to these particulars. Dr. Owen: " All worship is obedience; obedience respects authority; and authority exerts itself in commands. And if this authority be not the authority of God, the worship performed in obedience unto it is not the worship of GOD, but of him or them whose commands and authority are the reason and cause of it. It is the authority of God alone that can make any worship to be religious, or the performance of it to be an act of obedience unto him. God would never allow that the will and wisdom of any of his creatures should be the rise, rule, or measure of his worship, or any part of it, or any thing that belongs unto it. This honour he hath reserved unto himself, neither will he part with it unto any other. He alone knows what becomes his own greatness and holiness, and what tends to the advancement of his glory. Hence the scripture abounds with severe interdictions and comminations against them who shall presume to do or appoint any thing in his worship, besides or beyond his own institution.... Divine institution alone, is that which renders any thing acceptable unto God.... All divine service, or worship, must be resolved into divine ordination or institution. A worship not ordained of God, is not accepted of God.... It is a hard and rare thing to have the minds of men kept upright with God in the observation of the institutions of divine worship. Adam lost himself and us all by his failure therein. The Old [Testament] Church seldom attained unto it.... And at this day there are very few in the world who judge a diligent observation of divine institutions to be a thing of any great importance. By some they are neglected; by some corrupted with additions of their own; and by some they are exalted above their proper place and use, and turned into an occasion of neglecting more important duties.... Our utmost care and diligence in the consideration of the mind of God, is required in all that we do about his worship. There is nothing wherein men, for the most part, are more careless. Some suppose it belongs unto their own wisdom to order things in the worship of God, as it seems most meet unto them; some think they are no farther concerned in these things, than only to follow the traditions of their fathers. This, unto the community of Christians, is the only rule of divine worship. To suppose that it is their duty to enquire into the way and manner of the worship of God, the grounds and reasons of what they practise therein, is most remote from them.... It were no hard thing to demonstrate, that the principal way and means whereby God expects that we should give glory unto him in this world, is by a due observation of the divine worship that he hath appointed. For herein do we in an especial manner, ascribe unto him the glory of his sovereignty, of his wisdom, of his grace, and holiness; when in his worship we bow down to his authority alone; when we see such an impress of divine wisdom on all his institutions, as to judge all other ways folly in comparison of them; when we have experience of the grace represented and exhibited in them, then do we glorify God aright. And without these things, whatever we pretend, we honour him not in the solemnities of our worship."*——Turrettinus: "The appointment of God, is the highest law, the supreme necessity."†——Mr. Archibald Hall: " As we live under the gospel dispen-

---

* On Heb. i. 6; ix. 1; viii. 5.
† Institut. Theol. loc. xix. quæst. xiv. tom. iii. p. 441.

sation, all our worship must be regulated by gospel institution, that it may be performed according to the appointment of Christ, as king of the church." The same author, when speaking of baptism, says: "This ordinance should be observed with an honest simplicity, and kept pure and entire, as Christ hath appointed it. The rule given us in the word of God is our directory, and we do well to take heed to it in this duty, as much as in every other. How grand and awful is that weighty preface to the institution of Christian baptism! (Matt. xxvii. 18, 19.) Who is the daring insolent worm, that will presume to dispute the authority, or change the ordinances of him who is given to be head over all things to the church?.... The solemnity of this ordinance is complete, and all the great purposes of its institution are secured by the authority and blessing of Christ, who is a rock, whose work is perfect, and all his commandments are sure. His laws are not subject to any of those imperfections, which are attendants of the best contrived systems among men, and frequently need explanations, amendments, and corrections. It is most dangerous and presumptuous, to add any ceremony, or to join any service, on any pretence, unto heaven's appointment. This is the most criminal rashness; and, if it is not disputing the authority of Christ directly, it is mingling the authority of men with the authority of Him who has a name above every name.... When divine authority is interposed to point out the will of God concerning any service, which is enjoined for standing use among the saints, such a service ought to be observed without any regard to the manners and usages of mankind; because both the substance and the *manner* of it are the institution of Christ."*

Reflect. V. Concerning the *circumstances* of positive institutions, our Pædobaptist brethren speak as follow. Mr. Vincent Alsop: " Under the Mosaical law

---

* Gospel Worship, vol i. p. 32, 325, 326; vol. ii. p. 434.

God commanded that they should offer to him the daily burnt-offering; and, in this case, the *colour* of the beast (provided it was otherwise rightly qualified) was a mere *circumstance:* such as God laid no stress upon, and that man had proved himself a superstitious busy-body, that should curiously adhere to any one colour. But, for the heifer whose ashes were to make the *water of separation,* there the colour was no circumstance, but made by God's command a *substantial* part of the service. To be *red,* was as much as to be a *heifer:* for when circumstances have once passed the royal assent, and are stamped with the divine seal, they become substantials in instituted worship.... We ought not to judge that God has little regard to any of his commands, because the matter of them, abstracted from his authority, is little: for we must not conceive that Christ sets little by baptism, because the element is plain, fair water; or little by that other sacrament, because the materials thereof are common bread and wine.... For though the things in themselves be small, yet his authority is great.... Though the things be small, yet God can bless them to great purposes, (2 Kings v. 11.).... Nor are we to judge that God lays little stress upon his institutes, because he does not immediately avenge the contempt and neglect of them upon the violaters. (Eccles. viii. 11; Matt. v. 29; 1 Cor. xi. 30.).... As we must not think that God appreciates whatever men set a high value upon, so neither are we to judge that he disesteems any thing because it is grown out of fashion, and thereby exposed to contempt by the atheistical wits of mercenary writers.... If any of Christ's institutions seem necessary to be broken, it will be first necessary to decry them as poor, low, inconsiderable circumstances; and then to fill the people's heads with a noise and din, that Christ lays little stress on them; and in order hereto call them the *circumstantials,* the *accidentals,* the *minutes,* the *punctilioes,* and, if need be, the petty Johns of religion, that conscience may not kick at the contemning of them.... It would be injurious to conclude that God has very little respect to his own institutions, because he may suspend their exercise *pro hic & nunc*, rather than the duties imperated by a moral precept. *Mint, anise, and cummin*, are inconsiderable things, compared with *the weightier matters of the law, judgment, mercy, and faith;* and yet our Saviour tells them, (Matt. xxiii. 23,) 'These ought ye to have done, and not to have left the other undone'.... God is the sovereign and absolute legislator, who may suspend, rescind, alter his own laws at pleasure; and yet he has laid such a stress upon the meanest of them, that no man may, nor any man, but *the man of sin*, dares presume to dispense with them, much less to dispense against them.... *Positives* may be altered, changed, or abolished, by the legislator, when and how far he pleases; but this will never prove that he lays little stress upon them whilst they are not changed, not abolished: nor will it prove that man may chop and change, barter and truck one of God's least circumstantials, because the Lawgiver himself may do it. He that may alter one, may, for aught I know, alter them all, seeing they all bear the same image and supercription of divine authority.... If God was so rigorous in his animadversions, so punctual in his prescriptions, when his institutions were so numerous, his prescriptions so multiform; what will he be when he has prescribed us so few, and those so easy and useful to the observer? If we cannot be punctual in the observation of a very few positives of so plain signification, how should we have repined had we been charged with a numerous retinue of types and carnal rudiments! If Christ's yoke be accounted heavy, how should we have sunk under the Mosaical pædagogy!"*

Mr. Payne: "It is from the institution of the sacra-

---

* Sober Enquiry, p. 289—304.

ment [of the Lord's supper,] that we know what belongs to the substance of it, and is essential to it, and what is only circumstantial and accidental. I own, there were several things, even at the institution of it by Christ, which were only circumstantials; as, the place, the time when, the number of persons to whom, the posture in which he gave it; for all these are plainly, and in their own nature, circumstantial matters; so that nobody can think it necessary or essential to the sacrament, that it be celebrated in an upper room, at night after supper, only with twelve persons, and those sitting or lying upon beds, as the Jews used to do at meals; for the same thing which Christ bids them to do, may be done, the same sacramental action performed in another place, at another time, with fewer or more persons, and those otherwise postured or situated; but it cannot be the same sacrament or same action, if bread be not blessed and eaten, if wine be not blessed and drunken, as they were both then blessed by Christ, and eaten and drunk by his apostles. The doing of these is not *a circumstance*, but the *very thing itself*, and the very substance and essence of the sacrament; for without these we do not what Christ did; whereas we may do the very same thing which he did, without any of those circumstances with which he did it .... The command of Christ, *Do this*, does not in the least extend to these [circumstances,] but only to the sacramental action of *blessing bread and eating it; blessing wine and drinking it, in remembrance of Christ*: for that was the thing which Christ did, and which he commanded them to do.... He that does not plainly see those to be circumstances [before mentioned,] and cannot easily distinguish them from the thing itself which Christ did, and commanded to be done, must not know what it is to eat and drink, unless it be with his own family, in such a room of his own house, and at such an hour of the day: it is certainly as easy to know what

Christ instituted, and what he commanded, as to know this; and, consequently, what belongs to the essence of the sacrament, without which it would not be such a sacrament as Christ celebrated and appointed, as to know what it is to eat and to drink; and yet Monsieur de Meaux is pleased to make this the great difficulty, *to know what belongs to the essence* of the sacrament, and what does not, and to distinguish what is essential in it, from what is not."*——Mr. Arch. Hall: " The signs, and even every circumstance relative to the use of them, must be appointed by Christ, and not contrived by men: for here, as in every other duty, we must observe all things that Christ hath commanded us. It is equally presumptuous and vain, to teach for doctrines the commandments or inventions of men. The signs that are used in the sacraments have a natural fitness to bring the things they represent to our mind."†

Reflect. VI. With regard to positive institutions Protestant Pædobaptists farther inform us, that the Lord Jesus Christ is *jealous* of his honour; that what is not commanded, need not be *forbidden;* and that nothing is *lawful*, which is not a duty. The following instance may here suffice.—Dr. Witherspoon: Our obedience " must be implicit; founded immediately on the authority of God. We must not take upon us to judge of the moment and importance of any part of his will, farther than he hath made it known himself. It is a very dangerous thing for us to make comparisons between one duty and another; especially with a view of dispensing with any of them, or altering their order, and substituting one in another's place."‡——Dr. Owen: " Christ marrying his church to himself, taking it to that relation, still expresseth the main of their chaste and choice affections to him, to lie in their keeping his institutions and his worship according to his appointment.

---

* Preserv. against Pop. title vii. p. 110, 137, 138.
† Gospel Worship, vol. i. chap. vii. p. 235.
‡ Practical Discourses, vol. i. p. 335.

The breach of this he calls *adultery* everywhere, and *whoredom:* he is a *jealous* God, and he gives himself that title only in respect of his institutions. And the whole apostasy of the Christian church unto false worship, is called fornication, (Rev. xvii. 5,) and the church that leads the others to false worship, *the mother of harlots.* On this account, those believers who really attend to communion with Jesus Christ, do labour to keep their hearts chaste to him in his ordinances, institutions, and worship.... They will receive nothing, practise nothing, own nothing in his worship, but what is of his appointment. They know that from the foundation of the world he never did allow, nor ever will, that in any thing the will of the creatures should be the measure of his honour, or the principle of his worship, either as to matter or manner.... That principle, *That the church hath power to institute and appoint any thing, or ceremony belonging to the worship of God,* either as to matter or to manner, beyond the orderly observance of such circumstances as necessarily attend such ordinances as Christ himself hath instituted, lies at the bottom of all the horrible superstition and idolatry, of all the confusion, blood, persecution, and wars, that have, for so long a season, spread themselves over the face of the Christian world; and it is the design of a great part of the Revelation [of John] to make a discovery of this truth."*
——Mr. Arch. Hall: " God will bless nothing but his own institutions. The inventions of men, in serving God, are as unprofitable as they are wicked and presumptuous, (Deut. xii. 31, 32.).... We cannot think God will honour the inventions of men, however they may be dignified by the specious names of useful, decent, agreeable, or prudent contrivances; yet, if they are an addition to his system, will he not say, *Who hath required these things at your hands?*"†——Hoornbekius: " In

---

* Commun. with God, part ii. chap. v. p. 169, 170.
† View of Gospel Church, p. 33, 82.

what relates to the sacraments, and the affairs of religion, it is unlawful to do any thing that is not warranted by the command of God.*——Dr. Sherlock: " Our [Popish] author, and some of his size, who do not see half a consequence before them, think they have a mighty advantage of us, in demanding the same proofs from us to justify our rejecting their doctrines, which we demand of them to justify their belief of them. That is to say, as we demand of them a scripture-proof, that there is such a place as purgatory; they think they may as reasonably demand of us a scripture-proof, that there is *no* such place as purgatory: just with as much reason, as if one should tell me, that, by the laws of England, every man is bound to marry at twenty years old; and when I desire him to show me the law which makes this necessary, he should answer, Though he cannot show such a law, yet it may be necessary, unless I can show him a law which expressly declares that it is not necessary. Whereas nothing is necessary, but what the *law* makes so; and if the law has not made it necesssary, there is no need of any law to declare that it is not necessary."†——Dr. Owen: " What men have a *right* to do in the church, by God's institution, that they have a *command* to do."‡——Anonymous: " There is nothing relating to instituted worship, as such, that is lawful, but is our necessary duty; viz. necessary, *necessitate præcepti* instituting it."§

Reflect. VII. That the subjects of positive divine laws cannot *slight* or *neglect* them without offending God, is maintained with a decisive tone by our learned Pædobaptist brethren. Thus, for instance, Bp. Taylor: " The positive laws of Jesus Christ cannot be dispensed with by any human power. All laws given by Christ,

---

* Socin. Confut. tom. iii. p. 436.   † Preservat. against Pop. vol. ii. Appendix, p. 65.   ‡ On Heb. vii. 4, 5, 6, vol. iii. p. 127.   § Jerubbaal, p. 458

OF POSITIVE INSTITUTIONS. 33

are now made for ever to be obligatory."*——Mr. Joseph White, speaking of the ancient ceremonial law, says: "To slight any of its services, was to insult the authority which enjoined it."†——Dr. Waterland: "Positive duties stand upon a moral foot.... To obey God in whatsoever he commands is the first moral law, and the fundamental principle of all morality. The reason of things, and the relation we bear to God, require that God should be obeyed in matters otherwise *indifferent:* and such obedience is *moral,* and the opposite disobedience *immoral.....Positives,* therefore, while under precept, cannot be slighted without slighting *morals* also. In short, positive laws, as soon as enacted, become part of moral law; because, as I said, universal obedience to God's commands, is the first moral law into which all laws resolve.....Whenever positive duties are so performed as to become true obedience, they are as valuable in God's sight as any moral performances whatever, because obeying God's voice is all in all. Obedience was the thing insisted upon with Adam, with Abraham, with Saul, and with many others, in positive instances; and God laid as great a stress upon obedience there, as in any moral instances whatever. To conclude then, moral performances, without the obedience of the heart, are nothing; and positive performances, without the like obedience are nothing: but the sincere obeying of God's voice in both, is true religion and true morality."‡——Mr. Reynolds: "To call some law *moral,* in contradistinction from other law, as if it was not moral at all, is improper enough. Every law, properly so called, is *regula moralis,* or *regula morum;* an obliging rule for the moral creature to walk or act by.... Positive commands are more easily transgressed than those that bear

---

* Ductor Dub. b. ii. chap iii. p. 334.
† Sermons before University of Oxford, p. 130, edit. 2nd.
‡ Scripture Vindicated, part iii. p. 37, 71, 72.

hard upon the light and law of nature. The seeming indifferency of the subject, or matter, in which they are concerned, allays the awe, and fear, and distance, that attends more criminal matter."*——Mr. Wadsworth: " Some may say,—*Sure, God will not be so much concerned with a failure in so small a punctilio as a ceremony!* True, it [the Lord's supper] is a ceremony; but it is such a one that beareth the stamp of the authority of the Lord Jesus. If He appoints it, will you slight it, and say, *It is but a ceremony?*—It is but *a ceremony*, but you are greatly mistaken if you think that therefore there is no danger to neglect it. What was the tree of knowledge of good and evil, but a ceremony? Yet, for disobedience in eating thereof, do you not know and feel what wrath it hath brought on the whole race of mankind? And tell me, was circumcision any more than a ceremony? Yet it had almost cost Moses his life for neglecting to circumcise his son; for the angel stood ready with his sword to slay him, if he had not prevented it by his obedience, (Exod. iv. 24, 25, 26.) So, for the Lord's supper, as much a ceremony as it is, yet for the abuse of it, some of the church [at Corinth] were sick and weak, others fell asleep, that is, died: and if God did so severely punish the abuse, how think you to escape, that *presumptuously neglect* the use thereof? *But I am regenerate and become a new creature;—I do not fear that God will cast me away for the disuse of a ceremony.* Is this the reasoning of one *regenerate?* Surely, thou dost not understand what regeneration meaneth. Is it not the same with being *born of God?* And what is it to be obedient to the Father, but to do as he commandeth? And hath he not commanded you by his Son, to remember your Saviour in this supper? When you have considered this, then tell me what you think of this kind of reasoning: *I am a child of God, therefore*

---

* Enquiries concerning Angelical Worlds, p. 11, 12, 15.

I will presume to disobey him. He bids me remember Jesus in this supper, and I will not. Methinks thou blushest at the very mentioning of it. And what, if he should not cast thee quite off for this neglect? yet thou hast no reason to think, but that either outwardly, or inwardly, or both, he will scourge thee for this sin before thou diest."*——This reasoning, it is plain, *mutatis mutandis*, applies with equal force to a neglect of baptism: to which I will add the following passage from Dr. Owen: " Slaves take liberty *from* duty; children have liberty *in* duty. There is not a greater mistake in the world, than that the liberty of sons in the house of God consists in this, they can *perform* duties, or take the freedom to *omit* them: they *can* serve in the family of God, that is, they think they may if they *will*, and they can choose whether they will or no. This is a liberty *stolen* by slaves; not a liberty *given* by the Spirit unto sons."†

It is well observed by Chamier, and it is a dictate of common sense, " That no law derives its authority from the judgment [or the inclination] of those to whom it is given."‡ And it is equally clear, that when a law has been fairly promulged, ignorance of its demands cannot render a non-compliance innocent. For, as Dr. Waterland observes, the law presumes, " that when a man has done an ill thing, [or neglected his duty] he either *knew* that it was evil, or else *ought* to have known it. *Ignorantia juris non excusat delictum.*"§ It is therefore incumbent on every professor of Christianity, to make a diligent and impartial search into the records of the New Testament, that he may know and perform the will of his Lord respecting baptism. Nor has any one reason to consider himself as possessed of a pious and virtuous

---

* Supplem. to Morn. Exercise at Cripplegate, p. 243, 244.
† Communion with God, part ii. chap. x. p. 246.
‡ Panstrat. tom. i. l. vi. chap. xx. § 1.
§ Import. of Doct. of Trin. p. 164.

temper, while destitute of a disposition to make such an enquiry. Because " virtue," says Heineccius, " is always united with an earnest, indefatigable care to understand the divine law. The greater progress one has made in virtue, the more ardent is this desire in his breast." Nay, though a person should plead *conscience* for the omission or corruption of a positive institute, he would not be exculpated; for, as the last mentioned author justly observes, "Though he be guilty who acts contrary to his conscience, whether certain or probable, yet he cannot, for that reason, be said to act rightly and justly, who contends that he has acted according to his conscience. Conscience is not the *rule*, but it applies the rule to facts and cases which occur.... He who follows an erroneous conscience sins on this very account, *That he follows it rather than the will of the Legislator:* though he be more excusable than one who acts directly against conscience, yet he is guilty."* The morality of our conduct does not depend on the understanding; for our knowing, or being ignorant of a thing, is not the reason of its being good or evil, any more than the nature of an action does upon the will; because the willing a bad action to a good end, cannot render it innocent. Divine law is the rule of our conduct; and a want of conformity to that rule is a sin.

It appears, therefore, by the preceding reasoning, and from the authors produced, that none are worthy the name of Christians who are destitute of a disposition to acknowledge the authority of Christ by submission to his positive appointments; and, that ignorance of their nature, obligation, and use, is far from excusing, except it arise from *natural* incapacity, and not from a bad state of the will. Now, in regard to baptism, we have not only the command of our Lord, but his own *example* also, to enforce our observance of it; concerning which, Mr. Wesley very properly says : " Let our Lord's sub-

---

* Universal Law, b. i. chap. ii. § 37, 45.

mitting to baptism teach us a holy exactness in the observance of those institutions which owe their obligation merely to a divine command. Surely, *thus it becometh all his followers to fulfil all righteousness.*"* It has been justly remarked by a learned Lutheran, " That so great an honour was never conferred upon any ceremony,"† as there was upon baptism, when our Lord himself was immersed in Jordan, by the hands of John; when the divine Father, with an audible voice, proclaimed him his beloved Son; and when the Holy Spirit descended upon him.

I will conclude this part of our subject with the reasoning of Dr. Gerard. " A total disregard to the positive and external duties of religion, or a very great neglect of them, is justly reckoned more blameable, and a stronger evidence of an unprincipled character, than even some transgressions of moral obligation.... Even particular positive precepts, as soon as they are given by God, have something *moral* in their nature. Suppose the rites which are enjoined by them, perfectly indifferent before they were enjoined; yet from that moment they cease to be indifferent. The divine authority is interposed for the observance of them. To neglect them is no longer to forbear an indifferent action, or to do a thing in one way rather than another, which has naturally no great propriety: it is very different; it is to disobey God, it is to despise his authority, it is to resist his will. Can any man believe a God, and not acknowledge that disobedience to him, and contempt of his authority is *immoral*, and far from the least heinous species of immorality?.... All positive institutions of divine appointment, are means of cultivating moral virtue. Be the rites themselves what they will, their being enjoined by God, renders them proper trials of our obe-

---

* Note on Matt. iii. 16.
† Centur. Magdeb. cent. i. l. i. c. iv. p. 113.

dience to him, and renders our observance of them the means of cherishing a sense of his authority, and of improving a principle of subjection to it. A principle of subjection to the authority of God, is one of the firmest supports of all goodness and virtue; and positive institutions are the most direct means of cultivating it, for the observance of them proceeds solely from the principle of obedience; but in every moral virtue, other principles are conjoined with this. All the rites appointed by God, are likewise direct and very powerful means of improving many particular virtuous affections, all the affections which are naturally exercised in performing them. Neglect of the *means* demonstrates, in every case, indifference about the *end*. Disregard to external worship and positive institutions, shows the want of all concern for moral improvement. But unconcern for moral improvement is not the defect of a single virtue, is not a single vice; it is a corruption and degeneracy of the *whole soul*, and therefore must appear highly detestable to every person of sound and unbiassed judgment.... It is not they who reckon a regard to positive institutions essential to a good and unblemished character, that judge weakly, but they who reckon that regard of no importance. Vain are their pretensions to enlargement of sentiment, and elevation above prejudice; their minds are so contracted, that they can admit only a partial idea of the nature of positive duties; they consider but the mere matter of them; they comprehend not their moral principles, their sublime end, or their important signification."*

As the leading ideas in the preceding paragraphs are the *grand principles* of legitimate reasoning on the doctrine of positive institutions; as it is on these principles that our most eminent Protestant authors proceed, when exploding the superstitions of Popery; and as it

---

* Sermons, vol. i. p. 312—314, 316, 317, 320, edit. 2nd.

is our intention to examine Pædobaptism on these very principles; the reader is desired to keep them in mind, while perusing the following pages. It has been justly remarked by Bp. Taylor, that " men are easy enough to consent to a general rule ; but they will not suffer their *own case* to be concerned in it."* This observation is, doubtless, founded in fact, and it expresses an affecting truth. While, therefore, we consider the forementioned authors as having verified the remark by practising infant sprinkling, we shall endeavour to avoid a similar inconsistency.

---

* Ductor Dubitant. b. ii. chap. iii. p. 303.

CHAPTER II.

Concerning the Signification of the Terms, Baptize and Baptism.

[*N. B.* To prevent mistakes, the reader is desired to observe, that many of the following quotations are to be considered as *concessions* made by these learned authors; no inconsiderable part of them asserting, notwithstanding what they here say, that the word baptism signifies pouring and sprinkling, as well as immersion.]

Witsius.—" It cannot be denied, that the native signification of the word βαπτειν, and βαπτιζειν, is to plunge, to dip. So that it is, doubtless, more than επιπολαζειν, which is to swim lightly on the surface; but less than δυνειν, which is to go down to the bottom and be destroyed.... Yet I have observed, that the word καταδυσις is frequently used by the ancients, with reference to baptism." Œcon. Fœd. l. iv. c. xvi. § 13.

2. Salmasius.—" *Baptism* is immersion; and was administered, in ancient times, according to the force and meaning of the word. Now it is only *rhantism*, or sprinkling; not *immersion*, or dipping." De Cæsarie Virorum, p. 669.

3. Gurtlerus.—" *To baptize*, among the Greeks, is undoubtedly to immerse, to dip; and baptism, is immersion, dipping. Βαπτισμος εν Πνευματι άγιω, *baptism in the Holy Spirit*, is immersion into the pure waters of the Holy Spirit, or a rich and abundant communication of his gifts; for he on whom the Holy Spirit is poured out, is as it were immersed into him....Βαπτισμος εν πυρι, *baptism in fire*, is a figurative expression, and signifies casting into a flame, which, like water, flows far and wide; such as the flame that consumed Jerusalem....

The thing commanded by our Lord is baptism, immersion into water." Institut. Theol. cap. xxxiii. § 108, 109, 110, 115.

4. Danæus.—" Βαπτισμος, baptism, is derived απο του βαπτεσθαι, or βαπτιζεσθαι: the former of which properly signifies *to dye;* the latter, *to immerse*, especially in water. But, as that which emerges out of the water appears to be washed, and fair, and clean; so the term baptism is frequently used in the holy scripture, for washing and cleansing." In Leigh's Critica Sacra, under the word, Βαπτισμος, edit. 2nd.

5. Gomarus.—" Βαπτισμος and Βαπτισμα, signify the act of baptizing: that is, either plunging alone; or immersion, and the consequent washing." Opera, Disputat. Theolog. Disput. xxxii. § 5.

6. Buddeus.—" The words βαπτιζειν and βαπτισμος, are not to be interpreted of aspersion, but always of immersion." Theolog. Dogmat. l. v. c. i. § 5.

7. Dr. Bentley.—" Βαπτισμους, baptisms, dippings —Βαπτισον σεαυτον εις θαλασσαν, *dip yourself in the sea.*" Remarks on Disc. on Free Thinking, part ii. p. 56, 57, edit. 6.

8. Bp. Reynolds.—" The Spirit under the gospel is compared to water; and that not a little measure, to sprinkle, or bedew, but to *baptize* the faithful in, (Matt. iii. 11; Acts i. 5,) and that not in a font, or vessel, which grows less and less, but in a spring, or living river, (John vii. 39.).... There are two words which signify suffering of afflictions, and they are both applied unto Christ, (Matt. xx. 22.) Are ye able *to drink of the cup* that I shall drink of, or be *baptized* with that baptism that I am baptized with? He that drinketh hath the water *in* him; he that is dipped or plunged, hath the water *about* him: so it notes the universality of the wrath which Christ suffered." Works, p. 226, 407.

9. Calvin.—" The word baptize, signifies to immerse; and the rite of immersion was observed by

the ancient church." Institut. Christ. Relig. l. iv. c. xv. § 19.

10. Beza.—" Christ commanded us to be baptized; by which word it is certain immersion is signified.... Βαπτιζεσθαι, in this place, is more than χερνιπτειν; because *that* seems to respect the whole body, *this* only the hands. Nor does βαπτιζειν signify to wash, except by consequence: for it properly signifies to immerse for the sake of dyeing.... To be baptized in water, signifies no other than to be immersed in water, which is the external ceremony of baptism.... Βαπτιζω differs from the verb δυναι, which signifies, to plunge in the deep and to drown; as appears from that verse of an ancient oracle, Ασκος βαπτιζη, δυναι δε τοι ου θεμις εστι: in which these two terms are distinguished, as expressing different ideas." Epistola II. ad Thom. Tilium, (apud Spanhem. Dub. Evang. pars iii. Dub. 24.) Annotat. in Marc. vii. 4. Acts xix. 3; Matt. iii. 11.

11. Meisnerus.—" Βαπτιζειν and βαπτειν, are generally found used for plunging and a total immersion." Apud Spanhem. Dub. Evangel. pars iii. Dub. xxiv. § 2.

12. Danish Catechism.—" What is Christian dipping? Water in conjunction with the word and command of Christ. What is that command which is in conjunction with water? 'Go teach all nations,' and so on, (Matt. xxviii. 19; Mark xvi. 15, 16.) What is implied in these words? A command to the dipper and the dipped, with a promise of salvation to those that believe. How is this Christian dipping to be administered? The person must be deep-dipped in water, or overwhelmed with it, ' in the name of God the Father,' and so on." N. B. The gentleman who favoured me with this extract, observes: that βαπτιζω is translated, by the Germans, *teüff;* by the Dutch, *doop;* by the Danes and Swedes, *döbe;* all which signify, *to dip.*

13. Spanhemius.—" Βαπτιζειν and βαπτειν, are gene-

rally found used for plunging, or a total dipping." Dub. Evang. pars iii. Dub. xxiv. § 2.

14. Vitringa.—" The act of baptizing, is the immersion of believers in water. This expresses the force of the word. Thus also it was performed by Christ and his apostles." Aphorismi Sanct. Theolog. aphoris. 884.

15. Beckmanus.—" Baptism, according to the force of its etymology, is immersion, and washing, or dipping." Exercit. Theolog. exercit. xvii. p. 257.

16. Bucanus.—" Baptism, that is, immersion, dipping, and, by consequence, washing. Baptistery, a vat, or large vessel of wood, or stone, in which we are immersed, for the sake of washing. Baptist; one that immerses, or dips." Institut. Theolog. loc. xlvii. quæst. i. p. 605.

17. Bp. Patrick.—" I may say of him [Mr. John Smith] in Antoninus's praise, he was δικαιοσυνη βεβαμμενος εις βαθος, DIPPED *into justice,* as it were, over head and ears; he had not a slight superficial tincture, but was dyed and coloured quite through with it." Funeral Serm. for Mr. J. Smith of Cambridge, subjoined to his Select Discourses, p. 509.

18. Zanchius.—" Baptism is a Greek word, and signifies two things; first, and properly, immersion in water: for the proper signification of Βαπτιζω, is to immerse, to plunge under, to overwhelm in water.... And this signification properly agrees with our baptism, and has a resemblance of the thing signified." Opera, tom. vi. p. 217. Genev. 1619. N. B. Mr. De Courcy tells us, that the opinion of Zanchius ' is worth a *thousand* others.'" Rejoinder, p. 261.

19. Hoornbeekius.—" We do not deny that the word baptism bears the sense of immersion; or that, in the first examples of persons baptized, they went into the water and were immersed; or that this rite should be observed where it may be done conveniently and without endangering health." Socin. Confut. l. iii. c. ii. sect. i. tom. iii. p. 268.

20. Stapferus.—" By baptism we understand that rite of the New Testament church, commanded by Christ, in which believers, by being immersed in water, testify their communion with the church." Institut. Theolog. Polem. tom. i. cap. iii. § 1635.

21. Burmannus.—" Βαπτισμος and βαπτισμα, if you consider their etymology, properly signify immersion. 'And Jesus, when he was baptized, went up straightway out of the water,' (Matt. iii. 16. Compare Acts viii. 38.)" Synops. Theolog. loc. xliii. cap. vi. § 2.

22. Roell.—" Baptism, from βαπτω, signifies immersion." Explicat. Epist. ad Ephesios, ad cap. iv. 5.

23. Mr. John Trapp.—" 'Are ye able to—be baptized with the baptism;' or plunged over head and ears in the deep waters of affliction?" Comment. on Matt. xx. 22.

24. Limborch.—" Baptism is that rite, or ceremony, of the new covenant, whereby the faithful, by immersion into water, as by a sacred pledge, are assured of the favour of God, remission of sins, and eternal life; and by which they engage themselves to an amendment of life, and an obedience to the divine commands." Complete Syst. Div. b. v. chap. xxii. sect. i. Mr. Jones's translation.

25. H. Altingius.—" The word baptism properly signifies immersion; improperly, by a metonymy of the end, washing." Loci Commun. pars. i. loc. xii. p. 198.

26. Hospinianus.—" Christ commanded us to be baptized; by which word it is certain immersion is signified." Hist. Sacram. l. ii. c. i. p. 30.

27. Casaubonus.—" This was the rite of baptizing, that persons were plunged into the water; which the very word βαπτιζειν, *to baptize*, sufficiently declares; which, as it does not signify δυνειν, *to sink to the bottom and perish*, so, doubtless, it is not επιπολαζειν, *to swim on the surface*. For these three words, επιπολαζειν, βαπτιζειν,

and δυνειν, are of different significations. Whence we understand it was not without reason, that some long ago insisted on the immersion of the whole body in the ceremony of baptism; for they urge the word βαπτιζειν, *to baptize.*" Annotat. in Matt. iii. 6.

28. Diodati.—" *Baptized;* viz. plunged into water .... In baptism, being dipped in water according to the ancient ceremony, it is a sacred figure unto us, that sin ought to be drowned in us, by God's Spirit. Annotat. on Matt. iii. 6; Rom. vi. 4.

29. Calmet.—" Generally people [speaking of the Jews] dipped themselves entirely under the water; and this is the most simple and natural notion of the word baptism." Dict. of Bible, art. Baptism.

30. Luther.—"The term baptism, is a Greek word. It may be rendered *a dipping*, when we dip something in water, that it may be entirely covered with water. And though that custom be quite abolished among the generality (for neither do they entirely dip children, but only sprinkle them with a little water,) nevertheless they ought to be wholly immersed, and presently to be drawn out again; for the etymology of the word seems to require it. The Germans call baptism *tauff*, from *depth*, which they call *tieff*, in their language; as if it were proper those should be *deeply immersed*, who are baptized. And, truly, if you consider what baptism signifies, you shall see the same thing required: for it signifies, that the old man and our nativity, that is full of sins, which is entirely of flesh and blood, may be overwhelmed by divine grace. The manner of baptism, therefore, should correspond to the signification of baptism, that it may show a certain and plain sign of it." In Dr. Du Veil, on Acts viii. 38.

31. Schelhornius, when explaining 1 Cor. xv. 21, and understanding the word *baptized* in a metaphorical sense, as expressive of being overwhelmed in calamities, says; "The word βαπτιζεσθαι, which probably signifies

to be immersed, or plunged under water; though not so frequently used by profane authors in a metaphorical sense, is nevertheless not unusual."* Biblioth. Bremens. class. vii. p. 638.

32. Mr. Selden.—" In England, of late years, I ever thought the parson baptized his own fingers, rather than the child." Works, vol. vi. col. 2008.

33. Keckermannus.—" We cannot deny, that the first institution of baptism consisted in immersion, and not sprinkling; which is quite evident from Rom. vi. 3, 4." System. Theolog. l. iii. c. viii. p. 369.

34. Dr. Towerson.—"The third thing to be enquired concerning the outward visible sign of baptism is, how it ought to be applied; whether by an immersion, or an aspersion, or effusion;—a more material question

---

* In confirmation of which he produces the following authorities, which I will give in his own words. " Heliodorus, l. ii. c. iii. Æthiopic. Cnemon itaque cum omnino dolori illum succubuisse et *calamitate submersum* (συμφορα βεβαπ7ισμενον) esse intellexisset, metueretque, ne sibi aliquid mali consciceret. L. iv. c. xx. O vos, qui adestis, Charicli quidem et postea lugere licebit. Nos vero non *mergamur* (συμβαπ7ιζομεθα) hujus dolore, neque inconsideratè illius lacrymis, tanquam aquæ impetu auferamur, occasionem negligentes. L. v. c. xvi. Επειδη σε τα συμβεβηκο7α εβαπ7ιζεν, quoniam te casus tui obruebant ac *demergebant*. Ita et eo sensu venit (L. ii. c. xxvii.) ejusdem autoris verbum βυθιζεσθαι. Πλειονι κλυδωνι κακων βεβυθισμενοι, majore fluctu ærumnarum obruti——Libanius, (In Parent. Juliani, cap. cxlviii. p. 369.) Ea enim, quam ob Julianum sentimus, tristitia, animam *submergens* (βαπ7ιζεσα) mentemque obfuscans, tenebras quasdam oculis quoque offundit, nec multum ab iis, qui in tenebris nunc versantur, distamus.——Plutarchus: (De Puerorum Educatione, cap. xiii.) Sicut enim plantæ quidem mediocribus aquis nutriuntur, plurimis vero suffocantur: ad eundem modum anima quidem mediocribus augetur laboribus, sed immoderatis (βαπ7ιζε7αι) *submergitur*. Ita et Poeta anonymus: (Anthol. Gr. l. ii. c. xlvii.) Βαπ7ιζεσθαι ad somnum transfert——

Βαπ7ιζε7αι δ' ύπνω γει7ονι τȣ θανα7ȣ.

Vides heic βαπ7ιζεσθαι τῳ ύπνῳ esse per metaphoram somno *sepeliri*, quam phrasin etiam alicubi in Heliodoro legisse memini." Ut supra, p. 638, 639, 640.

[this] than it is commonly deemed by us, who have been accustomed to baptize by a bare effusion, or sprinkling of water upon the party. For in things which depend for their force upon the mere will and pleasure of him who instituted them, there ought, no doubt, great regard to be had to the commands of him who did so; as without which there is no reason to presume we shall receive the benefit of that ceremony, to which he hath been pleased to annex it. Now, what the command of Christ was in this particular, cannot well be doubted of by those who shall consider the words of Christ, (Matt. xxviii. 19,) concerning it, and the practice of those times, whether in the baptism of John, or of our Saviour. For the words of Christ are, that they should baptize, or *dip*, those whom they made disciples to him (for so, no doubt, the word βαπτιζειν properly signifies;) and which is more, and not without its weight, that they should baptize them *into* the name of the Father, and of the Son, and of the Holy Ghost: thereby intimating such a washing, as should receive the party baptized within the very body of the water, which they were to baptize him with. Though if there could be any doubt concerning the signification of the words in themselves, yet would that doubt be removed by considering the practice of those times, whether in the baptism of John, or of our Saviour. For such as was the practice of those times in baptizing, such in reason are we to think our Saviour's command to have been concerning it, especially when the words themselves incline that way; there being not otherwise any means, either for those, or future times, to discover his intention concerning it." Of the Sacram. of Bap. part iii. p. 53, 54, 55.

35. Dan. Grade.—" The word baptism generally denotes immersion, for the sake of washing or cleansing." In Thesaur. Theolog. Philolog. tom. ii. p. 560.

36. H. Clignetus.—" Baptism is so called from

immersion, or plunging into; because in the primitive times those that were baptized were entirely immersed in water." In Thesaur. Disputat. Sedan, tom. i. p. 769, 770. Genev. 1661.

37. Dr. Dan. Scott.—"The verb βαπτιζω expresses the form of admitting a proselyte into the Christian church, which tradition assures us was by a trine immersion, or plunging under water. But of late aspersion, or sprinkling, is admitted by the church of England instead of immersion, or dipping."* New Version of St. Matt. Gospel. Note on Matt. xxviii. 19.

38. Bossuet.—"To baptize signifies to plunge, as is granted by all the world." In Mr. Stennett, against Mr. Russen, p. 174.

39. Suicerus.—" He is said βαπτειν υδριαν, *to baptize a bucket*, who draws water out of a well or a river; which cannot be done except the bucket be entirely plunged under the water. Wool and clothes are said to be βαπτεσθαι, *baptized*, when they are dipped; because they are quite immersed in the dyeing fat, that they may imbibe the colour. Βαπτιζω, *to baptize*, hath properly the same signification.—Βαπτιζειν εαυτον εις θαλασσαν, in the ancient poet, is *to plunge himself into the sea.*—From the proper signification of the verb, *baptize*, baptism properly

---

* To fix the signification of βαπτιζω, he produces a number of passages from the following Greek authors: Joseph. Antiq. Jud. l. iv. c. iv. § 6, p. 207; l. xv. c. iii. § 3, p. 745. De Bell. Jud. l. i. c. xxii. § 2, p. 110; l. i. c. xxvii § 1; l. ii. c. xviii. § 4, p. 198; l. ii. c. xx. § 1; l. iii. c. ix. § 3, p. 251; l. iii. c. x. § 9, p. 259. Strab. Geogr. l. i. p. 44, B; l. xii. p. 809, D; l. xvi, p. 1108. Lucian. Ver. Hist. l. ii. p. 393, A. Plutarch. Quæst. Nat. tom. ii. p. 914, C. Orph. Argonaut. v. 510. Soph. Aj. v. 354. In the same learned author's Append. ad Thesaur. Græc. Ling. under the verb βαπτιζω, he quotes passages from the following Greek writers: Polyb. Hist. l. i. p. 73, ult. 545, 10, f; l. iii. p. 311, ult. Joseph. Antiq. l. ix. c. x. § 2. Vita, § 3. Diod. Sicul. Bibl. l. i. p. 23, 12. Strab. Geogr. l. i. p. 421, C; l. xiv. p. 982, D. Athen. Deipn. l. v. p. 221, c. 472, D. Lucian. Bacch. p. 853, A. Plat. Euthydem. i. 277, C. Diod. Sicul. l. i. p. 47, 4. Joseph. De Bell. l. iv. c. iii. § 3.

denotes immersion, or dipping into." Thesaurus Eccles. sub voce Βαπτισμα.

40. Venema.—" The word βαπτιζειν, *to baptize*, is no where used in the scripture for sprinkling; no not in Mark vii. 4, otherwise than appears to some." Institut. Hist. Eccles. Vet. et Nov. Test. tom. iii. secul. i. § 138.

41. Magdeburg Centuriators.—" The word βαπτιζω, *to baptize*, which signifies immersion into water, proves that the administrator of baptism immersed, or washed, the persons baptized in water." Cent. i. l. ii. c. iv. p. 382.

42. Anonymous.—" The word *baptize* doth certainly signify *immersion, absolute* and *total* immersion, in Josephus and other Greek writers. But this word is in some degree equivocal; and there are some eminent Greek scholars who have asserted, that immersion is not *necessarily* included in baptism. The examples produced, however, do not exactly serve the cause of those who think that a few drops of water sprinkled on the forehead of the child, constitute the essence of baptism. In the Septuagint it is said, that Nebuchadnezzar *was baptized with the dew of heaven:* and in a poem attributed to Homer (called) *The Battle of the Frogs and Mice,* it is said, that *a lake was baptized with the blood* of a wounded combatant. (Εβαπτετο δ' αιματι λιμνη πορφυρεῳ.) A question hath arisen, in what sense the word *baptize* can be used in this passage. Doth it signify immersion, properly so called? Certainly not: neither can it signify a partial sprinkling. A body wholly surrounded with a mist; wholly made humid with dew; or a piece of water so tinged with and discoloured by blood, that if it had been a solid body and dipped into it, it could not have received a more sanguine appearance, is a very different thing from that partial application which in modern times is supposed sufficient to constitute full and explicit baptism. The accommodation of the word

baptism to the instances we have referred to, is not unnatural, though highly metaphorical; and may be resolved into a trope or figure of speech, in which, though the primary idea is maintained, yet the mode of expression is altered; and the word itself is to be understood rather *allusively* than *really;* rather *relatively* than *absolutely.* If a body had been baptized or immersed, it could not have been more wet than Nebuchadnezzar's; if a lake had been dipped in blood, it could not have put on a more bloody appearance. Hitherto the Anti-Pædobaptists seem to have had the best of the argument, on the mode of administering the ordinance. The most explicit authorities are on their side. Their opponents have chiefly availed themselves of inferences, analogy, and doubtful construction." Monthly Review, for May 1784, p. 396.

43. G. J. Vossius.—" Βαπτιζειν, to baptize, signifies to plunge. It certainly therefore signifies more than επιπολαζειν, which is, *to swim lightly on the top;* and less than δυνειν, which is, *to sink to the bottom,* so as to be destroyed." Disputat. de Bap. disp. i. thes. i. p. 25. Amstelod. 1648.

44. Mr. De Courcy.—" It is readily allowed, that dipping is one of the included ideas in the original word [βαπτιζω]—We never denied, that dipping is not excluded from the signification of the original word." Rejoinder, p. 139, 143.

45. Turrettinus.—" The word *baptism* is of Greek origin, and is derived from the verb βαπτω; which signifies *to dip,* and *to dye:* βαπτιζειν, to baptize; to dip into, to immerse. Plut. de Superstit. βαπτισον σε εις θαλασσαν, *plunge yourself into the sea:* and, in the life of Theseus, he recites a Sibylline verse concerning the Athenians, which better agrees to the church:

Ασκος βαπτιζη, δυναι δε τοι ου θεμις εστι.

Mergeris uter aquis, sed non submergeris unquam.

Hence it appears, that βαπτιζειν is more than επιπολαζειν, which is *to swim lightly on the surface;* and less than δυνειν, which is *to go down to the bottom;* that is, to strike the bottom so as to be destroyed." Institut. loc. xix. quæst. xi. § 4.

46. Dr. Owen.—" Though the *original* and *natural* signification of the word [βαπτιζω] imports, to dip, to plunge, to dye; yet it also signifies to wash or cleanse." In Dr. Ridgley's Bod. Div. quest. clxvi. p. 608, note.

47. Bas. Faber.—" Baptism, is immersion, washing." Thesau. Erudit. Scholast. Lips. 1717.

48. Eras. Schmidius.—" Βαπτειν, is to dye, to immerse in water; also to wash, or to immerse for the sake of washing or cleansing." Annotat. in Matt. iii. 6. Norimb. 1658.

49. Mr. Daniel Rogers.—" None, of old, were wont to be sprinkled; and I confess myself unconvinced by demonstration of scripture for infants' sprinkling. It ought to be the church's part to cleave to the institution, which is dipping; and he betrays the church, whose officer he is, to a disorderly error, if he cleave not to the institution, which is to dip. That the minister is to dip in water, as the meetest act, the word βαπτιζω notes it: for the Greeks wanted not other words to express any other act besides dipping, if the institution could bear it. What resemblance of the burial or the resurrection of Christ is in sprinkling? All antiquity and scripture confirm that way. To dip, therefore, is *exceeding material* to the ordinance; which was the usage of old, without exception of countries, hot or cold." In Dr. Russel's Just Vind. of Doc. and Prac. of John, &c. Epist. Dedicat. p. 5.

50. Dr. Hammond.—" The word here used, βαπτιζεσθαι, (as it differs from νιπτεσθαι, verse 3,) signifies not only the washing of the whole body, (as when it is said of Eupolis, that being taken and thrown into the sea, εβαπτιζετο, he was immersed all over, and so **the**

baptisms of cups, &c., in the end of this verse, is putting into the *water all over*, rinsing them,) but washing any part as the hands here, by way of immersion in water, as that is opposed to affusion or pouring water on them." Annotations, on Mark vii. 4.

51. Ikenius.—" The Greek word βαπτισμος denotes the immersion of a thing, or a person, into something; either with a view to expiation, or for washing and cleansing. Here also [Matt. iii. 11, compared with Luke iii. 16.] the *baptism of fire*, or that which is performed in fire, must signify according to the same simplicity of the letter, an immission, or immersion, into fire for a similar end: and this the rather, because here, *to baptize in the Spirit*, and *in fire*, are not only connected, but also opposed to being baptized *in water;* and, therefore, the connection of the discourse, and the laws of opposition demand, that after whatever manner these two phrases denote baptism in water, and in the Spirit, to be performed, such must that be which is performed in fire. . . . The Jewish rites of purification were different; for either they were performed by an immersion of the whole body, which the Jews call טבילה, and the Greeks, βαπτισμον, baptism; or by the washing of some parts, as the hands, or the feet, which is called by the Greeks, εκνιψις; or by sprinkling; which, in Greek, is denominated ῥαντισμος, *rhantism*." Dissert. Philolog. Theolog. dissert. xix. p.325. Antiq. Hebraicæ, pars i. c. xviii. § 9.

52. Deylingius.—" The word βαπτιζεσθαι, as used by Greek authors, signifies immersion and overwhelming. Thus we read in Plutarch, (de Superstit. tom. ii. op. f. 166,) βαπτισον σεαυτον εις θαλασσαν, *dip* yourself in the sea: like as Naaman, (in 2 Kings v. 14,) who 'baptized himself seven times in Jordan,' which was an immersion of the whole body. So Strabo, (lib. xiv. p. 458,) when speaking about the soldiers of Alexander the Great, marching in the winter season between Climax, a mountain in Pamphylia, and the sea, says: They were

immersed, βαπτιζομενους, up to the waist. The same author, (lib. xii. p. 391,) speaking of Tatta, a marsh, situate between Galatia and Cappadocia, says: The water rises, παντι τῳ βαπτισθεντι εις αυτο, so as to *overwhelm* any thing. Diodorus Siculus, (lib. i. c. xxxvi.) when speaking of the Nile overflowing its banks, says: 'Many of the land animals perish, ὑπο του ποταμου περιληφθεντα διαφθειρεσθαι βαπτιζομενα, being overtaken and *overwhelmed* by the flood.' In Josephus, (Antiq. Jud. lib. xv. cap. iii.) βαπτιζοντες, persons baptizing, are persons plunging down. It has the same signification in the gospels, and in the writings of the apostles: if you except Luke xi. 38, where βαπτιζεσθαι seems to be used concerning washing the hands, which is done by sprinkling." Observat. Sac. pars iii. observ. xxvi. § 2. Lips. 1715.

53. Le Clerc. "' At that time came John the Baptizer.' He has been called the *Baptizer*, rather than *Baptist*, because the latter word is a proper name in the modern languages; whereas in this place it is an appellative, to signify a man that plunged in water those who testified an acknowledgment of his divine mission, and were desirous of leading a new life—' He shall baptize you in the Holy Spirit.' As I plunge you in water, he shall plunge you, so to speak, in the Holy Spirit." Remarques sur Nouv. Test. à Matt. iii. 1.

54. Danzius.—" Βαπτισμος, βαπτισμα, and βαπτισις, denote plunging, or dipping; also washing, or a bath." De Bap. Proselyt. Judaic. § 1, in Ugolini Thesauro Antiq. Sac. tom. xxii. p. 883.

55. Reiskius.—" To be baptized signifies, in its primary sense, to be immersed. Hence ναυς αβαπτιστος, a ship *unbaptized*, is a vessel not immersed in the waves; and, in Gregory Thaumaturgus, a person immersed in error, is called βεβαπτισμενος; and he who rescues such persons from their dangerous mistakes, is said τους βαπτιζομενους ανιμασθαι, *to lift up* or *draw out* the parties

that were so baptized." Dissertat. de Bap. Judæorum, cap. i. § 1.

56. Heideggerus.—" The words βαπτισμα and βαπτισμος, baptism, (from βαπτειν, to plunge, to immerse,) properly signify immersion." Corpus Theolog. Christ. loc. xxv. § 21.

57. J. J. Wetstenius.—" To baptize, is to plunge, to dip. The body, or part of the body, being under water, is said to be baptized." Comment. ad Matt. iii. 6.

58. Dr. Doddridge.—" I have, indeed, a most dreadful baptism to be baptized with, and know that I shall shortly be bathed as it were in blood, and plunged in the most overwhelming distress." Paraphrase on Luke xii. 50.

59. Zepperus.—" If we consider the proper meaning of the term, the word baptism signifies plunging into water, or the very act of dipping and washing. It appears, therefore, from the very signification and etymology of the term, what was the custom of administering baptism in the beginning; whereas we now, for baptism, rather have rhantism, or sprinkling." In Leigh's Crit. Sac. under the word βαπτισμος. Lond. 1646.

60. Mr. Poole's Continuators.—" To be baptized, is to be dipped in water; metaphorically, to be plunged in afflictions. I am, saith Christ, to be baptized with blood, overwhelmed with sufferings and afflictions." Annotations on Matt. xx. 22, edit. 1688.

61. Walæus.—" The external form of baptism is immersion into water, in the name of the Father, of the Son, and of the Holy Spirit." Enchiridium, p. 425.

62. Articles of Smalcald.—" Baptism is no other than the word of God, with plunging into water according to his appointment and command." Kromayeri Epitom. Lib. Concord. Christ. p. 107.

63. Anonymous.—" That the letter of the scripture is in favour of the Baptists (or, as they are still absurdly called Anabaptists,) cannot without evasion and equivo-

cation be denied." London Review, for June 1776, p. 489.

64. Gerhardus.—" Βαπτισμος and βαπτισμα, from βαπτιζειν, to baptize, to immerse, to dip, and that properly, into water: it has a likeness to the words βυθιζω and βαθυνω, each of which signifies to plunge down into the deep. Plutarch, βαπτισον σεαυτον εις θαλασσαν, *plunge yourself into the sea.* The same biographer, in the life of Galba, speaks metaphorically of being *baptized*, or immersed *in debt:* βεβαπτισμενος οφειλημασι. In his Morals, he speaks of being *baptized*, or oppressed, *by an accumulation of affairs:* βαπτιζεσθαι υπο των πραγματων. In his life of Phocion, of being *baptized in*, or plunged under *immoderate labours:* βαπτιζεσθαι τοις πονοις υπερβαλλουσι. Aphrod. l. i. probl. has the following expressions; βεβαπτισμενος τῳ σωματι, *plunged down in the body.* In this acceptation of immersing, it is used (2 Kings v. 14,) 'Then went he down and dipped (εβαπτισατο) himself seven times in Jordan'.... But because those who are immersed in water, and emerge out of it, appear washed and clean, therefore βαπτισμος and βαπτιζειν are consequentially used for any kind of ablution, whether it be performed by merely sprinkling, or pouring, or by a particular dipping. Βαπτιζειν is derived from βαπτειν, which signifies, in general, to dip, to wash, to dye, to immerse." Loc. Theolog. tom. iv. De Bap. p. 224.

65. Alstedius.—" Βαπτιζειν, to baptize, signifies only to immerse; not to wash, except by consequence." Lexicon Theologicum, cap. xii. p. 221,

66. Mr. Wilson.—" To baptize, to dip into water, or to plunge one into the water." Christian Dictionary, edit. 1678.

67. Mr. Bailey.—" Baptism, in strictness of speech, is that kind of ablution, or washing, which consists in dipping; and when applied to the Christian institution so called, it was used by the primitive Christians in no

other sense than that of dipping; as the learned Grotius and Casaubon well observe. But as new customs introduce new significations of words, in process of time it admitted the idea of sprinkling, as in the case of clinical baptism." Dictionary, Dr. Scott's edit. 1772.

68. Mr. Leigh.—" Βαπτιζω. The word *baptize*, though it be derived from βαπτω, to dip, or plunge into the water, and signifieth primarily such a kind of washing as is used in bucks, where linen is plunged and dipped; yet it is taken more largely for any kind of washing, rinsing, or cleansing, even where there is no dipping at all, (as Matt. iii. 11. and so on.)....The native and proper signification of it is, to dip into water, or to plunge under water, (John iii. 22, 23; Matt. iii. 16; Acts viii. 38.)" Critica Sacra.

69. Schoettgenius.—" Βαπτιζω, from βαπτω; properly, to plunge, to immerse; to cleanse, to wash." Lex. in Nov. Test. Krebsii, edit. 1765.

70. Mr. Parkhurst.—" Βαπτιζω, from βαπτω, to dip, immerse, or plunge in water. To baptize, to immerse in, or wash with water. Figuratively, *to be baptized*, immersed, or plunged in a flood, or sea, as it were, of grievous afflictions and sufferings."

71. Schrevelius.—" Βαπτιζω, to baptize, to plunge, to wash." Cantab. 1685.

72. Pasor.—" Βαπτιζω, to baptize, to immerse, to wash." Lips. 1735.

73. Trommius.—" Βαπτιζω, to baptize; to immerse, to dip." Concordantiæ Græcæ, sub voce.

74. Mintert.—Βαπτιζω, to baptize; properly, indeed, it signifies to plunge, to immerse, to dip into water: but because it is common to plunge or dip a thing that it may be washed, hence also it signifies to wash, to wash away....Βαπτισμος, *baptism:* immersion, dipping into; washing, washing away. Properly, and according to its etymology, it denotes that washing which is performed by immersion."

BAPTIZE AND BAPTISM. 57

75. Scapula.—" Βαπτιζω, to baptize; to dip, or immerse; as we immerse any thing for the purpose of dyeing, or cleansing in water. Also to dip, to plunge, to overwhelm in water. Likewise to wash away, to wash." Lond. 1652.

76. Hedericus.—" Βαπτιζω, to baptize; to plunge, to immerse, to overwhelm in water; to wash away, to wash.... Βαπτισμα, baptism; immersion, dipping into." Lond. 1778.

77. Constantinus.—" Βαπτισμος, baptism; the act of dyeing, that is, of plunging." Edit. 1592.

78. Mr. Robertson.—" Βαπτιζω, to baptize; to immerse, to wash." Thesaurus Græc.

79. Mr. William Young.—" *Baptize;* to dip all over, to wash, to baptize." Latin-English Dictionary.

80. Stockius.—" Βαπτισμα, baptism. Generally, and in virtue of its etymology, it signifies immersion, or dipping into. Particularly and properly, it denotes the immersion or dipping of a thing into water, that it may be cleansed or washed." Jenæ, 1735.

81. Stephanus.—" Βαπτιζω, to plunge, or immerse. To plunge; that is, to plunge under, or overwhelm in water. To cleanse, to wash." Thesaur. Græc. Ling. 1572.

82. Schwarzius. " Βαπτιζω, to baptize; to plunge, to overwhelm, to dip into.* To wash, by plunging,

---

* To authenticate this, as the native and primary meaning of the term, he produces the following authorities. "Polyb. iii. c. 72. Μολις εως των μαςων οι πεζοι βαπτιζομενοι διεβαινον, vix transibant pedites ad mammas usque *mersi.* Idem, v. c. 47. Αυτοι υπ' αυτων βαπτιζομενοι και καταδυνοντες εν τοις τελμασιν, ipsi a se ipsis mergebantur et deprimebantur in paludibus. Dio. xxxviii. p. 84. Παντελως βαπτιζονται, omnino *merguntur.* Idem. xxxvii. extr. p. 64. Χειμων τοιουτος εξαιφνης την χωραν απασαν κατεσχεν, ωςε—τα πλοια τα εν τω Τιβεριδι—βαπτισθηναι, tanta tempestas subito per totam regionem extitit, ut navigia in Tiberi *mergerentur.* Idem. l. p. 492. Πως μεν αν ουχ υπ' αυτου του πληθους των κωπων βαπτισθειη; quomodo non ipsa remorum multitudine, *submergatur?* Adde p. 502, 505. Porphyrius de Styge, p. 282. Οταν δε

(Luke xi. 38; Matt. vii. 4.) Sometimes to sprinkle, to besprinkle, to pour upon.* To purify and consecrate to God, by plunging. (Matt. iii. 6, 11, 13, 14, and elsewhere.).... Βαπτιστης, *the Baptist*, who sustained the singular and sacred office, of plunging men desirous

---

κατηγορουμενος επιβη, αναμαρτητος μεν ων αδεως διερχεται, αχρι των γονατων εχων το ύδωρ αμαρτων δε, ολιγον προβας βαπτιζεται μεχρι κεφαλης. Quum autem accusatus ingreditur lacum, secure, si peccati sit expers, transit, mersus usque ad genua. Sin peccarit, paulum progressus *submergitur* usque ad caput. Diodorus Siculus, i. p. 33. Των δε χερσαιων θηριων τα πολλα μεν ὑπο του ποταμου περιληφθεντα διαφθειρεται βαπτιζομενα, τινα δε εις τους μετεωρους εκφευγοντα τοπους διασωζεται. Animalium terrestrium multa a flumine Nilo correpta *mergendo* perduntur: alia in editos locos fugientia servantur. Adde Strabon. vi. p. 421. Joseph. Bell. Jud. p. 259, init. Activum quoque in significatione passiva est apud Joseph. Antiq. ix. c. x. § 2. Οσον ουπω μελλοντος βαπτιζειν του σκαφους, quum navis *mergeretur* tantum, quantum nondum coeperat."—I will here add another passage from Diod. Siculus, l. i. p. 67, as I find it quoted and translated by Dr. Sam. Chandler: "Τους δε ιδιωτας δια την εκ τουτων ευποριαν ου ΒΑΠΤΙΖΟΥΣΙ ταις εισφοραις. The people were not oppressed with taxes." Defence of Prime Minister of Joseph, p. ii. p. 388.

† His only authorities for the two latter of these ideas, are the following: "Æschyl. Prometh. Vinct. p. 53. Διδηκτον εν σφαγαισι βαψασα ξιφος, ancipitem gladium cædibus *tingens*. Apud Platon. in Conviv. p. 316. Aristophanes de se dicit, και γαρ και αυτος ειμι των χθες βεβαπτισμενων. Etenim ego quoque sum ex iis qui heri multum biberunt." Whether these passages do not confirm the idea of *plunging* and *overwhelming*, rather than that of *sprinkling*, or *pouring*, for which they were produced, let the learned judge. Respecting the latter of them, Dr. Daniel Scott says: "Plato uses this verb [βαπτιζω] of a person who had drunk freely, *drenched* himself in liquor." Note on Matt. xxviii. 19.—So Justin Martyr and Chrysostom speak of being *baptized in wine*; and Clemens Alexandrinus, of being *baptized in sleep*. Apud Suicerum, Thesaur. Eccles. tom. i. p. 623. And as the word *baptized*, in these connections, expresses the notion of being as it were *buried* in sleep, and *overwhelmed* in wine; so those corresponding adjectives, *ebrius*, *drunk*, and *drunken*, are allusively used to signify *soaked*, *dipped*, *drenched*. Thus Martial: "Lana sanguine conchæ EBRIA." Thus Jehovah: "I will make mine arrows drunk with blood." (Deut. xxxii. 42.) And Shakespeare thus: "Then let the earth be DRUNKEN with our blood." See Ainsworth and Johnson under the words.

of salvation, that they might know themselves to be devoted to God." Comment. Crit. et Philolog. Ling. Græc. See also Martini Lexicon Philologicum, sub voce, Baptismus. Riisenii Summa Theolog. loc. xvii. § 26. Glossarium Vetus, sub voce Βαπτιζω. Damm. Nov. Lex. Græc. sub voce Βαπτω. Dr. Macknight's Harm. part ii. p. 279, edit. 2nd. Petavii Theol. Dogmat. l. ii. de Pœnitent. c. i. § 11. Mr. S. Davies's Sermons, vol. ii. p. 169. edit. 3rd.

REFLECTIONS.

Reflect. I. It will be allowed, I think, by every competent and impartial judge, that many of the authors from whose writings these quotations are made, may be justly numbered among the first literary characters that any age has produced. Now, as all these concessions, declarations, and reasonings, proceeded from persons that practised pouring or sprinkling in the administration of the ordinance under consideration; so there is the highest reason to conclude, that nothing but the force of evidence, and a conscientious regard to truth, could have induced them thus to speak; for it is manifest, that such language has the appearance of supporting a contrary practice.

To the foregoing quotations from Pædobaptists, whom candour itself must suppose inclined to make as few concessions to the Baptists as the evidence of stubborn facts would permit, we will add the attestations of others, that may be justly considered as impartial spectators of our controversy about the right manner of administering baptism. The authors to whom I advert, belong to the denomination of people called Quakers; and their language is as follows.

1. Robert Barclay.—" Βαπτιζω signifies *immergo;* that is, to plunge and dip in; and that was the proper use of water baptism among the Jews, and also by John and the primitive Christians, who used it. Whereas our

adversaries, for the most part, only *sprinkle* a little water upon the forehead, which doth not at all answer to the word *baptism*: so that if our adversaries will stick to the word, they must alter their method of sprinkling." Apology, proposition xii. § 10.

2. John Gratton.—"John did baptize into water; and it was a baptism, a real dipping, or plunging into water, and so a real baptism was John's." Life of John Gratton, p. 231.

3. William Dell.—Speaking of baptism, he calls it, "the *plunging* of a man in cold water." Select Works, p. 389, edit. 1773.

4. Thomas Ellwood.—"They [the apostles, at the feast of Pentecost] were now baptized with the Holy Ghost indeed; and that in the strict and proper sense of the word *baptize;* which signifies *to dip, plunge,* or *put under.*" Sacred Hist. of the N. Test. part ii. p. 307.

5. Samuel Fothergill.—"By which [baptism of the Holy Spirit,] I understand such a thorough *immersion* into his holy nature, as to know him, the only begotten Son of God, to conform the soul to his own image." Remarks on Address to People called Quakers, p. 27.

6. Joseph Phipps.—The baptism of the Holy Spirit is "effected by spiritual immersion.... The practice of *sprinkling* infants, under the name of *baptism,* hath neither precept nor precedent in the New Testament." Dissertations on Bap. and Communion, p. 25, 30.

7. William Penn.—"I cannot see why the bishop [of Cork, in answer to whom he wrote,] should assume the power of unchristianing us, for not practising of that which he himself practises so unscripturally, and that according to the sentiments of a considerable part of Christendom; having not one text of scripture to prove that *sprinkling in the face* was the water baptism,—in the first times.—Then it was in the river *Jordan;* now in a *basin.*" Defence of Gospel Truths, against the Bishop of Cork, p. 82, 83.

8. George Whitehead.—"Sprinkling infants, I deny to be baptism, either in a proper or scripture sense. For sprinkling is *rhantism*, and not *baptism;* coming of ῥαντιζω, i. e. *aspergo*, to sprinkle, or to besprinkle, (Heb. ix. 13, 19, compared with Heb. x. 22; ῥαντισμος, a *besprinkling*, (and chap. xii. 24, and 1 Pet. i. 2.) But βαπτιζω, is *to baptize*, to *plunge* under water, to *overwhelm*. Wherefore I would not have these men offended at the word *rhantism*, it being as much English as the word baptism. And also βαπτισμους is translated *washing;* i. e. of cups, pots, brazen vessels, and tables, (Mark vii. 4.) Now if washing here should be taken in the common sense, cleanly people use not to do it only by sprinkling some drops of water upon them, but by washing them clean; so that rhantism can be neither *baptism*, nor *washing*, in a true or proper sense." Truth Prevalent, chap. ix. p. 116.

9. Elizabeth Bathurst.—" *Sprinkling* infants; this they [the Quakers] utterly deny, as a thing by men imposed, and never by God or Christ instituted." Life and Writings of Elizabeth Bathurst, chap. v. p. 44.

10. Thomas Lawson.—" Such as *rhantize*, or sprinkle infants, have no command from Christ, nor example among the apostles, nor the first primitive Christians, for so doing....The ceremony of John's ministration, according to divine institution, was by dipping, plunging, or overwhelming their bodies in water; as Scapula and Stephens, two great masters in the Greek tongue testify; as also Grotius, Pasor, Vossius, Minceus, Leigh, Casaubon, Bucer, Bullinger, Zanchy, Spanhemius, Rogers, Taylor, Hammond, Calvin, Piscator, Aquinas, Scotus....As for *sprinkling*, the Greeks call it *rhantismos*, which I render *rhantism:* for it is as proper to call sprinkling *rhantism*, as to call dipping *baptism*. This linguists cannot be ignorant of, that dipping and sprinkling are expressed by several words, both in Latin, Greek, and Hebrew. It is very evident,

if *sprinkling* had been of divine institution, the Greeks had their *rhantismos;* but as *dipping* was the institution, they used *baptismos;* so maintained the purity and propriety of the language.... To sprinkle young or old, and call it baptism, is very incongruous; yea, as improper as to call a horse a cow; for baptism signifies *dipping*. However, rhantism hath entered into, and among the professors of Christianity; and, TO GAIN THE MORE ACCEPTANCE, *it is called baptism*." Baptismalogia, p. 117, 118, 119.

11. Anthony Purver.—" *Baptized* is but a Greek word used in English, and signifying plunged." Note on 1 Cor. xv. 29.—Such is the harmonious and united testimony of these our impartial Friends: nor do I suppose that any sensible person of the same denomination would for a moment scruple to subscribe the preceding declarations.

Reflect. II. By the numerous quotations here produced from the most learned Pædobaptists, we are expressly taught, that immersion is the radical and obvious meaning of the term baptism, No. 1—82;—that the Danes, the Swedes, the Germans, and the Dutch, render the word $\beta\alpha\pi\tau\iota\zeta\omega$ by expressions that signify to dip, No. 12;—that it has no other signification in Mark vii. 4, No. 10, 40, 50, 82;—that the idea of immersion is retained when the term is used metaphorically of the Holy Spirit, No. 3, 8, 51, 53; of sufferings, No. 6, 8, 23, 58, 60, 70; and of other things, No. 42, 64, 82;—that $\beta\alpha\pi\tau\iota\zeta\epsilon\iota\nu$ is of a middle signification, between $\epsilon\pi\iota\pi o\lambda\alpha\zeta\epsilon\iota\nu$, *to swim on the surface,* and $\delta\upsilon\nu\epsilon\iota\nu$, *to go down to the bottom,* No. 1, 10, 27, 43, 45, 64;—that the word *baptism* is no where used in scripture to signify sprinkling, No. 40;—that it signifies immersion only, not washing, except by consequence, No. 65;—that the Greeks wanted not other words to have expressed a different action, if the institution would have borne it, No. 49;—that the manner of baptizing should correspond to the signification of the ordinance, No. 30;—that all antiquity and scripture confirm the idea of plunging, No. 49;—that sprinkling is rhantism, rather than baptism, No. 2, 59;—that new customs introduce new significations of words, No. 67;—that our opponents chiefly avail themselves of inferences, of analogy, and of doubtful construction, No. 42;—and that the Baptists have the advantage in point of argument, No. 42, 63.

Let us now review the testimonies of our impartial friends the Quakers. They assert, that the word in question signifies immersion, No. 1—11;—that the first administrator practised accordingly, No. 2, 7, 10;—that if sprinkling had been the institution, the Greeks had their *rhantismos*, but that dipping being appointed, *baptismos* was used in divine law, No. 10;—that sprinkling is neither baptism, nor washing, No. 8;—that there is neither precept nor precedent for sprinkling, No. 6, 7, 10; that the contrast between baptism and the rite which is now practised, is like that between the waves of Jordan, and the water in a portable basin, No. 7; that sprinkling of infants is a human invention, No. 9, 10; and that sprinkling is called baptism, to keep it in countenance, No. 10.—Such is the import of what the most learned Pædobaptists assert, and of what the impartial Quakers affirm, concerning the term in dispute; which, whether it be in our favour, I leave the reader to judge.

Reflect. III. Werenfelsius has well observed, in his excellent dissertation De Scopo Interpretis, that "some interpreters do not search the scripture so much for the meaning of the Holy Spirit, as for praise and honour; others, not so much for the sense of scripture, as for their own opinion; and others, not so much for the true meaning of scripture, as for one that is useful or agreeable."* Now as our enquiry here is concerning the sense of a term, an important enacting term of divine

---

* Opuscula Theolog. p. 373, 374.

law; and as the partiality and pride, so justly condemned by Werenfelsius, are too common to all theological writers; to avoid the appearance of predilection for a particular sense of the word in dispute, we will have recourse to the observations and rules of our opposers themselves, respecting the true meaning of inspired writers, and the expounding of laws. The following extracts may perhaps be useful to direct us in the present case, and are therefore submitted to the reader's consideration.

First, then, Buddeus.—" It is necessary, doubtless, that he who desires to be understood when he writes or speaks, should intend to convey only *one* meaning; which, if we obtain, we have the true and genuine sense."*——Chamier: "There is but one genuine sense of a text."†——Dr. Owen: "If it [the scripture] have not every-where one proper determinate sense, it hath none at all." ‡——Schelhornius: "The true sense of scripture, is not every sense the words will bear."§——Werenfelsius: "The true meaning of scripture, is not every sense the words will bear, and perhaps may excite in the reader's mind; nor yet every sense that is true in itself, but that which was really intended by the holy writer."||——Anonymous: " Laws being directed to the unlearned, as well as the learned, ought to be construed in their *most obvious* meaning, and not explained away by subtle distinctions; and no law is to suffer a figurative interpretation, where the proper sense of the words is as commodious, and equally fitted to the subject of the statute."¶——Dr. Sherlock: " When the words of the law are capable of different senses, and reason is for one sense, and the other sense against reason, there it is fit that a plain and necessary reason should expound

---

* Theolog. Dogmat l. i. c. ii. § 24.　　† Panstrat. tom. i. l. xiv. c. x. § 18.　　‡ On Heb. iii. 15, vol. ii. p. 155.
§ Bib. Bremens. class. vi. p. 468.　　|| Opuscula, p. 372.
¶ Encyclopæd. Britan. vol. vi. article Law, p. 41.

the law. But when the law is not capable of such different senses, or there is no such reason as makes one sense absurd and the other necessary, the law must be expounded according to the *most plain* and *obvious* signification of the words, though it should condemn that which we think there may be some reason for, or at least no reason against; for otherwise it is an easy matter to expound away all the laws of God."*——Bp. Taylor: " In all things where the precept is given in the proper style of laws, he that takes the *first* sense is the likeliest to be well guided.... In the interpretation of the laws of Christ, the *strict* sense is to be followed."†——Dr. Jonath. Edwards: " In words which are capable of two senses, the natural and proper is the primary; and therefore ought, in the first place and chiefly, to be regarded."‡——Dr. Horsley: " It is a principle with me, that the true sense of any phrase in the New Testament, is what may be called its standing sense; that which will be the *first* to occur to common people of every country and in every age."§——Vitringa: " This is accounted by all a constant and undoubted rule of approved interpretation ; that the *ordinary* and *most usual* signification of words must not be deserted, except for sufficient reasons."‖——Dr. Waterland: " Since words are designed to convey some meaning, if we take the liberty of playing upon words after the meaning is fixed and certain, there can be no security against equivocation and wile, in any laws, or any engagements whatever. All the ends and uses of speech will hereby be perverted."¶——Dr. William Sherlock: " In expounding scripture, we must confine ourselves to the *plain* and

---

* Preserv. against Pop. vol. ii. Appendix, p. 11.
† Duct. Dub. b. i. chap. i. p. 26 ; b. ii. chap. iii. p. 328.
‡ Preserv. against Socinianism, part iii. p. 52.
§ Reply to Dr. Priestley, lett. iv. p. 23.
‖ De Synag. Vet. l. i. pars i. c. iii. p. 110.
¶ Supplem. to Case of Arian Subscrip. p. 9, 10.

natural signification of the words... They [the Socinians] take and challenge to themselves a liberty of putting any sense upon the words of scripture which they can possibly bear, or are ever used in.... If we believe nothing but what the scripture does plainly and expressly teach, according to the most proper and usual acceptation of the words; if we believe amiss, it is none of our fault, unless just reverence to scripture be a fault.... It is impossible to prove, that *that* is not the sense of scripture, which is the *natural* interpretation of the words of any one text, and is not contradicted by any other text ....Can they [the Socinians] prove, that the words do *not* signify what we say they do? Or, that this is not the *most easy* and *obvious* sense of the words, and what every man would take to be the natural signification of them, who did not think himself concerned to try his skill to force some other sense on them? When the words are plain, and the sense plain and obvious, nothing can tempt any man to reject the plain sense of the words, for some obscure, laboured, and artificial interpretations, but a dislike of the doctrine which the plain and obvious sense of the words teaches."*——Dr. Doddridge: "I am more and more convinced, that the vulgar sense of the New Testament, that is, the sense in which an honest man of plain sense would take it, on his *first* reading the original, or any good translation, is almost every where the true general sense of any passage....I chose to follow the plainest and most obvious and common interpretation; which, indeed, I generally think the best ....As it is certain that $αρχη$ has not always that signification, [for which some contend] I judge it safe to give what is more commonly the sense of it."†—Once more: —Mr. Alsop says, " No cogent reason can be assigned, why we should depart from the plain, ordinary,

---

* Scripture Proofs of our Saviour's Div. p. 64, 65, 130, 131, 132.
† Fam. Exp. Note on Matt. xviii. 17 ; 2 Cor. viii. 1 ; Rev. iii. 14.

primary acceptation of the word *Christ*, for a figurative, improper and *secondary* acceptation."*——Were I to produce all the passages of this kind, from learned Pædobaptists, with which observation has furnished me, I should fill several more pages:† but I forbear, considering these as quite sufficient.

The leading idea of the foregoing paragraph is not a merely speculative principle: it is considered and treated, by great numbers of learned Pædobaptists, as of the highest importance. In all controversies, where an appeal is made to divine revelation, every one is ready to avail himself, as much as possible, of the primary, obvious, and most common sense of inspired language, both as to single terms and complete propositions. A sensible disputant is never willing to waive this advantage; nor, so far as I have observed, will he deliberately violate this principle, except when maintaining such hypotheses as he knows would be injured, if not subverted by it. Of the *latter*, Socinians are extremely culpable; and, indeed, we need not wonder at it: for the very life of their cause consists in explaining some of the most capital terms of scripture, in an improper and a secondary, a far-fetched and an arbitrary sense. They make exceptions to the clearest evidence of scripture testimony; insisting, that this or the other emphatical term, on which the argument very much depends, *may* be understood in a sense extremely different from its natural and obvious meaning: and then, without any reason, besides the support of their own hypothesis, they argue and infer any thing that suits their purpose. Thus deserting at every turn the radical and common acceptation of the most important scrip-

---

* Antisozzo, p. 35.   † See, among others, Dr. Owen, On the Nature of a Gosp. Church, p. 142. Ikenii Dissertat. Philolog. Theolog. p. 69, 361. Jos. Placæi Opera, tom. ii. p. 91, 255, 777, 875. Francof. 1703. Luther, De Servo Arbitrio, p. 115, 184. Argent. 1707.

tural expressions, they are never at a loss for an evasion. Against this conduct their numerous opponents have made very loud complaints; of which I will produce a few examples. "Their whole design and endeavour," says Dr. Owen, "is to put in exceptions against the *obvious* sense and interpretation of the words; not fixing on any determinate exposition of [the passage in question] themselves, such as they will abide by, in opposition unto any other sense of the place. Now this is a most *sophistical* way of arguing upon testimonies, and suited to make controversies endless. Whose wit is so barren, as not to be able to raise one exception or other, against the plainest and most evident testimony? So the Socinians deal with us, in all the testimonies we produce to prove the deity and satisfaction of Christ. They suppose it enough to evade their force, if they can but pretend that the words are capable of *another* sense; although they will not abide by it, that *this* or *that* is their sense: for if they would do so, when that is overthrown, the truth would be established. But every testimony of the scripture hath *one determinate* sense. When this is contended about, it is equal those at difference do express their apprehensions of the mind of the Holy Spirit, in the word which they will abide by. When this is done, let it be examined and tried, whether of the two senses pretended unto, doth best comply with the signification and use of the words, the context or scope of the place, other scripture testimonies, and the analogy of faith.... The words *may* have another sense; therefore [say the Socinians] nothing from them can be concluded; whereby they have left nothing stable, or unshaken in Christian religion.... How will they prove that [εγενετο] *may* be rendered by *fuit, was?* They tell you, it is so in two other places in the New Testament. But doth that prove that it *may* so much as be so rendered here? The proper sense and common usage of it is, *was made;* and because it is once or twice used in a peculiar sense, *may* it be so rendered here (John i. 14,) where nothing requires that it be turned aside from its most usual acceptation?.... The various signification of a word, used *absolutely* in any other place, is sufficient for these men to confute its *necessary* signification in any context."*——Dr. John Edwards: "Certainly, never men made such ill use of grammar and criticism as these [Socinians] do; for they make use of them only to deprave the true sense of the holy writ. To avoid and put by the force of some plain and express places, how do they stickle, how do they tug! To lexicons, dictionaries, and glossaries they resort, and enquire into and pick up all possible senses of the words and phrases which they meet with in scripture, but what are most agreeable to the matter and scope of the places they are concerned in. If a word have any other meaning in any author whatsoever, they make this a sufficient warrant to depart from the true and genuine sense of the place."†——Volkelius having asserted that, by the term *Godhead* (Col. ii. 8,) "neither the nature of God, nor of Christ, but the knowledge of the divine will, and the manner of worshipping God, *may* be, and therefore *must* be understood;" Mr. Alsop replies, "The reader is now satisfied why it *must* be so. It *may* be so, and therefore necessarily it *must* be so:" and, in a similar case, he says: "From *may* be in the premises, to *must* be in the conclusion, is a high leap."‡——Once more: Dr. Horsley says, "It is the particular happiness of the Unitarian writers, that they are never found at a loss for an expedient."‡

Farther: When Protestant Pædobaptists are disputing with Roman Catholics about the meaning of that

---

* Nature of Gospel Church, p. 144. Mystery of the Gospel vindicated, p. 160, 218; see also p. 228, 275, 303. Exposit. of Heb. vol. iii. p. 468. † Discourse concerning Truth and Error, p. 301. ‡ Antisozzo, p. 37, 44. § Reply to Dr. Priestley, lett. v. p. 30.

capital term *justification*, they constantly maintain the necessity of abiding by its primary, obvious, and most common acceptation, which is forensic; in opposition to any real or pretended secondary sense, for which the Papists earnestly plead. Of this I will give the following instances. Turrettinus: "*Properly* the verb *justify*, is forensic; and signifies, to *absolve* any one in judgment, or to *account* and *declare just*.... The Roman Catholics do not deny, that the word *justification*, and the verb *justify*, are frequently used in a forensic sense; yet they will not allow this to be the constant sense of the terms, but maintain that they often signify the real production, acquisition, and increase of righteousness; and that this acceptation of the words takes place in a particular manner, with reference to the justification of man before God.... But though the word justification, in some passages of scripture, depart from its proper signification, and take a sense that is not forensic; it does not follow that we do ill by taking it in a judicial sense, because its *proper sense* is to be regarded in those places which are the seat of the doctrine."*——Buddeus: "It may be demonstrated, that the forensic sense of the word *justification*, is the constant and perpetual signification of it in holy scripture. Yet were it very clearly shown, that in one or two places the word is used in a different sense, our cause would not be injured; for it would still be a fact, that the forensic sense is *more usual*, and chiefly perspicuous in the sacred writings.†"
——Dr. Owen, when endeavouring to vindicate the forensic sense of the word *justify*, against the exceptions of a learned man, makes the following preliminary observation: " I shall premise that which I judge not an unreasonable demand; namely, that if the signification of the word in any, or all the places which he mentions, should seem doubtful unto any, (as it doth not unto me)

---

* Institut. loc. xvi. quæst. i. § 4, 5, 9.
† Theolog. Dogmat. l. iv. c. iv. § 11, p. 953.

that the uncertainty of a very few places should not make us question the proper signification of a word, whose sense is determined in so many, wherein it is clear and unquestionable."*

Once more: Our learned Pædobaptist brethren apply the same principle to the interpretation of Greek particles. Thus Dr. Doddridge: "It seems desirable, where it can be done, to interpret the *particles* in their *most usual* sense."†——Mr. James Hervey, when disputing the signification of a Greek particle with Mr. J. Wesley, says: "I am ready to grant, that places may be found where the preposition εν must be understood according to your sense. But then every one knows that this is not the native, obvious, literal meaning; rather a meaning swayed, influenced, moulded by the preceding or following word.... He will not allow the Greek preposition εν to signify *in;* though I can prove it to have been in peaceful possession of this signification for more than two thousand years."‡

Reflect. IV. If we examine the present prevailing practice of pouring, or sprinkling, upon those principles, rules, and reasonings, which the most eminent Pædobaptists have laid before us in the preceding quotations; or if we pay any regard to the decision of those who have no interest in this dispute, and may therefore be justly considered as quite impartial; we must conclude, that neither sprinkling, nor pouring, is warranted by the word *baptism*. For our learned opponents themselves assure us, without so much as one exception occurring to observation in the course of my reading, that the primary meaning of the term in dispute, is *immersion;* and many distinguished characters among them unite in

---

* Doct. of Justif. chap. iv. Vid. Gomari Opera, pars ii. p. 92. Walæi Enchirid. Relig. p. 337, 338. Mastricht. Theolog. l. vi. c. vi. § 19. Witsii Œcon. Fæd. l. iii. c. viii. § 5—14.

† Note, on Mark ix. 49.

‡ Letters to Mr. J. Wesley, lett. ii. p. 26; lett. x. p. 232.

directing us, to interpret words and laws agreeably to the primary, obvious, and most usual sense of the terms. Now Pædobaptism, as practised in these northern parts of Europe, is not agreeable to the native, obvious, and common acceptation of the word *baptism*. It adopts a supposed secondary, remote, and obscure sense of the term. It represents our divine Legislator as having more meanings than one, under the same enacting term, of the same law, and at the same time; for so far as I have observed, none deny that *immersion* is warranted by that commanding word. It confronts an established principle upon which, among other things, the great doctrine of justification is defended against the Papists; a principle on which every confutation of Socinian error must proceed. And it opposes the grand rule of all interpretation, *that the ordinary and most usual signification of words must not be deserted, except for cogent reasons;* which rule is no other than the language of reason, of observation, and common sense. Pædobaptism, however, has nothing to plead for departing from this rule but—*its own existence.*

Reflect. V. Dr. Addington has justly observed, that " if there are two translations of a word, one of which is certainly true, and the other may be false, it is easy to say which the wise and candid would prefer."[*] Now, on the authorities here produced—authorities of commentators, of critics, and of lexicographers the most respectable—we may venture to assert, that the word baptism *certainly* signifies immersion, whatever meaning it may have besides; consequently, both candour and prudence require us to embrace that acceptation in preference to any other. But supposing, without granting, that the word under consideration is occasionally used by inspired writers, by the Septuagint translators, or by Greek classics, to signify *washing*, where there is no immersion, or even to denote *sprinkling;* yet while it is al-

---

[*] Christian Minister's Reas. p. 34.

lowed by so many of the first characters for sacred criticism, that its primary and obvious meaning is immersion; there is no reason to depart from it in the administration of a divine ordinance; except it can be proved, that the design of the institution will not comport with it, or that the practice of the apostles was a departure from it; concerning both which, we shall hear the verdict of learned men in subsequent chapters. Nay, if the numerous authors produced be not under a gross mistake, in fixing the natural and primary meaning of the term *baptism;* though many incontestable instances could be brought, that βαπτιζω, in certain connections, signifies *to wash*, without including the idea of dipping; and that on some occasions it also signifies to *pour*, and to *sprinkle;* yet immersion would still be the grand ruling idea. Surely, then, we ought not hastily, or for trivial reasons, to desert the original, the natural and proper sense of a term which was chosen by the unerring Spirit, when a new branch of holy worship was appointed; especially seeing that very term was intended to direct the church in all future ages, *how* the worship should be performed.

It should be well observed, that when our Lord after his resurrection says, *Go—baptize;* he does not mention baptism by way of allusion, or incidentally. No, he speaks the language of *legislation:* he delivers DIVINE LAW. He mentions and appoints baptism as an ordinance of God, and as a branch of human duty. Where then must we expect precision in the use of terms, if not on such an occasion? Can it be supposed, without impeaching the wisdom or the goodness of Christ, that he enacted a law relating to his own worship, the *principal* term in which is obscure and ambiguous? Can it be imagined that he *intended* an ambiguity so great in the term baptism, which prescribes the duty to be performed, as equally to warrant the use of immersion, of pouring, or of sprinkling, which are three different actions? We may safely challenge our opposers to produce an instance of this kind out of the Mosaic ritual.—Does Jehovah, when giving his positive laws, make use of a term that properly signifies *dipping*? He means as he speaks, and requires immersion, in contradistinction to pouring and sprinkling. Does he, on the other hand, employ a word which, properly understood, signifies *pouring*? Or does he choose an expression, the radical idea of which is no other than *sprinkling*? He still means as he speaks, and enjoins what he mentions, in distinction from every other action.

That dipping, pouring, and sprinkling, denote three different actions, in the language of divine law, as well as in the estimate of common sense, we have many examples in the writings of Moses. The following are selected for the reader's notice. " And the priest shall dip, βαψει, (Septuag.) his finger in the blood, and SPRINKLE, προσρανει, of the blood seven times before the Lord, before the veil of the sanctuary. And the priest shall——POUR, εκχεει, all the blood of the bullock at the bottom of the altar."* " Moses took the anointing oil—and he SPRINKLED, ερρανεν, thereof upon the altar seven times,—and he POURED, επεχεε, of the anointing oil upon Aaron's head." " Moses SPRINKLED, προσεχεε, the blood upon the altar round about—and he WASHED, επλυνεν, the inwards and the legs in water.† He DIPT, εβαψε, his finger in the blood —and poured out, εξεχεεν, the blood at the bottom of the altar.—And Aaron's sons presented unto him the blood, which he SPRINKLED, προσεχεεν, round about upon the altar—And he did WASH, επλυνε, the inwards."‡ " As for the living bird, he shall take it, and the cedar wood, and the scarlet, and the hyssop, and shall DIP them, βαψει αυτα, and the living bird, in the blood of the bird that was killed——And he shall SPRINKLE,

---

* Levit. iv. 6, 7; see v. 17, 18.   † Chap. viii. 11, 12, 19, 21.
‡ Chap. ix. 9, 12, 14.

περιρβανει, upon him that is to be cleansed from the leprosy seven times——And he that is to be cleansed shall WASH, πλυνει, his clothes, and shave off all his hair, and WASH HIMSELF, λουσεται, in water, that he may be clean.* And whosoever toucheth his bed shall WASH, πλυνει, his clothes, and BATHE HIMSELF, λουσεται, in water." See the following verse.†—So in the New Testament, washing the feet is distinguished from bathing the whole body, washing a part of the body from being baptized, and baptism from washing; as appears by the following instances. "He that is WASHED (or has been bathing, ὁ λελουμενος,) needeth not, save to WASH HIS FEET, ποδας νιψασθαι." "He took them the same hour of the night and WASHED, ελουσεν, their stripes; and was BAPTIZED, εβαπτισθη, he and all his straightway." "Arise and be BAPTIZED, βαπτισαι, and WASH AWAY, απολουσαι, thy sins."‡ By which it appears, that as *tasting*, in the language of scripture, is distinguished from *drinking*;§ so are *washing* the feet, from *bathing* the whole body, and washing *a part* of the body, from being *baptized*. So that ancient patron of Pædobaptism, Cyprian, expressly distinguishes between *washing* and *sprinkling*, when professedly pleading for the latter, in what he thought a case of necessity. In his letter to Magnus he intimates that some doubted, whether those who received the clinical baptism, "were to be accounted legitimate Christians; eo quod aquâ salutari non loti sint, sed perfusi, because they were not *washed*, but *sprinkled*, with the salutary water."‖ Whence it appears, that in Cyprian's time sprinkling was quite a novel practice; that it was used only in favour of those who were confined by illness; and that baptismal *washing*,

---

* Lev. chap. xiv. 6, 7, 8.
† Chap. xv. 5, 6; see also, Numb. xix. 4, 7, 18, 19; Deut. xxi. 6, 7.
‡ Job xiii. 10. See Dr. Doddridge *in loc.*; Acts xvi. 33, and xxii. 16. § Matt. xxvii. 34. ‖ Epist. lxxvi.

in the language of Cyprian, is no other than plunging. Mr. Cleaveland also has very lately distinguished between dipping, sprinkling, and washing, in the following manner: "We *dip* our hand in water, though not all over, to baptize a person by *sprinkling*, or to *wash* our face."* With what reason or shadow of propriety, then, can any one pretend that the term baptism, is equally expressive of these different actions?

Were the leading term in any human law to have an ambiguity in it equal to that for which our brethren plead, with regard to the word *baptism;* such law would certainly be considered as betraying either the weakness or wickedness of the legislator; and be condemned as opening a door to perpetual chicane and painful uncertainty. Far be it, then, from us to suppose, that our gracious and omniscient Lord should give a law relating to divine worship, and obligatory on the most illiterate of his real disciples, which may be fairly construed to mean, *this*, *that*, or the *other* action—a law, which is calculated to excite and perpetuate contention among his wisest and sincerest followers—a law, in respect of its triple meaning, that would disgrace a British parliament, as being involved in the dark ambiguity of a pagan oracle. It must, therefore, be at our peril, if we indulge a wanton fancy in the interpretation of that law which is now before us. For, as Mr. Charnock observes, "It is a part of God's sovereignty to be the interpreter, as well as the maker, of his own laws; as it is a right inherent in the legislative power among men. So that it is an invasion of his right to fasten a sense upon his declared will, which doth not *naturally flow* from the words. For to put any interpretation, according to our pleasure, upon divine as well as human laws, contrary to their true intent, is a virtual usurpation of this power; because if laws may be interpreted accord-

---

* Infant Baptism from Heaven, p. 63. Salem, 1784.

ing to our humours, the power of the law would be more in the interpreter than in the legislator."*

Were the same licence of interpretation used in construing the law of the sacred supper, as numbers practise on the term baptism; we should probably soon behold an obsolete and superstitious custom revived: the custom, I mean, of employing a reed, a glass tube, or something similar, by which to *suck* the wine out of the cup.† When our Lord instituted the holy supper, his order concerning the wine was; Πιετε εξ αυτου παντες, "DRINK ye all of it," (Matt. xxvi. 27.) Now none will dispute, that πιετε is from πινω; or that the natural and proper signification of it is, *to drink*; in the full and most proper sense, *to* DRINK. Nay, it will be allowed, I suppose, that if πινω does not signify that precise idea, there is never a word in the Greek Testament that can express it. Yet the learned lexicographer Schwarzius tells us, that it signifies not only to *drink;* but also to SUCK, to *imbibe*, to *admit*, to *receive*, for which he refers to Heb. vi. 7.

Our brethren ought not to forget, that the principal terms of a law, and especially of a law relating to divine worship, should be understood in their natural, obvious, primary sense; from which it is dangerous to depart, except some glaring absurdity would follow. This remark is perfectly agreeable to the doctrine of Sir William Blackstone, who lays it down as a rule of legal interpretation; "that the words of a law are generally to be understood in their *usual* and *most known* signification; not so much regarding the propriety of grammar, as their general and popular use:"—but, "where words bear either none, or a very absurd signification, if literally understood, we must a little deviate from the received sense of them." ‡ This, we may venture to say,

---

* Of Man's Enmity to God, p. 98. † Hospiniani Hist. Sac. l. iv. c. ii. p. 248. Venem. Hist. Eccles. tom. vi. p. 193.

‡ Commentaries, vol. i. Introduct. sect. ii.

is a rule of good sense, as well as of legal knowledge; and should be constantly regarded in our interpretation of laws, whether divine or human. Whereas, if we wantonly depart from it, almost any hypothesis may be supported; for by taking such a liberty, there is no word in any language that might not have the whole of its natural and primary sense expounded away.

Reflect. VI. While our brethren maintain that the term baptism, when relating to the institution so called, means any thing short of immersion; it behoves them to inform us, which of our English words is competent to express its adequate idea. I have observed, indeed, that they seldom fix upon any particular term and abide by it, as answering to the word baptism; but rather choose to use, *washing*, *pouring*, or *sprinkling*, just as their cause requires. Now, as those three expressions, in their native signification, denote three different actions, it looks as if they were fearful of being embarrassed, were they to select one of them and uniformly to employ it, in preference to the other two. As they do not pretend our divine Lawgiver meant, that washing, pouring, and sprinkling, should *all* be performed on the same person to constitute baptism; so, while they believe that any action short of immersion is warranted by his command, they ought, as fair disputants, to tell us what that action is, and by what name we should call it. (See the quotations from Dr. Owen, Reflect. iii. p. 68, 69.) At present, however, we can only ask, Is it *washing?* If so, we may consider that word as a proper translation of it,* and a complete substitute for it, wherever the ordinance before us is mentioned by the sacred writers.†

---

* *Baptism* is the Greek word, with an English termination; concerning which Mr. Lewis says, "Our last translators were directed by the king to retain the old ecclesiastical words," of which baptism was one. Hist. of Eng. Translations, p. 317, 326, edit. 2nd.

† It is an old rule, Definitiones debent cum definito reciprocari: that is, A definition and the thing defined should be convertible.

BAPTIZE AND BAPTISM. 79

Let us make the experiment on a few passages. We will take, for instance, the words of Ananias to Saul, (Acts xxii. 16,) which must be read thus: "Arise and be WASHED, and WASH away thy sins:" and those of Paul, (Rom. vi. 3, and Gal. iii. 27,) "Know ye not, that so many of us as were WASHED into Jesus Christ, were WASHED into his death? As many of us as have been WASHED into Christ, have put on Christ."—Is it *pouring?* Then we must read (Mark i. 9, and Acts ii. 38, 41,) thus; "Jesus came from Nazareth of Galilee, and was POURED of John in (εις, into) Jordan."—"Repent and be POURED every one of you."—"Then they that gladly received his word, were POURED."—Is it *sprinkling?* Then we must read (John iii. 23; Rom. vi. 4; Col. ii. 12,) thus: "John also was SPRINKLING in Enon near to Salim, BECAUSE THERE WAS MUCH WATER there: and they came and were SPRINKLED."—"Therefore we are BURIED with him by SPRINKLING into death."—"Buried with him by SPRINKLING." These few examples may suffice to show, what an awkward appearance the noble sense and masculine diction of inspiration wear, when expressed according to this hypothesis. Whereas, if instead of *washing*, *pouring*, or *sprinkling*, you employ the word *immersion*, the preceding passages will make a very different figure, and read thus: "Arise and be IMMERSED, and wash away thy sins."—"Know ye not, that so many of us as were IMMERSED into Jesus Christ, were IMMERSED into his death?"—"As many of us as have been IMMERSED into Christ, have put on Christ." —"Jesus came from Nazareth of Galilee, and was IMMERSED of John in (or into) Jordan."—"Repent and be IMMERSED every one of you."—"Then they that gladly received his word were IMMERSED."—"John also was IMMERSING in Enon near to Salim, because there was much WATER there: and they came and were IMMERSED."—"Therefore we are buried with him by IMMERSION into death."—"Buried with him by

IMMERSION." Here we have, if I mistake not, both dignity of sentiment, and propriety of language. Hence it appears, that the word βαπτιζω is connected with such particles (εν and εις) as forbid our concluding that either *wash, pour,* or *sprinkle,* is a proper substitute for it. The form of expression adopted by evangelists and apostles, is always, if I mistake not, baptizing *in* or *into* something. Thus, for example, εν or εις, *in* or *into* Jordan;* εν, *in* water, *in* the Holy Spirit;† εις, *into* the name,‡ *into* Moses,§ *into* Christ, ‖ *into* his death.¶ Εις, in the case of baptism, cannot be rendered *to* or *towards;* because it would be absurd to say, that John baptized *to* or *towards* Jordan; nor in regard to this affair can εν be translated *with* or *by;* because it would be awkward to say, John baptized *with* or *by* Jordan; besides, εις, which is used of the same administration, cannot be so rendered. Baptism, therefore, being always expressed as performed *in,* or *into* something, must be immersion, and not pouring, or sprinkling; for *persons* cannot be sprinkled or poured *into* water, though they may be plunged *into* it.

Let us now apply the same terms to the different *metaphorical* baptisms of which we read in the New Testament. There we have, the baptism of *sufferings,* of the *Spirit* and of *fire,* of the *cloud* and the *sea.* According to our brethren, the passages to which I refer must be read, either thus: " I have A WASHING to be WASHED WITH, and how am I straitened till it be accomplished."—" He shall WASH you with (rather in, εν,) the Holy Spirit and in fire."—" And were all WASHED unto Moses in the cloud and in the sea."** Or thus: " I have a POURING to be POURED with, and how am I straitened till it be accomplished!"—" He shall POUR

---

* Matt. iii. 6; Mark i. 9. † Matt. iii 11.
‡ Matt. xxviii. 19. § 1 Cor. x. 2. ‖ Gal. iii. 27.
¶ Rom. vi. 3. See Mr. M'Lean's Nature and Import of Baptism, p. 6. ** Luke xii. 50; Matt. iii. 11; 1 Cor. x. 2.

you in the Holy Spirit and in fire."—" And were all POURED unto Moses, in the cloud and in the sea."—Or thus: " I have a SPRINKLING to be SPRINKLED with, and how am I straitened till it be accomplished!"—" He shall SPRINKLE you in the Holy Spirit and in fire."— " And were all SPRINKLED unto Moses, in the cloud and in the sea." According to us, the manner of reading these passages will be this: " I have an IMMERSION to be IMMERSED with, and how am I straitened till it be accomplished!"—" He shall IMMERSE you in the Holy Spirit and in fire."—" And were all IMMERSED unto Moses, in the cloud and in the sea." In regard to Luke xii. 50, if you render the word baptism by the term washing, you not only sink the vigorous idea, but convey a sentiment foreign to the text. For the term *washing* plainly suggests the notion of cleansing; whereas it is manifest, that our Lord here speaks of *himself* personally—of himself, not as to be *cleansed* from sin, but *punished* for it; or, as the apostle asserts, MADE A CURSE FOR US. To adopt the word *pouring*, would exceedingly dilute and impoverish the marvellous meaning, if not to render the passage absolutely unintelligible; and, from using the term *sprinkling*, common sense turns abhorrent; as it would render the emphatical and admirable text quite ridiculous. For who can seriously imagine that our Lord intended to represent his most bitter sufferings by the act of sprinkling a few drops of water on a person? No; he designed to express his being " baptized, or plunged, into death," as Bugenhagius interprets the passage.* So that, though the term baptism is here used by way of allusion; and, though I am far from thinking that the allusive sense of a word should be the rule of interpreting the same expression in a positive divine law; yet, as all pertinent metaphors have a literal and proper sense for their foundation, we may conclude, that if it

---

* In Biblioth. Bremens. class. ii. p. 665.

be possible for any word, when used metaphorically, to express the idea of *immersion, plunging, overwhelming*, we have it here in the term baptism. The same observations will apply to a similar text, (Matt. xx. 22,) "Are ye able to be baptized with the baptism that I am baptized with?" which Dr. Doddridge thus paraphrases: "Are you able to be baptized with the baptism, and *plunged* into that sea of sufferings with which I am shortly to be baptized, and, as it were, *overwhelmed* for a time?"—In respect of the two other passages, whether our sense of the word in question, or that of Pædobaptists, be more emphatical, and the language more agreeable, my reader will determine.

Farther: If it be lawful to administer the ordinance before us by pouring or sprinkling, equally as by immersion; it must be, because that diversity of administration is warranted, either by the command of our divine Lawgiver, or by the practice of his apostles. But if so, is it not very surprising that the sacred penmen of the New Testament, when recording precepts and facts for our direction in this affair, have never used a term, the *natural* and *primary* meaning of which is pouring, or sprinkling? This is the more surprising, as, in other cases, apparently of much less consequence to the purity of divine worship, they frequently employ such words as are adapted to express those ideas without any ambiguity. If *pouring*, for instance, be a legitimate way of performing the rite, what can be the reason that βαλλω, εκχεω, επιχεω, εκχυνω, καταχεω, προσχεω, or προσχυσις, (all which are found in the apostolic writings,) are never used in the New Testament, concerning the administration of baptism? Or, if *sprinkling* be a proper mode of proceeding, how comes it that ραντιζω, ραντισμος, or some other term of the same signification, does not appear in any command or precedent, relating to the subject of this controversy? Why should those Greek words I have just mentioned, and all others of a similar meaning, (whether used by Pagan classics, or the Septuagint translators) be excluded from precepts and examples of the institution before us; while βαπτιζω, βαπτισμα, and βαπτισμος, are appropriated to that service, if pouring or sprinkling had been at all intended by our Lord, or ever practised by his apostles? See No. 49.—It must not be supposed, as Jos. Placæus has justly observed in another case, that this was done by inspired writers without design:* and on our principles the reason is plain. The great Legislator intended that his followers should be IMMERSED, " in the name of the Father, and of the Son, and of the Holy Spirit:" in pursuance therefore of this design, such words are used concerning the ordinance, as *naturally* and *properly* convey that idea.—We have, I think, as much reason to conclude that βαπτιζω and ῥαντιζω are terms of opposite significations, as that βαπτιστηριον and περιρραντηριον denote things intended for opposite uses. The former of these names, it is well known, was applied by ancient Christians to the baptismal font; because candidates for communion were *immersed* in it: the latter, it is equally clear, was appropriated by Pagan Greeks to the vessel which contained their holy water; because thence the idolatrous priest *sprinkled* the consecrated element upon each worshipper.† What then would the learned say, were any one pretending to an acquaintance with Christian and Greek antiquities, designedly to confound the two latter expressions, as if they were convertible terms? Be the just censure what it might, I cannot help thinking it is due to those who confound the two former, by labouring to prove them equivalent, in regard to the ordinance before us. Though our brethren maintain the lawfulness of *pouring* and *sprinkling*, they cannot produce one instance from the divine rubric of this institution, of any

---

* Opera, tom. ii, p. 267.
† Suiceri Thesaurus Eccles. tom. i. p. 659. Dr. Potter's Antiquities of Greece, vol. i. chap. iv. p. 195.

word being used which primarily and plainly expresses either of those actions.—It is very remarkable, that while few or none of our learned opponents dare deny, that the term baptism conveys the idea of immersion; and while none of them, so far as I have observed, venture to assert, that it never means any thing besides pouring or sprinkling; yet, in their *practice*, pouring, or sprinkling, is constantly used. Thus what is allowed by learned men in general to be the *radical* idea of a capital term in divine law, is entirely kept out of sight; while a presumed *secondary* sense, is the only thing that appears in their mode of proceeding.

Dr. Addington, indeed, says: "We have not met with *one* text, in the whole Bible, that requires the immersion of the whole body."* Just so, I remember, Socinus declared, that he could not find one text which requires either immersion or sprinkling. The people called Quakers adopt similar language. Nor could the whole Council of Trent meet with so much as one text that enjoins those whom they call the laity, to partake of wine at the Lord's table.† "So hard a thing is it," says Mr. Reeves, "to find any text plain enough for some men!"‡ But though Dr. Addington has not met with one text, which he considers as requiring immersion, many of those learned authors with whose language the reader has been entertained, seem to be of a different opinion: and if the native signification of the term baptism, be immersion, the action so called must be *required*, wherever divine law enjoins the administration of baptism. This must be the case, except it can be proved, that the leading terms of a law should be understood in a real, or supposed, secondary sense. Has, then, Dr. Addington met with any text which requires *pouring*, or *sprinkling*, in opposition to immersion? Has he found any passage of sacred writ, that *enjoins* pour-

---

* Christian Minister's Reasons, p. 176.   † Sess. xxi. cap. i.
‡ Apologies, vol. i. Preface, p. 84, edit. 1709.

ing or sprinkling water on the *face*, in contradistinction to plunging the whole body? He will not, I think, dare to assert either the one or the other. But if immersion be not *required*, in contradistinction to pouring and sprinkling; and if pouring or sprinkling be not *required*, in opposition to immersion; we should consider it as a favour, if this opponent would inform us what *is* required. For the question relates to the *mind of* CHRIST: it regards the meaning of a *divine* LAW: nor can we forbear thinking, that *something* is required, *really* and in *earnest* required, which is called *baptism;* or else our Protestant principles would exclaim against us, for performing any thing under that name as a branch of holy worship. While, therefore, any of our opposers deny that *immersion* is required, they are obliged to prove, either, that their own mode of proceeding has the sanction of a *divine requisition*, exclusively of ours; or, that the most High has, for once, consulted the honour of the human will, by leaving the manner of performing a positive rite of religion entirely at the option of his worshippers. The former will be an arduous task; the latter is pregnant with impious absurdity.

Reflect. VII. While the Pædobaptists maintain that our great Lawgiver intended any thing less than *dipping* the subject of the ordinance, whether it be washing, pouring, or sprinkling; it is necessary for them to consider, whether his design was, that water should be applied, in any of these ways, to the *whole body*, or to some *particular part*. If the former, why do they not comply with his requisition? Why make such a partial application of the element? If the latter, what part must it be? Some pour water on the *back part* of the head, and call it baptism.* Others have *washed the face*, pronounced the prescribed form of words, and thought the institution was rightly administered.† What, if others were to

---

* Bp. Burnet's Second Letter of his Travels, p. 85.
† Mr. Neale's Hist. Purit. vol. i. p. 543, 544, octav. edit.

wash the *hands* of a candidate, call it baptism, and plead, that washing the hands was a religious rite appointed by Jehovah?* Nay, what if some should wash the *feet*, pronounce it baptism, and appeal to John xiii. 10, in justification of their conduct?† I leave the reader to consider, whether a minister has not as good a warrant from the New Testament thus to proceed, as to pour water upon, or to sprinkle the *face*; and then to conclude, that the party is duly baptized.—It has been the opinion of some, that a child is baptized, on whatever part of his body the water may fall:‡ and we may justly demand, By what law of Christ, or by what example of the apostles, is any one authorized to apply water to the face, or the head; rather than to the hands, the feet, or any other part of the body? It should never be forgotten, that the institution about which we treat, is of a positive kind; and that we are not at liberty to perform it as we please, but are bound to observe the law of administration enacted by our divine Sovereign. See chap. i.

In opposition to this partial application of water, it may be farther observed, that when Jehovah appointed circumcision, he expressly mentioned the part on which it should be performed. When also he commanded a topical application of the sacrificial blood and the anointing oil, he did not fail to describe the parts intended:§ and such was the obligation of his directions in refe-

---

* Deut. xxi. 6. † The *pedilavium* practised in early times, was actually considered by some, in the beginning of the fourth century, as a proper substitute for baptism; on which account, washing of the feet by the bishop was forbidden by the Council of Eliberis. See Dr. Gill, on John xiii. 15.—The church of Milan practised washing of the feet, " because Adam was *supplanted* by the devil, and the serpent's poison was cast upon his *feet;* therefore men were washed in that part for greater sanctification, that he might have no power to supplant them any farther." Mr. Bingham's Orig. Ecclesiast. b. xii. chap. iv. § 10.

‡ Venem. Hist. Eccles. tom. vi. p. 192. § Lev. xiv. 14, 17

rence to these affairs, that if Abraham had circumcised a *finger*, instead of the *foreskin;* or had the blood and the oil been applied to any other parts of the body, than those that were specified; guilt would have been contracted, and the anger of the Lord incurred. So, on the other hand, when God enjoined the priests or the people to *bathe*, had they only sprinkled the *face*, poured water on the *hands*, or washed the *feet*, they would have been equally culpable. Now, baptism being a positive institution, as well as those ancient rites, what reason can be assigned, if water should be applied only to a particular part of the body, why that part was not mentioned, either in the institution of the ordinance, or in some apostolic example of its administration? yet I do not remember to have observed, that any of our opponents pretend that it is.

Reflect. VIII. That extraordinary communication of spiritual gifts and of divine influence, which the disciples of Christ received at the feast of Pentecost, being called the *baptism* of the Holy Spirit; and the Holy Spirit being represented as *poured out*, and *falling upon*, those first ministers in the Messiah's kingdom; our brethren have often pleaded these facts in opposition to us, and in favour of their own practice. In answer to which, I would propose the following things to consideration.

The word *baptism* is here manifestly used in an improper and allusive sense; for there is no more literal propriety in speaking of the Holy Spirit being *poured*, or *sprinkled*, upon those first disciples of our ascended Lord, than in representing them as *immersed* in the Holy Spirit. Must we, then, expound the principal term of a divine law, which is to be literally understood, by a merely *allusive* expression? so expound it, as to depart from its native, primary, and obvious meaning? It has been common for learned men to examine the propriety of metaphorical and allusive terms, upon the foundation of their literal and primary meaning; but never, that I have observed, to consider an allusive application of them, as the standard of their literal sense. Yet this is the case here. For our dispute is about the meaning of the term baptism, in a *proper*, *literal* sense, and as occurring in divine *law:* to determine which, our brethren appeal to an *improper*, and an *allusive* sense of the word as used with reference to a supernatural fact. This, we think, is very extraordinary. For if the command to baptize need any explanation from subsequent facts, it seems natural for us to have recourse—not to the language of metaphor, nor to any expression that is merely allusive,—but, to apostolic practice in the administration of baptism; because, by making allusive expressions the rule of interpreting literal commands, any divine law may soon be explained away.—For instance: Had the mode of interpretation adopted by our opponents been approved and applied by the ancient Hebrews to the command of circumcision, they might have evaded the painful rite. They would, it is likely, have reasoned thus: "The law of circumcision is plainly symbolical; and the chief moral instruction suggested by it, is the circumcision of *the heart*. But that is not the mutilating, or the impairing, of *natural* power: it is no other than the superinducing of mental purity, by an alteration of moral qualities. If, then, there be a just correspondence, as doubtless there is, between the rite itself and its principal moral design, the præputium should not be *cut off*, but some way or other *purified*." Thus the order of Jehovah might have been evaded under a fair pretext, and the divine rite essentially altered. I cannot help thinking, therefore, that when our brethren, in the case before us, make such appeals to miraculous agency and metaphorical expression, they tacitly confess that the obvious meaning of the word baptism, and primitive practice, afford their cause but little assistance.

Again: As it is not uncommon for us to speak of

being *immersed* in debt, in business, or in care; and of being *plunged* in grief, or in ruin; so we are never considered as using these metaphorical expressions with elegance, or with propriety, except so far as the analogical sense, in which we employ them, points to their literal and primary meaning. The following rules, among various others, have in this case been given. "It ought to be remembered, that all figurative ways of using words or phrases suppose a natural and literal meaning."*
"The figurative sense must have a *relation* to that which is proper; and the more intimate the relation, the figure is the more happy—The proper sense of the word ought to bear some proportion to the figurative sense, and not soar much above it, nor sink much below it—To draw consequences from a figure of speech, as if the word were to be understood literally, is a gross absurdity."†—Pertinent, on this occasion, is the language of Chrysostom, who speaks of "being BAPTIZED, *or immersed*, in cares innumerable;" μυριαις βαπτιζομενος φροντισιν: and again, to the same effect, υπο πληθος φροντιδων τον νουν βεβαπτισμενον εχοντες. So Basil the Great, describing a person who stands immovably against the storms of temptation and persecution, calls him αβαπτιστος ψυχη, "a soul *unbaptized*, or not overwhelmed."‡ See No. 31, 82.—Now here the very term in question is used in a metaphorical way; yet so used, as plainly to retain its obvious and primary meaning. But how disagreeably would it sound, seriously to say of a man that owes but a few pence, He is *immersed* in debt? or, of one whose heart is broken with sorrow, He is *sprinkled* with grief? The most illiterate would be struck with such a glaring impropriety. When, therefore, we

---

* Dr. Reid's Essays on the Intellectual Powers of Man, p. 74.

† Encyclopæd. Britan. under the article FIGURE of Speech. See also Dr. Ward's System of Oratory, vol. i. p. 386.

‡ Apud Schelhornium, Biblioth. Brem. class. vii. p. 638. Vid. Suiceri Thesaur. Eccles. tom. i. p. 623.

consider this metaphorical use of the term baptism, as expressive of that divine energy, and that assemblage of wonderful gifts, which were granted in the primitive times to fit the apostles for their arduous work; the analogical sense of the word *baptism*, will appear much more elegant and much more emphatical on our principles, than on those of our opposers. Dr. Ward has observed, that " we say, *floods* of fire, and *clouds* of smoke, for large quantities;"* so when the scripture speaks of being *baptized* with, or *in*, the Holy Spirit, the *great abundance* of his gifts and graces must be intended. One of our English authors has used the words, "*dipped in scandal.*"† Now thus to represent a person is much more expressive of that opprobrium under which he lies, than if it were said: His character is greatly *aspersed;* or, infamy is *poured* upon him; because it immediately leads us to think of his being *overwhelmed* with reproachful charges.—Dr. Owen speaks of " being *baptized into* the spirit of the gospel."‡ As it is plain that the word *baptized* cannot here mean poured, or sprinkled; (for what sense is there in representing a *person* as poured, or sprinkled, *into* any thing?) so it is equally plain, that the author's words more strongly express the sanctifying power of the gospel on the human heart, than if he had talked of the spirit of the gospel being poured or sprinkled upon a professor of religion.—Thus, in the present case, we have a much stronger idea of that sacred influence, and of those heavenly donatives, with which the apostles were indulged at the feast of Pentecost, by retaining the primary meaning of the word in question; than by thinking of some possible, but remote sense of the term. For as the analogical signification of the same word, when used of our Lord's unparalleled sufferings, would be so diluted as to become ridiculous, or

---

* Ut supra, p. 404.
† Notes on Mr. Pope's Dunciad, p. 123, edit. 1729.
‡ Discourse on the Holy Spirit, b. iv. chap. i. p. 334.

unintelligible, were we to consider the allusion as made to the act of pouring, or of sprinkling, a few drops of water upon any person; so, in regard to the baptism of the Holy Spirit, we must either abide by the natural sense of the term, or greatly impoverish the scriptural notion of that wonderful fact. Though all true believers are partakers of a divine influence, yet they are not all baptized in the Holy Spirit. For as those afflictions which are common to the disciples of Christ, are not the baptism of sufferings; so neither are those communications of divine influence, which are common to real saints, the baptism of the Holy Spirit.

Farther: Our brethren themselves I think will allow, that a person may be *so* surrounded with subtle effluvia; that a liquid may be *so* poured, or it may *so* distil upon him, that he may be *as if* immersed in it. A certain writer, when speaking about the different applications of electricity for the cure of diseases, says: "The first is the electrical *bath;* so called, because it surrounds the patient with an atmosphere of the electrical fluid, in which he is *plunged*, and receives positive electricity."* This philosophical document reminds me of the sacred historian's language, where narrating the fact under consideration. Thus he speaks: "And when the day of Pentecost was fully come, they were all with one accord in one place. And suddenly there came a sound from heaven as of a rushing mighty wind, and it FILLED ALL THE HOUSE WHERE THEY WERE SITTING. And there appeared unto them cloven tongues, like as of fire, and it sat upon each of them. And they were all filled with the Holy Ghost.†" Now if the language of medical electricity be just, it cannot be absurd, nay, it seems highly rational, to understand this language of inspiration as expressive of that idea for which we contend. Was the Holy Spirit *poured out*, did the Holy Spirit *fall upon* the apostles and others at that memo-

---

* Monthly Review, vol. lxxii. p. 486.   † Acts ii. 1, 2, 3, 4.

rable time? it was in such a manner, and to such a degree, that they were like a patient in the electric bath, *as if immersed* in it. Did our opposers thus consider the term *pour*, in this connection, we should not object; because the primary and evident meaning of the word *baptism* would be still preserved in their explanation of its allusive sense. But to suppose that the pouring a *very small* quantity of water, or the falling of *a few drops* on the face of a person, is a just emblem of that metaphorical baptism, is quite incongruous; as it enervates and almost annihilates that grand idea which the scripture gives of the marvellous fact. See No. 42.

Once more: We have the pleasure to find that various authors, who were not under the influence of Antipædobaptist sentiments, express themselves agreeably to our view of the case. Cyril of Jerusalem, about the middle of the fourth century, speaks thus: "As he, ὁ ενδυνων εν τοις ὑδασι, who is plunged in water and baptized, is encompassed by the water on every side; so are they that are wholly baptized by the Spirit."*——Casaubon: "Βαπτιζειν, is to immerse; and in this sense the apostles are truly said to be baptized; for the house in which this was done was filled with the Holy Ghost, so that the apostles seemed to be plunged into it, as into a fishpool."†——Grotius: "To be baptized here, is not to be slightly sprinkled, but to have the Holy Spirit abundantly poured upon them."‡——Cor. *a* Lapide, Menochius, and Tirinus: "A copious effusion of the Holy Spirit, is called the baptism of the Holy Spirit."§——Witsius: "A very great communication of the fiery or purifying Spirit, is called baptism, because of its abundance."∥——Dr. Doddridge: "He [Christ] shall baptize you with

---

* In Dr. Gill's Exposit. on Acts i. 5.
† In Dr. Gill's Ancient Mode of Baptizing, p. 22, 23.
‡ Apud Poli Synopsin, ad Act. i. 5.   § Ibid.
∥ Miscel. Sac. tom. ii. p. 535.

a most plentiful effusion of the Holy Spirit."*——
Mr. Leigh: "*Baptized;* that is, drown you all over, dip you into the ocean of his grace; opposite to the sprinkling which was in the law."†—— Bp. Hopkins: "Those that are baptized with the Spirit, are as it were plunged into that heavenly flame, whose searching energy devours all their dross, tin, and base alloy."‡ See No. 3, 8, 51, 53.—To all which I may add, As the baptism of water was administered, εν ὑδατι, IN *water*;§ *in* Jordan;‖ and *in* Enon;¶ so the New Testament uniformly represents the recipients of this heavenly baptism, as baptized εν πνευματι ἁγιῳ, IN *the Holy Spirit;*** which unavoidably leads us to the proper and primary sense of the word baptism, rather than to any supposed secondary meaning that can be imagined.

Reflect. IX. In opposition to all these authorities and all this reasoning, Mr. John Horsey is of opinion, that the word baptism is "an equivocal, open, general term;" that nothing is determined by it farther "than this, that water should be applied to the subject *in some form or other;*" that "the mode of use," is "only the ceremonial part of a positive institute; just as, in the supper of our Lord, the time of day, the number and posture of communicants, the quality and quantity of bread and wine, are circumstances not accounted essential by any party of Christians;" that "sprinkling,

---

* Paraphrase on Matt. iii. 11.   † Annotat. on Matt. iii. 11.
‡ Works, p. 519.   § Matt. iii. 11; Mark i. 8; John i. 26, 31, 33. So Montanus; so the Vulgate, Syriac, Arabic, and Ethiopic versions; and so Le Cene, Simon, and others in their French versions, together with Wetham's English translation, published at Douay, render Matt. iii. 11, with whom Tindal's translation, Cranmer's Bible, and the Bishops' Bible, as they are usually called, agree.—N. B. What is here said respecting the French versions, and our old English translations, depends on the observation of a friend.   ‖ Matt. iii. 6; Mark i. 9.   ¶ John iii. 23.
** Matt. iii 11; Mark i. 8; Luke iii. 16; John i. 33; Acts i. 5, and xi. 16.

pouring, and plunging, are perfectly equivalent, equally valid; and, that if our Lord had designed to confine his followers to a particular mode, exclusive of all others," he would hardly have used "an open general term, (βαπτιζω)" but "a word decided and limited in its import." He adds, "the Greek language would have furnished him with terms indisputably precise and exact. Of this kind have been reckoned, and I think properly, καταβυθιζω, καταποντιζω, καταδυνω or καταδυω, not to say δυπτω and βυθιζω."*——Mr. Edward Williams, when adverting to the same subject, says: "As the most eminent critics, commentators, and lexicographers are divided in their verdict, respecting the acceptation of the term *baptizo*, and consequently the intention of our Saviour's command *to baptize;* and as the *practice* of the disciples, whence we should gather in what sense they understood it, is attended with considerable difficulty, when reduced to any one invariable method—we should vary it according to circumstances, and in proportion as demonstrable evidence is wanting, refer the mode to the private judgment of the person or persons concerned." † Such are the views and such is the language of Messrs. Williams and Horsey: to whom I may say, as the Athenians to Paul, "You bring certain strange things to our ears, we would know therefore what these things mean."

The word *baptizo*, then, is *an equivocal, open, general term;* so *equivocal and* so *obscure,* that the most learned authors are divided about its meaning, in our Lord's command *to baptize*. This, however, is mere assertion; and, indeed, I should be sorry to see it proved, because it would greatly impeach the legislative character of Jesus Christ. For, as Baron Montesquieu observes, " The style [of laws] should be plain and simple; a

---

* Infant Baptism Stated and Defended, p. 15, 16, 17, edit. 2nd.
† Notes on Mr. Maurice's Social Relig. p. 131.

direct expression being always better understood than an indirect one.... It is an essential article that the words of the laws should [be adapted to] excite in every body the same ideas.... The laws ought not to be subtle; they are designed for people of common understanding, not as an art of logic, but as the plain reason of a father of a family."* Now can it be supposed that our Lord would give a positive law of divine worship—a law that is obligatory on the most illiterate of his real disciples, in the very first stage of their Christian profession; and yet express it in such ambiguous language, that the most wise and eminent of his followers cannot now understand it? Love to his character and zeal for his cause forbid the thought! That ambiguity of which our brethren speak, must, if real, have arisen in our great Legislator's conduct, either from *incapacity*, from *inadvertency*, or from *design*. Not the *first;* for he was undoubtedly able clearly to have expressed his own meaning. Not the *second;* for no incogitancy could befal Him, in whom are *all the treasures of wisdom and knowledge*. Not the *last;* for it would ill become One who declared himself possessed of *all authority in heaven and in earth*, to give a law of perpetual obligation, with an intention that nobody now should understand it.— A little to illustrate this, it may be observed, that his order to baptize, is a *law;* a law of equal force with that of the holy supper. This law extends its obliging power to all that are *taught;* so taught, as to be his disciples. For them to neglect or transgress it, therefore, must be a sin; and all sin exposes to punishment. If, then, the grand enacting term of this law be so equivocal, that no one can tell with certainty what it means, we may suppose it probable that, in ten thousand instances, a transgression of it has proceeded, not from any thing wrong in the hearts of our Lord's disciples, but from the *designed* obscurity of the law itself. Now

---

* Spirit of Laws, b. xxix. chap. xvi.

a law designedly obscure is fitted for nothing so much as to multiply crimes and punishments. Such a law is unjust and cruel; consequently, could not proceed from our divine Sovereign.

Again: According to Mr. Williams's view of the case, we may safely conclude, that the law of baptism is now *obsolete;* nay, in regard to us, that it never was *promulged.* The former, because when the enacting terms of a statute become unintelligible, it is high time to consider the law as antiquated. For to what purpose is a law considered as obligatory, when the most learned, sagacious, and impartial cannot understand it? Here we are landed at downright Quakerism, so far as baptism is concerned in it. With regard to the latter, let the following things be observed. It is generally agreed, if I mistake not, that no positive law is obligatory till promulged; in other words, it is not a *law.* For what is meant by the term *law,* but *a rule of action* prescribed by sovereign authority? It cannot, however, be a *rule of action,* any farther than it is made known. Agreeable to this is the following language of Sir William Blackstone: " A bare resolution, confined in the breast of the legislator, without manifesting itself by some external sign, can never be properly *a law.* It is requisite that this resolution be notified to the people who are to obey it."* See Chap. I. No. 12.—Now if any law, requiring a *single act* of obedience, as in the case before us, do not specify the act intended in such a manner as to be understood by those who read and study it without partiality, it is absurd to talk of its promulgation. For what is meant by promulging a law, but publicly making known the commanding will of the legislator, with regard to this or the other affair? Yet this, according to Messrs. Horsey and Williams, has not been done, respecting the law of baptism; for the principal word in that law is an *equivocal, open, general* term, and so

---

* Comment. vol. i. Introduct. sect. ii.

obscure, that the *most eminent* authors are divided about its meaning. Nor does the apostolic practice explain it. Our Lord, indeed, gave a command *to baptize;* by which it is universally understood, that he designed the performance of *a single action;* for nobody supposes, that sprinkling, pouring, and plunging, must all be united to constitute baptism. But what particular action he meant by the Greek verb, is quite as uncertain as what the Psalmist intended by the Hebrew term, *Selah.* All we can learn is this: As the latter seems to contain a direction to those concerned in the sacred music, to perform that music *in some way or other;* so, the former denotes an application of water to the subject, " *in some form or other;*" for, on the authority of Mr. Horsey, nothing farther is determined by it. Such is the *ne plus ultra* of its meaning! *The trumpet gives an uncertain sound, and who shall prepare himself to the battle?* It follows, therefore, on the principles opposed, that the law of baptism has not, with regard to us, been promulged. We have been used to think that the *laws* of Christ were equally determinate, fixed, and plain, with the *gospel* of Christ; and Paul informs us, that the gospel which he preached *was not yea and nay*, but always affirmative and always the same. Not so the law of baptism, if our opposers be right; for it is *this, that,* and the *other,* but nothing determinate, nothing certain.

The principal enacting word in a positive law of the New Testament, an equivocal term; and so obscure, that the most eminent writers are divided about its meaning! Strange, indeed. For, fond as our brethren are of this idea, were either of them the legislator in a civil state, and to act a similar part, he would soon be accounted either a fool or a tyrant. But I am persuaded, that his wisdom, his rectitude, and his benevolence, would all revolt at the thought of such a procedure. Admitting this representation of our Lord's conduct in his legislative capacity to be just and fair, mankind may think themselves happy that he has not, in this respect, had more imitators among the petty sovereigns of the earth. Britons, at least, would quickly be disposed to execrate the measures of parliament, were the three estates to adopt the idea and act upon it. How often and how justly have the canons and decrees of the Council of Trent been severely censured for their studied ambiguity! Thus Bp. Stillingfleet, concerning that matter: " This was one of the great arts of that council, to draw up their decrees in such terms as should leave room enough for eternal wranglings among themselves; provided they agreed in doing the business effectually against the heretics, as they were pleased to call them."*——Thus Werenfelsius: " Integrity was wanting in the fathers of the Trent synod, when they studiously left ambiguity and obscurity in a great part of their canons and decrees."† Whether, in thus acting, they had the supposed ambiguity of our Lord's canon concerning baptism in their eye, we dare not assert; but every one must allow, if Messrs. Horsey and Williams be right, that they might have pleaded the most venerable example for such a conduct.

Βαπτιζω, *an equivocal, open, general term;* a term which, with equal facility, admits the idea of plunging in Jordan, of pouring from the palm of the hand, and of sprinkling from the ends of the fingers! Our author might as well have asserted, that its derivative, βαπτιστηριον, equally signifies a *bath*, large as King Solomon's brazen sea; a *font*, small as those in our modern-built parish churches; and a *basin*, precisely of the same dimensions with those he commonly uses when sprinkling infants. But what would learning, what would impartiality have said, had he made such an assertion?

A capital word in positive divine law, an equivocal term

---

* Preservative against Popery, vol. ii. Appendix, p. 103.

† Opuscula, p. 580.

—a term, so ambiguous and so obscure, that the most learned and upright do not with certainty know what it means! Then we have need of an infallible judge; and were there one at Rome, it would be worth our while to visit his holiness, that we might have the obscurity all removed. For while the Legislator considers himself as having fairly promulged his law, whether we view its enacting terms as equivocal or univocal, it will prove a serious fact, that they who neglect or transgress it will not be held innocent. With the idea of ambiguity, however, some of our brethren seem delighted. But so were not the ancient Athenians: for Abp. Potter informs us, that it was considered as *criminal*, for any person among them to propose a law in ambiguous terms.* I have heard, indeed, that some of our pettifogging lawyers boast the great uncertainty of our English law, with regard to the issue of numerous causes. Nor do I wonder at it. But that such worthy characters, as Messrs. Horsey and Williams, should seek a refuge for their cause in the supposed uncertainty of divine law, is truly amazing! Were they disputing with Roman Catholics, or discussing almost any subject of a theological kind, except that of infant sprinkling, they would labour to establish against every opposer, the certainty, the precision, and the sufficiency of divine law and apostolic example. This at least has been the common practice of Protestants. For instance: Turrettinus (de Baptismo) speaks to the following effect: It is not lawful to suppose that Christ, in a very important affair of Christianity, would so express himself, that he could not be understood by any mortal.†—— Dr. Ridgley: " In order to our yielding obedience, it is necessary that God should signify to us, in *what* instances he will be obeyed, and the *manner how* it is to be perform-

---

* Antiquities of Greece, vol. i. chap. xxv. edit. 1697.
† Institut. loc. xix. quæst. xviii. § 4.

ed; otherwise it would rather be fulfilling of our own will than his."*——Dr. Owen: "The sole reason why he [the apostle] did make use of it [the word *surety*] was, that from the nature and notion of it among men in other cases, we may understand the signification of it, what he intends by it—It is not for us to charge the apostle with such obscurity, and expressing his mind in such uncouth terms."†——Mr. Benjamin Bennet: "It is a *reproach* to the lawgiver, *blasphemy* against him, to suppose that any of his upright sincere subjects, cannot find out the meaning of his laws, with all their care and diligence, even in the necessary essential points of their faith and obedience."‡——Mr. Bradbury: "The words [of our Lord, Matt. xxviii. 19,] ought to be taken in their plain and natural sense, because they are a lasting form to the end of time. For Christ to give us expressions that people cannot understand, would be only to *abuse* them. It is unworthy of Him who is the light of the world, in whose mouth there was no guile.....[Such] is the plain and natural sense of the words; and therefore to twine and torture them with conjectures and *maybe's*, is making Christ, not a teacher, but a *barbarian*, by not uttering words that are easy to be understood."§——Anonymous: "A confusion in terms would at length produce entirely the same effect, as the confusion of languages; vague and equivocal expressions would render the most accurate notions liable to continual contradictions, and expose truth itself to perpetual cavils. As the first intention of words is to make known our ideas to each other, the principal merit of every language [and of every discourse] must consist in the clearness and precision of its terms."∥——Bp. Taylor: "It is certain

---

* Body of Div. quest. xci, xcii. p. 491.
† On Heb. vii. 22, 26, vol. iii. p. 222, 256.
‡ Irenicum, p. 60. § Duty and Doct. of Bap. p. 150, 173.
∥ Monthly Review, vol. lxxiv. p. 537, 538.

God put no disguises upon his own commandments, and the words are meant plainly and heartily; and the farther you remove from their *first* sense, the more you have lost the purpose of your rule."*——Samuel Fothergill, one of the people called Quakers: "Thou [Mr. Pilkinton] concludest, that *water baptism may be properly administered in any decent and convenient manner whatsoever*. Pray, who must be judge of this decency and convenience? Any thing subjected to human decision, with respect to decency and convenience, wants, in my judgment, those characters of divine institution which become the religion of the holy Jesus; which is, 'not of the will of the flesh, nor of the will of man, but of God.'† Hence it appears, that the plea of our brethren for a latitude of administration, from the supposed ambiguity of the law, is not only contrary to the avowed sentiments of Protestants in other cases, but an encouragement to those who entirely reject the ordinance. See Reflect. III. and Chap. I. No. 4, 8, 12, 13, 20. Reflect. II, III.

The following quotation, *mutatis mutandis*, will here apply with peculiar force. Thus, then, Mr. Vincent Alsop: "I cannot imagine what greater reproach he [Dr. Goodman] could throw upon these famous [Thirty-nine] Articles and their worthy compilers, than to suggest that they were calculated for all meridians and latitudes; as if the Church did imitate Λοξιας, the Delphian Apollo, whose oracles wore *two faces* under one hood, and were penned like those amphilogies, that cheated Crœsus and Pyrrhus into their destruction; or as if, like Janus, they looked, προσσω και οπισσω, *backwards and forwards;* and like the untouched needle, stood indifferently to be interpreted through the two and thirty points of the compass. The Papists do never more

---

* Ductor Dubitant. b. i. chap. i. p. 26. Vid. Chamierum, Panstrat. tom. i. l. xv. c. iv. § 16; c. ix. § 2.

† Remarks on an Address to the People called Quakers, p. 6, 7.

maliciously reproach the scripture, than when they call it *a Lesbian rule, a nose of wax, a leaden dagger, a pair of seaman's trowsers, a moveable dial,* you may make it what o'clock you please: and yet they never arrived at that height of blasphemy, as to say it was *industriously* so penned by the amanuenses of the Holy Ghost. I dare not entertain so little charity for an assembly of holy and learned men, convened upon so solemn an occasion, that they would play *leger-de-main,* and contrive us a system of divinity which should be *instrumentum pacis non veritatis.* The conventicle of Trent, indeed, acted like themselves, that is, a pack of jugglers, who, when they were gravelled and knew not how to hush the noise and importunate clamour of the bickering factions, the craftier leading men found out *a temper,* as they called it, to skin over that wound which they could not heal, and durst not search. And what was the success of these carnal policies? only this, both parties retained their differing opinions, believed just as they did before; and yet their opinions were directly contrary to one another, though both supposed to agree with the decree of the council.... If *the trumpet gives an uncertain sound,* it is all one as if it were not sounded. That which is every thing and every where, is nothing and no where. That which has no determinate sense, has no sense; and that is very near akin to nonsense. The Jews indeed have a tradition, that the manna was what every man's appetite could relish; and such a religion would these men invent as should be most flexible.... Strange it is, that religion, of all things in the world, should be unfixed, and like Delos or O-Brazile, float up and down in various and uncertain conjectures!"* Perfectly similar are the animadversions of Dr. Edwards on Bp. Burnet's *Exposition of the Thirty-nine Articles;* for, among other things, he says: " He hath made the articles of our

---

* Sober Enquiry, p. 60, 61.

church a nose of wax, and accordingly he bends and wrests them which way he pleases.... According to this learned prelate, we do not know the meaning of a great part of our articles, and consequently they are of no use, for what is unintelligible is so.... This way of dealing with the articles seems to me to be a very severe reflection on our first reformers, the pious and learned compilers of these articles, as if they were not able to write or dictate sense; or could not speak grammatically, and so as to be understood; or as if they purposely designed obscurity, and that in some of the most considerable points of our religion; as if they studied to perplex men's minds and ensnare their consciences.... If the words and expressions be voted doubtful and of uncertain signification, the thing itself, the matter couched in them, will soon be insignificant and vain."*

But why should the word *baptism* be esteemed so equivocal and so obscure? Is it because, in different connections, it is used in various acceptations; such as immersion, washing, pouring, and sprinkling? For the sake of argument, and for that only, we admit the reality of those various acceptations. But is that a sufficient reason for pronouncing the word *equivocal*, and for considering the sense of it in divine law as *uncertain?* If so, we shall find comparatively but few terms in any language that are not equivocal and of dubious meaning. The reader needs only to dip into a Hebrew or a Greek Lexicon; into Ainsworth's Latin, or Johnson's English Dictionary, to be convinced of this. The following instances, which have some affinity with the subject of our dispute, may serve as a specimen.

מול is the word most commonly used, to signify *the act* of circumcising; and if that idea be not expressed by it,

---

* Discourse concerning Truth and Error, p. 425, 429.

we may safely conclude there is never a term in the Hebrew language which can express it. Yet besides that sense, and its prepositional acceptations, which are various, it has the general signification of *cutting off, cutting down,* and *cutting to pieces.* So it is used in Psalm lviii. 7; xc. 6; cxviii. 10, 11, 12, and in other places. נמל is another word sometimes used for the same action: but, besides its being equally various in its acceptation, as a verb, it is the name of an *ant,* or of some little insect, that is very sagacious and provident; and is supposed to *cut* or *nibble* grains of corn to fit them for being stowed up in the earth.—On these two Hebrew roots the learned Gussetius has the following remark: "Though they do not occur in the conjugation Kal, except in the sacramental or typical signification of circumcising; yet this is not to be considered as their primary sense, but only as a species of their general signification of *cutting;* which, therefore, is their proper meaning. The genuine, general signification is to be fetched from Psalm xc. 6, and cxviii. 10."*—ערל is used for the *foreskin,* but its general and leading idea is, as Dr. Taylor informs us, *a superfluous incumbrance;* and Mr. Julius Bate says its primary meaning is, *the top,* or *protuberance.* Mr. Bate farther observes, "מל we render, *to circumcise;* but there is no *circum* in the Hebrew. It is to cut off *the top,* or *protuberance;* for so ערל, which was cut off, signifies."†— "The words מול *Mul,* and נמל *Namal,*" says Quenstedius, "do not necessarily signify such an amputation of the foreskin that no part of it remains; and therefore it may be true circumcision if the extremity of it be cut off.— The scripture says, 'Ye shall circumcise the flesh of your foreskin.' Had the *whole* præputium been strictly to be understood, it would have been said, either, *all the*

---

* Comment. Ebraicæ, sub Rad. מול.
† See Dr. Taylor's Heb. Concord. Rad. 1165, 1414. Mr. Bate's Critica Heb. p. 315, 453, 454 Alberti Port. Ling. Sanct. sub Rad. מול.

flesh of your foreskin; or, *the flesh of your whole foreskin.*"*

Now had there been any controversy among the Jews, in the latter times of their civil state, about the manner of performing circumcision, they might, on the principles of our opposers, have reasoned thus: " The forementioned words of our law are *equivocal, open, general* terms; by which nothing is determined, but that a *superfluous incumbrance* (the *top,* or *protuberance,* of something pertaining to the subject) should be, *in some form or other,* cut, or cut off. We may therefore cut, or pare, the nails of our fingers, or of our toes, instead of circumcising the foreskin. For the cutting required, is merely the *ceremonial* part of a positive institute; and therefore only a *circumstance,* like that of number, of time, of gesture, or of place, in various other affairs. If a sharp instrument be but applied to any part of our bodies, so as to make an incision,* or an amputation of something belonging to our own persons, it is *perfectly equivalent, equally valid,* with cutting off the *præputium.*— Besides, the latter is *harsh, severe,* and *indecent,* especially with regard to adult persons: it *shocks* our feelings, and exposes us to a thousand reproaches amongst our Gentile neighbours. We have indeed our doubts, whether it was *originally* practised in that rigid sense for which some of our brethren plead. But were it incontestably proved, that our father Abraham actually circumcised his foreskin, and that his immediate descendants followed his example, there are, we conceive sufficient reasons for our adopting a different method. The

---

‡ Antiq. Bib. Ecclesiast. pars. i. c. iii. p. 270. Witteberg. 1699. See Ainsworth's Latin Dict. under the words *Circumcido,* and *Circumcisus,* for the various acceptations of those Latin terms.

† The learned Vander Waeyen informs us, that circumcision, as performed by the Arabians and some others, is only an *incision* made in the præputium, which afterwards is entirely healed. Varia Sacra, p. 332, 333.

faith and obedience of the renowned Abraham, we all know, were tried in a *singular* manner on various occasions; and, perhaps, the blessed God might give him some intimation of his will respecting the rite in question, which, not being intended for general obligation, was not recorded by the inspired writer. But it is the language of God as penned by Moses, that is the rule of our conduct; and it is plain that the words are of an equivocal, open, general meaning, and far from being confined to the circumcising of the præputium. It should be carefully remembered also, that our great progenitor and his immediate offspring, lived in times when civilization, and a sense of delicacy were far from having arrived at their present stage of refinement: nor had our venerable fathers much intercourse with the nations around them. Now it is evident, that what was considered as decent, or not much disgustful, in a rude uncultivated age, may become, in a course of time, quite the reverse. This we apprehend is a fact in the case before us. So that were we to insist on performing the ceremony in that sanguinary and painful manner, for which some few contend, it would be an insuperable bar to the polished Greeks and Romans around us becoming proselytes to our divine religion, and an occasion perhaps of their final ruin. But who can imagine that the God of Israel would be pleased with such scrupulosity, as tended to continue the Heathens in their idolatry? a scrupulosity too, about that which is no where *precisely* and *incontrovertibly* required. We remember with pleasure, nor can we forget that condescending declaration of God, recorded by one of our minor prophets: ' I desired mercy and not sacrifice; and the knowledge of God, more than burnt offerings.' To enforce the rite in a manner so disgusting to the delicacy and ease of our polite neighbours, who may be at any time inclined to forsake their old superstitions, and to shelter themselves under the wings of the Schechina, would be like *putting new wine into old bottles*, and greatly retard the progress of our holy religion." Thus, on the principles of our brethren, and in their language, *mutatis mutandis*, might the Jews have reasoned away a divine command.

Again: Were our opposers to apply their principles and reasonings concerning the word *baptism* to one of those Greek verbs that were used by our Lord in the institution of his last supper, many of them would be presented with a new discovery, both of the nature and the design of the ordinance; for, when contemplating its administration, they would soon behold, with Roman Catholics and some others, the officiating minister wearing the character of a *priest*, and *offering* a sacrifice to God. The original word, to which I advert, is the verb ποιειν; which signifies *to do*, as plainly as βαπτιζειν signifies *to dip*. Ποιειν, however, in different connections, admits a great number of acceptations; no fewer, even in the New Testament, according to Mr. Parkhurst, than *twenty-six*: and among others, like *facere*, to which it answers, it undoubtedly signifies, in some passages of the Greek classics and of the Septuagint version, *to offer*, or *present an oblation* to God. On this remote sense of the term, the propriety of talking about a *priest* at the Lord's table; about his *offering* the bread and wine; about an *altar*, and a *sacrifice*, chiefly depends: just as the practice of pouring or sprinkling, instead of immersion, depends on a supposed secondary sense of the word βαπτιζειν. But let us hear Dr. Brett on the subject.

"There is yet," says he, "a more evident proof to be found in the scripture, even in the very words of the institution, to prove that we are required to *offer* the bread and wine to God, when we celebrate the holy eucharist, 'This DO in remembrance of me.' Dr. Hickes, in his Christian Priesthood, p. 58, &c., proves, by a great many instances, that the word ποιειν, *to do*, also signifies *to offer*, and is very frequently used both by profane authors, and by the Greek translators of the Old Testament in that sense; and so also is the Latin word *facere.* I will transcribe a few of those instances, and those who desire more may consult Dr. Hickes's book. Herodotus, lib. i. cap. cxxxii. says: 'Without one of the Magi it is not lawful for them, ποιεισθαι, to offer a sacrifice.' And in the Septuagint translation of the Old Testament, which all the learned know is followed by the writers of the New Testament, even where they cite the words and speeches of our Saviour, it is so used; as Exod. xxix. 36, 'Thou shalt offer, ποιησεις, a bullock:' verse 38, 'This is that which, ποιησεις, *thou shalt offer* upon the altar:' verse 39, 'The one lamb, ποιησεις, *thou shalt offer* in the morning, and the other lamb, ποιησεις, *thou shalt offer* in the evening.' So likewise Exod. x. 25. In all which places the word, which is translated *offer*, and which in this last text is translated *sacrifice*, and which in these and many other places will bear *no other* sense, is the very word which in the institution of the eucharist is translated DO. And even our English translators have sometimes used the word DO in this sacrificial sense; as particularly Lev. iv. 20. Here our English translation is, 'And he shall *do* with the bullock, as he *did* with the bullock for a sin offering, so shall he *do* with this.' Here indeed they have put in the word *with*, without any authority: the Greek is, *he shall* DO *the bullock, as he* DID *the bullock, so shall he* DO *this:* where DO plainly signifies *offer*.... That the words of the institution, τουτο ποιειτε, *do this*, are to be understood in this sacrificial sense, is manifest from the command concerning the cup, which is, 'This DO ye, as oft as you drink it, in remembrance of me.' For except we understand the words in such a sense, they will be a plain tautology. But translate it, as I have showed the words will very probably bear, *Offer this:* make an oblation or libation of this, *as oft as ye drink it in remembrance of* ME, and the sense is very good.... A *priest* therefore is necessary and *essential* to the due administration of this sacrament."*—On this reasoning Dr. Doddridge remarks: "Because the word ποιειν signifies, in some few instances, *to sacrifice*, Dr. Brett would render it, [τουτο ποιειτε] *sacrifice this;* whence he infers, that the eucharist is a *sacrifice.*"† But though Dr. Doddridge very justly considers the argument of Dr. Brett as quite inconclusive, I may be permitted to observe; that he has proved the *sacrificial* sense of the term ποιειν, in certain connections, by far better evidence than I have ever yet seen produced by our opposers, in favour of that secondary sense of the word βαπτιζειν, on which their constant practice proceeds. The reasoning of Dr. Brett may therefore teach them the necessity of abiding by the natural and obvious meaning of the term in dispute; for it is impossible, I think, to confute him on any other ground.

Farther: To show the impropriety of our brethren's conduct when reasoning on the word before us, we will suppose our Lord to have used the term νιπτω, which, in its primary acceptation, signifies a partial application of water to a person, by *washing his hands*. Now had this been our Legislator's commanding term, its native and most common signification would undoubtedly have been pleaded against an immersion of the whole body. But, on the principle of interpretation adopted by our opposers, the argument might easily have been evaded. For we might have replied, Νιπτω is an equivocal, open, general term. It signifies not only to wash the hands, but also the *feet* and the *face*. Nay, it is manifestly used to express an *entire plunging*. For thus it is written: *Every vessel of wood shall be* RINSED, νιφησεται, *in water*, (Lev. xv. 12.) Agreeably to which, Mr. Parkhurst says, it signifies, (in John ix. 7, 11, 15,) to wash *the whole body;* and so Schwarzius understands it. So equivocal is the

---

* True Scrip. Account of the Eucharist, p. 81, 82, 83, 131.
† Note on 1 Cor. xi. 24.

term, and of such various application, that the Septuagint uses it, as Mintert observes, to express the idea of *raining down*, or of *sending a shower*, (Job. xx. 23.) —Again: We will suppose our Lord to have expressed his law in Latin, and that he used the word *perfundo*, instead of the Greek βαπτιζω. We will farther suppose, that the primary meaning of the Latin verb is pleaded against us. In this case we might have replied, It not only signifies *to sprinkle* and *to pour*, but also *to bathe:* in proof of which, we appeal to Ainsworth, and to the authorities produced by him.*

We will indulge imagination and suppose, on the contrary, that our Lord had caused his law of baptism to be written in modern English; and that, instead of the word βαπτιζω, we had found the term *bathe* or *dip;* even this would have been liable to similar objections. Our opposers might still have recurred to their old exception: It is an equivocal, open, general term; and signifies to *sprinkle*, to *wet*, or *bedew*, as well as to *plunge*. In confirmation of which they might have said: "As to the word *bathe*, it is frequently used by our correctest writers and speakers, in such connections where plunging cannot possibly be intended. Nothing, for instance, is more common among us than to say, Such an one's cheeks are *bathed* in tears; when we only mean, that the tears trickle plentifully down his cheeks: by which the idea of *sprinkling* is conveyed, rather than that of plunging. To *bathe*, signifies also to supple or soften by the outward application of warm liquors, as Dr. Johnson informs us: for which he produces the authority of Mr. Dryden, who says, *I'll* bathe *your wounds in tears for my offence*. Still the word bathe is rather in favour of sprinkling than of immersion."—As to the term *dip*, they might have said: "It is plain the word is often used where a total immersion cannot be designed. So we read that Jonathan ' put forth the end of the rod which

---

* To which may be added, Virg. Georg. I. 194. Æn. VIII. 589.

BAPTIZE AND BAPTISM. 111

was in his hand, and DIPPED it, εβαψεν αυτο, in a honeycomb.'* Again, 'Send Lazarus that he may DIP, βαψη, the tip of his finger in water.'† It is also common for us to speak of *dipping* a pen in the ink. Sometimes also the word is used allusively, in a sense equally foreign from the idea of an entire immersion. For example, thus: I have just *dipped* into the works of such an author. Now this, far from signifying that I feel my mind, as it were, *immersed* in the author's writings, only means, as Johnson tells us, that I have entered *slightly* into them. Nay, sometimes, when the term *dip* is used with reference to a liquid, it means no more than to *moisten*, to *wet*, as the same celebrated author informs us; who confirms that sense of the word, by appealing to the following lines of our famous English classic, Milton:

> ' And tho' not mortal, yet a cold shudd'ring dew
> *Dips* me all o'er, as when the wrath of Jove
> Speaks thunder.'

Evident proofs, they might have added, that the words *dip* and *bathe*, as well as βαπτω and βαπτιζω, are equivocal, open, general terms; which do not determine any thing farther, than that water should be applied to the subject in some form or other."—On such principles, and by such reasonings, the natural and primary meaning of any word, in any law, or in any language, might be quickly explained away. Were this principle of interpretation universally admitted and applied, no law upon earth could maintain its authority, or obtain its end. The obligation of laws, and obedience to lawgivers, would be little more than empty names. Nor could any doctrine, or any fact, contained in the Bible, stand its ground against the operation of this principle. For by rejecting the natural sense of inspired terms, whenever we find it uncompliant with our inclination; and by adopting a secondary, uncommon, or allusive acceptation

---

* 1 Sam. xiv. 27. Septuag.   † Luke xvi. 24.

of them, as often as we find occasion; it is an easy thing for the most ungodly person to manufacture a creed, as well as ritual, entirely to his own liking, out of those materials which the scripture furnishes, let the real meaning of prophets and apostles be what it may. Yes, he must be a dull genius who cannot, by proceeding on this principle, frame a theological system to suit his own taste, in such a manner as to leave but little room for the subjecting of his understanding, his conscience, and his will to divine authority; or so as to have but little occasion for the practice of that self-denial, which is represented by our Lord as a distinguishing mark of true godliness. For, grant but the liberty of taking the principal words of a law, of a narrative, or of a doctrine, in a secondary and remote sense, where metaphor and allusion are out of the question, and a person of genius might safely engage to evade any law, to subvert any doctrine, and essentially to misrepresent any fact, contained in the Bible.—My acquaintance, indeed, with languages, ancient or modern, is very contracted; but yet I may venture to conclude, on the ground of analogy, that there are few terms in any language which are not as liable to an improper, allusive, and secondary acceptation, as the word *baptism*. Why, then, in the name of common sense and of common impartiality— why should that emphatical and enacting term βαπτίζω, be singled out as remarkably *equivocal?* Why represented as obscure to such a degree, "that the most eminent critics, commentators, and lexicographers are divided in their verdict about"—what? Its *primary* meaning? far from it. Here we think Mr. Williams is under a gross mistake; for, on the authority of those numerous testimonies which have been laid before the reader, we may safely assert, that there is hardly any verb in the Greek Testament, about the natural, obvious, primary meaning of which, the most eminent authors appear to be less divided. I do not, indeed, recollect so much as one learned writer, in the whole course of my reading, who denies that the primary sense of the term is to *dip:* and as to the different acceptations for which our opposers plead, we may ask, with Mr. Locke, "What words are there not used with great latitude, and with some deviation from their strict and proper significations?"*

The *manner of using* water, when baptism is administered, is a *mere circumstance*, according to Mr. Horsey; for he compares it with various particulars in the administration of the holy supper, that are entirely circumstantial. This, if I mistake not, neither agrees with his own principles; with the doctrine of positive institutes, as contained in scripture and acknowledged by Protestants; nor with common sense.—Not with *his own principles*. For when he baptizes a child, in *what* does he consider the act of baptizing to consist? In taking the infant in his arms? he never imagined it. In pronouncing the solemn form of words? by no means; for then he must consider himself as baptizing the subject without any water at all. In putting his fingers into the water? no such thing; for still no water is applied. In verbal addresses to God for a blessing upon the child, or in exhortations to the parents? far from it; because the same consequence would follow. In what, then, but the *very act* of sprinkling, or of pouring, *in the name of the Father*, and so on? But how can that, in which the very act of baptizing consists, be a mere *circumstance* of baptism? Let a man's notions of baptism be what they may, he always considers, and cannot but consider, the act of applying water to a person, or of plunging him into water, not as a *circumstance* of baptism, but as *baptism itself.*——If any of our Pædobaptist brethren still hesitate, let them ask their own consciences, whether they consider themselves as performing

---

* Essay on Human Understanding, b. ii. chap. xxxii. § 1.

a circumstance no way essential to baptism, when, "in the name of the Father, and of the Son, and of the Holy Spirit," they apply water to a child? The answer, doubtless, will be in the negative. With equal reason, therefore, might Mr. Horsey have told us, that eating bread and drinking wine at the Lord's table, are circumstances of receiving the sacred supper, or that walking is a circumstance of local motion; as that plunging, pouring, or sprinkling, is a circumstance of baptism: for no minister of Christ can consider his performance of sprinkling, of pouring, or of plunging, in the sublimest of all names, as any thing but the *very act* of baptizing.

Not with *the doctrine of positive institutes*, as contained in scripture and acknowledged by Protestants. If there be any force or propriety in what our opponent says, it must be on supposition that what he represents as a circumstance, is not enjoined by our divine Lord; for whatever he requires cannot be indifferent, and therefore is not a circumstance. Had the time of day, the number and posture of communicants, or the quality and quantity of bread and wine, been appointed by the great Lawgiver, with reference to his holy supper, not one of those particulars would have been a circumstance: for, it is manifest, they would all have been so many *parts* of one institution; nor would it have been lawful to vary from them. Many particulars of a similar nature were appointed by Jehovah in the ordinance of the ancient passover: but, being appointed, they were of divine obligation, even though the *minutiæ* of the institution extended to "the time of day" when that festival should commence.—The Roman Catholics, like our author in the present case, would fain persuade us, that a participation of wine at the Lord's table is a mere *circumstance;* but they have been constantly told by Protestants, that it is an essential part of the institution: yet not more so, than the use of water, in baptism, let "the mode of use" be whatever it may. Besides, our opponent here begs the question in dispute between us, respecting the term *baptism*.—Again: Omitting various divine appointments which might be mentioned on this occasion, how multifarious were the rites enjoined for the cleansing of an Israelitish leper, as particularized in Leviticus the fourteenth! They are too numerous to be given in detail; but every reader of the heavenly statute may soon perceive, that, according to Mr. Horsey, many of them were such *ceremonial* parts of one positive institute, as may be called *circumstances:* for there is no reason to doubt but the original words there used are as equivocal as the term *baptism*.—As to the avowed *sentiments of Protestants*, relating to the doctrine of positive institutions, I would refer my reader to the preceding chapter, No. 2, 6, 10, 11, 15, 16, 20. Reflect. II, III, V, VI, VII.

Not with *common sense*. For if the manner of using water be a *circumstance* of baptism, what in the world can baptism *itself* be? The *circumstances* of a thing are always considered as different from the *thing itself*. They attend, they accompany, or, if you please, they *stand about* a thing; but they are never considered as THE thing. I should be glad to know, on these premises, what baptism, real, identical baptism is. It is not *sprinkling* of water; it is not *pouring* of water; nor is it *plunging* into water: for these are only so many modes of using water; and the mode of use is no more of the essence of baptism, than the number of communicants at the Lord's table is of the essence of the sacred supper. Now as, according to Mr. Horsey, the manner of using water is only a circumstance of baptism; as the word βαπτιζω is an equivocal, open, general term; and as, according to Mr. Williams, the most eminent authors are divided in their verdict about what our Lord meant by it; all we can learn concerning the ordinance is this: baptism is an *unknown something*, which has a connection with water,* and was practised by the apostles in obedience to Jesus Christ; for on the authority of Mr. Horsey, whether you sprinkle, or pour, or plunge, in the name of the eternal Trinity, it is only a *circumstance*, and not *baptism itself.*—Sprinkling, pouring, or plunging, as much a circumstance of baptism, as the *number* of communicants at the holy table is of the sacred supper! One step farther, and *baptism* itself (whatever the equivocal word means) will be esteemed a circumstance of something else, and its obligation confined, as by the Quakers, to the ministry of John. Far be it that I should imagine Messrs. Williams and Horsey intended to relax the obligation of this positive rite; but whether their manner of speaking has not a tendency so to do, I leave the reader to judge.

It may, perhaps, be objected, " Baptism signifies *washing;* which may be performed by plunging, pouring, or sprinkling: and it is in this view that the different modes of proceeding are called *circumstances.*" That *washing* is the native, primary, and obvious meaning of the term, we do not believe, nor can we admit, except for the sake of argument. Let it be granted, however, that baptism is no other than washing. What follows? That these three different ways of solemnly using water are mere *circumstances* of washing? nothing less. Because whether one or another of these various modes be adopted, it is *the washing itself*, and not a circumstance of it; or else there is nothing in the whole solemnity that has the least appearance of any such thing. Nor can our opposers themselves deny it. For whether they pour water on the head, or sprinkle the face, it is all the washing they pretend to perform. Consequently, on their own principles, it is not a circumstance; nor can they without absurdity consider it in

---

* Mr. Horsey's words are, " connection with a river;" but his practice, I presume, is in connection with a basin. See his Sermon, p. 19.

that light, while they are obliged to acknowledge, that the circumstances of a thing are always different from the thing itself.—That various particulars relating to baptism are merely circumstantial, we readily allow. For instance: the *age* of the candidate, provided he make a credible profession of repentance and faith.— The *time* of administration: it may be in the morning, at noon, in the evening, or at midnight, as in the case of the Philippian jailor.—The *place:* it may be in a river, a pond, or a baptistery.—The *number* of spectators: they may be many or few. These, and other things of a similar kind, we look upon as indifferent; as, properly speaking, *circumstances:* because, not being included in the law of baptism, they make no part of the institution. These may greatly vary, while the qualifications of the candidates, the whole form of administration, and the gracious purposes to be answered by the ordinance, are essentially the same. But it is quite otherwise, as to the solemn use of water. For if that be omitted, baptism itself is wanting: if used contrary to divine order and primitive example, the ordinance is corrupted, so corrupted, as not to deserve its original name. See Chap. I. No. 15, and Reflect. V.—These things being duly regarded, it will appear surprising that so many of our opposers inadvertently speak of immersion, pouring, and sprinkling, as if they were *mere circumstances* of the appointment under dispute: an idea, so contrary to scripture, to fact, and to common sense, that it may be considered as the last refuge of a desperate cause.

Sprinkling, pouring, and plunging, are PERFECTLY EQUIVALENT, EQUALLY VALID, says Mr. Horsey. " Those that are baptized, are either *plunged* into the water, or water is *poured* upon them, or they are *sprinkled* with water: now which soever of these three ways is observed, we ought to believe baptism to be *valid,*" says the Council of Trent.* If plunging, pouring, and

---

* Catechism of the Council of Trent, part ii. Of Bap. § 17.

sprinkling, be *equally valid*, it must be because they are *equally enjoined* by divine law. But they are three *different* actions, as before proved, and as all the world will acknowledge, in reference to any other affair. How then shall a single term, understood in its proper and primary sense, *equally* respect three different actions? yet an equal respect they must have from a single term of positive divine law, to render them " perfectly equivalent, equally valid." Before Mr. Horsey pretends to evince, that the word βαπτιζω has this plenitude of signification, we wish him to prove, that any term, in any language, either does or can equally and naturally signify three different actions. A word that has *three* senses, equally proper and natural to it, is indeed equivocal; nor has it, properly speaking, any determinate sense at all. It is a mere term without an idea, and deserves to be banished from the language to which it belongs. See Reflect. III.—There have been many disputes concerning what is *the proper* and *true* sense of a word; but none, that I have read, about the *number* of true and proper senses which the same word bears, in the same connection. Disputes also have been multiplied, about the *real* meaning of such or such a clause in divine and human law; but theologians and civilians have seldom taken it into their heads to contend, whether the legislator had *three* meanings, or only *one*, in any enacting clause. It is pleasing, however, for us to reflect, that *plunging* is valid; for so it is, by the confession of Mr. Horsey, and by that of the whole Council of Trent, whatever becomes of sprinkling or pouring.—But though Mr. Horsey assures us, that plunging is perfectly equivalent, equally valid, with pouring or sprinkling; and though he has done it in emphatical *capitals*, yet he quickly insinuates, that there is great *severity* in plunging; that it must be often *inconsistent* with the mild genius of the Christian religion; and that it is *harsh, painful*, and *terrifying*.* He repents, alas! he repents of his honest

---

* Infant. Bap. Stated, p. 20.

concession. He no sooner grants us the sanction of his opinion, than he resumes it with eagerness, by endeavouring to deprive us of all its authority. But does this worthy author imagine that plunging is valid, independent of divine authority? Or, that Jesus Christ would exert his authority to sanction a rite that is *inconsistent* with his own religion? This, I confess, appears to me as incompatible and unaccountable, as our great Legislator having *three* meanings in the same enacting term of his positive law.

Sprinkling, pouring, and plunging, perfectly equivalent, equally valid! As, by plunging, Mr. Horsey means an immersion of the whole body; and as we have no reason to think, that he is for sprinkling or pouring water *all over* the human frame; so, by his not mentioning any particular part, on which the water should be poured or sprinkled, we are led to conclude that, in his opinion, it is quite indifferent on what part the water may fall. Here, then, the administrator has full scope for his inclination to operate; and he may sprinkle any part, from the crown of the head to the soles of the feet, just as his sovereign will directs. How contrary this to the whole analogy of positive divine law in the Old Testament! If Mr. Horsey be right, the law of baptism is a leaden rule, that will bend and take any form; rather, it is *no* law—it is *no* rule; and with regard to the use of water, every one may do that which seems right in his own eyes. But as it is absurd to suppose, that the primary sense of the same word will equally apply to three different objects; so it must be incongruous for any to imagine, that the same enacting clause or term of a law, can equally require three different actions, and at the same time be completely satisfied with any one of them. Before Mr. Horsey had inadvertently fixed an imputation of this kind on a positive law of Jesus Christ, he should have well considered, whether the whole history of legislation (sacred, civil, or ecclesiastical) could have furnished him with a single instance of such a fact. That many tyrants and fools have given laws to secular kingdoms, and have even presumed to legislate for Jesus Christ himself, is a fact; that some of their laws have been marked with tyrannical subtlety, and others with egregious folly, is also a fact; but that any of them ever were so crafty, as to contrive a law which, by a single enacting term, equally required *three different* acts of obedience; and yet were so compliant, as to feel themselves perfectly satisfied with having *any one* of those acts performed, I do not believe.

Vary the mode of administration according to circumstances!—Refer the manner of performance to the private judgment of the person or persons concerned! Strange positions, from the pen of a Protestant Dissenter! How inimical to the grand principle of Nonconformity, and to that of the Reformation! Surely, no law of either God or man was ever so condescending to the will of the subject, as the law of baptism. It is reported, indeed, that those who sit as judges in the court of Inquisition, may interpret the laws against heretics, if there be any thing doubtful in them, according to their own pleasure.* Nor do I wonder at it. But that a Protestant, and a Protestant Dissenting brother, should first pronounce the divine law of baptism *obscure*, and then assure us that we may understand and act upon it, with regard to the use of water, *just as we please*, is very amazing! Mr. Williams, I presume, did not recollect the manner in which our great Legislator introduces the sovereign mandate, nor the words that immediately follow it. "ALL AUTHORITY ($\epsilon\xi o \upsilon \sigma \iota \alpha$) is given unto me in heaven and in earth"—introduces the law under consideration. "Teaching them to OBSERVE ALL THINGS WHATSOEVER I HAVE COMMANDED YOU"—are the immediately following words. If ever our Lord expressed himself in the high legislative tone,

---

* Venema Hist. Eccles. secul. xiii. § 217.

if ever he spake like one who in earnest demands an implicit and punctual obedience, it was on this occasion. Can it then be supposed, that the Lord Redeemer assumed such an air of divine majesty, and such a style of divine authority, in giving a law of religious worship, when he *intended* that his followers should administer the rite just as they pleased? We may say with Chillingworth, in another case, " He that *can* believe it, let him."

Vary the mode of administration according to circumstances! Refer the manner of performance to the private judgment of the administrator, or of the candidate! Incidental circumstances, then, or the caprice of those concerned, must be the rule of proceeding. On this principle, who can set bounds to that variety of administration which may be lawfully practised? The Council of Trent is of opinion that water should be applied, not to any part of the body, but to the *head*, because it is the seat of sensation.*——Mr. Cleaveland thinks the *face* is the most proper part, because it is always naked.†——Deylingius is confident that sprinkling may be performed, once or thrice, on the *head*, the *forehead*, or the *breast*.‡——The Eunomians, it is reported, " baptized only the upper parts of the body as far as the breast; and this they did in a very preposterous way, as Epiphanius relates, τους ποδας ανω, και την κεφαλην κατω, *with their heels upwards, and their head downward. Which sort of men are called Histopedes, or Pederecti*."§ Now here is variety, great variety; yet Mr. Williams's principle will admit of a much larger latitude in the course of baptismal practice. It has indeed no other bounds than the caprice and fancies of men are pleased to affix. They only can say, *Hitherto shalt thou go, and*

---

* Catechism of the Council of Trent, part ii. Of Sac. of Bap. § 18.
† Infant Bap. from Heaven, p. 88, 89.
‡ De Prudent. Past. pars iii. c. iii. § 25.
§ Bingham's Origines Ecclesiast. b. xi. chap. xi. § 4.

no farther. Were an adult, therefore, or any parent on behalf of his child, to request of Mr. Williams an application of baptismal water in any of these ways, he could not refuse without confronting his own principle. Or, were any one to prefer the use of water in imitation of the ancient episcopal unction; which was applied to the forehead, the eyes, the ears, the nose, the mouth, and the breast; he could not decline it without departing from his own rule.* Nor could Mr. Horsey, because it would be an application of water " in some form or other;" which is all, according to him, that the word βαπτιζω determines: " the *mode* of use" being as much a circumstance, as the *number* of communicants at the Lord's table is of the holy supper.——It is observed by the laborious and learned Chamier, " That no man in his senses will believe that to be the true religion, the law of which is no more fixed and certain, than the rule of conduct contained in these lines:

" Cùm fueris Romæ, Romano vivito more:
Cùm fueris alibi, vivito sicut ibi."†

But, whatever this great opposer of papal usurpation and superstition might think about a rule of *true religion*, Messrs. Horsey and Williams have given what they consider as a rule of *true baptism*, which has little more fixedness or certainty in it, than that in the Latin distich, which the learned Frenchman holds in such contempt. For it is plain, that the application " of water *in some form or other*," will readily comply with the custom of any age, or of any country; and referring " the mode to the *private judgment of the persons concerned*," will politely oblige any inclination. This reminds me of what Cardinal Cusanus affirms. " The scripture," says he, " is fitted to the time, and variably understood: so that at one time, it is expounded according to the current fashion of the church; and when

---

* Bingham's Origines Ecclesiast. b. xii. chap. ii. § 2.
† Panstrat. tom. i. l. ii. c. xiv. § 9.

that fashion is changed, the sense of scripture is also changed.... No wonder if the practice of the church do take the scripture, one time one way, and another time another; for the sense of it keeps pace with the practice."*—Were these our Dissenting brethren, however, to enter the lists of controversy with a sensible Roman Catholic, they would soon find themselves obliged, either to proceed on different principles, and speak in a different manner, or, in various articles, to give up the Protestant cause.

Were my judgment of the term *baptism* to be formed on those documents which Messrs. Horsey and Williams have given us, I should be ready to say: It is the strangest and most unaccountable word in the world, when used respecting a divine institution. For, though I never heard that learned men were much at a loss to fix its meaning, when found in the Greek classics, in Josephus, or in ancient ecclesiastical authors; though cold bathing was abundantly practised by many nations in former times; and though, in our own country, it is frequently used by both sexes, for medical purposes and for amusement, without any suspicion of danger or of indecency; yet we no sooner consider the term as making a part of divine law, and as prescribing an act of Christian worship, than all is *darkness*, as to its meaning, and all is *terror*, if considered as enjoining immersion.—If, when used in this connection, you desire to *fix* its meaning, commentators, critics, and lexicographers are searched in vain. It is a mere Proteus, or a chameleon; for it will assume almost any appearance. In general, however, it is quite complaisant; altering its colour, or shape, just as you please. If you prefer *sprinkling*, it is your devoted servant; and you may sprinkle the head or breast, the hands or the feet, for it makes no objection. Have you a predilection for *pouring?* still it is at your service: for whether you pour much or little, on

---

* In Mr. Clarkson's Pract. Divinity of Papists, p. 379.

the face or the neck, on the fingers or the toes, it will sanction your deed. Are you for *washing*, such washing as cleanses from exterior pollution? you may dip a towel in the basin, instead of your fingers, and apply it to the face or the hands, or to any part of the body you please: for it will be quite satisfied if you do but apply the water *in some form or other*, and you are at your option. Nay, if you happen to be *fond* of water, and to prefer *plunging*, this good-natured word will stamp legality on the act; for plunging is *perfectly equivalent, equally valid*, with pouring and sprinkling. But here, alas! its complaisance takes leave of the plungers. For though it will sturdily defend the *perfect validity* of their practice against every opposer; yet they must shift for themselves as well as they can, if their conduct happen to be suspected of *severity*, of *harshness*, or of any thing *terrifying*. While, therefore, I cannot but admire the versatility of this identical word, *baptism*, I am constrained to lament, that it is not quite so impartial in its regards as one might have imagined; for its beautifully varying aspect is chiefly turned towards our opponents.

Once more: Mr. Horsey is of opinion, that if our Lord had intended to confine his followers to the practice of immersion, he would probably "have used a word that is decided and limited in its import:" and he thinks, that βυθιζω or καταβυθιζω, δυπτω, καταδυνω or καταδυω, or, finally, καταποντιζω, would have been "indisputably precise and exact," for such a purpose. Let us enquire, therefore, into the opinion of lexicographers, concerning the import of these expressions; and we will begin with the famous Henry Stephens. " Βυθιζω, to cast into a gulf, (the deep, or the sea,) to plunge down: καταβυθιζω signifies the same, and is more commonly used."—— Pasor : (Schoettgenii edit.) " To plunge down, to cast into the deep, (1 Tim. vi. 9; 2 Maccab. xii. 4; Luke v. 7.)"——Hedericus: " To plunge; from βυθος, a whirlpool, a bottomless pit, or the deep. Καταβυθιζω, to cast into a gulf, or the deep, to plunge down; to throw down, to ruin." See also Mintert, Schwarzius, Leigh, and Parkhurst, under the word Βυθιζω.——Hedericus: " Δυπτω, to go under, or into, water; to plunge."——Schrevelius: " To go under, or into, water; from which the English terms, *dip* and *dive*, seem to have been derived."——H. Stephens: " Καταδυνω, or καταδυω, to enter within, or into a more interior place; to enter into a gulf, or the deep."——Hedericus: " To go into a more interior place, to enter into a gulf, or the deep; to hide one's self, to lie hid; to be ashamed, to blush; to plunge down, to plunge under; to fall down; to put on."——Pasor: " To plunge, to destroy, to descend, (Amos ix. 3; Ezek. xxvi. 13; Exod. xv. 5.) Καταδυσις, a descent; a cave in which idolaters worshipped their gods, (1 Kings xv. 13.)"——H. Stephens: " Ποντιζω, to plunge into the sea: καταποντιζω is most frequently used, and signifies to plunge down into the sea, to plunge under."——Hedericus: " To plunge down into the sea, to plunge under, (Matt. xviii. 6.) Καταποντιστης, is one who plunges others into the sea; a pirate, who, after making his capture, plunges the men under the water."——Schwarzius: " To plunge down." See Mintert and Parkhurst, under the word, καταποντιζω. —Such, according to these learned authors, are the significations of the words before us: on which I would make the following remarks.

These chosen terms are far from being so univocal and precise in their import, in comparison with the word βαπτιζω, as Mr. Horsey represents them to be; for several of them have secondary senses, *more distant* from their primary acceptation, than sprinkling is from plunging. This, in a particular manner, is the case with καταδυνω or καταδυω. The natural sense of δυπτω, and a secondary acceptation of others, nearly coincide with the acknowledged primary meaning of βαπτιζω; as the reader may easily observe. Were these terms perfectly well adapted precisely to express a total immersion, without any disagreeable idea attending it, as our opponent supposes, it might be expected, that one or another of them would have been frequently employed by the seventy translators, in their version of the Mosaic institutes. But it does not appear, by the Concordance of Trommius, that any one of these verbs is ever used by them, to express those *bathings* which are so frequently mentioned in the Hebrew ritual. No; for as νιπτω is their usual word to enjoin washing the *hands* and the *feet*,* and as πλυνω is their term for washing of *garments*, so λουω is the verb they use for bathing the *whole body*. Of this, the following passage is a remarkable instance: " Whomsoever he toucheth that hath the issue, (and hath not rinsed, νενιπται, his hands in water,) he shall wash, πλυνει, his clothes, and bathe himself, λουσεται το σωμα, in water."† Perfectly agreeable to which, is the observation of Dr. Duport: " The grammarians remark a difference between λουειν, and πλυνειν, and νιπτειν; that λουειν is spoken of the *whole body*, πλυνειν of *garments* and *clothes*, and νιπτειν of the hands."‡ Λουω and βαπτιζω are used by the Seventy as equivalent. For thus it is written: " Go, and wash, λουσαι, in Jordan seven times.—Then went he down, and DIPPED himself, εβαπτισατο, seven times in Jordan, according to the saying of the man of God."§ As to βυθιζω, καταβυθιζω, and δυπτω, according to Trommius, they are not so much as once used in the Septuagint; and as to καταδυνω and καταποντιζω, though used by the Seventy, yet in a sense quite foreign to the nature of a positive rite. For instance: " Pharaoh's chariots and his host hath he cast into the sea: his chosen captains also are drowned (κατεποθησαν; but other copies

---

* Sometimes also the *face*, both in the Seventy and in the New Testament. See Gen. xliii. 31, and Matt. vi. 17.

† Lev. xv. 11; see also verse 5, 8, 13, 21, 22, 27; chap. xvi. 26, 28; and xvii. 15; Numb. xix. 7, 8, 19.

‡ In Mr. Parkhurst's Greek Lexicon, under the verb Λουω. Vid. Mintert, sub voce Νιπτω. § 2 Kings v. 10, 14.

read, κατεποντισεν;) in the Red Sea. The depths have covered them: they SANK into the bottom, κατεδυσαν εις βυθον, as a stone."*—" Why wilt thou SWALLOW UP, καταποντιζεις, the inheritance of the Lord? Far be it, that I should SWALLOW UP, καταποντιω, or destroy."† So, in the New Testament, καταποντιζω is used only in the sense of *sinking in the deep*, and of *drowning*. Thus, for instance, concerning Peter, when walking on the sea: " He was afraid; and beginning to SINK, καταποντιζεσθαι, he cried, saying, Lord, save me!"—" It were better for him that a millstone were hanged about his neck, and that he were drowned, καταποντισθη, in the depth of the sea."‡ Βυθιζω is used likewise in the Apocrypha, and in the New Testament, for *sinking in the deep*, and for *drowning*.—Thus an apocryphal author: " When they were gone forth into the deep, they DROWNED, εβυθισαν, no less than two hundred of them."§—Thus an evangelist: " They came and filled both the ships, so that they began to SINK, βυθιζεσθαι αυτα." ∥—Thus the apostle Paul: " They that will be rich, fall into temptation and a snare, and into many foolish and hurtful lusts, which DROWN, βυθιζουσι, men in destruction and perdition."¶ —And thus Clemens Romanus: " Pharaoh and his host, and all the rulers of Egypt—were *drowned*, εβυθισθησαν, in the bottom of the Red Sea, and perished."** Hence it appears, that all those Greek verbs which are selected by Mr. Horsey, except δυπτω, manifestly convey the idea of danger, of injury, or of destruction to the subject upon which an agent performs the action that is naturally expressed by them; yet of these terms, he thinks it probable that our Lord would have chosen one or another, had he designed to confine his followers to the practice of immersion! As if no word could be decidedly for

---

* Exod. xv. 4, 5. † 2 Sam. xx. 19, 20. See Ps. lv. 9; Septuag. liv. 9; Lament. ii. 2, 5; and many other places.
‡ Matt. xiv. 30, and xviii. 6. § 2 Maccab. xii. 4.
∥ Luke v. 7. ¶ 1 Tim. vi. 9.
** Epist. ad Corinth. § 51.

dipping, if it did not, in its primary acceptation, denote *sinking in the deep,* or *drowning!* With much greater critical propriety might he have mentioned λουω, than any of the words proposed; because that is the verb which, above all others, the seventy translators adopted, to signify the bathing of *the whole body.* Yet here, alas! the old exception would have recurred; for λουω signifies to *wash*; and washing, they would have said, may be performed by pouring or sprinkling. From what the learned assert, concerning the native and obvious acceptation of ραντιζω, εκχεω, βαπτιζω, and most of the terms Mr. Horsey has mentioned, there seems to be much the same difference between them, as there is between *sprinkling, pouring, dipping,* and *drowning,* in our own language.

But what would Mr. Horsey and others have said, had any of his chosen terms, except δυπτω, been used by our Lord to express that immersion about which we contend? They would soon, I suppose, have exclaimed: "What, will nothing satisfy our opposers, but plunging a candidate for the appointed rite into a *gulf,* or the *sea!* Nothing short of what will put life itself into the most imminent danger! Must we always go to the sea, or to some abyss of water, to administer the ordinance! Severe, harsh, terrifying! The very thought shocks our feelings and plunges us in horror. Impossible, that the law of our gracious and condescending Lord should be rightly understood by these dismal and cruel plungers. It *must* have another meaning; for common sense requires it."——
Here a secondary and remote acceptation of the word in question (suppose καταδυνω, or καταδυω,) would have been sought. In which case, two copies of the Septuagint version of Psalm cxix. 136, would have furnished them with an instance much to their purpose: for there the word κατεδυσαν is used to express *a copious flow and fall of tears;* which might have been very

happily applied to prove, that the term, among other acceptations, means *to sprinkle.** Nay, they might have pleaded the use of the word by the author of the Apostolical Constitutions, Basil the Great, Chrysostom, Theophylact, Damascene, and other ecclesiastical Greek writers, as tantamount to the term βαπτιζω.† For, as no one doubts but they had a tolerable acquaintance with their own language; as nobody dreams of their administering baptism, by plunging people into the depths of the sea; and as Mr. Horsey thinks he has proved that the word *baptize* signifies to sprinkle; so it follows, by an easy consequence, that the verb καταδυνω, stubborn and terrifying as it may appear, would have been quite as pliable and obliging to our opponents as the term βαπτιζω. There is reason to think, however, that it would be a much easier task for any one to prove, that βαπτιζω signifies, in certain connections, *to sink in the deep,* or *to drown* and *destroy;* than that it is ever used by Greek authors to express the idea of pouring or of sprinkling *a few drops of water* on the head or the face. See No. 52, 55, 64, and the note subjoined to No. 82.—Agreeable to which is the language of Damascene, and of Tertullian. By the former, Noah's flood is called *a baptism;* and by the latter, *the baptism of the world.*‡

Mr. Horsey, when pleading the want of a word more decidedly expressive of plunging than βαπτιζω is, reminds me of an evasion sometimes used by Arian subscribers to the Thirty-nine Articles of the English church. " Had the compilers, or imposers," they say, " intended to have been more determinate upon any point, they ought to have been *more explicit and par-*

---

* See Bos's Septuagint.

† See No. 1 of this Chap. Suiceri Thesaur. Eccles. sub voce, Αναδυω; and Spanhemii Dub. Evang. pars. iii. dub. xxiv. p. 70.

‡ Apud Suicerum, Thesaur. Eccles. tom. i. p. 623.

ticular."* Now, as it is not so much a want of precision in the Articles and Liturgy of the national establishment which occasioned this exception, as a dislike to the doctrines they contain; so I suspect, that it is not so much a defect of *meaning* in the word βαπτιζω, to signify immersion, as a disapprobation of that *very immersion*, which was the reason of our opponent's remark. It may, on our part, with reason be asked, if our Lord intended, and if the apostles practised pouring or sprinkling, why was not such or such a word used, which, in its *obvious* and *primary* acceptation, signifies to pour or to sprinkle? But it is quite foreign to the purpose, and proves nothing so much as the want of better arguments, to think of another word to express the idea of immersion, when that is the radical and obvious meaning of the term βαπτιζω. The following observation of Mr. Alsop will therefore apply, *mutatis mutandis*, to the case before us. "If λυτρον, αντιλυτρον, and αντιλυτρον ὑπερ, will not evince a *proper price* paid by way of ransom for another, we must despair of ever expressing truth with that clearness, but it shall be liable to misconstruction, by the possibility of another meaning: and it is in vain to seek a remedy against that evil for which there is no help in nature."†

Reflect. X. Before I conclude this chapter, I will present the reader with a pertinent quotation from Dr. Waterland. "In all manner of controversy which depends upon interpretation of dead writings, he that undertakes to prove a point, or to establish a doctrine, lies under this disadvantage; that, as long as there appears any *possibility* of a different interpretation, an adversary may still demur and demand farther evidence. Now, considering the great latitude and am-

---

* In Dr. Waterland's Supplem. to Case of Arian Subscrip. p. 34.
† Antisozzo, p. 644.

biguity of words and phrases, in all languages, (if a man would search into all the senses they are possibly capable of,) and that even the most full and *express* may be often eluded by having recourse to tropes and figures, or to some other artificial turn of wit or criticism; I say, considering this, there may be always something or other plausibly urged against any thing almost whatever."*—Now, though every person of reading and observation must acknowledge this remark to be just, yet we may venture to affirm, that if the preceding authorities produced from the Quakers, whose hypothesis is not affected by any particular sense of the term in dispute—from the most learned Pædobaptists themselves, whose cause is deeply interested in the meaning of the word—and, by some of our opposers, from Greek authors,†—do not sufficiently warrant our sense of the word under consideration, we may justly challenge our brethren to fix and authenticate the meaning of any expression in the original scriptures, against any opponent whatever. Nay, if the term baptism do not determinately signify that the ordinance should be administered by immersing the subject in water, we should be glad of information what other expression *could* have conveyed that idea, without being liable to similar exceptions with those against which we now contend. It may therefore be safely concluded, that if there be nothing in the design of the ordinance, nor in the apostolic practice, inconsistent with the notion of dipping, we do not deserve reproach for insisting, that *baptism* and *immersion* are terms equivalent.

---

* Eight Sermons, Pref. p. 4, 5, edit. 2nd.

† To the authorities produced from Greek authors, No. 31, 45, 52, 55, 64, and 82, a multitude of others might be added; as the reader may see by consulting Dr. Gale's Reflections upon Dr. Wall's Hist. of Inf. Bap. lett. iii.

CHAPTER III.

The Design of Baptism; or the Facts and Blessings represented by it, both in regard to our Lord and his Disciples.

Witsius.—" Our Lord would be baptized, that he might conciliate authority to the baptism of John; that he might manifest himself to be equally the head of those who are baptized, as of those who are circumcised; that he has communion with both, and came that of both he might make one; that by his own example, he might commend and sanctify our baptism equally as other sacraments to which he submitted; that men might not be loth to come to the baptism of the Lord, seeing the Lord was not backward to come to the baptism of a servant; that by his baptism, he might represent the future condition both of himself and his followers—first humble, then glorious; now mean and low, then glorious and exalted; *that* represented by immersion, *this* by emersion; that by the use of this sacrament, the promises of the covenant, which was between himself and the Father, might be confirmed to him, concerning the entire expiation of those offences which he took on himself, the justification and sanctification of those persons whom he represented, and concerning a glorious resurrection, by which he should soon emerge out of the waters of tribulation, (Psalm cx. 7;) and, finally, to declare, by his voluntary submission to baptism, that he would not delay the delivering up of himself to be immersed in the torrents of hell, yet with a certain faith and hope of emerging ....Immersion into the water is to be considered by us, as exhibiting that dreadful abyss of divine justice, in which Christ for our sins, which he took on himself, was for a time as it were absorbed; as in David, his type, he complains, (Psalm lxix. 3.) More particularly, seeing such an immersion deprives a person of light, and of other things pertaining to this world, it excellently represents the death of Christ, while his continuance under water, however short, denotes the burial of Christ, and the lowest degree of his humiliation; when, being laid in a sepulchre that was sealed and guarded by the Roman soldiers, he was considered as entirely cut off. Emersion out of the water, exhibits an image of his resurrection, or of the victory which, being dead, he obtained over death in his own dark domains, that is, the grave. All these things the apostle intimates, (Rom.. vi. 3, 4.) Besides, baptism also represents those *benefits*, both present and future, which believers obtain in Christ. Among the present benefits, the principal is, communion with the death, burial, and resurrection of Christ; and, which is consequent upon it, the mortification and burial of our old, and resurrection of the new man, in virtue of the blood and Spirit of Christ. For immersion into the water, represents the death of the old man, in such a manner as shows, that he can neither stand in judgment to our condemnation, nor exercise dominion in our bodies, that we should obey his lusts. In respect of the former, the death of the old man pertains to our justification; in regard to the latter, it belongs to our sanctification. The continuance under the water, represents the burial of the body of sin, by which all hope of its revival is cut off; so that it shall never be able afterwards, either to condemn the elect, or to reign over them." Miscel. Sac. tom. ii. exercit xv. § 63. Œcon. Fœd. l. iv. c. xvi. § 25—29.

2. Dr. Robert Newton.—" Baptism was usually performed by immersion, or dipping the whole body under water, to represent the death, and burial, and resurrection of Christ together; and therewith to signify

the person's own dying to sin, the destruction of its power, and his resurrection to new life. St. Paul plainly refers to this custom, (Rom. vi. 4.)" Pract. Exposit. of Catechism, p. 297, 298.

3. A. H. Frankius.—" The baptism of Christ represented his sufferings, (Matt. xx. 22,) and his coming up out of the water, his resurrection from the dead." Programmata, program. xiv. p. 343, 344.

4. Mr. Rich. Baxter.—" In our baptism, we are dipped under the water, as signifying our covenant profession, that as he was buried for sin, we are dead and buried to sin.... They [your lusts] are dead and buried with him, for so your baptism signifieth; in which you are put under the water, to signify and profess, that your old man is dead and buried.... We are raised to holiness by his Spirit, as we rise out of the water in baptism—(Col. ii. 11, 12, 13, where note,)—that the putting of the body under the water did signify our burial with Christ, and the death, or putting off of our sins. And though we now use a less quantity of water, yet it is to signify the same thing, or else we should destroy the being of the sacrament: so also our rising out of the water signifieth our rising and being quickened together with him. Note also, that it is not only an engagement to this *hereafter*, but a thing presently done. They were in baptism buried with Christ; and put off the body of sin, and were quickened with him: and this doth all suppose their *own present* profession to put off the body of sin, and their consent to be baptized on these terms." Paraphrase on the New Test. at Rom. vi. 4; Col, ii. 12; 1 Pet. iii. 21. Disput. of Right to Sacram. p. 58.

5. M. Saurin.—" Paul says, ' We are buried with him by baptism into death;' that is, the ceremony of wholly immersing us in water, when we were baptized, signified, that we died to sin; and that of raising us again from our immersion signified, that we would no

more return to those disorderly practices, in which we lived before our conversion to Christianity." Sermons, vol. iii. p. 171. Mr. Robinson's Translat.

6. Dr. T. Goodwin.—" The eminent thing signified and represented in baptism, is, not simply the blood of Christ, as it *washeth* us from sin; but there is a farther representation therein of Christ's death, burial, and resurrection, in the baptized's being first buried under water, and then rising out of it; and this is not in a bare conformity unto Christ, but in a representation of a communion with Christ, in that his death and resurrection. Therefore it is said, 'We are BURIED with him in baptism;' and, 'Wherein you are RISEN with him.' It is not simply said, *like as* he was buried and rose, but *with him*. So that our communion and oneness with him in his resurrection, is represented to us therein, and not only our conformity or likeness unto him therein. And so baptism representeth this to us, that Christ having once in himself sustained the persons of all the elect, in his burial and resurrection; that now, upon the party himself who is baptized, is personally, particularly, and apparently reacted the same part again in his baptism; thereby showing what his communion with Christ before was, in what was then done to Christ; that he then was buried with Christ, and rose with him; and upon that ground is now, in this outward sign of baptism, (as in a show, or representation) both buried and also riseth again." Christ set forth, sect. iii. chap. vii. p. 82, 83.

7. Turrettinus.—" The passage of the Israelites through the Red Sea, wonderfully agrees with our baptism, and represents the grace it was designed to express. For as, in baptism, when performed in the primitive manner, by immersion and emersion, descending into the water, and again going out of it, of which descent and ascent we have an example in the eunuch, (Acts viii. 38, 39;) yea, and what is more, as by this rite, when persons are immersed in water, they are over-

whelmed, and as it were buried, and in a manner buried 'together with Christ;' and again, when they emerge, seem to be raised out of the grave, and are said to rise again with Christ, (Rom. vi. 4, 5; Col. ii. 12;) so in the Mosaic baptism, we have an immersion, and an emersion; that, when they descended into the depths of the sea; this, when they went out and came to the opposite shore. The former, was an image of death; the latter, of a resurrection. For, passing through the bottom of the sea, were they not near to death? And escaping to the opposite shore, were they not as if revived from the dead?....As in former times, the persons to be baptized were immersed in the water, continued under the water, and emerged out of it, (Matt. iii. 16; Acts viii. 38;) so the old man died in them and was buried, and the new man arose, (Rom. vi. 4; Col. ii. 12.) As now, persons to be baptized, are sprinkled with water; so they are sprinkled with the blood and Spirit of Christ, to the washing away of sin, (Acts xxii. 16; Ephes. v. 26, 27; Heb. ix. 14.)"* Disputat. de Bap. Nubis et Maris, § ·24. Institut. Theolog. tom. iii. loc. xix. quæst. xi. § 14.

8. Bp. Patrick.—" They [the primitive Christians] put off their old clothes, and stripped themselves of their garments; then they were immersed all over, and buried in the water, which notably signified the 'putting off the body of the sins of the flesh,' as the apostle speaks, and their entering into a state of death or mortification after the similitude of Christ; according to the same apostle's language elsewhere, 'We are baptized into his death—We are buried with him in baptism.'—Though we by going into the water profess that we are willing to take up the cross and die for Christ's sake; yet, on God's

---

* "I should think that man's reasoning very weak," says Mr. Bradbury, "who would pretend to prove sprinkling from [those words,] ' your hearts sprinkled from an evil conscience.' This is mere jingling upon words." Duty and Doct. of Bap. p. 158.

part, this action of going into and coming out of the water again, did signify that he would bring such persons to live again," at the general resurrection. Discourse of the Lord's Supper, p. 421, 422, 436, edit. 5th.

9. Mr. Polhill.—" Where baptism is in the right use, there is a seal of union with Christ.... They have the power of his death in mortification, and the power of his resurrection in a divine life: the one, is notably adumbrated in the baptismal immersion into the water; the other, in the eduction out of it." Mystical Union, chap. vii. p. 202, 203.

10. Mr. Scudder.—" Baptism—doth lively represent the death, burial, and resurrection of Christ, together with your crucifying the affections and lusts; being dead and buried with him unto sin, and rising with him to newness of life, and to hope of glory. (Rom. vi. 3, 4, 5; Col. ii. 11, 12, 13.)" Daily Walk, chap. v. p. 95.

11. Gerhardus.—" As plunging may signify that we are baptized with Christ into his death, (Rom. vi. 3;) and that our old man is drowned in baptism, (Rom. vi. 6;) so aspersion may signify that we are sprinkled in baptism with the blood of Christ, and cleansed from all sin, (1 Pet. i. 2; 1 John i. 8.)" Loci Theolog. tom. iv. De Circumcis. § 96.

12. Botsaccus.—" Baptism is a sepulchre: 'We are buried with Christ, by baptism into death,' (Rom. vi. 4.)" Promptuarium Allegoriarum, § 1295.

13. Mr. Marshall.—" Baptism signifieth the application of Christ's resurrection to us, as well as his death; we are raised up with him in it to newness of life, as well as buried with him, (Rom. vi. 4, 5, 10, 11.)" Gospel Mystery of Sanct. direct. iii. p. 50.

14. Mr. Alexander Ross.—" Immersion into the water, represents to us the death and burial of Christ, and therefore our mortification: likewise the very emersion out of the purifying water, is a shadow of the re-

surrection of Christ, and of our spiritual quickening." Annotat. in Wollebii Compend. Theolog. l. i. c. xxiii. p. 150.

15. Chamierus.—" They who are baptized represent the death of Christ, and at the same time their own, (Rom. vi. 3, 4.)" Panstrat. tom. iii. l. xxvi. c. xix. § 12.

16. Buddeus.—"Immersion, which was used in former times, was a symbol and an image of the death and burial of Christ; and at the same time it informs us, that the remains of sin, which are called the *old man*, should be mortified." Dogmat. Theolog. l. v. c. i. § 8.

17. Dr. Whitby.—"'Therefore we are buried with him by baptism,' plunging us under the water, *into* a conformity to his *death*, which put his body under the earth; 'that like as Christ was raised up from the dead, by the glorious power of the Father, even so we also,' thus dead in baptism, 'should' rise with him, and 'walk in newness of life.'" Paraphrase on Rom. vi. 4.

18. Bp. Hall.—" Ye are, in baptism, buried together with Christ, in respect of the mortification of your sins, represented by lying under the water; and in the same baptism, ye rise up with him in newness of life, represented by your rising up out of the water again, through that faith of yours which is grounded upon the mighty power of God, who hath raised him from the dead." Hard Texts, on Col. ii. 12, edit. 1633.

19. Pictetus.—" That immersion into, and emersion out of the water, practised by the ancients, signify the death of the old, and the resurrection of the new man, (Rom. vi.; Col. ii.)" Theolog. Christ. l. xiv. c. iv. § 13.

20. Bp. Davenant.—" In baptism, the burial of the body of sin, or of the old Adam, is represented, when the person to be baptized is put down into the water; as a resurrection, when he is brought out of it." Expos. Epist. ad Coloss. in cap. ii. 12.

21. Dr. Boys.—" The dipping in holy baptism has three parts: the putting into the water, the continuance

in the water, and the coming out of the water. The putting into the water, doth ratify the mortification of sin by the power of Christ's death, as Paul, (Rom. vi. 3,) 'Know ye not that all we which have been baptized into Jesus Christ, have been baptized into his death, and that our old man is crucified with him?' The continuance in the water, notes the burial of sin; to wit, a continual increase of mortification by the power of Christ's death and burial, (Rom. vi. 4.) The coming out of the water, figured our spiritual resurrection and vivification to newness of life, by the power of Christ's resurrection, (Rom. vi. 4; Col. ii. 12.)" Works, p. 294, edit. 1629.

22. Mastricht.—" As in the baptismal washing, especially when performed by immersion, we are plunged in water, abide in it a little while, and then emerge; so Christ was immersed for us in death, continued under its dominion the space of three days, and then emerged by his resurrection....As in the baptismal washing, especially when performed by immersion, we are planted in water; so we are planted both in the blood and body of Christ, when we are baptized into his mystical body, (1 Cor. xii. 13:) and as we, in a manner, put on water, so also do we put on Christ, (Gal. iii. 27.) Again: As Christ, by that baptism of his own blood, (Matt. xx. 22,) died, was buried, and rose again; so we are planted in him, spiritually die with him to sin, are buried and rise again, (Rom. vi. 3—6. Col. ii. 11, 12, 13.) Further: As by water the body is cleansed, (1 Pet. iii. 21,) so by the blood and Spirit of Christ the soul is purified, (1 John i. 7.) Finally: As in baptism we emerge out of a sepulchre of water, and pass, as it were, into a new life; so also being delivered from every kind of death, we shall be saved to eternal life, (Mark xvi. 16.)" Theoret. Pract. Theolog. l. vii. c. iv. § 10.

23. Grotius.—" 'Buried with him by baptism.' Not only the word *baptism*, but the very *form* of it, intimates

this. For an immersion of the whole body in water, so that it is no longer beheld, bears an image of that burial which is given to the dead. So Col. ii. 12....There was in baptism, as administered in former times, an image both of a burial and of a resurrection; which, in respect of Christ, was external; in regard to Christians, internal, (Rom. vi. 4.)" In Rom. vi. 4; Col. ii. 12.

24. Mr. Burkitt.—" 'We are buried with him by baptism into death.' The apostle alludes, no doubt, to the ancient manner and way of baptizing persons in those hot countries, which was by immersion, or putting them under water for a time, and then raising them up again out of the water; which rite had also a mystical signification, representing the burial of our old man, sin in us, and our resurrection to newness of life." Expos. Notes on Rom. vi. 4.

25. Vitringa.—"To be immersed in water, and to be under water, represent the death and burial of our old man, in virtue of the death of Christ. To be washed with water, denotes our being justified and sanctified. To emerge out of the water, signifies our being saved from death, in virtue of Christ's death; our being regenerated to a lively hope; and our being raised again to a new life, that shall never cease." Aphorismi Sanct. Theolog. aphor. 891.

26. Confession of Sueveland.—" As touching baptism we confess, that which the scripture doth in divers places teach thereof, that we by it are buried into the death of Christ, made one body, and do put on Christ." Chapter xvii. in Harmony of Confess. p. 410. Cambridge, 1586.

27. Bucanus.—Our Lord was baptized of John " to signify that he was sent to be *baptized*, that is, plunged in death; and that he might wash away our sins with his own blood....Immersion into water, or aspersion, plainly denotes the sprinkling of the blood of Christ for the remission of sins, and the imputation of righteous-

ness: and the continuance under water, however short, the death and burial of our native corruption, (in virtue of our Lord's death and burial,) that is, the mortification of the old Adam, which is the first part of our regeneration; but emersion, the rising of the new man, or quickening and newness of life; and so, analogically, our future resurrection is, as it were, presented to view. (Rom. vi. 3, 4, and iv. 5, 13.)" Institut. Theolog. loc. xlvii. p. 621, 631.

28. Zanchius.—" Baptism is a sign of the mortification and burial of the old man.... For immersion into the water, which was used of old, represented this mortification, death, and burial; in which infants remain, as it were, under the water, when baptized. I speak agreeably to the ancient practice of the church. The apostle, therefore, says: 'We are crucified with Christ, and buried, by baptism into death.'" Opera, tom. iv. p. 437, 438.

29. Limborch.—" Baptism is a figure and mark of our spiritual burial. For by that immersion into water, and continuance under the water, which represent a burial, baptized persons express their being buried to sin." Comment. in Epist. ad Rom. ad cap. vi. 4.

30. Castalio.—" 'Else what shall they do who are baptized for the dead?'—That you may understand this place of Paul, consider the manner and nature of baptism, as described, (Rom. vi.) in these words: 'As many of us as have been baptized into Jesus Christ, were baptized into his death.' And a little after, 'For if we have been planted together in the likeness of his death, we shall be also in the likeness of his resurrection.' This, therefore, is the argument of Paul; when Christians are baptized, they are baptized for this purpose, that they may die with Christ, and then rise again." In 1 Cor. xv. 29.

31. Schoettgenius.—" The apostle forms a comparison between baptism and death. He that is bap-

tized, is entirely under water, and no longer seems to live. When, therefore, we Christians are baptized, it is into the death of Christ; namely, that we should become imitators of his death. Baptism obligeth us to become like our Lord in his death and resurrection." Horæ Hebraicæ, ad Rom. vi. 4, p. 515.

32. Hoornbeekius.—" The apostle, speaking of what was notorious and certain, says: 'Know ye not, that so many of us as were baptized into Jesus Christ, were baptized into his death?' (Rom. vi. 3,) referring to what is performed in baptism; namely, the entrance into water, and the going out of it. For he immediately adds: 'Therefore, we are buried with him by baptism.' And, (Col. ii. 12,) 'Buried with him in baptism, wherein also ye are risen with him.' As, in respect of Christ, his death was followed by his resurrection from the dead, so our conformity to him consists in dying and rising again with him. This is clearly presented to our view and sealed, by that immersion and emersion which are in baptism." Theolog. Pract. l. ix. c. xxii. tom. ii. p. 388.

33. Tilenus.—" The ceremony in baptism is three-fold; immersion into the water, a continuance under the water, and a rising out of the water.... The internal and essential form of baptism is no other than that analogical proportion of the signs, already explained, with the things signified. For as it is a property of water to wash away the filth of the body, so it represents the power of Christ's blood in the cleansing from sin. Thus immersion into the water declares, by the most agreeable analogy, the mortification of the old man; and emersion out of the water, the vivification of the new man.... The same plunging into the water exhibits to our view that dreadful abyss of divine justice, in which Christ, on account of our sins, was for a time in a manner swallowed up. Abiding under the water, however short the time, denotes his descent to hell; that is, as we have

elsewhere declared, the lowest degree of abasement, when, in a sealed and guarded sepulchre, he was considered as one entirely cut off. Emersion out of the water, presents us with an image of that victory which he, though dead, obtained over death, even in his own pavilion; that is, the sepulchre. Thus, therefore, it is right that we who are *baptized into his death,* and buried with him, should also rise again with him, and walk in newness of life. (Rom. vi. 3, 4; Col. ii. 12.)" Syntag. Disputat. pars ii. disp. xli. § 15, 32, 34.

34. Stapferus.—" The apostle explains the sacrament of baptism, by communion with the death and resurrection of Christ, (Rom. vi. 3, 4; Col. ii. 12.)" Institut. Theolog. Polem. tom. i. cap. iii. § 1638.

35. Burmannus.—" The external rite, in baptism, having the image, as well of overwhelming and suffocation, as of washing, bears also a twofold figure: and it signifies, partly, the death and burial of Christ, and our communion with them;—partly, the washing away of sin, by the blood and Spirit of Christ, or the justification and sanctification of a sinner. (Rom. vi. 4; 1 Pet. iii. 20; Acts ii. 38; Tit. iii. 5.)" Synops. Theolog. tom. ii. loc. xliii. c. viii. § 3.

36. Roell.—" The signification of baptism is taught, (Rom. vi.) namely, that it is a sign and seal of the death, burial, and resurrection of Christ, and of our communion with them. For he that is immersed in water, which has the power of suffocating, is considered as in a state of death; and likewise, as long as he continues immersed, he is there buried. But when he rises out of the water, he rises, as it were, from a state of death, and begins to live afresh. Of what kind this newness of life is, baptism also at the same time distinctly represents. For as water has the power of washing and purifying, it signifies that, in virtue of our Lord's death, the person baptized is cleansed from sin, and that he ought to live a new and a pure life without the pollution of sin. . . .

When persons are baptized in faith, they are *buried with Christ;* to signify that they are no longer under the curse. They rise with Christ, or rather they are raised; as they that are baptized, after immersion into water, rise again out of the water, when they repent and so rise again from a death in sin. Thus also they rise again to a new life and are quickened: they live with Christ here in grace, and shall for ever live in glory." Explicat. Epist. ad Ephes. in cap. iv. 5. Exegesis Epist. ad Coloss. in cap. ii. 13.

37. Lampe.—" Water, in the sacrament of baptism, represents the passive obedience and death of Christ, and the communion of believers with them." Prolegom. in Joan. l. i. c. ii. § 23.

38. Abp. Leighton.—" That baptism doth apply and seal to the believer his interest in the death and resurrection of Christ, the apostle St. Paul teaches to the full, (Rom. vi. 4,) 'We are buried with him by baptism into death; that like as Christ was raised up from the dead by the glory of the Father, even so we also should walk in newness of life.' Where the dipping into water is referred to, as representing our dying with Christ; and the return thence, as expressive of our rising with him." Comment upon 1 Pet. iii. 21.

39. Braunius.—" By baptism we are plunged under the water, and, as it were, buried; but we do not continue in a state of death, for we immediately rise again from thence: to signify that we, through the merits of Christ, and with Christ, mortify the old man, are buried with Christ, and with him arise to newness of life. 'We are buried with him by baptism into death; that like as Christ was raised from the dead, to the glory of the Father, so we also should walk in newness of life,' (Rom. vi. 4, 5.)" Doct. Fœd. pars iv. cap. xxi. § 11.

40. Dr. Manton.—"'We are buried with him in baptism into his death:' the like expression you have, (Col. ii. 12,) 'Buried with him in baptism, wherein also

ye are risen with him.' The putting the baptized person into the water, denoteth and proclaimeth the burial of Christ, and we by submitting to it are baptized [buried] with him, or profess to be dead to sin; for none but the dead are buried: so that it signifieth Christ's death for sin, and our dying unto sin." Sermon on Rom. vi. 4.

41. Church of England.—"As we be buried with Christ by our baptism into death, so let us daily die to sin, mortifying and killing the evil motions thereof. And as Christ was raised up from death by the glory of the Father, so let us rise to a new life, and walk continually therein." Homily of the Resurrec.

42. H. Altingius.—" As in ancient times the persons to be baptized were immersed into water, continued under water, and emerged out of the water, (Matt. iii. 16; Acts viii. 38;) so the old man in them died and was buried, and the new man rose again, (Rom. vi. 4; Col. ii. 12.) As, now, the persons to be baptized are sprinkled with water, so they are sprinkled with the blood and Spirit of Christ, to the washing away of sin, (Acts xxii. 16; Ephes. v. 25, 26; Heb. ix. 14.)" Loci Commun. pars. i. loc. xii. p. 200. Explicat. Catechis. Palat. pars ii. quæst. lxix. p. 311, 312.

43. Wolfius.—" Immersion into water, in former times, and a short continuance under the water, practised by the ancient church, afforded the representation of a burial in baptism." Curæ, ad Rom. vi. 4.

44. G. J. Vossius.—" In our baptism, by a continuance under water, the burial of the body of sin, or the old Adam, is represented. The similitude consists in this: That as a corpse is overwhelmed and pressed by the earth; so, in baptism, a man is overwhelmed with water; and as a man is pressed with water, so the power of sin should be pressed in us and enervated, that it may no longer drive us whither it pleases, or hinder our salvation." Disputat. de Bap. disp. iii. thes. 4.

45. Dr. Cave.—" As in immersion there are in a

manner three several acts, the putting the person into water, his abiding there for a little time, and his rising up again; so by these were represented Christ's death, burial, and resurrection; and in conformity thereunto, our dying unto sin, the destruction of its power, and our resurrection to a new course of life. By the person's being put into water, was lively represented the putting off the body of the sins of the flesh, and being washed from the filth and pollution of them. By his abode under it, which was a kind of burial in the water, his entering into a new state of death or mortification, like as Christ remained for some time under the state or power of death. Therefore, ' as many as are baptized into Christ,' are said to be ' baptized unto his death,' and to be ' buried with him by baptism into death;' that the ' old man being crucified with him, the body of sin might be destroyed, that henceforth he might not serve sin ;' for that ' he that is dead is freed from sin,' as the apostle clearly explains the meaning of this rite. And then by his emersion, or rising up out of the water, was signified his entering upon a new course of life, differing from that he lived before; ' that like as Christ was raised up by the glory of the Father, even so we also should walk in newness of life.'" Primitive Christianity, part i. chap. x. p. 204, edit. 6th.

46. Luther.—" That the minister dippeth a child into the water, signifieth death; that he again bringeth him out of it, signifieth life. So Paul explains it, (Rom. vi.).... Being moved by this reason, I would have those that are to be baptized, to be entirely immersed, as the word imports and the mystery signifies." In Dr. Du Veil, on Acts viii. 38. Vid. Lutheri Catechis. Minor.

47. Bp. Fowler.—" Christians being plunged into the water in baptism, signifies their obliging themselves, in a spiritual sense, to die and be buried with Jesus Christ, (which death and burial consist, in an utter re-

nouncing and forsaking of all their sins,) that so, answerably to his resurrection, they may live a holy and godly life." Design of Christianity, sect. i. chap. viii. p. 79, edit. 4th.

48. Dr. Sam. Clarke.—"'We are buried with Christ by baptism into death; that like as Christ was raised up from the dead by the glory of the Father, even so we also should walk in newness of life,' (Rom. vi. 4.) In the primitive times, the manner of baptizing was by immersion, or dipping the whole body into the water. And this manner of doing it, was a very significant emblem of the dying and rising again, referred to by St. Paul, in the abovementioned similitude." Exposition of the Church Catechism, p. 294. edit. 6th.

49. Cajetan.—"'We are buried with him by baptism into death.' By our burying he declares our death, from the ceremony of baptism; because he who is baptized, is put under the water, and by this bears a likeness of him that is buried, who is put under the earth. Now because none are buried but dead men, from this very thing, that we are buried in baptism, we are assimilated to Christ when he was buried." In Mr. Hen. Laurence's Treatise of Bap. p. 71, 72.

50. Cornelius à Lapide.—"We are baptized into a similitude of the death of Christ. For they who are put under the water, allegorically represent Christ dead and buried." In Mr. Hen. Laurence's Treatise of Bap. p. 73, 74.

51. Dr. Hammond.—" It is a thing that every Christian knows, that the immersion in baptism refers to the death of Christ; the putting the person into the water, denotes and proclaims the death and burial of Christ." On Rom. vi. 3.

52. Bp. Nicholson.—" The ancient manner in baptism, the putting of the person baptized under the water, and then taking him out again, did well set forth these two acts; the first his dying, the second his rising again

.... Into the grave with Christ, we went not; for our bodies were not, nor could be buried with his: but in our baptism, by a kind of analogy or resemblance, while our bodies are under the water, we may be said to be buried with him." In Mr. Davye's Bapt. of Adult Believ. p. 114.

53. Heideggerus.—" Baptism signifies the death and burial, both of Christ and of believers, in the abolition of the old man, as well initial, in this life, as perfect, in laying down the body of the sins of the flesh; the resurrection and vivification, first of Christ, then of ourselves; the obedience of Christ, even to death, which has the power of justifying and of delivering from death; regenerating grace, and the Spirit, purifying our hearts; our union with Christ, and the communion of believers with him; and lastly, a resurrection to life." Historia Patriarch. tom. i. p. 565.

54. Momma.—" As baptism represents the death and burial of our Lord, so also his resurrection, and seals our communion with him. Paul therefore teaches, (Col. ii. 12,) that 'we are buried with him by baptism.' For the baptismal water, so far as it suffocates, is a manifest emblem of death; as it covers, of a burial; as it purifies, of a resurrection." De Statu Eccles. tom. ii. c. v. § 199.

55. Rigaltius.—" Dipping into the baptismal water, denotes the person to be deeply tinctured with the Christian faith; his being overwhelmed, signifies his cleansing from moral stains and filth; and his rising up out of the water, his resurrection." In Mr. Stennett against Mr. Russen, p. 71.

56. Anonymous.—" The apostle seems here (Rom. vi. 4,) to allude to the manner of baptism; indicating that this, as well as the words made use of at the time, signified a kind of death: for the body being wholly immersed in water at baptism, so that it no longer appeared, represented its being buried.... And the body rising

from the water, after it had been wholly immersed in it, so as to be, as it were, buried under it, was in some degree a figure, or representation, of Christ's rising from the grave." Illustration of the Bible, on Rom. vi. 4.

57. Dr. Wells.—" St. Paul here alludes (Rom. vi. 4,) to immersion, or dipping the whole body under water, in baptism: which he intimates did typify the death and burial (of the person baptized) to sin; as his rising up out of the water did typify his resurrection to newness of life." On Rom. vi. 4.

58. Mr. Hardy.—"'Therefore we are buried with him by baptism.' He alludes to the rite of immersing, which bears an image of our Lord's burial. 'That like as Christ was raised.' For the rising again of the body out of the water, bore an image of that fact." Annotat. in Rom. vi. 4.

59. Dr. Barrow.—" The action is *baptizing*, or immersing in water. The object thereof, those persons of any nation, whom his ministers can by their instruction and persuasion render disciples; that is, such as do sincerely believe the truth of his doctrine, and seriously resolve to obey his commandments.... The mersion also in water, and the emersion thence, doth figure our death to the former [worldly defilements,] and receiving [reviving] to a new life." Works, vol. i. p. 518, 520, edit. 1722.

60. Dr. John Edwards.—" Some of the fathers hold, that the apostle's argument in the text (1 Cor. xv. 29,) is of this sort: *If there shall be no rising of the dead* hereafter, why is baptism so significant a symbol of our dying and rising again, and also of the death and resurrection of Christ? For those that were proselytes to the Christian religion, were interpreted to make an open profession of these, in their being plunged into the baptismal water, and in being there overwhelmed and buried, as it were, in the consecrated element. The immersion into the water, was thought to signify the death of

Christ; and their coming out, denoted his rising again, and did no less represent their own future resurrection. On which account, the minister's putting in of the Christian converts into the sacred waters, and his taking them out thence, are styled by St. Chrysostom, 'The sign and pledge of descending into the state of the dead, and of a return from thence.' And thus because the washing and plunging of the newly admitted Christians was a visible proof and emblem, first of Christ's, and then of their resurrection from the grave; the forementioned fathers have been induced to believe, that this passage of our apostle, which I am speaking of, hath a particular respect to that, and is to be interpreted by it. Nay, this seems to agree exactly with the language and tenour of our apostle himself, who may be thought to be the best interpreter of his own words: 'Know ye not,' saith he, 'that so many of us as have been baptized into Christ were baptized into his death? Therefore we are buried with him by baptism,' &c. (Rom. vi. 3, 4.)" Enquiry into four Remarkable Texts, p. 143, 144.

61. Peter Martyr.—" As Christ, by baptism, hath drawn us with him into his death and burial; so he hath drawn us out unto life. This doth the dipping into the water, and the issuing forth again, signify, when we are baptized." Oration concerning the Resurrection of Christ, subjoined to Comm. Places, p. 11, edit. 1574.

62. E. Spanhemius.—" As immersion signifies the death of the old man, and emersion the life of the new man; so sprinkling signifies and seals the sprinkling of the blood of Christ, (1 Pet. i. 2.)" Disputat. Syntag. Disp. de Bap. § 21.

63. Cocceius.—" 'We are buried with him by baptism into death,' (Rom. vi. 3, 4, 5.) We are baptized into death, by which the servitude of sin is laid aside; and thus a seal of our communion with him is bestowed on us, that we may be considered as buried with him.

.... In baptism there is a resemblance of our Lord's death." Summa Doct. de Fœd. c. vi. § 209.

64. Bp. Taylor.—"'We are buried with him in baptism,' saith the apostle. 'In aqua tanquam in sepulchro caput immergentibus vetus homo sepelitur et submergitur, deinde nobis emergentibus novus resurgit inde.'—So S. Chrysostom : 'The old man is buried and drowned in the immersion under water; and when the baptized person is lifted up from the water, it represents the resurrection of the new man to newness of life.' In this case, therefore, the contrary custom [of pouring, or sprinkling,] not only being against an ecclesiastical law, [of the church of England] but against the analogy and mysterious signification of the sacrament, IS NOT TO BE COMPLIED WITH; unless in such cases that can be of themselves sufficient to justify a liberty in a ritual and ceremony, that is, a case of necessity." Ductor Dubitantium, b. iii. c. iv. rule xv. p. 645.

65. Sir Norton Knatchbull.—" The proper end of baptism ought not to be understood, as if it were a sign of the *washing away* of sin—but, properly, it is the sign of *a resurrection*, by faith in the resurrection of Jesus Christ, of which baptism is a very lively and expressive figure; as was also the ark of Noah, out of which he returned, as it were out of a sepulchre to a new life.... And so was the whale's belly, out of which Jonah arose, after a three days' burial; and the cloud and the Red Sea, in which the people of Israel are said to have been baptized; that is, not washed, but buried. For all these were types of the same thing with baptism; not of the *washing away* of sin, i. e. *the putting off the filth of the flesh*, but of the *death* and *resurrection* of Christ, and at the same time of ours. To this truth, apostles, fathers, schoolmen, and almost all interpreters, give their suffrage. The thing is indeed so manifest, that there is no need of testimonies to confirm it: but because there are not a few that otherwise teach, it will not be super-

fluous, (that I may not seem to speak without proper authority) out of innumerable testimonies to produce a few. We begin with St. Paul. ' Know ye not that so many as were baptized into Jesus Christ were baptized into his death? Therefore we are buried with him by baptism into death, that like as Christ was raised from the dead by the Father of glory, even so we also should walk in newness of life,' (Rom. vi. 3, 4, and Col. ii. 12; as also 1 Cor. xv. 29.) ' Else what shall they do who are baptized for the dead, if the dead rise not at all?' As if he had said, If there be no resurrection, to what purpose are we baptized? In vain does the church use the sign of baptism, if the dead rise not. Similar testimonies frequently occur in the fathers. For instance: ' That believing on his death, by his baptism ye may be rendered partakers of his resurrection.' Ignat. Ep. ad Tral.—' Baptism was given,' or appointed, ' to set forth the death of our Lord.' Ep. ad Philadel. in the name of Ignat.—' In baptism we perform the signs of his passion and resurrection.' Just. Mart.—' We know one saving baptism, seeing there is but one death for the world, and one resurrection from the dead, of which baptism is a type.' Basil. Mag.—' Hear Paul speaking aloud, They passed through the sea, and were all baptized in the cloud and in the sea. He calls their passage through the sea, BAPTISM; for it was an escape from death accomplished by water.' Basil. Seleuc.—' To be baptized and plunged, then to return and emerge, are a sign of our descent to Hades, and of an ascent from it.' Chrysost.—' Baptism is a pledge and figure of the resurrection.' Ambros.—' Baptism is an earnest of the resurrection.' Lactan.—' Dipping bears the resemblance of death, and of a burial.' Bern.—I might accumulate innumerable testimonies; but these, I think, are abundantly sufficient to prove, that baptism is properly a type of the death and resurrection of Jesus Christ;—and also of all believers that are baptized into the faith of him, from a death in sin to newness of life; which if they do in this world, they have a most firm hope, that after death they shall, with Christ, arise to glory." Animadvers. in Lib. Nov. Test. ad 1 Pet. iii. 20, 21, p. 178, 179, 180. Oxon. 1677.

66. Bp. Hoadly.—" This latter expression [*buried* with Christ and *rising* with him] made use of by St. Paul, with relation to baptism, is taken from the custom of immersion in the first days, and from that particular manner of baptizing proselytes; by which they were first covered with water, and in a state, as it were, of death and inactivity, and then arose out of it into a sort of new state of life and action. And if baptism had been then performed as it is now amongst us, we should never have so much as heard of this form of expression, of *dying* and *rising again* in this rite." Works, vol. iii. p. 890.

67. Dr. Scott. — " Those phrases, ' buried with Christ,' and ' risen with Christ,' are only the sense and signification of that eastern custom in baptism, viz. of plunging the baptized person under water, and raising him up again—and the significancy of them, the apostle here (Rom. vi. 3, 4, 5,) plainly tells us, wholly refers to the death, and burial, and resurrection of Christ; and therefore the plunging under water must necessarily refer to Christ's death and burial, and the raising up again to his resurrection." Works, vol. i. 446, edit. 1718.

68. Anonymous.—" The water [of baptism] symbolically expresses, by immersing into it, the death of Christ, or—*being baptized*—into his death, (Rom. vi. 3;) emersing out of it, his resurrection, and our rising with him unto righteousness—the whole body of sin, with all its members, dying with him to sin by immersion, and by emersion rising with him to newness of life." Cure of Deism, vol. i. chap. iv. p. 120, 121, 124.

69 Mr. Doutrin.—" What did this dipping in [in the administration of baptism] signify? By the dipping

in, and remaining for a little space under, and rising up out of the water, was signified the communion of believers with Christ, in his death, burial, and resurrection. (See Rom. vi. 3, 6.)" Scheme of Div. Truths, chap. xxii. quest. 25.

70. Dr. Balguy.— " Baptism represents to our view a purification from sin. The apostle indeed carried his idea farther, and considered the act of immersion in water as signifying a *burial;* the termination of our sinful life: and the rising again from the water as a new birth; as an entrance, that is, on a life of piety and virtue." Discourses on Various Subjects, p. 302.

71. Dr. Towerson.—" One other particular there is, wherein I have said the water of baptism to have been intended as a sign; and that is in respect of that manner of application, which was sometime used, I mean the *dipping* or *plunging* the party baptized in it. A signification which St. Paul will not suffer those to forget, who have been acquainted with his Epistles. For with reference to that manner of baptizing, we find him affirming, (Rom. vi. 4,) that we are ' buried with Christ by baptism into death; that like as Christ was raised up from the dead by the glory of the Father, even so we also should walk in newness of life.' And again, (verse 5,) that ' if we have been planted together in the likeness of his death, we shall be also in the likeness of his resurrection.' To the same purpose, or rather yet more clearly, doth that apostle discourse, where he tells us, (Col. ii. 12,) that as we are ' buried with Christ in baptism,' so we do 'therein rise also with him through the faith of the operation of God, who hath raised him from the dead.' For what is this but to say, That as the design of baptism was to oblige men to conform so far to Christ's death and resurrection, as to die unto sin, and live again unto righteousness; so it was performed by the ceremony of immersion, that the person immersed might, by that very

ceremony, which was no obscure image of a sepulture, be minded of the precedent death; as, in like manner, by his coming again out of the water, of his rising from that death to life, after the example of the Institutor thereof?....The thing signified by the sacrament of baptism, *cannot* otherwise be well represented, than by an immersion; or, at least, by some more general way of purification, than that of effusion, or sprinkling. For though the pouring, or sprinkling of a little water upon the face, may suffice to represent an internal washing, which seems to be the general end of Christ's making use of the sacrament of baptism; yet can it not be thought to represent such an *entire* washing, as that of new-born infants was, and as baptism may seem to have been intended for, because represented as *the laver of regeneration:* That, though it do [not] require an immersion, yet requiring such a general washing at least, as may extend to the whole body; as other than which cannot answer its type, nor yet that general, though internal purgation, which baptism was intended to represent. The same is to be said yet more upon the account of our conforming to the death and resurrection of Christ, which we learn from St. Paul, to have been the design of baptism to signify. For though that might, and was well enough represented, by the baptized person's being buried in baptism, and then rising out of it, yet can it not be said to be so, or at least but very imperfectly, by the pouring out, or sprinkling the baptismal water on him. But, therefore, as there is so much the more reason to represent the rite of immersion, as the ONLY LEGITIMATE rite of baptism, because THE ONLY ONE that can answer the ends of its institution, and those things which were to be signified by it; so, especially if (as is well known, and undoubtedly of great force,) the general practice of the primitive church was agreeable thereto, and the practice of the Greek church to this very day. For who can think either the one or the other would have been so tenacious of so troublesome a rite, were it not that they were well assured, as they of the primitive church might very well be, of its being the ONLY INSTITUTED AND LEGITIMATE ONE?" Of the Sacram. of Bap. part. iii. p. 51, 52, 53, 56, 57, 58.

72. Bengelius.—"He that is baptized puts on Christ, the second Adam; he is baptized, I say, into a whole Christ, and therefore also into his death: and it is like as if, in that very moment, Christ suffered, died, and was buried for such a man; and such a man suffered, died, and was buried with Christ." Gnomon, ad Rom. vi. 3.

73. Bochartus.—"The plunging performed in baptism, signifies a death to sin; and the emersion, a new life." Opera, tom. i. p. 1029, edit. 1682.

74. Daille.—"In the primitive church, the greater part of those that were baptized, being persons of age, were unclothed, and then plunged into the water, whence they immediately came forth;—whereby they testified that they did put off the body of sin, the habit of the first Adam, and buried it in the saving waters of Jesus Christ, as in its mystical grave, and came forth thence risen up to a new life." Sermons on Epist. to Coloss. chap. ii. 12, p. 245.

75. Venema.—"It is generally agreed among divines, that the communion of a believer with Christ and the effects of his obedience, by which the guilt, the pollution, and the punishment of sin are taken away, and so the remission of sin, sanctification, and glorification are conferred, are presented to view in baptism; yet they do not sufficiently show the way and manner in which that representation is made, and frequently speak with but little consistency. If, in baptism, the appearance of nothing but *washing* offered itself to our consideration, the thing would be easy. For seeing we are delivered from sin by the

BLESSINGS REPRESENTED BY IT. 157

obedience of Christ, that would be readily understood by every one, as the cause of our purification, and as represented by water, in which there is a cleansing virtue; especially, as the scripture usually comprehends it under the emblem of water. But washing is neither the only idea, nor, as I think, the principal one, of this sacrament; but more truly that of *suffocating*, and of bringing *death* on the flesh, an effect which water produces, seems here to be intended: as well, because the apostle asserts it in express words, (Rom. vi. 3, 4; Col. ii. 12,) as that baptism is elsewhere compared to the deluge and the Red Sea, (1 Pet. iii. 21; 1 Cor. x. 1, 2.) Why? Because in the former passage Peter calls baptism αντιτυπον, the *antitype* of the water of the deluge; which word there, in a special and peculiar sense, denotes *a parallel;* by which is declared, that the deluge and baptism depict the same spiritual thing, and in a mystical representation answer one another: and, lastly, because the apostle (1 Pet. iii. 21,) seems to derive the idea of washing, from that power of *killing* which there is in water. For the death of sin, and of the flesh, really and properly consists in the washing away of spiritual filth; and therefore is rightly comprehended under the appearance of *putting to death*. When, therefore, Peter had compared baptism to the deluge, and so had attributed to it the power of cleansing; he immediately beholds in it σαρκος αποθεσιν ῥυπον, *a putting off the filth of the flesh*. Farther: That the idea of *washing* is not the first and the principal signification of baptism, plainly appears from the rite of *immersion;* in which way it used to be administered by the apostles and first Christians; for that leads us to think, not so much of *washing*, as of *putting to death*. Once more: The phrase, *laver of regeneration*, which is used by Paul, (Tit. iii. 5,) does not so properly signify washing, as *renovation from death*.

" Let us try, then, in this way to unfold the mystery.

The water, as is manifest, both from the immersion of Christ, and the comparison with the deluge and the Red Sea, denotes what is called, the *punishing justice* of God; by which a sinner is not acquitted, without the public sanctification of Jehovah's name, which is usually denominated the *wrath* of God. Into this justice Christ was immersed. He took it on himself, when he was perfected by sufferings and put to death; by which he not only bore, but placated the wrath of God. So that, being freed from the sins which were laid upon him, he rested in the sepulchre in peace; for the curse was then taken from the earth. But he obtained a more excellent sign of sin being expiated, and of justice being satisfied, in his resurrection from the dead; when he was not only justified, but also obtained the whole promised glory, which is his most complete emersion. This is the *baptism* of Christ, concerning which he speaks, (Matt. xx. 22;) and this was represented by the baptism of water, that was administered to him by John. This is the righteousness of Christ, accomplished by his obedience and death; by which, being released from a charge of guilt, he received a right to the promised blessings. Hence, farther, a judgment must be formed concerning the baptism of believers; seeing their communion, not only with the righteousness of Christ, but also with the manner of obtaining it, is, in a certain way, signified and sealed; in which the mystery of baptism consists.

"That this may a little more plainly appear, it must be maintained, that the aforesaid communion with Christ consists both in the imputation of his righteousness, as it is usually called in the schools, and in a real communication of it. The former, for the sake of Christ's righteousness, confers justification by the gracious sentence of God, and implies that believers were comprehended in their Sponsor; so that whatever Christ suffered, they may be esteemed as having underwent.

According to this benign interpretation, they are themselves reputed as immersed in the justice of God; and, in Christ, they also possess a right of acceptance in a more excellent manner than if they themselves had obtained it: which great mystery of our faith is first of all presented to view in baptism, and is made sure to believers by a seal and pledge....This, if I may so speak, is our *imputative* immersion in the justice of God, and emersion out of it; our death and resurrection, which baptism exhibits to view." Dissertat. Sac. l. ii. c. xiv. § 9, 10, 11, 12.—See also Dr. Watts's Hymns, b. i. No. 122. Mr. Marchant's Exposit. of New Test. on Col. ii. 12. Vander Waeyen Varia Sacra, in Gal. iii. 27, p. 84. H. Hulsii Comment. in Israel. Pris. Prærog. p. 801. Mr. T. Bradbury's Duty and Doct. of Bap. p. 83. Hist. of Popery, vol. i. p. 196.

REFLECTIONS.

Reflect. I. Baptism being a gracious appointment of God, it must have an important meaning; and as it is a positive ordinance, the whole of its design must be fixed by divine institution: for we have no more authority to invent a signification for any rite of holy worship than we have to appoint the rite itself. The design of baptism, therefore, must be learned from the New Testament, and from such parts of that sacred volume as have an immediate reference to it. See Chap. I. No. 2, 16, 20.

Were we divested of partiality and prepossession, there is reason to conclude, that it would not be very difficult to discover the chief design of our Lord in his positive appointments. The following words of Dr. Owen are here worthy of notice. " This was a great part of the imperfection of legal institutions, that they taught the things which they signified and represented *obscurely*, and the mind of God in them was not learned but with much difficulty....But all the ordinances and institutions of the gospel do give light into, and exhibit the things themselves unto the minds and faith of belivers. Hereon they discern the reasons and grounds of their use and benefit; whence our whole worship is called our *reasonable service*, (Rom. xii. 1.)"*

That positive ordinances derive all their utility from divine institution, and that it is of great importance to know and comply wth the revealed intention of God in their appointment, Pædobaptists have abundantly taught. Thus Dr. Hunter, for instance: " Positive and arbitrary institutions derive all their value and use, from a right understanding of their meaning and the design of their author."†——Dr. Owen: " There is nothing in religion that hath any efficacy for compassing an end, but it hath it from God's appointment of it to that purpose.... God may in his wisdom appoint and accept of ordinances and duties unto one end, which he will refuse and reject when they are applied unto another.... To do a thing appointed unto an end, without aiming at that end, is no better than the not doing it at all; in some cases much worse."‡ Mr. Baxter: " We must not take liberty, upon our own fancies, to add new ends to God's ordinances:"§ nay, he represents the annexing of a new design to the ordinance before us, as the inventing of *a new baptism.* ‖ To these declarations we cordially assent without the least hesitation.

Reflect. II. These learned authors are almost unanimous in considering baptism as principally intended, by the great Legislator, to represent the *death, burial*, and *resurrection* of Christ; the *communion* his people have with him in those momentous facts; and their *interest* in the blessings thence resulting. To confirm and illustrate which, they agree in applying the declarations

---

* On Heb. vii. 11, vol. iii. p. 171. † Sacred Biography, vol iii. p. 215. ‡ Mortification of Sin, chap. iii. On Heb. x. 5—10, and on Heb. ii. 1. § Plain Scrip. Proof, p. 301, edit. 4th.
‖ Disputations of Right to Sac. p. 162.

of Paul, recorded in Rom. vi. 4, and Col. ii. 12. Now, if such be the chief design of the ordinance; if these passages of holy writ be pertinently applied; and if there be any correspondence between the sign and the things that are signified by it, immersion must be the mode of administration. Nay, supposing our *purification from sin* by the blood of Christ were the first and principal thing intended and suggested by baptism, yet the same consequence would naturally follow; for that purification must be either partial, or complete. Not the former, our opposers themselves being judges: it must, therefore, be the latter. Of perfect purification, then, baptism is either an expressive emblem, or it is not. If not, why such a ritual service appointed in preference to any other that might have exhibited the blessing in a far more striking point of light? To this reasoning Pædobaptist authors give attestation. Thus, for example, Stapferus: " Between an arbitrary sign and the thing signified, there may be an agreement, or similitude; which is the reason of one sign being chosen rather than another. And by how much the more a sign is fitted to excite certain thoughts, and to represent the thing signified, by so much the better, or more useful, it is. Whence it follows, that the illustration of an invisible thing, *depends on the* LIKENESS *there is between the* SIGN *and the* SPIRITUAL OBJECT *to be represented in the mind.*"*——Mr. Blake: "They [sacraments] are analogical signs, such as carry analogy and proportion with the thing signified; they have ever an aptness in them for resemblance. That of Austin is famous: ' If sacraments carry no resemblance of the things whereof they are sacraments, they are no sacraments at all.' "†——Jacob. Laurentius: " In all sacraments there ought to be some similitude, or analogy, between

---

* Institut. Theolog. Polem. tom. i. cap. iii. § 1625.

† Covenant sealed, p. 45.

the sign and the thing signified."*——Mastricht: "Similitude and analogy, between the sign and the thing signified, are necessarily supposed in every sacrament."†—Chamierus, when handling this particular, and having produced the saying of Austin that is mentioned by Mr. Blake, immediately adds: "In which all divines have acquiesced, as in an oracle."‡—If in baptism, then, there be an expressive emblem of *perfect* purification from sin, immersion must be the mode of administration; because nothing short of that represents a total washing. I may here venture an appeal to the common sense of mankind; whether pouring or sprinkling a little water on the *face*, or an immersion of the *whole body*, be better adapted to excite the idea of an entire cleansing. See No. 71.

Reflect. III. Dr. Addington tells us, that "the supposition of Paul's alluding here (Rom. vi. 3, 4,) to the mode of immersion in baptism, as bearing a resemblance to the burial and resurrection of Christ, is entirely founded on a mistaken interpretation of the passage. Without referring in the least to that, or any other mode of administering the ordinance, Paul gives us an account of the *nature* and design of it; as figuring, not any scenes through which our Redeemer passed, but that great change on the heart of the true Christian convert, which is effected by the washing of regeneration."§ If, then, the apostle gives "us an account of the *nature*" of baptism as well as of its design, he must speak of baptism *itself*; which cannot but include the mode of administration. This he does when representing it under the notion of a *burial* with Christ.—Yet were we, in opposition to these numerous and respectable authors, to understand the passage as referring only to the design of the ordinance, immersion would still be the proper

---

* Dialog. Eucharist. cap. iv. § 51. † Theologia, l. vii. c. iii. § 8. ‡ Panstrat. tom. iv. l. i. c. xi. § 29.
§ Christian Minist. Reas. p. 44, 45.

mode of administration. For supposing, though far from granting, that Paul means only to give an account of the ordinance, as figuring that great change on the heart of a real convert; yet, while it is allowed that he speaks of this important change under the notion of a death, a burial, and a resurrection; and while it is maintained that baptism is a *figure* of that change, we are naturally led to conclude, that immersion is the only suitable mode. What *figure*, what *resemblance* is there, of a death, a burial, and a resurrection, in sprinkling a few drops of water on the face of a person? or, if there be any similitude between the act and the things intended, it is of that kind which Dr. Addington himself describes, when he says: " A strong imagination, or a prejudiced mind, may find an object, and then point out a resemblance in many particulars; but no reader of judgment and caution will strain so obscure an allusion."* See Chap. II. No. 1, 33, 36, 71, 75.—Mr. Henry having given a view of the passage similar to that of Dr. Addington, Mr. Jenkins replies: "A Quaker would thank him for the remark, that *our conformity to Christ lies not in the sign, but in the thing signified;* and prove from his own words, that this text does not intend water-baptism, but some inward work so expressed; as also, that the Lord's supper means no external ordinance, but an inward conformity to Christ's death." †—The people called Quakers, when commenting on the passage before us, express themselves in the following manner. William Dell: " You see, that the same baptism of the Spirit that makes us die with Christ, doth also quicken us into his resurrection, and deprives us of our own life; not that we may remain dead, but that it may communicate to us a better life than our own, even the life of Christ himself." ‡—— John Gratton: " Can any man conclude, that Paul here speaks of water-baptism? Is it not plainly said,

---

* Ut supra, p. 37.   † Inconsistency of Infant Sprinkling with Christian Bap. p. 98.   ‡ Select Works, p. 404, 405.

into Christ? Not into water, but into Christ, into death."*——Robert Barclay considers Rom. vi. 3, 4; Gal. iii. 27; and Col. ii. 12, as expressing the *effects* of what he calls the baptism of the Spirit.† So nearly does the sense of the passage, according to Dr. Addington, coincide with that of the Quakers. We may therefore conclude, that whether baptism was intended to represent a purification from sin, by the blood of Christ; or the death of the old, and the quickening of the new man, by the Spirit of God; or the death, burial, and resurrection of our divine Sponsor; immersion is the only proper way of its administration. By this mode of proceeding, *all* those ideas are fully and strongly expressed; which cannot be affirmed of pouring or sprinkling, because neither the one nor the other is adapted to the allusions in the sacred text. Besides, it is highly probable, as Bp. Hoadly has well observed, that if pouring or sprinkling had been practised in the apostolic times, "we should never have so much as heard of *dying*, and *rising again*," in baptism. See No. 66.

Reflect. IV. Witsius has observed, that there is little or no analogy between *wafers*, which are used in the holy supper by Roman Catholics, and the *bread* which our Lord appointed for that purpose.‡ It has also been maintained, that real bread should not only be used, but *broken*, at the Lord's table, to preserve and exhibit the intended analogy. With reference to this, Heidegger says: "Between the *breaking* of bread and the *crucifixion* of the body of Christ, there is an analogy, or likeness; which analogy sufficiently demonstrates the necessity of *breaking* the bread in the sacred supper."§ So, likewise, various eminent Pædobaptists have pleaded for the baptismal immersion, to prevent the gracious

---

* Life of John Gratton, p. 171, edit. 1720.
† Apology, proposition xii. § 4.   ‡ Œcon. l. iv. c. xvii. § 7.
§ Corp. Theolog. loc. xxv. § 83.

design of our Lord in the ordinance from being obscured and lost. Thus Wolfius: " There have been some learned Christians, who were of opinion, that the rite of plunging should be recalled into practice, lest the mystical signification of baptism *should be entirely lost*."* Sir Norton Knatchbull observes, that the true and genuine reason of baptism being appointed "*is almost lost*," by the change of immersion into pouring or sprinkling.† The very famous Buddeus, after having given a summary view of the arguments for immersion, from Zeltnerus, adds: " He who accurately considers these things, will be of opinion, that they are by no means to be blamed, who, though they do not reject sprinkling, yet *wish that immersion had never been deserted;* or, if possible, that it might be restored: among whom is Spenerus, nay, Luther himself. . . . That all doubts and scruples may be removed, the advice of Zeltnerus, a very learned divine of Altorf, should certainly be received; who persuades to the use of *a larger affusion*, that by so doing the want of immersion may be compensated."‡—Now, reader, what think you of these declarations from the pens of Pædobaptists, whose characters are high in the learned world, and in the Protestant churches? Could they have spoken more strongly in our favour, without pronouncing pouring and sprinkling a mere nullity? What but evidence of the strongest kind could induce persons of such a character implicitly to condemn their own practice, as insufficient to answer the design of baptism? The Papists, indeed, may as well pretend that the bread, or the wine, used alone at the Lord's table, fully represents the design of the ordinance, as for any to say that the intention of baptism is completely answered by pouring or sprinkling a few drops of water on any part of the body; and as well might Franciscus (a Sancta Clara) reconcile the Thirty-nine Articles to

---

* Curæ, ad Rom. vi. 4. † Annotat. ad 1 Pet. iii. 21.
‡ Theolog. Dogmat. l. v. c. i. § v. p. 1055.

the canons of the Council of Trent,* as any of our brethren accommodate Rom. vi. 3, 4, and Col. ii. 12, to their own practice. Dr. Nichols, in defiance of common sense, when defending the custom of kneeling at the Lord's table, asserts, that the Dissenters themselves, " by their posture of *sitting*, no more represent a feast, than we [of the church of England] do by *kneeling:*"† and it is with equal propriety pretended by some, that a death, a burial, and a resurrection, are exhibited to view, as well by pouring or sprinkling, as by immersion.

Hence it is that some of those learned Pædobaptists, produced in the preceding pages, finding it hard, if not impossible, to reconcile the obvious and genuine meaning of Rom. vi. 3, 4, and Col. ii. 12, with the natural import of their own practice, manifestly speak, as if the ordinance of baptism represented *one* thing in the apostolic times, and *another* now. See No. 7, 42.—What can be the reason of this? If there be only *one* baptism, as the apostle asserts; and if that institution be not altered since the time of Paul, it must have the very same signification, and that in the same degree; because it must represent the same objects, with an equal perspicuity, and in the same way, as when administered by that ambassador of Christ. It must be entirely the same, whether practised in Judea, or in Britain; in the first, or in the eighteenth century. How lamentable it is to think, that such great men as H. Alting, F. Turrettin, and various others, should sacrifice thus to the love of hypothesis!

Reflect. V. Some of these eminent Pædobaptists, far from viewing the metaphorical baptism of which the apostle speaks, (1 Cor. x. 2,) as militating against the necessity of immersion; represent it as conveying the same leading idea with Rom. vi. 4, and Col. ii. 12; which latter passages are undoubtedly much in our favour.

---

* See Dr. Waterland's Importance of Doct. of Trinity, p. 211.
† In Mr. Peirce's Vindicat. of Dissenters, part iii. p. 206.

See No. 7, 65, 75.—To the opinion of Turrettin, Knatchbull, and Venema, on 1 Cor. x. 2, we may add the sentiments of several others, whose characters are high in the learned world. Grotius, on the passage, expresses himself thus: "The cloud hung over the heads of the Israelites; and so the water is over those that are baptized. The sea surrounded them on each side; and so the water encompasses those that are baptized."—Witsius, when remarking on the text, speaks to this effect: "How were the Israelites *baptized in the cloud, and in the sea*, seeing they were neither immersed in the sea, nor wetted by the cloud? It is to be considered, that the apostle here uses the term baptism in a figurative sense; yet there is some agreement even in the external sign. The sea is water, and a cloud differs but little from water. The cloud hung over their heads; and so the water is over those that are baptized. . . . The sea surrounded them on each side; and so the water, in regard to those that are baptized."*—Braunius, in perfect agreement with No. 7, 65, 75, says: "The Israelites are said to be *baptized in the cloud and in the sea;* and it represented a death, and a resurrection (1 Pet. iii. 21; Rom. vi. 3, 4.†)"—Still more fully Mr. Gataker: "The going down of the Israelites into the bottom and middle of the sea, and their coming up from thence to dry ground, have a great agreement with the rite of Christian baptism, as it was administered in the first times: seeing the persons to be baptized went down into the water, and again came up out of it; of which *going down* and *coming up*, express mention is made in the baptism of the Ethiopian eunuch, (Acts viii. 38, 39.) Nay, farther, as in the Christian rite, when persons are baptized, they are overwhelmed, and, as it were, buried in water, and seem in a manner to be *buried with Christ;* and again, when they emerge, they arise as out of a sepulchre, and are repre-

---

* Œcon. Fœd. l. iv. c. x. § 11. Vid. ejusdem Miscell. Sac. tom. ii. p. 529.   † Doctrina Fœd. loc. xviii. c. x. § 7.

sented as risen again with Christ, (Rom. vi. 4, 5; Col. ii. 12;) so the Israelites might seem, when passing through the waters of the sea, that were higher than their heads, to be overwhelmed, and, as it were, buried; and again to emerge and arise, when they escaped to the opposite shore."*——Mr. Poole's Continuators: "Others most probably think, that the apostle useth this term [baptism] in regard of the great analogy betwixt baptism, as it was then used; the persons going down into the waters, and being dipped in them, and the Israelites going down into the sea, the great receptacle of water: though the waters at that time were gathered on heaps, on either side of them, yet they seemed *buried* in the water, as persons in that age were when they were baptized."——Dr. Hammond: The cloud was "a concave body over their heads, and so coming down to the ground like wings inclosing and encompassing them on every side—and dry ground being left them in the midst of the channel, and the sea encompassing them on every side, before them, behind them, on the right hand, and on the left, and so the cloud environed them in like manner; the sea environed them also."——Dr. Whitby: "They were *covered with the sea on both sides*, (Exod. xiv. 22.) So that both the cloud and the sea had some resemblance to our being covered with water in baptism. Their going into the sea, resembled the ancient rite of going into the water; and their coming out of it, their rising up out of the water."——Hulsius: "Baptism, and indeed immersion in the sea, continued for a time; but they were baptized longer under the cloud."†——Bp. Patrick: "God, by the covering of the cloud, took them under his wings and protection, owning them for his people; and they, passing through the heart of the sea, the waters enclosing them round about, did profess to trust in God, and there to drown all the thoughts of

---

* Adversar. Miscel. cap. iv.
† Comment. in Israel. Prisc. Prœrog. dissert. ii. § 25.

Egypt, which sometimes they feared, and sometimes they loved over much."*——Mr. Burkitt: " The Israelites are here said to be *baptized in the cloud, and in the sea:* that is, the cloud which overshadowed them, did sometimes bedew and sprinkle them; and the Red Sea, through which they passed, had its waters gathered into two heaps, one on the right hand, and the other on the left, betwixt which the Israelites passed, and in their passage seemed to be buried in the waters; as persons in that age were put under the water, when they were baptized: and thus were Israel baptized in the cloud and in the sea."

Other learned Pædobaptists there are, who, when commenting on the text, do not seem to have the least suspicion of its being inimical to the necessity of immersion. For instance: Camero, on the passage, says: " How were the Israelites baptized in the cloud and in the sea? for they were neither dipped in the sea, nor wetted by the cloud."——Bengelius: "They were baptized in the cloud, inasmuch as they were under it; and in the sea, seeing they passed through it: but neither the cloud nor the sea wetted, much less immersed them, (though some conjecture, from Psalm lxviii. 9, and cv. 39, that a miraculous rain fell from the cloud,) nor is the appellation, *baptism*, extant in the narrative of Moses. Nevertheless, Paul very agreeably denominates it thus, because a cloud and the sea are both of a watery nature; therefore Paul says nothing of the fiery pillar: and because the cloud and the sea withdrew the fathers from sight and returned them, almost in a similar manner as the water does those that are baptized."†——Marckius: "The Israelites were covered with the cloud from above under the conduct of Moses, so that they were as if immersed in those heavenly waters: and this was intended, not to prefigure the future external baptism of water in the

---

* Discourse of the Lord's Supper, p. 417, 418.
† Gnomon, in loc.

Christian church, as many, both ancients and moderns, have rashly thought; but to intimate the same grace of Christ which baptism now seals to us.*" See Chap. IV. No. 20.—Now, either these learned authors were extremely inadvertent, or they were very generous to their opponents, in giving up an argument well adapted to defend their own practice; or our opposers proceed on a gross mistake, when they plead this passage against us. Besides, as every one sees the term *baptized* is here used merely by way of allusion; and as the allusive acceptation of a word should never be made the standard of its literal and proper sense; it must be very incongruous to produce this passage in favour of sprinkling, and shows great poverty of argument in defence of the common practice. See Chap. II. Reflect. VIII.

Reflect. VI. If then so many of the most eminent Pædobaptists agree, that the term baptism, properly speaking, signifies immersion; and if, to so great a degree, they farther unite in declaring, that the principal facts represented by the ordinance are, the death, burial, and resurrection of Christ, as the substitute of his chosen people; their communion with him in those facts, and their interest in the blessings procured by them; we have reason to conclude, on their own principles and concessions, that there neither is, nor can be, any valid plea for pouring or sprinkling, as a proper mode of administration. This must be the case, except it should appear on farther enquiry, that the apostles and first Christians did not practise what the name of the ordinance is allowed to imply, and the design of the institution seems to require. We must therefore consider, in the following chapter, what some of the most learned Pædobaptists have to say on that part of the subject.

---

* Bib. Exercitat. exercit. viii. § 12.

CHAPTER IV.

The Practice of John the Baptist, of the Apostles, and of the Church in succeeding Ages, in regard to the Manner of administering the Ordinance of Baptism.

[*N. B.* Candour demands we should here acknowledge, that though these numerous and learned authors have expressed themselves in the following manner; yet many of them insist upon it as highly probable, that the apostles did sometimes administer baptism by pouring or sprinkling.]

WITSIUS.—" It is certain that both John the Baptist, and the disciples of Christ, ordinarily practised immersion; whose example was followed by the ancient church, as Vossius hath shown, by producing many testimonies from the Greek and Latin writers. Disp. I. de Baptismo, thes. vi., and also Hoornbeek, de Baptismo Veterum, sect. iv." Œcon. Fœd. l. iv. c. xvi. § 13.

2. L'Enfant.—" ' In the water—in the Holy Ghost.' These words do very well express the ceremony of baptism, which was at first performed by plunging the whole body in water, as also the copious effusion of the Holy Ghost on the day of Pentecost." Note on Matt. iii. 11. Eng. translat.

3. Anonymous.—" If we have regard to the manner in which the idea of baptism is naturally adapted to the situation of a guilty creature, zealous to express his abhorrence of sin; or to the general practice of the Jewish, as well as other eastern nations; to the example of our Lord, and of his disciples; and to the most plain and obvious construction of the Greek language; we shall be inclined to believe that infant *sprinkling* is not an institution of Christianity, but a deviation from the original rite, which was performed by dipping, or

plunging into water....The arguments by which the Pædobaptists support their practice and doctrine, appear to us to be so forced and violent, that we are of opinion, nothing but the general prevalence of infant sprinkling could have so long supported it." English Review, for Nov. 1783, p. 351.

4. Gurtlerus.—" The action in this element of water, is immersion; which rite continued for a long time in the Christian church, until, in a very late age, it was changed into sprinkling: of which an example is hardly to be found in ancient history, except what relates to the clinics, or sick persons, who, when confined to their beds, were to be initiated by the sign of the covenant of grace. Hence baptized persons are said to have 'descended into the water,' and to be 'buried with Christ into death,' (Matt. iii. 16; Acts viii. 38; Rom. vi. 4;) for they who are immersed in water are covered with it, and as it were buried in it, until they arise out of it." Institut. Theolog. cap. xxxiii. § 117, 118.

5. Bp. Davenant.—" In the ancient church, they not only sprinkled, but immersed those whom they baptized." Expos. Epist. ad Colos. in cap. ii. 12.

6. Pictetus.—" As to the manner of administering baptism, it was usual in ancient times for the whole body to be immersed in water; as appears from Matt. iii. 6, 16; John iii. 23; and Acts viii. 38. This rite might be used in those warm countries; and it must be confessed, that such a rite most happily represented that grace by which our sins are, as it were, drowned, and we raised again from the abyss of sin." Theolog. Christ. l. xiv. c. iv. § 17. Genev. 1696.

7. Dr. Robert Newton.—" It must be confessed, that in the primitive times, and in those hot countries where the gospel was first preached, baptism for the most part was administered by dipping or plunging the person baptized into water....This ceremony of washing with water was the usual way among the Jews of receiving

proselytes—and from thence it was introduced by our Saviour into his church." Pract. Exposit. of Catechism, p. 294, 295.

8. Piscator.—" Ὕδατα πολλα, signifies *many rivers;* as ὕδωρ, in the singular number, denoted the river Jordan. This is mentioned to signify the ceremony of baptism which John used; that is, immersing the whole body of a person standing in the river. Whence Christ, being baptized of John in Jordan, is said to *ascend out of the water,* (Matt. iii.) The same manner was observed by Philip, (Acts viii. 38.)" Ad Joh. iii. 23, in Mr. Henry Lawrence's Treatise of Bap. chap. v. p. 64.

9. Abp. Secker.—" Burying, as it were, the person baptized in the water, and raising him out of it again, without question, was anciently the more usual method: on account of which St. Paul speaks of baptism, as representing both the death, and burial, and resurrection of Christ, and what is grounded on them, our being dead and buried to sin, renouncing it, and being acquitted of it; and our rising again to walk in newness of life." Lectures on the Catechism, lect. xxxv.

10. Mastricht.—" The sign representing, or the element in baptism, is water;—the sign applying, is washing,—whether it be performed by immersion, (Matt. iii. 6, 16; John iii. 23; Acts viii. 38,) which ONLY was used by the apostles and primitive churches; because it is not only more agreeable in the warm eastern countries, but also more significant, (Rom. vi. 3, 4, 5;) or whether it be performed by sprinkling, which is not destitute of its foundation and analogy, (1 Pet. i. 2; Heb. x. 22; compare Isa. lii. 15, and Ezek. xxxvi. 25,) and is more agreeable in these countries." Theologia, l. vii. c. iv. § 9.

11. Calvin.—" From these words, (John iii. 23,) it may be inferred, that baptism was administered by John and Christ, by plunging the whole body under water .... Here we perceive how baptism was administered among the ancients; for they immersed the whole body

in water. Now it is the prevailing practice for a minister only to sprinkle the body or the head. In Joan. iii. 23; Comment. in Act. viii. 38.

12. Spanhemius.—" To be baptized is denominated by Paul, a being *buried*, according to the ancient manner of baptizing. For immersion is a kind of burial; and emersion, a resurrection, to which the apostle alludes, Col. ii. 12. So Christ, being baptized, *went up out of the water*, (Matt. iii. 16.) The same is related concerning the Ethiopian eunuch, (Acts viii. 38.)" Dubiorum Evang. pars. iii. dub. xxiv. § 2.

13. Vitringa.—" The act of baptizing, is the immersion of believers in water. This expresses the force of the word. Thus also it was performed by Christ and the apostles." Aphorismi Sanct. Theolog. aph. 884.

14. Bp. Patrick.—" They [the primitive Christians] put off their old clothes, and stript themselves of their garments; then they were immersed all over, and buried in the water." Discourse of the Lord's Supper, p. 421.

15. Marloratus.—" From these words (John iii. 23,) it may be gathered, that baptism was performed by John and Christ, by plunging of the whole body." Comment. ad Joan. iii. 23.

16. Mr. Stackhouse.—" The observation of the Greek church, in relation to this matter [the baptism of Christ] is this: That he who ascended out of the water, must first descend down into it; and consequently, that baptism is to be performed, not by sprinkling, but by washing the body. And indeed, he must be strangely ignorant of the Jewish rites of baptism who seems to doubt of this; since, to the due performance of it, they required the immersion of the whole body to such a degree of nicety, that if any dirt was upon it, that hindered the water from coming to the part, they thought the ceremony not rightly done. The Christians, no doubt, took this rite from the Jews, and followed them in their manner of performing it. Accordingly, several authors

have shown, that we read no where in scripture of any one's being baptized, but by immersion; and from the acts of councils and ancient rituals have proved, that this manner of immersion continued (as much as possible) to be used for *thirteen hundred years* after Christ. But it is much to be questioned, whether the prevalence of custom, and the over fondness of parents, will, in these cold climates especially, ever suffer it to be restored." History of the Bib. b. viii. chap. i. p. 1234, 1235, Note. See also Dr. Whitby, on Matt. iii. 16.

17. Mr. Burkitt.—" Observe the manner of the administration of baptism to the eunuch; he *went down into* the water, and was baptized by Philip. In those hot countries it was usual so to do, and we do not oppose the lawfulness of dipping in some cases, but the necessity of dipping in all cases." Expos. Notes on Acts viii. 38.

18. Mr. John Wesley.—" Mary Welsh, aged eleven days, was baptized according to the custom of the first church, and the rule of the church of England, by immersion. The child was ill then, but recovered from that hour..... ' Buried with him;' alluding to the ancient manner of baptizing by immersion." Extract of Mr. J. Wesley's Journal, from his embarking for Georgia, p. 11, edit 2nd; Note on Rom. vi. 4.

19. Confession of Helvetia.—" Baptism was instituted and consecrated by God; and the first that baptized was John, who dipped Christ in the water, in Jordan." Harmony of Confess. p. 395.

20. Zanchius.—" The ancient church used to immerse those that were baptized. Thus Christ went down into Jordan and was baptized; as also others that were baptized by John. Of this thing, and of immersion, the passage of the people through the midst of the sea was a type; concerning which the apostle speaks, 1 Cor. x. 2. ' They were baptized,' says he, ' in the sea.'" Opera, tom. vi. p. 217.

21. Hoornbeekius.—" We do not deny that, in the first examples of persons baptized, they went into the water and were immersed." Socin. Confut. l. iii. c. ii. sect. i. tom. iii. p. 268.

22. Daille.—" It was a custom heretofore in the ancient church, to plunge those they baptized over head and ears in the water.... This is still the practice, both of the Greek and the Russian church, even at this very day." Right Use of the Fathers, b. ii. p. 148.

23. Salmasius.—" The ancients did not baptize otherwise than by immersion, either once, or thrice." Apud Witsium, Œcon. Fœd. l. iv. c. xvi. § 13.

24. Mr. Bower.—" Baptism by immersion, was undoubtedly the apostolical practice, and was never dispensed with by the church, except in case of sickness, or when a sufficient quantity of water could not be had. In both these cases baptism by aspersion, or sprinkling, was allowed, but in no other." Hist of the Popes, vol. ii. p. 110, Note. See also p. 121, Note.

25. Mr. Poole's Continuators.—" A great part of those who went out to hear John were baptized, that is, dipped in Jordan.... It is true, the first baptisms of which we read in holy writ, were by dippings of the persons baptized. It was in a hot country, where it might be at any time without the danger of persons' lives; where it may be, we judge it reasonable, and most resembling *our burial with Christ by baptism into death:* but we cannot think it necessary, for God loveth mercy rather than sacrifice; and the thing signified by baptism, viz. *the washing away the soul's sins with the blood of Christ,* is in Scripture expressed to us by pouring and sprinkling, (Ezek. xxxvi. 25; Heb. xii. 14; 1 Pet. i. 2).... It is from this (John iii. 23,) apparent, that both Christ and John baptized by dipping the body in water; else they need not have sought places where had been a *great plenty* of water.... He [Paul] seems here (Rom. vi. 4,) to allude to the manner of baptizing in those

warm eastern countries, which was to dip, or plunge the party baptized; and, as it were, to bury him for a while under water. See the like phrase, Col. ii. 12." Annotations on Matt. iii. 6, and xxviii. 19, 20; John iii. 21; Rom. vi. 4.

26. Ravanellus.—" In the first institution of baptism, when adult persons were chiefly baptized, and that in a warm country, immersion was used; as appears from Matt. iii. 16; Acts viii. 36, 38, 39; Rom. vi. 4, 5. But in the present age, in which infants are generally baptized, and that in cold countries, aspersion is practised, according to the law of charity, yet without any injury to the nature of the sacrament." Bibliotheca, sub voce, Baptismus. Genev. 1652.

27. Marckius.—" The action to be performed in the administration of baptism, is washing the body with water; which we think is rightly done, I. by immersion. (1) As in that act there is the greatest washing of the whole body. To signify which, the word is therefore (2) most frequently used. (3) It was commonly practised by John the Baptist, the disciples of Christ, (Matt. iii. 6, 16; John iii. 23; Acts viii. 38,) and the first Christians; and (4) to which reference is had, Rom. vi. 3, 4; Gal. iii. 27; Col. ii. 12." Compend. Theolog. Christ. cap. xxx. § 11. Vid. ejusdem Bib. Exercitat., exercit. xxvii. § 2, 3.

28. Mosheim.—" The exhortations of this respectable messenger [John the Baptist] were not without effect; and those who, moved by his solemn admonitions, had formed the resolution of correcting their evil dispositions and amending their lives, were initiated into the kingdom of the Redeemer by the ceremony of immersion, or baptism, (Matt. iii. 6; John i. 22).... The sacrament of baptism was administered in this [the second] century, without the public assemblies, in places appointed and prepared for that purpose, and was performed by immersion of the whole body in the baptismal

font.... Those adult persons, that desire to be baptized [among the collegiants] receive the sacrament of baptism, according to the ancient and primitive manner of celebrating that institution, even by *immersion*." Eccles. Hist. cent. i. part i. chap. iii. § 3; cent. ii. part ii. chap. iv. § 8; and cent. xvii. sect. ii. part ii. chap. vii. § 1.

29. Bp. Taylor.—" The custom of the ancient churches was not sprinkling, but immersion; in pursuance of the sense of the word [baptize] in the commandment, and the example of our blessed Saviour. Now this was of so sacred account in their esteem, that they did not account it lawful to receive him into the clergy, who had been only sprinkled in his baptism, as we learn from the Epistle of Cornelius to Fabius of Antioch, apud Euseb. lib. vi. cap. xliii." Ductor Dubitantium, b. iii. chap. iv. rule xv. p. 644.

30. Clignetus.—" In the primitive times, persons baptized were entirely immersed in water. Thus Christ was baptized, as we are informed Matt. iii. 16, where it is said that Christ 'went up out of the water;' for a coming out, supposes a going in. To which form of baptizing Paul seems to have referred, (Rom. vi. 4; Col. ii. 12,) where he says, that 'we are buried with Christ by baptism:' for a death and burial are better expressed by immersion, than by sprinkling." In Thesaur. Disputat. Sedan. tom. i. p. 769, 770.

31. Mr. Doutrin.—" How is this [baptismal] water administered to the baptized? Formerly it was done by dipping quite in; but in our climate only by sprinkling." Scheme of Div. Truths, chap. xxii. quest. 24.

32. Mr. David Martin.—" As baptism was performed by immersion, or plunging the entire person in a great depth of water, Jesus Christ has here (Mark x. 38,) used this expression in the same sense as the prophets have mentioned gulphs and great waters, metaphorically to represent great afflictions." Note sur Marc. x. 38.

33. Dr. Priestley.—" This rite appears to have

been generally, though probably not always, performed by dipping the whole body in water.... It is certain that in very early times there is no particular mention made of any person being baptized by sprinkling only, or a partial application of water to the body." Hist. Corrupt. vol. ii. p. 66, 67.

34. Burmannus.—" Immersion was used by the Jews, the apostles, and the primitive church, especially in warm countries. To this various forms of speaking used by the apostles refer, (Rom. vi. 3, 4; Col. ii. 12; Gal. iii. 27.) But in the west, and colder parts of the world, sprinkling prevailed." Synops. Theolog. tom. ii. loc. xliii. c. vi. § 9.

35. Mr. John Trapp.—" There were, saith one, many ceremonies in baptism used in the primitive church; viz. putting off old clothes, drenching in water, so as to be buried in it, putting on new clothes at their coming out, to which Paul alludeth in these words." Commentary on Col. ii. 12.

36. Grotius.—" That baptism used to be performed by immersion, and not by pouring, appears both from the proper signification of the word, and the places chosen for the administration of the rite, (John iii. 23; Acts viii. 38;) and also from the many allusions of the apostles, which cannot be referred to sprinkling, (Rom. vi. 3, 4; Col. ii. 12.)" Apud Polum, Synops. ad Matt. iii. 6.

37. Castalio and Camerarius.—"*And were baptized;* that is, they were immersed in water." Apud Poli Synopsin, ad Matt. iii. 6.

38. Beza.—" *Ye have put on Christ*—This phrase seems to proceed from the ancient custom of plunging the adult, in baptism." Annotat. ad Gal. iii. 27.

39. Mr. Bingham.—" The ancients thought that immersion, or burying under water, did more lively represent the death, and burial, and resurrection of Christ, as well as our own death unto sin, and rising again unto righteousness; and the divesting or unclothing of the

person to be baptized, did also represent the putting off the body of sin, in order to *put on the new man, which is created in righteousness and true holiness*....Persons thus divested, or unclothed, were usually baptized by immersion, or dipping of their whole bodies under water ....There are a great many passages in the epistles of St. Paul, which plainly refer to this custom; as this was the original apostolical practice, so it continued to be the universal practice of the church for many ages, upon the same symbolical reasons as it was first used by the apostles....It appears from Epiphanius and others, that almost all heretics, who retained any baptism, retained immersion also....The only heretics against whom this charge [of not baptizing by a total immersion] is brought, were the Eunomians, a branch of the Arians." Origin. Eccles. b. xi. chap. xi. § 1, 4.

40. Buddeus.—" Concerning baptism, it is particularly to be observed, that in the apostolic church it was performed by immersion into water: which, not now to mention other things, is manifest from this: The apostle seeks an image, in this immersion, of the death and burial of Christ, and of mortifying the old man and raising up of the new, (Rom. vi. 3, 4.) There are, indeed, some authors who think otherwise, and contend that sprinkling was practised in the apostolic church: to convince us of which, Dr. Lightfoot has left no stone unturned. But what may be said in answer to his arguments, has already appeared in my Institut. Theolog. Dogmat. l. v. c. i. § 5." Ecclesia Apostolica, cap. vii. p. 825, 826.

41. Heidanus.—" That John the Baptist and the apostles immersed, there is no doubt, (Matt. iii. 6, 16; John iii. 23; Acts viii. 38;) whose example the ancient church followed, as is most evident from the testimonies of the fathers." Corp. Theol. Christ. loc. xiv. tom. ii. p. 475.

42. Mr. Twells.—" 'Therefore we are buried with

him' by being plunged into a sort of death. [So the author of the New Text and Version of the New Testament renders Rom. vi. 4.] What blundering explication is here! He should rather have said, by being plunged into a sort of grave, viz. the waters of baptism." Critical Examination, part. i. p. 98.

43. Menochius and Estius.—"The apostle, in Rom. vi. 4, alludes to the rite of immersion, when the body is, as it were, buried, and in a little while drawn out again, as from a sepulchre." Apud Poli, Synops. ad Rom. vi. 4.

44. Lampe.—"'Because there was much water there.' That plenty of water was necessary to the administration of baptism by immersion, to a very great multitude of people, is readily acknowledged." Comment. in Evangel. secund Joan. ad cap. iii. 23.

45. Limborch.—"Baptism, then, consists in washing, or rather immersing the whole body into water, as was customary in the primitive times.... The apostle alludes to the manner of baptizing, not as practised at this day, which is performed by sprinkling of water; but as administered of old, in the primitive church, by immersing the whole body in water, a short continuance in the water, and a speedy emersion out of the water." Complete Syst. of Divin. B. V. chap. xxvii. sect. i. Comment. in Epist. ad Rom. in cap. vi. 4.

46. Sir Thomas Ridley.—"The rites of baptism, in the primitive times, were performed in rivers and fountains; and this manner of baptizing the ancient church entertained from the example of Christ, who was baptized of John in Jordan." In Thomas Lawson's Baptismalogia, p. 105.

47. Mr. John Claude.—"In his baptism, he [Christ] is plunged in the water." Essay on Compos. of Serm. vol. i. p. 272.

48. H. Altingius.—"This baptismal washing, in warm countries and ancient times, was performed by

immersion into water, a continuance under the water, and an emersion out of the water; as the practice of John the Baptist, (Matt. iii. 6, 16; John iii. 23;) of Christ's apostles, (John iii. 22, and iv. 1, 2;) and of Philip, (Acts viii. 38;) and also the signification of these rites teach, (Rom. vi. 4.)" Loci Commun. pars i. loc. xii. p. 199.

49. Hospinianus.——" John the Baptist baptized Christ in Jordan, and Philip baptized the eunuch in a river, (Acts viii.) Lydia also, together with her household, seems to have been baptized in a river, near to Philippi, at which prayers were usually made, (Acts xvi.)" De Templis, l. ii. c. iv. p. 80.

50. Curcellæus.——" Baptism was performed by plunging the whole body into water, and not by sprinkling a few drops, as is now the practice. For 'John was baptizing in Ænon, near to Salim, because there was much water; and they came and were baptized,' (John iii. 23.) Nor did the disciples that were sent out by Christ administer baptism afterwards in any other way: and this is more agreeable to the signification of the ordinance, (Rom. vi. 4). I am therefore of opinion, that we should endeavour to restore and introduce this primitive rite of immersing, if it may be done without offence to the weak; otherwise it seems better to tolerate this abuse, than to raise a disturbance in the church about it....They are now ridiculed who desire to be baptized, not by sprinkling, but as it was performed by the ancient church, by an immersion of the whole body into water." Relig. Christ. Institut. l. v. c. ii. et apud HEIDEGG. Libert. Christ. a Lege Cib. Vet. c. xiv. § 3.

51. Wolfius.——" That baptismal immersion was practised in the first ages of the Christian church, many have shown from the writings of the ancients.... Some learned Christians therefore have judged, that the same rite of immersion should be recalled into practice

at this day, lest the mystical signification of the ordinance should be lost.... Here the apostle alludes to immersion in baptism, practised of old." 'Curæ, ad Rom. vi. 4, et Col. ii. 12.

52. G. J. Vossius.—"That John the Baptist and the apostles immersed persons whom they baptized, there is no doubt. For thus we read: 'And they were baptized in Jordan.... And Jesus, when he was baptized, went up straightway out of the water,' (Matt. iii. 6, 16. It is also written, (John iii. 23:) 'John also was baptizing in Ænon, near to Salim, because there was much water there.' And (Acts viii. 38,) it is said: 'They went down both into the water, both Philip and the eunuch.' And that the ancient church followed these examples, is very clearly evinced by innumerable testimonies of the Fathers." Disputat. de Bap. disp. i. § 6.

53. Sir Peter King.—"To me it seems evident, that their [the primitive Christians'] usual custom was, to immerse, or dip, the whole body." Enquiry into the Constitut. of Prim. Church, part. ii. chap. iv. § 5.

54. Abp. Tillotson.—"Anciently, those who were baptized, put off their garments, which signified the putting off the body of sin; and were immersed and buried in the water, to represent their death to sin; and then did rise up again out of the water, to signify their entrance upon a new life. And to these customs the apostle alludes, Rom. vi. 2—6; Gal. iii. 27." Works, vol. i. serm. vii. p. 179, edit. 8vo.

55. Frid. Spanhemius, F.—"This rite of immersion, and of bringing out of the baptismal water, was common and promiscuous in the apostolic age. Whence the apostle alludes to it, as a rite common to all Christians, Rom. vi. 4; Col. ii. 12." Disputat. De Bap. pro Mortuis, p. 16, annexed by Dr. Du Veil, to his Literal Exposition of the Acts.

56. Bp. Pearce.—"I think the most probable

meaning of the phrase [*baptized for the dead,*] is to be fetched from Matt. xx. 22; Luke xii. 50; and Mark x. 38; in all which places βαπτίζεσθαι signifies to die a violent death, by the hands of persecutors. It seems to have been a metaphor taken from the custom of those days in baptizing; for the person baptized went down under the water, and was (as it were) buried under it. Hence, St. Paul says, (in Rom. vi. 4, and Col. ii. 12,) that they 'were buried with Christ by baptism.' So that this custom probably gave occasion to our Saviour to express his being to suffer death by the hands of the Jews, in the phrase of *a baptism* that he was to be baptized with. And St. Paul seems to have taken up the same phrase with a little variation, but still with the same meaning." Note on 1 Cor. xv. 29.

57. Abp. Usher.—" Some there are that stand strictly for the particular action of diving or dipping the baptized under water, as the only action which the institution of the sacrament will bear; and our church allows no other, except in case of the child's weakness; and there is expressed in our Saviour's baptism, both the descending into the water, and the rising up." Sum and Subs. of the Christ. Relig. p. 413, edit. 6th.

58. Momma.—" They were wont to go down into the water. Philip and the eunuch 'went down into the water,' (Acts viii. 38; compare verse 39.) Christ also, being baptized, *went up from the water*, (Matt. iii. 16;) therefore, he *went down into the water* to be baptized." De Statu Eccles. tom. ii. c. v. § 193.

59. Theod. Hasæus.—" Though, in the time of the apostles, the custom was not known which prevailed in the following ages; namely, that persons, immediately after their baptism, were clothed with white garments which they wore for a week afterward, and thence were called, *Albati, Candidati;* yet seeing they were entirely immersed in water, they could not be baptized without

putting off, and again putting on, their clothes." Biblioth, Bremens. class. iv. p. 1042, 1043.

60. Mr. Rich. Baxter.—"We grant that baptism then, [in the primitive times] was by washing the whole body; and did not the differences of our cold country, as to that hot one, teach us to remember, 'I will have mercy and not sacrifice,' it should be so here.... It is commonly confessed by us to the Anabaptists, as our commentators declare, that in the apostles' times, the baptized were dipped over head in the water, and that this signified their profession, both of believing the burial and resurrection of Christ; and of their own *present* renouncing the world and flesh, or dying to sin and living to Christ, or rising again to newness of life, or being buried and risen again with Christ, as the apostle expoundeth, in the forecited texts of Col. iii. [Col. ii.] and Rom. vi. And though (as is before said) we have thought it lawful to disuse the manner of dipping and to use less water, yet we presume not to change the use and signification of it.... For my part, I may say as Mr. Blake, that I never saw a child *sprinkled;* but all that I have seen baptized had water *poured* on them, and so were washed." Paraphrase on the New Test. at Matt. iii. 6. Disputations of Right to Sacram. p. 70. Plain Script. Proof, p. 134.

61. Bp. Burnet.—"They [the primitive ministers of the gospel] led them into the water, and with no other garments but what might cover nature; they at first laid them down in the water, as a man is laid in a grave, and then they said those words: 'I baptize thee in the name of the Father, Son, and Holy Ghost.' Then they raised them up again, and clean garments were put on them; from whence came the phrases of being 'baptized into Christ's death;' of our being 'buried with him by baptism into death;' of our being 'risen with Christ,' and of our 'putting on the Lord Jesus Christ;' of 'putting off the old man,' and 'putting on the new,' (Rom.

vi. 3, 4, 5; Col. ii. 12; Col. iii. 1, 10; Rom. xiii. 14.) After baptism was thus performed, the baptized person was to be farther instructed in all the specialities of the Christian religion, and in all the rules of life that Christ had prescribed." Expos. Thirty-nine Articles, p. 374, 375.

62 Braunius.—" Christ went down into Jordan, to be baptized by John, (Matt. iii.) The same thing seems to be intimated by the apostle, when he speaks of being 'buried by baptism,' (Col. ii. 12; Rom. vi. 3, 4; Gal. iii. 27.)" Doctrina Fœd. pars. iv. cap. xxi. § 8.

63. Mr. De Courcy.—" I grant, that the word [baptize] signifies to dip, and that the ordinance might have been administered by immersion in the ancient church." Rejoinder, p. 265, 266.

64. Mr. Weemse.—"When [in the primitive times] they were baptized, they went down into the water, and were baptized all over the body." Exposit. of Laws of Moses, b. i. chap. xliv.

65. Mr. T. Wilson.—"Baptism was performed in the primitive times by immersion." Archæolog. Dict. article, Baptism.

66. Assembly of Divines. — "'Were baptized.' Washed by dipping in Jordan, (as Mark vii. 4; Heb. ix. 10.). . . .'Buried with him by baptism.' (See Col. ii. 12.) In this phrase the apostle seemeth to allude to the ancient manner of baptism, which was to dip the parties baptized, and, as it were, to bury them under the water for a while, and then to draw them out of it, and lift them up, to represent the burial of our old man, and our resurrection to newness of life." Annotations on Matt. iii. 6, and Rom. vi. 4.

67. Mr. Joseph Mede.—"There was no such thing as sprinkling, or ῥαντισμος, used in baptism in the apostles' days, nor many ages after them." Discourse on Tit. iii. 5. Works, p. 63, edit. 1677.

68. Dr. Cave.—" The party to be baptized was

wholly immerged, or put under water, which was the almost constant and universal custom of those times; whereby they did more notably and significantly express the three great ends and effects of baptism." Primitive Christianity, part i. chap. x. p. 203.

69. Dr. Towerson.—"What the practice of those [primitive] times was.... will need no other proof than resorting to rivers, and other such like receptacles of waters, for the performance of that ceremony, and that too, 'because there was much water there.' For so the scripture doth not only affirm concerning the baptism of John, (Matt. iii. 5, 6, 13; John iii. 23;) but both intimate concerning that which our Saviour administered in Judea (because making John's baptism and his to be so far forth of the same sort, John iii. 22, 23,) and expressly affirm concerning the baptism of the eunuch, which is the only Christian baptism the scripture is any thing particular in the description of. The words of St. Luke (Acts viii. 38,) being, that 'both Philip and the eunuch went down into a certain water,' which they met with in their journey, in order to the baptizing of the latter. For what need would there have been either of the Baptist's resorting to great confluxes of water, or of Philip and the eunuch's going down into this, were it not that the baptism both of the one and the other, was to be performed by an immersion? A very little water, as we know it doth with us, sufficing for an effusion, or sprinkling." Of the Sacram of Bap. part iii. p. 55, 56.

70. Bossuet.—"The baptism of St. John the Baptist, which served for a preparative to that of Jesus Christ, was performed by plunging.... When Jesus Christ came to St. John, to raise baptism to a more marvellous efficacy in receiving it, the scripture says, that 'he went up out of the water' of Jordan, (Matt. iii. 16; Mark i. 10.).... In fine, we read not in the scripture that baptism was otherwise administered; and we

are able to make it appear by the acts of councils, and by the ancient rituals, that for THIRTEEN HUNDRED YEARS baptism was thus administered *throughout the whole church*, as far as was possible." In Mr. Stennett *against* Russen, p. 175, 176.

71. Mr. Chambers.—" In the primitive times this ceremony was performed by immersion; as it is to this day in the oriental churches, according to the original signification of the word." Cyclopædia, article, Baptism, edit. 7th.

72. Mr. George Whitefield.—" It is certain, that in the words of our text (Rom. vi. 3, 4,) there is an allusion to the manner of baptism, which was by immersion; which our own church allows, and insists upon it, that children should be immersed in water, unless those that bring the children to be baptized assure the minister that they cannot bear the plunging." Eighteen Sermons, p. 297.

73. Dr. Doddridge.—" And after Jesus was baptized, as soon as he 'ascended out of the water' to the bank of Jordan.... And John was also at that time baptizing at Ænon, which was a place near Salim, a town on the east side of Jordan; and he particularly chose that place, because there was *a great quantity* of water there, which made it very convenient for his purpose. Nothing, surely, can be more evident, than that πολλα υδατα, *many waters*, signifies *a large quantity of water;* it being sometimes used for the Euphrates, (Jer. li. 13. Septuag.) To which I suppose there may be an allusion, Rev. xvii. 1. Compare Ezek. xliii. 2, and Rev. i. 15, xiv. 2, xix. 6; where 'the voice of many waters' does plainly signify the roaring of a high sea*.... Considering how frequently bathing was used in those

---

* Dr. Bentley has given the following criticism on the words επι των υδατων των πολλων, (Rev. xvii. 1.) *Upon the many waters;* "upon the vast, wide, and spacious waters: for it is known, that πολυς is

hot countries, it is not to be wondered, that baptism was generally administered by immersion; though I see no proof that it was essential to the institution. It would be very unnatural to suppose that they [Philip and the eunuch] *went down to the water*, merely that Philip might take up a little water in his hand to pour on the eunuch. A person of his dignity had, no doubt, many vessels in his baggage, on such a journey through so desert a country; a precaution absolutely necessary for travellers in those parts, and never omitted by them. (See Dr. Shaw's Travels, Pref. p. 4.).... 'Buried with him in baptism.' It seems the part of candour to confess, that here [Rom. vi. 4,] is an allusion to the manner of baptizing by immersion, as most usual in those early times; but that will not prove this particular cicumstance essential to the ordinance.... They who practise baptism by immersion, are by no means to be condemned on that account; since, on the whole, that mode of baptism is evidently favoured by scripture examples, though not required by express precept." Fam. Expos. on Matt. iii. 16; John iii. 23; Acts viii. 38; Rom. vi. 4. Lectures, proposit. cliii. corol. 1.

74. M. Jurieu.—" The ancients used to plunge persons into the water, calling on the adorable Trinity." In Dr. Gale's Reflect. on Dr. Wall's Hist. Inf. Bap. p. 193.

75. Mr. Le Clerc.—" The manner of baptizing at that time, by plunging into the water those whom they baptized, was an image of the burial of Jesus Christ." In Dr. Gale's Reflect. p. 193.

76. Venema.—" It is without controversy, that baptism in the primitive church was administered by immersion into water, and not by sprinkling; seeing John is

---

often applied to continued quantity, as well as to discontinued; to magnitude and dimensions, as well as to number." Sermon upon Popery, p. 6. Camb. 1715.

said to have baptized *in Jordan*, and where there was *much water*, as Christ also did by his disciples in the neighbourhood of those places, (Matt. iii. and John iii.) Philip also *going down into the water* baptized the eunuch, (Acts viii.) To which also the apostle refers, Rom. vi. .... Nor is there any necessity to have recourse to the idea of sprinkling in our interpretation of Acts ii. 41, where *three thousand souls* are said to be added to Christ by baptism; seeing it might be performed by immersion, equally as by aspersion, especially as they are not said to have been baptized at the same time.... The essential act of baptizing, in the second century, consisted, not in sprinkling, but in immersion into water, in the name of each Person in the Trinity. Concerning immersion the words and phrases that are used sufficiently testify; and that it was performed in a river, a pool, or a fountain.... To the essential rites of baptism, in the third century, pertained immersion, and not aspersion; except in cases of necessity, and it was accounted a *half*-perfect baptism.... Immersion, in the fourth century, was one of those acts that were considered as essential to baptism;—nevertheless, aspersion was used in the last moments of life, on such as were called *clinics*, and also where there was not a sufficient quantity of water.... Beveridge, on the fiftieth *Apostolical Canon*, asserts, that the ceremony of sprinkling began to be used instead of immersion, about the time of Pope Gregory, in the sixth century; but without producing any testimony in favour of his assertion; and it is undoubtedly a mistake. Martene declares, (in his Antiq. Eccles. Rit. l. i. p. i. c. i.) that in all the ritual books, or pontifical MSS. ancient or modern, that he had seen, immersion is required; except by the Cenomanensian, and that of a more modern date, in which pouring on the head is mentioned. In the council of Ravenna also, held in the year thirteen hundred and eleven, both immersion and pouring are left to the determination of the administrator: and the council of Nismes, in the year one thousand two hundred and eighty-four, permitted pouring, if a vessel could not be had; therefore only in case of necessity.... The council of Celichith, in the beginning of the ninth century, forbade the pouring of water on the heads of infants, and commanded that they should be immersed in the font.... Baptism was administered by immersion, in the twelfth century.... In the thirteenth century, baptism was administered by immersion, thrice repeated; yet so, that one immersion was esteemed sufficient, as appears from Augerius de Montfaucon. That was a singular synodal appointment under John de Zurich, bishop of Utrecht, in the year one thousand two hundred and ninety one, which runs thus: "We appoint, that the head be put three times in the water, unless the child be weak, or sickly, or the season cold; then water may be poured, by the hand of the priest, on the head of the child, lest, by plunging, or coldness, or weakness, the child should be injured and die." Hist. Eccles. secul. i. § 138; secul. ii. § 100; secul. iii. § 51; secul. iv. § 110; secul. vi. § 251; secul. viii. § 206; secul. xii. § 45; secul. xiii. § 164.

77. Altmannus.—"In the primitive church, persons to be baptized were not sprinkled, but entirely immersed in water; which was performed according to the example of John the Baptist. Hence all those allusions: seeing, by immersion, they plainly signified a burial; by the following emersion out of the water, a resurrection; and agreeably to these ideas are those passages of scripture to be explained which refer to this rite. (See Rom. vi. 3, 4, 5; Col. ii. 12, and Gal. iii. 27.)" Meletem. Philolog. rit. tom. iii. exercit. in 1 Cor. xv. 29, § 8.

78. Magdeburg Centuriators.—"The Son of God was dipped in the water of Jordan, by the hand of John the Baptist.... Philip baptized the eunuch in a river, (Acts viii. 38.) It seems also, that Lydia and her household at Philippi were baptized in a river, at which prayers

were usually made, (Acts xvi. 13, 16.)" Cent. i. l. i. c. iv. p. 118; l. ii. c. vi. p. 381.

79. Dr. Hammond.—John baptized "in a river, in Jordan, (Mark i. 5;) in a confluence of *much water*, (John iii. 23;) *because*, as it is added, *there was much water there:* and therefore as the Jews, writing in Greek, call those lakes wherein they wash themselves κολυμβηθραι; so, in the Christian church, the βαπτιστηριον, or vessel which contained the baptismal water, is oft called, κολυμβηθρα, a *swimming* or *diving* place." Annotations on Matt. iii. 1.

80. Chamierus.—"Immersion of the whole body was used from the beginning, which expresses the force of the word *baptize*; whence John baptized in a river. It was afterwards changed into sprinkling, though it is uncertain when or by whom it commenced." Panstrat. Cathol. t. iv. l. v. c. ii. § 6.

81. Bp. Fell.—"The primitive fashion of immersion under the water, representing our death, and elevation again out of it, our resurrection, or regeneration." On the Epistles of Paul. Note on Rom. vi. 4.

82. Dutch Annotators.—"'Because there was much water there.' Because they that were baptized by John, went into the water with their whole bodies. (See Matt. iii. 16; Acts viii. 38.).... The apostle seems here [Rom. vi. 3,] to allude to the manner of baptizing, much used in those warm eastern countries; where men were wholly dipped into the water, and remained a little while under water, and afterwards rose up out of the water: to show that their dipping into and remaining in the water, is a representation of Christ's death and burial; and the rising up out of the water, of his resurrection." On John iii. 23, and Rom. vi. 3.

83. Bp. Stillingfleet.—"Rites and customs apostolical are altered; therefore men do not think that apostolical practice doth bind: for if it did, there could be no alteration of things agreeable thereunto. Now let

any one consider but these few particulars, and judge how far the pleaders for a divine right of apostolical practice do look upon themselves as bound now to observe 'them: as dipping in baptism, the use of love-feasts, community of goods, the holy kiss, by Tertullian called 'signaculum orationis:'* yet none look upon

---

* I will here subjoin a quotation from that spirited writer, Mr. Vincent Alsop: "The *feasts of love* and the *holy kiss*," he replies, in his answer to Dr. Goodman, " were not at all *institutions* of the apostles. All that the apostle determined about them was, that supposing in their civil congresses and converses they salute each other, they should be sure to avoid all levity, wantonness, all appearance of evil: for religion teaches us not only to worship God, but to regulate our civil actions in subordination to the great ends of holiness, the adorning of the gospel, and thereby the glorifying of our God and Saviour. I say the same concerning the *feast of love*. The apostle made it no *ordinance*, either temporary or perpetual; but finding that such a civil custom had obtained among them—he cautions them against gluttony, drunkenness, all excess and riot, to which such feasts, through the power of corruption in some, and the remainders of corruption in the best, were obnoxious: which is evident from 1 Cor. xi. 21. The apostle Paul, (1 Tim. ii. 8,) commands that *men pray every where lifting up holy hands:* can any rational creature imagine, that he has thereby made it a duty as oft as we pray to *elevate our hands?* That was none of his design to that age, or the present: but under a ceremonial phrase he wraps up an evangelical duty. As if he had said, Be sure you cleanse your hearts; and if you do *lift up your hands,* let them be no umbrage for unholy souls.

"Concerning *deaconesses,* I can find no such order or constitution of the apostles. It is true, they used in their travels and other occasions the services and assistances of holy women, who cheerfully administered to their necessities, and are thence called διακοναι, and said διακονειν. But how childish is it to conclude an order or institution from so slippery a thing as *an etymology?* The angels are called λειτουργικα πνευματα, *ministering spirits,* (Heb. i. 14.) Will any from hence infer that they read *the liturgy?* Magistrates are styled λειτουργοι του Θεου, and διακονοι Θεου, (Rom. xiii. 4, 6;) and yet it is no part of their office to *read divine service*..... In a word, the duty of saluting with a holy kiss; the order of all our feasts of love to God's glory; the ministering in our respective places to the necessities of the saints, are as much in force as ever, unless holiness be grown out of fashion." Sober Enquiry, p. 285, 286.

themselves as bound to observe them now, and yet all acknowledge them to have been the practice of the apostles." Irenicum, part ii. chap. vi. p. 345.

84. H. Hulsius.—" Some interpret 1 Cor. xv. 29, concerning the baptism of *clinics,* or persons confined to their beds; but this baptism changed dipping into sprinkling, and was not practised in the time of Paul." Comment. in Israel. Pris. p. 819.

85. Deylingius.—" It is manifest, that while the apostles lived, the ordinance of baptism was administered, not out of a vessel, or a baptistery, which are the marks of later times; but out of rivers and pools: and that, not by sprinkling, but by immersion....So long as the apostles lived, as many believe, immersion only was used; to which afterwards, perhaps, they added a kind of pouring, such as the Greeks practise at this day, having performed the trine immersion." Observat. Sac. pars ii. observ. xliv. § 3; par iii. obs. xxvi. § 2.

86. Heideggerus.—" Plunging, or immersion, was most commonly used by John the Baptist and by the apostles....It is of no importance whether baptism be performed by immersion into water, as of old in the warm eastern countries, and even at this day; or by sprinkling, which was afterward introduced in colder climates." Corpus Theolog. Christ. loc. xxv. § 35.

87. Mr. Edward Leigh.—" The ceremony used in baptism, is either dipping, or sprinkling: dipping is the more ancient. At first, they went down into the rivers; afterwards they were dipped in the fonts....Zanchius and Mr. Perkins prefer (in persons of age and hot countries, where it may be safe) the ceremony of immersion under the water, before that of sprinkling, or laying on the water, as holding more analogy to that of Paul, Rom. vi. 4." Body of Div. b. viii. chap. viii. p. 665.

88. Mr. Hardy.—" 'They were baptized;' that is, they were immersed in water. That this rite was commonly performed by plunging, and not by pouring, is

indicated both by the proper meaning of the word, and by the passages relating to the ordinance; for the custom of sprinkling seems to have prevailed somewhat later, in favour of those who desired to give up themselves to Christ, or to be baptized, when lying ill of disease; whom others called *clinics*. . . . *In baptism:* The allusion is to the ancient custom of baptizing, when the body was immersed in water; and therefore putting off the clothes was required: whence those phrases, *putting off the old*, and *putting on the new man*, had their origin. This rite was a figure and an image, both of a burial and a resurrection; as well of Christ, which were conspicuous, as of what is internal, in Christians. (Rom. vi. 4.)" Annotat. in Matt. iii. 6; Col. ii. 12.

89. Mr. Locke.—" We Christians, who by baptism were admitted into the kingdom and church of Christ, were baptized into a similitude of his death: We did own some kind of death, by being buried under water, which being buried with him, *i. e.* in conformity to his burial, as a confession of our being dead, was to signify, that as Christ was raised up from the dead, into a glorious life with his Father, even so we, being raised from our typical death and burial in baptism, should lead a new sort of life." Paraphrase on Rom. vi. 4.

90. J. J. Wetstenius.—"John baptized in the river Jordan, in Ænon, 'because there was *much water*,' (John iii. 23;) and Christ, when he was baptized, 'went down *into the water*,' (Matt. iii. 16.) And Christians, in baptism, are said to *put off their clothes*, (Gal. iii. 27;) to be *washed*, (Tit. iii. 5;) and to be *buried under the water*, (Rom. vi. 4:) all which are expressive, not of sprinkling, but of dipping." Comment. ad Matt. iii. 6.

91. Roell.—" It is certain that immersion into water, and emersion out of it, were practised—in Christian baptism, in the beginning." Exegesis Epist. ad Col. in cap. ii. 12.

92. Mr. Walker.—" Mr. Rogers was for retrieving

the use of dipping, as witnessed to by antiquity, approved by scripture, required by the church, (as then it was, except in case of weakness,) and symbolical with the things signified in baptism: Which I could wish as well and as heartily as he, in order to making of peace in the church, if that would do it. If I may speak my thoughts, I believe the ministers of the nation would be glad if the people would desire, or be but willing, to have their infants dipped, without fear of being destroyed." In Dr. Wall's Hist. Inf. Bap. part ii. chap. ix. p. 475.

93. Dr. Whitby.—"It being so expressly declared here, [Rom. vi. 4,] and Colos. ii. 12, that we are 'buried with Christ in baptism,' by being buried under water; and the argument to oblige us to a conformity to his death, by dying to sin, being taken hence; and this immersion being religiously observed BY ALL CHRISTIANS FOR THIRTEEN CENTURIES, and approved by our church, and the change of it into sprinkling, even without any allowance from the Author of this institution, or any licence from any council of the church, being that which the Romanist still urgeth to justify his refusal of the cup to the laity; it were to be wished, that this custom might be again of general use, and aspersion only permitted, as of old, in case of the clinici, or in present danger of death." Note on Rom. vi. 4.

94. Bp. Nicholson.—" The sacrament of baptism was anciently administered by plunging into the water, in the western as well as the eastern part of the church; and that the Gothic word........ (Mark i. 8, and Luke iii. 7, 12,) the German word *Tauffen*, the Danish word *Dobe*, and the Belgic *Doopen*, do as clearly make out that practice, as the Greek word βαπτιζω." In Dr. Gale's Reflect. on Dr. Wall's Hist. Inf. Bap. p. 121, 192.

95. Quenstedius.—" It is highly probable, if not certain, that John the Baptist and the apostles immersed

the persons to be baptized into water. For thus we read, (Matt. iii. 6, 16,) 'And they were baptized in Jordan. When Jesus was baptized, he immediately came up' (or, as Grotius renders it, he had scarcely ascended) 'out of the water.' Our Saviour, therefore, when he was baptized, first went down into the river, was plunged into the water, and afterwards came up out of it.... That immersion into the water was practised by John, is gathered also from that reason of the evangelist, (John iii. 23,) 'John was baptizing in Ænon near to Salim, because there was much water there'.... With St. Paul, *to be baptized is to be buried*, (Rom. vi. 3, 4.) Immersion is, as it were, a burial; emersion, a resurrection; to which the apostle alludes, Col. ii. 12. It is written, (Acts viii. 38, 39,) that Philip *went down* with the eunuch *into the water*, and there baptized him; and it is added, that, the ordinance being administered, they both *came up out of the water*.... Both the eastern and the western churches were very observant of the rite of immersion, for a great number of years.... Nor is there any instance among the more ancient writers, that I have observed, of baptism being administered by a simple aspersion." Antiq. Bib. pars. i. c. iv. sect. ii. num. i. § 1, 2, 4.

96. Dr. Wall.—" Their [the primitive Christians'] general and ordinary way was to baptize by immersion, or dipping the person, whether it were an infant, or grown man or woman, into the water. This is so plain and clear by an infinite number of passages, that as one cannot but pity the weak endeavours of such Pædobaptists as would maintain the negative of it; so also we ought to disown and show a dislike of the PROFANE SCOFFS which some people give to the English Antipædobaptists, merely for their use of dipping. It is one thing to maintain, that that circumstance is not absolutely necessary to the essence of baptism; and an-

other, to go about to represent it as ridiculous and foolish, or as shameful and indecent; when it was, in all probability, the way by which our blessed Saviour, and for certain was the most usual and ordinary way by which the ancient Christians did receive their baptism.... It is a great want of prudence, as well as of honesty, to refuse to grant to an adversary what is certainly true, and may be proved so. It creates a jealousy of all the rest, that one says.... It is plain that the ordinary and general practice of St. John, the apostles, and primitive church, was to baptize by putting the person into the water, or causing him to go into the water. Neither do I know of *any Protestant* who has denied it; and but *very few* men of learning that have denied, that where it can be used with safety of health, it is the most fitting way.... John iii. 23; Mark i. 5; Acts viii. 38, are *undeniable proofs* that the baptized person went ordinarily into the water, and sometimes the baptist too. We should not know by these accounts, whether the whole body of the baptized was put under water, head and all, were it not for two later proofs, which seem to me to put it out of question. One, that St. Paul does twice, in an allusive way of speaking, call baptism *a burial;* which allusion is not so proper, if we conceive them to have gone into the water only up to the armpits, &c. as it is if their whole body was immersed. The other, the custom of the near succeeding times.... As for *sprinkling*, I say as Mr. Blake, at its first coming up in England, *Let them defend it that use it.*....They [who are inclined to Presbyterianism] are hardly prevailed on to leave off that SCANDALOUS custom of having their children, though never so well, baptized out of a basin, or porringer, in a bed-chamber; hardly persuaded to bring them to church; much farther from having them dipped, though never so able to endure it." Hist. of Inf. Bap. part ii. chap. ii. p. 462, 463. De-

fence of Hist. Inf. Bap. p. 129, 131, 140, 147.*—
See also Dr. Robertson's Hist. Emp. Charles V. vol iii.
p. 78. Œderi Cateches. Racoviens. Profligat. p. 98.
Milton's Parad. Lost, b. xii. l. 438, 441, 442. Ency-
clopæd. Britan. art. Baptism, vol. ii. p. 995. Thesaur.
Theolog. Philolog. tom. ii. p. 569. Leydeckeri Idea
Theolog. l. vii. c. v. § 7. Petavii Theol. Dogmat.
l. ii. de Pœnitent. c. i. § 11. Episcopii Respons. ad
Quest. xxxv. Dr. Grabe's Unity of the Church, and
Expediency of Forms of Prayer, Preface. Cajetani
Annotat. ad Matt. iii. 16. Cases to Recover Dissenters, vol. iii. p. 31. Dict. of the Bible, (three vols.
octavo) vol. ii. p. 709. Brandt's Hist. Reform. b. xlviii.
vol. iv. p. 56. Mr. Ostervald's Grounds and Principles
of Christ. Relig. p. 311, edit. 6th. Scheuchzeri Physica
Sacra, tab. dclxiv.

REFLECTIONS.

Reflect. I. Here we have a great number of the
most respectable characters for solid learning, and many
of them for eminent piety. They appear to testify what
they know and what they believe concerning an ancient
fact; a fact, in an acquaintance with which, the purity
of a divine institution, and obedience to the will of our
Lord are not a little involved. The principal question
on which they are cited to give their opinion, is: Whether John the Baptist, and the apostles of Christ, admi-

---

* The anonymous author of a book entitled, Le Baptême Retabli, gives us the following remarkable anecdote respecting immersion, as performed by one of the Roman pontiffs. "Pope Be-
nedict XIII. having occasion, more than once, to baptize adult persons, and among others, nine Jews and Turks at one time; he instructed them himself, and after that he *immersed* them. With a
view to every thing being performed in its natural and proper order, he made use of the ancient rituals; which so much displeased
the cardinals, that not one of them would assist at the ceremony.
This is what I myself, as well as others, have read under the article
Rome, in the public newspapers." Le Bap. Retab. part ii. p. 92, 93.

nistered baptism by immersion? A question this, which regards both fact and right. Because, in whatever manner those venerable men, and lights of the world, performed that institution, we are bound to believe it was right; for they had too much knowledge and too much integrity to administer this branch of holy worship in a wrong way. Besides, they were not ignorant that their practice, in this respect, was to be viewed as a pattern, and to be considered as law, by the succeeding disciples of Christ. The character and profession of those authors, who appear to give their thoughts on this important subject, leave no room for suspicion that they were biassed in favour of the Baptists: because partiality itself must confess, that if their judgment was under the influence of predilection, it most probably lay on the contrary side. Many of them also are beyond the reach of suspicion, in regard to their knowledge of ecclesiastical antiquity.

Let us now see what our impartial friends, the Quakers, have to say on this part of the subject.

1. Thomas Lawson.—" John the Baptist, that is, John the *dipper;* so called because he was authorized to baptize in water.... Such as *rhantize,* or sprinkle infants, have no command from Christ, nor example among the apostles, nor the first primitive Christians for so doing .... See the author of *rhantism,* that is, sprinkling; not Christ, nor the apostles, but Cyprian; not in the days of Christ, but some two hundred and thirty years after." Baptismalogia, p. 7, 75, 117.

2. Thomas Ellwood.—" Philip went down with him [the eunuch] into the water, and baptized him; which was no sooner done, and they come up out of the water again, but the Spirit of the Lord caught away Philip." Sacred Hist. of the New Test. part ii. p. 335.

3. John Gratton.—" Down into the water he [Jesus] goes, and fulfilled John's dispensation, or that righteousness required by it, and having fulfilled it, he went up

straightway out of the water." Life of John Gratton, p. 150. See Chap. II. Reflect. I. No. 1, 7.—Such is the language of those who have no perceivable interest in the decision of this dispute.

On a brief review of the preceding quotations from learned Pædobaptist authors, it appears, that immersion was practised by John the Baptist, by the apostles of Christ, and by the primitive Christians, No. 1—94;—that our Lord himself was immersed by the venerable John, No. 6, 7, 8, 10, 12, 16, 19, 20, 26, 27, 29, 30, 37, 41, 46, 47, 52, 57, 58, 62, 70, 73, 76, 78, 90, 95, 96;—that some of them expressly assert, and many of them implicitly allow, that the scripture no where speaks of any being baptized, but by immersion, No. 10, 16, 23, 31, 36, 50, 67, 69, 71, 76, 80, 83, 85;—that the practice of immersion gave occasion for some very singular and emphatical phrases to be used by the apostles, No. 9, 12, 18, 30, 34, 36, 40, 45, 54, 55, 61, 66, 73, 82, 88, 89;—that the baptism of the three thousand affords no objection to the universal practice of immersion in those times, No. 76;—that plunging was the general and almost universal practice, for a long course of ages, No. 4, 70, 76, 93;—that the churches of Helvetia acknowledge, and the church of England, in common cases, requires immersion, No. 19, 57, 93;—that one of these authors knew of no Protestant, who had denied immersion to have been the general practice of apostolic times; and of but very few learned men, who denied its being the fittest, if a regard to health do not forbid, No. 96;—that the custom of sprinkling is absolutely indefensible, ibid.;—that they who ridicule the practice of immersion deserve censure, ibid.;—that sprinkling of infants is not an institution of Christ, No. 3, 67;—that it is uncertain when, and by whom, sprinkling was introduced, No. 80;—and, that a restoration of the primitive practice is very desirable, No. 50, 51, 92, 93. See Chap. III. Reflect. IV.—Such is the verdict which these Pædobaptists give on the cause before us.

Reflect. II. Now is it not strange, strange to astonishment, that so many eminent men should thus agree in bearing testimony to immersion, as the apostolic example; when it is notorious that their own practice was very different? Just so the Papists acknowledge, that the apostolic church communicated at the Lord's table in both kinds; while they themselves unite in a contrary practice. Thus Toletus, for instance: " It was an ancient custom in the church, from the times of the apostles, to communicate under both species. About this there is no controversy. This ancient custom is manifest from the words of Paul, 1 Cor. x. and xi."——Salmero: " No one denies that the Corinthians communicated under both species; yet we deny that custom to have the force of a divine precept."* At what these veterans in the cause of superstition may say, we have little reason indeed to be surprised; but is it not a wonderful phenomenon in the religious world, that such a number of the most learned Lutherans, Calvinists, and Arminians, abroad; together with English Episcopalians, Presbyterians, and Independents; should all unite in one attestation, respecting the primitive mode of administering this ordinance; even while they opposed the Baptists, for considering immersion as absolutely necessary to a compliance with the divine command; and while they greatly differed among themselves, in respect of several particulars relating to the subjects and the design of baptism? To what can this remarkable agreement with us, as to the primitive mode of proceeding, be ascribed? And what is the reason of their differing so much among themselves? The true reason, I take to be this: When they unite in declaring their views of the apostolic pattern, they have clear, strong, indubitable evidence, arising from the meaning of the name

---

* Apud Laurentium, Dialog. Eucharist. c. ii. § 62, 63.

which the ordinance bears, and the inspired narrative of the first Christian churches. Each of them feels the ground on which he treads. Hence their union; and here they agree with us.—On the other hand, when they differ among themselves, about the foundation of an infant's claim on the ordinance; concerning the degree of necessity and the utility of Pædobaptism; about sponsors, the sign of the cross, and so on; they argue on general principles and moral considerations. This kind of argumentation is quite foreign to the nature of positive rites; and yet, by a long train of deductions from such principles, they infer their various rules of proceeding in the administration of baptism. Hence they differ among themselves. Nor need we wonder. For as moral considerations are exceedingly various, and as the application of each to practice may be greatly diversified; so, according to the complexion of the principle adopted as the foundation of an argument, will the natural inference be, whether it regard the mode or the subject of any ordinance. Whenever ideas, therefore, of moral fitness, of expediency, or of necessity, usurp the place of divine precepts and apostolic examples, relating to positive institutions of the Christian church; the most learned and the best of men will always differ in their conclusions, and that in proportion as their notions of what *is* fitness, expediency, or necessity, vary. For it is notorious, that while one esteems this or the other thing extremely proper and highly useful to the cause of religion; another despises it as absurd, or detests it as injurious. But when our divine Lord, addressing his disciples in a positive command, says, ' It *shall* be so;' or when, speaking by an apostolic example, he declares, ' It *is* thus;' all our own reasonings about fitness, expediency, or utility, must hide their impertinent heads. The finest powers of reason have nothing to do, in this case, but only to consider the natural, the obvious import of his language, and then submit.

To reason any farther here, is only to seek a plausible excuse for rebellion against the sovereign majesty of HIM who is king in Zion.

Reflect. III. It is, I think, a good rule which Dr. Owen gives, relating to divine institutions, when he says: "That which is *first* in any kind, gives *the measure* of what follows in the same kind."*—With Dr. Owen, Abp. Tillotson perfectly agrees. He expresses himself thus: "This is reasonable, that the *first* in every kind should be the *rule* and *pattern* of the rest, and of all that follow after, because it is likely to be the most perfect. In process of time, the best institutions are apt to decline, and, by insensible degrees, to swerve and depart from their first state; and therefore it is a good rule to preserve things from corruption and degeneracy, often to look back to the *first institution*, and by that to correct those imperfections which almost unavoidably creep in with time."†—To the judgment of these two eminent authors, I will add the suffrage of Mr. Henry, who speaks with a professed regard to baptism in the following manner: "When a question was put to our Lord Jesus, by the Pharisees, concerning marriage, he refers them to the institution and original law, (Matt. xix. 3, 4,) to teach us to go by the *same rule* in other ordinances. Run up the stream of the observation (which in a long course sometimes contracts filth) to the spring of the institution, and see *what it was from the beginning.*"‡—These directions perfectly coincide with that maxim of unerring wisdom, to which Mr. Henry adverts: *From the beginning it was not so.* A maxim this of such importance, that whoever can is ready to avail himself of it. For, as Mr. Blake justly observes, "If we can but say, *From the beginning it was not*

---

* Enquiry into Orig. Nat. and Constitut. of Churches, Pref. p. 54.
† Works, vol. ii. p. 170, fol. 1722.
‡ Treatise on Bap. p. 18.

so—we have sufficient."*—To which I will add the suffrage of Dr. Ridgley: "The example of our Saviour and his apostles ought to be a rule to the churches in all succeeding ages."† Consequently, if at the beginning of the Christian church baptism was immersion, as appears by the foregoing testimonies, it ought to be so now.‡ This must be the case, except there be evidence of our sovereign Lord having repealed his first order, and altered the original plan of proceeding: but no such pretence is made by our brethren.—Perfectly agreeable to this, is the following language of a learned Pædobaptist in opposition to the church of Rome. "If so then, [in the apostolic times] why not now? Does not that reason still hold good? Who hath made this change? Who hath sown these new tares in the church? How crept in this false doctrine? How grew up this corrupt absurd practice? Certainly, from no other than that abominable root, which gives being to the whole body of Popery, viz. pride and usurpation."§

It must, indeed, be acknowledged, that though the numerous and learned authors just produced, consider immersion as practised by the apostles; yet many of them think it highly probable, that pouring or sprinkling was used on some occasions, in those primitive times. A supposition this, too much like that of the Roman Catholics, when they speak to the following effect: "Though wine was *commonly* used by those who partook of the holy supper, in the apostolic age; yet a participation of that element is not essential to the ordinance: nor is it demonstrable that the apostles

---

* Covenant Sealed, p. 111. Vid. Vitring. De Synag. Vet. Prolegom. p. 75. † Body of Div. quest. 168, 169, 170. Vid. Dr. Owen, on Church Government, p. 62, 92.

‡ Id esse verum quodcunque prius : id esse adulterum, quodcunque posterius, says Tertullian. That is, *Whatever was first, is true* : *Whatever was introduced afterwards, is a* corruption.

§ Hist. of Popery, vol. i. p. 160.

always used it when they celebrated the death of their Lord. Nay, the contrary seems rather to be implied, when they call the administration of that solemn appointment, *Breaking of* BREAD."—Mr. Payne has justly observed, with regard to the holy supper, that it would have been very strange had the apostles acted contrary to its institution in the course of their practice, and in so short a time after its first appointment:* which observation may be applied to the subject before us.—But we answer more directly, by asking: Whether the apostles and their associates did not administer baptism in obedience to divine law? Whether the commanding terms in every law, divine or human, should not be understood in their most commonly received sense; except there be some intimation of a different acceptation being intended? Whether the primary and most common meaning of the word *baptism*, be not immersion? And, whether the act of solemnly immersing a person does not more fully express the great design of the ordinance, than pouring or sprinkling? Now, if learning and impartiality unite in demanding an affirmative answer to these queries, as appears from quotations already produced; there is not the least reason to doubt, but the apostles always practised immersion.

Very few of our opposers, if I mistake not, have dared absolutely to deny, either the lawfulness of immersion, or that the apostles ever used it. But if lawful, it must be so in virtue of a divine command, or of some authentic example; because it is a positive rite, and when performed by us, it is as a religious duty. If, then, a divine precept require immersion, by what authority is pouring or sprinkling at all used? for that plunging, pouring, and sprinkling, are three different actions, will not admit of a doubt. Or, does our Lord, in the same enacting term of the same law, warrant *all* those different modes of proceeding, and compliment the human will

---

* Preservative against Popery, title vii. p. 111.

with a liberty of choosing that which is most agreeable? Were that the case, it would be a strange law indeed, when considered as enacted by our divine Sovereign! Have we any instance of this kind in the sacred records? Nay, the majesty of a human legislator would be disgraced by such a conduct.—On the other hand, if pouring or sprinkling be *naturally* inferible from our Lord's command (and he must be of a perverse turn, who pleads for an inference confessedly *unnatural*;) and if the apostles, or the primitive church, ever practised the one or the other; it is hard to imagine how they came to use immersion at all: either of the former, considered simply in itself, being more easy, and more agreeable to human feelings, both in regard to the administrator and the candidate. So, had Abraham and his male posterity been left at their option to circumcise either a *finger*, or the *foreskin*, we might have safely concluded, without express information, which they would have preferred— so preferred, as never to have practised the other. It is far more natural therefore to conclude, that immersion was changed into *sprinkling*, than that sprinkling was laid aside for *immersion:* and of this Pædobaptists themselves will furnish us with sufficient evidence in a following chapter.

Farther: Had the apostles practised pouring or sprinkling, a *basin*, or something similar, must have been frequently used on the solemn occasion. Is it not then a wonder that the sacred historians, when recording so many instances of the ordinance being administered, no where *mention* such a domestic utensil, nor any thing like it, as employed by the administrator? Our brethren perhaps may say: "This was a trifling circumstance, and not worthy of particular notice." We find, however, that when our Lord washed the feet of his disciples, as he made use of a basin, it is expressly mentioned.* Now that pedilavium being a single instance, not intended as

---

* John xiii. 5; see Exod. xii. 22, and xxiv. 6.

an ordinance of divine worship, nor yet, in a literal sense, as a binding example on the followers of Christ; it is quite unaccountable that the inspired historic pen should so expressly mark the use of a basin on that occasion, and yet pass over in silence its very frequent service at the administration of baptism : for its use must have been frequent indeed, had the mode of proceeding adopted by our opposers been then practised. Besides, there would have been the greatest propriety in mentioning a circumstance of this kind, had pouring or sprinkling been the mode of administration; because it would have been a plain intimation, that the term *baptism* was not to be understood in its primary and obvious, but in a secondary and remote acceptation. Of what importance was it for us to know, that our Lord *poured water into a basin*, before he performed the condescending act; in comparison with an explicit account of something similar, if any thing similar there had been, prior to the administration of baptism, and preparatory to it ? How comes it that these expressions, or others equivalent : " Peter, or Paul, or Philip (for instance) *poured water into a basin, and baptized such a one*, are entirely unknown to the New Testament? How came the inspired page to speak, not of *basins*, but of *rivers;* not of a *little*, but of *much water;* not of *bringing* water to the candidate, but of his *going to*, and *into* the water; not of *wetting*, but of *burying;* when the administration and the design of the ordinance are described ? Were one of our opponents to publish a history of his own practice, in regard to baptism, he must either use different language from that of inspiration, respecting this matter ; or expose himself to a violent suspicion of having deserted the cause he once espoused. His character would certainly appear problematical among his brethren, and his conduct bear a dispute, whatever he might intend. If therefore the sacred historians practised aspersion, their conduct as writers was extremely

THE CHURCH IN FOLLOWING AGES. 209

remarkable: for though, on that supposition, they set the example which our opposers follow, as to the mode of administration; yet, in their narrations, they adopt such expressions, and mention such circumstances relating to baptism, as would make a very singular figure from the pen of an English Pædobaptist, when describing his own conduct and views in reference to that institution. Were my reader to peruse a narrative of baptismal practice, penned by a foreigner, or by any anonymous author, of whom he had no knowledge but what was obtained from his writings;—were he to find him speak of choosing a place for the administration of baptism, in preference to others, because there was *much water* there—of his baptizing in a *river*—of *going down* with the candidate *into*, and *coming up out of the water;* —were he to find him reminding baptized persons of their having been *buried* and *raised* with Christ in baptism; and were he to observe, that the author always uses a word for the ordinance, which, in its primary acceptation, signifies *immersion,* but never talks of *bringing water* to the candidate, or of using a *basin,* as preparatory to the administration; he would, I presume, be ready to say: "This author, whoever he be, writes like a *Baptist.* He speaks the language of one that considers baptism as nothing short of immersion. If, however, contrary to all appearances, he practise *aspersion,* and intended to inform the public of that particular, he has chosen a very singular method in which to do it, and has expressed himself in the most awkward manner imaginable." Now, supposing the apostles to have practised pouring, or sprinkling, it is highly reasonable for us to conclude, that the inspired penmen *intended* to inform us of it. But if so, how comes it that a serious and uniform adoption of their expressions, by an unknown author, respecting the administration and meaning of the sacred rite, is enough to raise an immediate suspicion that he approves of *immersion?* And how comes it, that our present opposers never talk of going to a place where there is *much water*, of going *into* the water, and of *coming up out of* the water, when they speak of performing the solemn service? A similarity of *practice*, in other cases, usually produces a similarity of *language*, when that practice is narrated. This, therefore, is a presumptive evidence, that the apostolic practice was different from theirs. For while they avoid the use of this remarkable apostolic language, it looks as if they were conscious that it would not properly express the facts to which it should be applied.

To illustrate the point and confirm the argument, it may be observed, that when Justin Martyr describes the manner of proceeding in his time, he speaks of the candidates being " brought *to a place of water*,"* that they might be baptized. A kind of language this which is not at all used, that I recollect, by Pædobaptists in our country. The ancient apologist, however, saw reason for such expressions. Was it, then, because he *designed* to inform the Roman emperor how baptism was practised in those times? Undoubtedly; and we have equal grounds to conclude, that the apostles *intended* to inform posterity how baptism was administered by John, and by themselves. Is this phraseology of Justin like that of the New Testament in similar cases? None, with any appearance of reason, can deny it; and hence it has been inferred, that religious practice, in this respect, was the same in the second as it was in the first century. What then has been the opinion of learned men concerning the mode of administration, as intimated in these remarkable words of the martyr? They have, I think, universally understood him, as meaning to convey the idea of *immersion*. Mr. Reeves, for instance, in his Note on this very passage, has the following words. " It is evident, from this place of Justin, and that of

---

* Mr. Reeves's Apologies, vol. i. p. 105. Vid. Buddei Theol. Dogmat. l. v. c. i. § 5.

Tertullian (De Cor. Mil. c. iii.) that *ponds* and *rivers* were the only baptisteries or fonts the church had for the first two hundred years."*— But whether the apostles and Justin administered the ordinance by plunging or sprinkling, one thing is plain; Various remarkable expressions, found in the writings of those ancients relative to baptism, are seldom, if ever, used in the same connection by our opposers, though common enough among such as practise immersion. This reminds me of what is reported concerning some Popish priests in Scotland, who imagined that the New Testament was composed by Martin Luther.† A wild imagination, doubtless. It may be supposed to have arisen, however, from that similarity of sentiment and of expression, which they perceived to exist, between the apostolic writings and those of the great reformer. Now, as it is natural for persons to make use of language that is agreeable to their own religious practice; and as the obvious meaning, not only of Justin's expressions, but of inspired phraseology, relating to baptism, is much more agreeable to the practice of plunging, than to that of pouring or sprinkling a little water upon the face; I cannot but think, that both the apologist and the apostles constantly practised immersion.

That the principle of reasoning adopted in the two preceding paragraphs is not peculiar to us, appears by the following extract from Dr. Waterland; which, *mutatis mutandis*, will apply in the present case. "The Arians never use any expressions like to some which they subscribe to. They will never say from the press, or from the pulpit, or in common conversation, that Father, Son, and Holy Ghost are *one God;* that they are *coequal, coeternal,* and so on. They allow of these expressions as often as they subscribe, but never else....

---

* Mr. Reeves's Apologies, vol. i. p. 105. Vid. Buddei Theol. Dogmat. l. v. c. i. § 5.

† Mr. Clarkson's Practical Div. of Papists, p. 79.

Should any man of them, in a treatise or sermon, throw out any such shocking assertions, (shocking, I mean, to *them*,) he would be looked upon as a *deserter* by the party, and a *betrayer* of the cause which he had undertaken to defend."*

Reflect. IV. It has been sometimes objected, that there is no mention of any *change of raiment* at the administration of baptism; which must have taken place, and would probably have been mentioned, had immersion been the common practice. Various learned and eminent Pædobaptists have taught us, however, that in the apostolic writings there are *plain allusions* to such change of raiment. See No. 54, 59, 61.—But supposing no such allusive expressions to have been used, yet as the inspired writers inform us, that John baptized our Lord *in*, or *into Jordan;* that Philip and the eunuch *went down into the water*, and that the latter was *baptized;* we should not have wanted any farther information respecting that affair. Who can doubt whether the Syrian leper changed his garments, when, according to the order of the man of God, he *dipped himself seven times in Jordan*, though the sacred historian is silent as to that particular? Nor is any mention made of changing the raiment, that I recollect, either in the laws or in the history of legal purification by bathing, among the ancient Israelites; yet that mode of purification often occurs in the Old Testament.†

Reflect. V. To favour the cause of sprinkling, some Pædobaptists have given such a representation of the manner in which John performed the sacred rite, as is quite ludicrous. Dr. Guise, for instance, when speaking of the multitude baptized by our Lord's harbinger, says: " It seems therefore to me, that the people stood *in ranks near to, or just within the edge of the river;* and John, passing along before them, *cast water* upon

---

* Case of Arian Subscription, p. 33.
† See Mr. Martin's Letters to Mr. Horsey, p. 145, 146.

their heads or faces, with his hands, or some proper instrument; by which means he might easily baptize many thousands in a day."* Of this Mr. J. Wesley has been the humble transcriber; † and Mr. Arch. Hall gives Dr. Guise's Note the sanction of his express approbation.‡—Mr. Horsey also adopts the same view of the fact, when he says: " I presume, that the multitude stood *in ranks* at the brink, or just within the edge of the river, while the administrator sprinkled or poured the *running* water upon them." §—Very different, however, is the following language of that eminent and learned Lutheran, Buddeus: " Though a great multitude was baptized by John, yet thence it does not follow that they could not be baptized by immersion; seeing nothing hinders but they might be baptized separately, one by one." ǁ—That so grave an author as Dr. Guise should give such a puerile and farcical turn to the conduct of him who came in the spirit and power of Elijah, when administering a solemn ordinance of divine worship, is matter of wonder. Nor can I account for its being approved by others, but on a supposition, that they feel themselves embarrassed, when attempting to reconcile their own practice with the natural and obvious meaning of what the evangelists have said concerning John's administration of the rite. If, however, the credit of sprinkling cannot be supported without burlesquing the sacred history, and exposing in this manner one of the most exalted human characters to the ridicule of infidels, it ought for ever to sink in oblivion. But what will not the love of hypothesis do, when cherished by any writer! To justify my censure, let the following things be considered.

This account of the fact represents him who was more than a prophet, as less than a man—represents

---

* Note on Matt. iii. 6. † Ibid. Compare No. 18.
‡ Gospel Worship, vol. i. p. 271. § Inf. Bap. Stated and Defended, p. 20. ǁ Theolog. Dogmat. l. v. c. i. § 5.

him, who was all severity in his manners, and all solemnity in his ministry, as acting the part of a playful boy. According to these authors, there was not half the solemnity in John's baptism, which there is in that annual festival of the Romish church, which is called *The Benediction of Horses.* Concerning the latter, Dr. Middleton says: "It is always celebrated with much solemnity in the month of January, when all the inhabitants of the city and neighbourhood send up their horses, asses, and so on, to the convent of St. Anthony, near St. Mary the Great; where a priest in his surplice at the church-door *sprinkles with his brush* all the animals singly, as they are presented to him, and receives from each owner a gratuity proportionable to his zeal and ability. Amongst the rest, I had my own horses blest at the expense of about eighteen-pence of our money; as well to satisfy my own curiosity, as to humour the coachman."*— Whether Dr. Guise, and those who follow him in this particular, imagine the son of Zacharias to have used his naked hand, a scoop, a squirt, a brush, or a bunch of hyssop, I cannot say; though the last, I think, is most likely, on the principle of Mr. Horsey's reasoning.† This, however, is clear: The priest of superstition in his white

---

* In Conformity of Ancient and Modern Cerem. Pref. p. 5, 6.

† Mr. Gay has mentioned another instrument that is well fitted to sprinkle a multitude expeditiously. These are his words:

" When dext'rous damsels twirl the *sprinkling mop*."

See Dr. Johnson's Dict. under the verb SPRINKLE. Whether this was the instrument used by John, we leave our opposers to judge. But how strange it is to hear of *casting* water on the head or face with an *instrument!* It leads one to think, rather of a pagan priest, than of the Messiah's harbinger—of ancient heathenism, rather than Christian baptism. For an account of the *aspergilla,* or instruments of sprinkling, used in the rites of paganism, Lomeierus De Vet. Gent. Lustrat. Syntag. cap. xxxv. may be consulted; but whither the reader must have recourse for intelligence concerning the *aspergillum* of John, or of any apostle, I confess myself entirely ignorant; because the only authors that mention it, have not condescended to give us the least description of it.

surplice, appears to act with more care and more solemnity, than the servant of God in his hairy garment. The former, though paid for his labour at so much per head, cautiously *sprinkles the cattle one by one:* the latter, though mortified to secular gain, burning with zeal for God, and full of love to the souls of men, being all in a hurry to finish his business, *casts water* on half a dozen or half a score at a time. Of this haste, it may be supposed, the consequence was, that the water was very unequally divided among the candidates. How many *deep* the ranks were, our authors indeed have not informed us; but according to them there must have been more than *one* rank, because they speak in the plural. It is plain, therefore, that the front rank must have had the most copious application of the liquid element: while many individuals, we may justly suppose, that were farther distant from the administrator, had little or none at all. This presumed conduct of John, considered in one view, presents us with a *mercenary drudge* in the service of God, who cares not how slovenly the solemnities of holy worship are performed, provided they do but appear in full tale: in another, with a *wanton boy*, who makes himself sport by squirting water upon all that are near him: in every view, not only with something quite inimical to the character of John, but also to the solemn and gracious import of that ordinance which he administered. But, as the learned Chamier observes, "there is nothing so extraordinary, nothing so unusual, nothing so obscure, that is not urged by one or another against a divine appointment."*—Dr. Hammond informs us, that the manner of immersing proselytes among the Jews "is said to be, that they should sit in water *up to the neck*," and in that situation, "learn some of the precepts of the law, both hard and easy.†" Now, after such a representation of John's baptism, who could have ima-

---

* Panstrat. tom. iv. l. viii. c. vi. § 28.   † Note on Matt. iii. 1.

gined these very authors to consider it as originating in the proselyte bathing; yet so it is!

The people stood in RANKS, *near to, or just within the edge of the river; and John, passing before them* CAST *water upon their heads or faces.* But had this been a fact, there is reason to think it would have been mentioned: because, when our Lord miraculously fed five thousand men with a few loaves and fishes, we are expressly told that the hungry multitude were seated *in ranks*.* As John was the first administrator of baptism, and as his example, in the use of water, was to be a pattern for the church in following ages; it was apparently of much more importance for us to have been informed, had it been a fact, that the people were *baptized* when standing in ranks, than it was to be told in what position the five thousand were placed, when they partook of miraculous food. Because the former concerned a standing ordinance of New Testament worship: the latter, it is plain, was an extraordinary and transient fact. Yet the sacred historians have not said a word about the people *standing* in ranks when John baptized them, though *sitting* in ranks be so plainly mentioned respecting the miracle. It may be observed also in regard to the latter case, that a great multitude were to be served by a few disciples, and to be fed when the day was far advanced. Expedition, therefore, was highly necessary, that the people might be refreshed, and afterward go to their own habitations. In reference to this affair, the idea of *expedition* forces itself upon us; but not at all, in regard to John's baptizing a multitude, farther than was consistent with deep solemnity; for it is no where said, that he baptized them all in a day. What then would serious readers have thought, if Dr. Guise had represented Jesus Christ as giving his disciples the broken loaves and the divided fishes to *fling* among the ranks, and leave the hungry thousands to scramble for them?

---

* Mark vi. 40.

I cannot help supposing, that they would have execrated the representation as a vile impeachment of our Lord's conduct, and as worthy of a Woolston, rather than a Guise. My reader will apply this to the case before us.

Again: Do any of our opponents imagine that our Lord, standing in one of these ranks, was baptized by having a little water *cast* upon him in this random way? Or, do they suppose that John baptized him in a singular manner? Few, I think, will assert the former; and as to the latter, there is no appearance of evidence. For, are we informed that the people of Judea and of Jerusalem were all baptized by John *in the river Jordan?* We are assured by the same authority, that Jesus came from Nazareth of Galilee, and was baptized of John *in Jordan.** Such is the testimony of Matthew and of Mark; with which the language of sacred history in the Old Testament, as given by the Seventy, may be compared. Of Naaman, it is written: " Then went he down and dipped himself, εβαπτισατο, seven times in Jordan."† With equal reason therefore might we suppose, that the Syrian general went only to the *brink,* or *just within the edge* of Jordan, and there cast water upon his head or his face; as adopt the imagination of these authors, respecting the manner of John's proceeding. When the Seventy interpreters express the idea of coming TO *Jordan,* their words are, εως του Ιορδανου : ‡ when they convey the notion of standing BY *Jordan,* they use the terms, επι του Ιορδανου : § and when they represent a person standing *upon the brink,* or *just within the edge of Jordan,* their language is, επι του χειλους του Ιορδανου.|| But when the evangelists mention Jordan, in connection with John's baptizing, they represent him as performing the rite, εν τω Ιορδανη, IN *Jordan;* or as baptizing, εις τον Ιορδανην, INTO *Jordan.*¶ As coming *to the brink* of Jordan, and

---

* Mark i. 5, 9 ; Matt. iii. 6. † 2 Kings v. 14.
‡ 2 Sam. xix. 15 ; 2 Kings vi. 2, and vii. 15.
§ 2 Kings ii. 7. || 2 Kings ii. 13. ¶ Matt. iii. 6 ; Mark i. 9.

being *in* that river, manifestly denote different situations; so they are plainly distinguished in the Septuagint. "When ye are come TO THE BRINK, επι μερους, of the water of Jordan, ye shall stand still, εν Ιορδανη, IN JORDAN."* So, in the history of the Ethiopian eunuch, it is written, "As they went on their way, they came TO A CERTAIN WATER, επι τι υδωρ;" which is an approach to the brink: but when the act of baptizing was to be performed, "they went down both into the water, εις το υδωρ, both Philip and the eunuch;"† which, doubtless, expresses an idea somewhat different from the eunuch standing *on the brink*, or *just within the edge* of the water, that Philip might *cast* a few drops upon his head or his face.

Or, if the sacred historians designed to inform us, that our Lord accompanied John into Jordan, that he might be baptized by having a little water, not *cast* in his face, but *poured* upon his head; how comes it that none of them says a word about that memorable, solemn, and significant *pouring?* It is manifest they were not so sparing in their narratives on other occasions, though of much less importance to our instruction, and to the purity of a divine institution. Is ointment *poured* on the head of our Lord, once and again? it is expressly mentioned by those very evangelists who represent him as baptized *in Jordan.*‡ Yet none can doubt that it was of much greater moment for us to know, in what manner he was baptized; than it was precisely to be informed, how two godly women applied their costly ointment to his sacred person.

The people stood in ranks, near to, or just within the edge of the river; and John, passing before them, cast water upon their heads or faces. Such, according to these authors, was the truly primitive mode of proceeding! But if any of our opposers really believe this, why do they not imitate an example of such antiquity and so well recommended? Why, when called to admi-

---
* Josh. iii. 8.   † Acts viii. 36, 38.   ‡ Matt. xxvi. 7; Mark xiv. 3.

nister baptism, do they not go to a river, or some collection of water, place the candidate on the brink, and then, standing in the liquid element, *cast* some of it upon his head or his face? This would be a compliance with what these authors consider as *original* practice.—It may be observed, however, that their own representation of John's proceedings does not give us a very strong idea of his baptizing infants. For mere infants could not *stand* in ranks, either on the brink, or just within the edge of Jordan. Were they then *laid* in ranks? our opposers, I think, will not assert it. They, it may be presumed, if present for the purpose of being baptized, must have been held in the arms; of which, nevertheless, there is no mention. Nor could the administrator take them into his arms one by one; for that, according to this representation, his expedition in baptizing multitudes would not permit. If, therefore, he sprinkled infants along with adults, it must have been while they were in the arms of their parents, or of their friends; of which there is no intimation, or shadow of probability. It is to be feared, therefore, that this remarkable anecdote of primitive sprinkling, of which some Pædobaptists are so fond, has a tendency to exclude infants from a share in the rite. However, be that as it may, for any of our Protestant Dissenting brethren to fix the idea of original example in opposition to us, and *never to imitate* that example, has but an awkward look; as it is too much like the conduct of Roman Catholics, respecting the holy supper. Whoever believes the divine mission of John, cannot have any just reason to be ashamed of doing as he did, in regard to the use of baptismal water. Yet were I informed that Mr. Horsey, for instance, frequently goes *into a river*, merely to sprinkle an infant, or an adult; I should certainly impeach, either the *credibility* of my information, or the *intellects* of the administrator. Nor would a consideration of all I have read in Mr. Horsey's Discourse, concerning John's being *the son of a priest*, concerning *legal purifications*, and *running water*, at all relieve my anxiety about the punctuality of my informant, or the sanity of my friend. Because, when John baptized, it was, not as the son of a priest, but as the forerunner of Christ; not as influenced by Jewish customs, but as feeling the force of divine authority. Besides, were it granted that *mere* water was ever sprinkled with a view to legal purification, which nevertheless cannot be proved; it would be as hard to evince, that the Jewish priests went *into a river* to sprinkle the running water, as it would be to demonstrate that they purified any person by *plunging* him in water. Nor, among all the laws of ceremonial purification, do I recollect one, that enjoined pouring water on the *head*, or sprinkling it on the *face:* much less, that the officiating priest should thus apply the liquid element, when standing on the brink, or just within the edge of a stream.

It may perhaps be said: John chose a river for the purpose of sprinkling, not only because it was *running* water, but also on account of the *multitude* that came to his baptism; and therefore his example in entering a river does not, in common cases, oblige. So the Roman Catholics tell us, that in primitive times, when the sacred supper was administered to a small number of communicants, they might all partake of the cup without inconvenience; but afterward, when communicants became numerous, it was necessary to make an alteration in that particular.—The futility of this plea will farther appear, if it be considered, that a basin, or a pail, would have contained a sufficient quantity of water for the sprinkling of great numbers. See No. 69.—Besides, we are informed, that when Philip baptized a single individual, both he and the candidate *went into the water*. Were Mr. Horsey, therefore, to act upon that representation of John's baptism which he has given, I cannot help thinking, that serious Pædobaptist spectators would find themselves in a predicament not much different from that of the poet:

"To *laugh* were want of goodness and of grace;
And to be *grave* exceeds all power of face."

If our Lord's harbinger discovered no more solemnity and caution in hearing a profession of repentance made by the candidates, and in declaring by what authority and for what purposes they were to be baptized, than these our opponents represent him as having when he used the water; there was, we may venture to conclude, but little appearance of his baptism being *from heaven*, or of much devotion subsisting in his heart. The love of hypothesis must surely be very great, when it impels godly and sensible men to seek refuge for their cause in such extravagant fancies as these. But, as Mr. Alsop observes, "when men are pressed with express scripture, and yet are resolved (cost what will) to adhere to their own conclusions, it is advisable to cast about, to turn their thoughts into all shapes imaginable, to hunt for the extremest possibilities. If a word, a phrase, an expression, is but capable of another sense, let it be probable or improbable, true or false, agreeable to the scope of the place, or alien, all is a case; something must be said, that they may not seem to say nothing: and if they can say, *It is possible it may be otherwise*, (as who cannot?) though they do not believe themselves, they hug themselves for their ready wit, and applaud themselves for grave respondents."*

Reflect. VI. The baptism of the *three thousand* † has been frequently pleaded, as a presumptive evidence in favour of pouring, or of sprinkling. The Roman Catholics also imagine, that they find a warrant in the same fact, for persons who do not bear the ministerial character to administer baptism, when a supposed necessity urges; because they conclude that the apostles

---

* Antisozzo, p. 549, 550.   † Acts ii. 41.

could not baptize so great a number in so short a time.* Agreeable to which is the following language of Mr. Ferdinando Shaw: "Many learned men are of opinion, that the believers, the brethren, lay-christians, assisted the apostles in baptizing them; without which it is hard to be conceived how it could be done in so short a time."† One very learned, sagacious, and impartial writer, already quoted, (No. 76,) frankly acknowledges, that the passage is far from affording an argument against immersion; to whom I will now add a few more Pædobaptists. Thus then, Mr. Marchant: "The only question is, how such a multitude of converts could be baptized in one day? To which some reply, that this rite of initiation into the Christian church was then performed by way of sprinkling, as it is among us: but whoever looks into history will find, that the form of baptism among the Jews was plunging the whole body under water; and that in conformity to them, the primitive Christians did, and the eastern church even to this day does administer that sacrament in this manner. There is no necessity, therefore, for us to suppose, that all those proselytes to the Christian faith were baptized in one day. St. Luke delivers in the gross, what might possibly be transacted at several times."‡——Buddeus: "When those three thousand persons that were brought to repentance in one day, by the preaching of Peter, were to be baptized, they were led to another place; and might be baptized, [i. e. immersed] by the apostles, by others in company with them, and also by the seventy disciples. For though Luke has not mentioned this, yet we cannot thence infer that it is not a fact, seeing many circumstances are frequently omitted for the sake of brevity."§

---

* Forbesii Instruct. Hist. Theol. l. x. c. xiii. § 13.
† Valid. of Bap. by Dissent. Ministers, p. 92, edit. 2nd.
‡ Exposit. in loc.   § Theolog. Dogmat. l. v. c. i. § 5.

THE CHURCH IN FOLLOWING AGES. 223

––—Bp. Wilson: "*The same day*, i. e. at that time, on account of that sermon; though they might not all be baptized in one day, but were at that time converted."*——Bp. Taylor: " Aquinas supposes the apostles did so, [that is, used sprinkling instead of immersion,] when the three thousand, and when the five thousand, were at once converted and baptized. But this is but a conjecture, and hath no tradition and no record to warrant it."†——Bossuet: " It appears not, that the three thousand and the five thousand, mentioned in the Acts of the Apostles, who were converted at the first sermons of St. Peter, were baptized any other way [than by immersion;] and the great numbers of those converts is no proof that they were baptized by sprinkling, as some have conjectured. For, besides that nothing obliges us to say that they were all baptized on the same day; it is certain that St. John the Baptist, who baptized no less numbers, seeing all Judea flocked to him, baptized no other way than by dipping: and his example shows us, that to baptize a great number of people those places were chosen where there was abundance of water. Add to this, that the baths and purifications of the ancients rendered this ceremony easy and familiar at that time."‡

People who are but little accustomed to cold bathing, either for amusement, for medical purposes, or with religious views, may wonder how such multitudes could be accommodated, if they were immersed in water; but when it is considered that this was done at Jerusalem, where immersion was quite familiar, and must, by the laws of Judaism, be daily practised, not only there, but in all parts of the country, their amazement will cease. For, as Bp. Patrick observes, " There are so many washings prescribed [in the law of Moses,] that it is reason-

---

* Note in loc. † Duct Dub. b. iii. chap. iv. p. 644.
‡ In Mr. Stennett's Answer to Mr. Russen, p. 175, 176.

able to believe, there were not only at Jerusalem, and in all other cities, but in every village, several bathing places contrived for these legal purifications, that men might, without much labour, be capable to fulfil these precepts."*——Thus also D'Outreinius: "Whoever considers the number of unclean persons, who daily had need of washing, and he who reads the Talmudic Treatises concerning purifications, and collections of water convenient for those purposes, will be easily persuaded, that Bethesda and other pools at Jerusalem subserved that design."†

Again: We are informed by the sacred historian, that when king Solomon dedicated his magnificent temple, *he offered two and twenty thousand oxen, and a hundred and twenty thousand sheep.* Now, supposing a Deist were to question the truth of this historical fact, on account of the great number of animals that were offered; it would soon be replied by our opponents themselves: " A great number of priests were employed; nor was the work performed in one day."‡ Why then may not a similar answer suffice in the present case? All the Jewish males were enjoined, by divine law, to appear before the Lord in Jerusalem three times in a year. Now it may be asked, How could that metropolis contain such multitudes as came up from all parts of the country, at each of their grand festivals? Though far from thinking this difficulty insurmountable, yet I am persuaded, that it is full as easy to account for the three thousand being immersed in one day, as it is to conceive how such a prodigious concourse of strangers were accommodated with lodgings, in the city and suburbs of Jerusalem. But as, in the one case, there is no necessity of supposing that the strangers were turned into the fields to sleep with cattle; § so, in the other,

---

* On Lev. xv. 12.   † Biblioth. Bremens. class. i. p. 614.
‡ See Mr. Martin's Letters to Mr. Horsey, p. 150, 151.
§ See Dr. Jennings's Jewish Antiq. vol. ii. p. 169, 170.

there is no occasion to imagine that plunging was converted into sprinkling.

Farther: Were the method of arguing adopted by our opposers with reference to this passage legitimate, and their inference valid, it might be rendered highly probable, that the first instance of circumcision was performed, not by *cutting off* the foreskin, but by making *a slight incision* in that pellicle. For Moses assures us, that Abraham circumcised himself and his son Ishmael, together with all the males that were born in his house and bought with his money, on the very same day that he received the divine order.* We are also informed by the sacred historian, that long before Abraham received the command of circumcision, he had *three hundred and eighteen* male servants, who were *born in his own house*, and able to bear arms;† consequently, it is highly probable the whole number of males that were born in his house, and then living, was four hundred or upwards; besides those that were *bought with his money*, concerning the number of whom we have no information. Nor is there any reason to think that his household was diminished, but rather increased, when he obeyed the heavenly mandate under consideration. Now if we may estimate the time required for circumcising four or five hundred persons, by the time spent, exclusive of devotional exercises, when the modern Jews perform the same rite upon an infant; we may safely consider the difficulty as much greater in the case of Abraham's circumcising his numerous household in one day, than that which attends the immersion of three thousand. For, by an instance of circumcision which the author saw performed, he cannot help thinking that the time employed in merely cutting off the foreskin, and taking care of the part with a view to its healing, would have sufficed for the solemn immersion of at least four

---

* Gen. xvii. 23, 24. † Gen. xiv. 14.

persons.* It must indeed be admitted, as exceedingly probable, that the precautions used by Abraham to abate the pain and to heal the part, were different from those of the modern Jews in similar cases; but some care, doubtless, must have been *immediately* necessary, supposing the præputium of each to have been cut off, especially with regard to grown persons in that hot country. But how to account for one man doing all this in a single day, I do not perceive. The difficulty will increase if it be admitted, as I think it ought, that Abraham set the first example in his own person, for, as there is no intimation of any thing miraculous on that occasion, the soreness and the pain must greatly incommode him, while performing the rite upon others. On the principle of reasoning here opposed, we might therefore infer, that the venerable patriarch did not *cut off*, but only made a *trifling incision* in the part specified. But, whatever difficulties may attend speculation upon the fact, I have not heard that any of the Jews ever doubted whether their great progenitor performed a real circumcision upon the males of his very numerous household; nor that they ever declined an imitation of the original example, on account of any inconveniences which attended it. See Chap. II. Reflect. IX.—It may perhaps be said; There is no necessity to conclude, that the hoary patriarch himself circumcised all the males of his numerous family; because he might be said to do what was performed by his order. To which it may be replied; The record of the fact expressly marks both the performer and the time; nor will it, I conceive, admit of such an interpretation; for it is written, "Abraham *took* Ishmael his son, and *all* that were born in his house, and *all* that were bought with his money, *every* male among the men of Abraham's house, and *circumcised* the flesh of their foreskin in the *selfsame day*, as

---

* See Leo Modena's Hist. of the Rites and Customs of the Jews, part iv. chap. viii.

God had said unto him." Now it is plain, that this language ascribes to Abraham the whole performance of the rite, exclusive of any assistant; for it was the patriarch himself who *took* Ishmael, and *every male* in his house, and *circumcised* them. That all this was performed by Abraham in one day, we have no doubt; because the fact rests upon divine testimony: but that speculation when employed upon it is embarrassed, except we admit of a trifling incision instead of circumcision, must I think be acknowledged. When our opposers, therefore, have clearly accounted for the aged patriarch's circumcising four or five hundred persons in one day, they will not be much at a loss to conceive of twelve apostles, and seventy disciples, immersing three thousand in the same space of time.

That three thousand should be solemnly immersed at such a place as Jerusalem, and at a time when, as the sacred historian remarks, the disciples *had favour with all the people*, even supposing them all to have been baptized in one day, is not half so strange as various accounts relating to facts of the same nature, that we find in the page of history. Thus, for example, Mr. Marchant: " Peter [and his companions in the ministry] baptizing in one day three thousand persons by immersion, need not be wondered at; since we read in the authentic life of Gregory, the apostle of the Armenians, that he baptized *twelve thousand* together, by immersion, in the river Euphrates: which Isaac, the patriarch of that nation, confirms in his first invective."*——Mr. Bingham: "Palladius observes, in the life of St. Chrysostom, that at Constantinople *three thousand* persons were baptized at once, upon one of [their] greater festivals." †——Dr. J. G. King: " Wolodimer, a Russian prince, was baptized by the name of Basilius; and it is said *twenty thousand* of his subjects were baptized the same day." ‡——Mr.

---

* Exposit. on Matt. iii 7. † Origines Eccles. b. xi. chap. vi. § 9.
‡ Rites and Cerem. of Greek Church, p. 4.

John Fox informs us, that Austin, the monk, " baptized and christened *ten thousand* Saxons, or Angles, in the West river, that is called Swale, beside York, on a Christmas day."*——Dr. Robertson: "A single clergyman baptized in one day above *five thousand* Mexicans, and did not desist till he was so exhausted by fatigue, that he was unable to lift up his hands."†—Nay, Salmero asserts, (with what credibility the reader will judge,) that " Francis Xavier, among the Indians, baptized *fifteen thousand* in one day." Upon which the learned Chamier pertinently asks, " Could fifteen thousand be baptized by one person; and might not three thousand be baptized by many?"‡—Respecting the administration of baptism, Dr. Doddridge says: I think " the office was generally assigned to *inferiors*, as requiring no extraordinary abilities, and as being attended with some trouble and inconvenience, especially where immersion was used, as I suppose it often, though not constantly, was." § That persons much inferior to the apostles in office and gifts were sometimes employed by them to baptize those who professed faith, we have no doubt: but that it was because of any *trouble* or *inconvenience* which attended the administration, we do not believe; nay, we consider such an idea as unworthy the character of those laborious and self-denying ambassadors of Christ.

Our opponents, however, seem to forget that the principal difficulty, in regard to *time*, does not lie in such a multitude being *baptized*, whether by plunging or otherwise; but in their making a *satisfactory profession* of repentance and faith. For the three thousand were adults; and our opposers agree, that all adults, previous to baptism, should make such a profession. It is

---

* Acts and Mon. under A.D. 602.
† Hist. of South America, vol. ii. p. 384, quarto.
‡ Panstrat. tom. iv. l. v. c. xiv. § 39.
§ Note on 1 Cor. i. 16. Vid. Turrett. Institut. loc. xix. quæst. xiv. § 11.

much easier to conceive of their being immersed in the course of a day, by such a number of administrators, and with such conveniences as were then at Jerusalem; than it is to imagine how those administrators could receive a profession of faith in the Son of God, from each of the candidates, in an equal space of time. I may here venture an appeal to Pædobaptist ministers, Whether, when adults apply for baptism, they do not spend more time in hearing a declaration of the grounds of their faith and hope, than they themselves would think necessary for the solemn immersion of such candidates, a river, a pond, or a baptistery being at hand? The passage before us, therefore, might be adduced with much more appearance of argument, in opposition to the necessity of personally professing faith previous to baptism, than it can in favour of pouring or sprinkling.—But why should our opposers raise an objection, which, as Mr. Martin observes, if it have any force, militates against the idea of pouring, as well as of plunging? For, as but one person could be baptized at once, and as the same form of words must have been used at the baptism of each, the difference in respect of time between their being plunged, and having water poured or sprinkled upon them, must be considered as very small. Besides, according to another branch of that hypothesis which we oppose, it seems as if many of these three thousand must have had their children sprinkled in the same space of time; which will greatly increase the number, and more than counterbalance the extra time required for immersion.—Should it be objected, There is no occasion for supposing that the children of those believers were baptized on the *same* day: it may be replied, Neither does Luke say that the three thousand were *baptized*, but *added* to the church, the same day. Besides, an objection of that kind would be a departure from their usual way of stating the matter; for they have often told us, that infants were baptized *along with their parents;* and it is full as likely that those children whose parents were among the three thousand should be baptized at the same time, as that the jailor's infants, if he had any, should have their sweet repose disturbed by being baptized at *midnight*. Yet this their argument, from the latter of these facts, implies.—I will add a remark of Mr. Ditton's: " If the evidence be good," says he, " by all the laws of human nature, I do not care for ten thousand difficulties, if they were ever so insuperable, provided they are not such as infer simple impossibility, or palpable absurdity."*

Once more: Supposing it appeared with indisputable evidence, that the three thousand were baptized by pouring or sprinkling; yet, according to Protestant Pædobaptists, it would not prove the lawfulness of such an administration in common practice, except it appeared to agree with divine law, or to have been the appointment of Christ. For this was undoubtedly an *extraordinary* case; and learned Pædobaptists assure us, when disputing with Roman Catholics about the sacred supper, That a scriptural example in an extraordinary instance, must not be considered as the rule of general conduct.—Thus Mr. Steele: " The relation of an example in an extraordinary case, [is not] sufficient to cancel a direct precept and clear example with it."†——Chemnitius thus: " A general rule must not be taken from extraordinary examples;—for that should be derived from the institution of the sacraments."‡——Mr. Payne, in answer to an argument of the Papists for communion in one kind, which is drawn from supposed instances of such a practice in the ancient church, thus reasons: " What will this signify, [could it be proved] to the justifying the *constant* and public communions in one kind, when there are no such particular or extraordinary

---

* Discourse on the Resurrection of Christ, part iii. sect. lxix.
† Morning Exercise against Popery, p. 774.
‡ Exam. Concil. Trident. p. 216. Vid. p. 327.

reasons for it?....The doing this, is as if the Jews, because whilst they were in the wilderness they could not so well observe the precept of circumcision, and so were at that time, for a particular reason, excused from it, should ever after have omitted it as unnecessary. This, sure, had been making too bold with a positive precept, although there might be a particular case, or instance, wherein it was not so exactly to be observed.... David's eating the show-bread, which it was not lawful but for the priests ordinarily to eat, is approved by our Saviour; not upon the account of tradition, or the judgment of the high-priest, but the extreme hunger which he and his companions were then pressed with, and which made it lawful for them to eat of the hallowed bread, when there was no other to be procured. But did this make it lawful afterwards for the high-priest, or the Sanhedrim, to have made the holy bread always common to others when there was no such necessity?"*

Reflection VII. If the numerous and learned authors, in the beginning of this chapter, be not under a gross mistake, with regard to apostolic practice, my reader has reason to be surprised, offended, shocked, at the following reflection which is cast on immersion; because he cannot but perceive it to fall on some of the most venerable and excellent persons that ever appeared in the world. "To baptize *naked*, or *next* to naked, (which is SUPPOSED, and GENERALLY *practised* in immersion) is against the law of modesty; and to do such a thing in public solemn assemblies, is so far from being tolerable, that it is abominable, to every chaste soul: and especially to baptize *women* in this manner."†— When, in perusing the treatise, I came to these words, I paused, I was astonished, I was almost confounded. What, thought I, is this the language of the amiable and

---

* Preserv. against Popery, title vii. p. 124, 149.
† Mr. Matt. Henry's Treatise on Baptism, p. 138, 139.

excellent Mr. Henry? Does immersion SUPPOSE the subject of the ordinance NAKED, or NEXT *to naked?* Is this PRACTISED, GENERALLY *practised, practised in* PUBLIC SOLEMN ASSEMBLIES, and that upon WOMEN too? Where have you been, ye sons of sensuality! that you have not crowded around our baptisteries, when we have immersed any of the fair sex? How many fine opportunities have you missed, of feasting your lascivious eyes, and exulting in the wonderful sight! And what are you about, ye infidels; ye who laugh at every thing sacred, and take a malignant pleasure in exposing Christianity to ridicule! what, I again ask, are ye about, that you have not published our praise for gratifying your enmity to the religion of Jesus Christ! For on the word of an author, who has long been held in a high degree of esteem by the religious public, we have often committed the most enormous outrage—I will not say, on the *solemnities of religion,* because you do not regard them—but, on *the laws of decorum,* and on the *modest feelings* of the tender sex; even while professing to act by the authority and example of Christ. What, are *ye* silent, *all* silent on such an interesting occasion; while the pen of a Christian minister, of a sacred expositor, and of a Protestant Dissenting BROTHER, is thus officiously employed? *This,* ah! this—but I forbear; and shall only add a salutary prohibition, a gentle reprehension, and a candid extenuation. THOU SHALT NOT BEAR FALSE WITNESS AGAINST THY NEIGHBOUR; is the prohibition of JEHOVAH, the God of Israel. "We ought to DISOWN and show a DISLIKE of the PROFANE SCOFFS which some people give to the English Antipædobaptists, merely for their use of DIPPING;" is the reprehension of Dr. Wall, the Episcopalian. See No. 96.—*I wot that* THROUGH IGNORANCE *ye did it;* is the extenuation of Peter the apostle, when the most unjustifiable conduct was under his notice.

I will now subjoin the remark of a Pædobaptist writer upon this passage of Mr. Henry. "This *calumny* against immersion," says one of the Monthly Reviewers, "might possibly have had some grounds in the practice of a few enthusiasts in the last age. Mr. Baxter uses almost the same words, when speaking of the indecency, as well as the danger, of administering baptism by immersion, as Mr. Henry; and indeed the latter appears to have copied from him. The reflection, however, should by no means be extended to the general practice of the Antipædobaptists, especially those of modern times. We almost question if it *ever* had a foundation: we are *certain* it hath none at present."*——It has, indeed, been supposed by many of the learned, and there seems to be some evidence of it, that the ancients did sometimes administer the ordinance to persons of both sexes, *in puris naturalibus:* against this, however, the famous Voetius has entered his protest, as a mistake of the moderns, and a misrepresentation of ancient practice.† But, admitting the fact, all whom I have observed agree, that a becoming decorum was constantly observed, as far as the nature of the case would permit. Thus, for instance, Dr. Wall: "They took great care for preserving the modesty of any woman that was to be baptized. There was none but women came near, or in sight, till she was undressed, and her body in the water: then the priest came, and putting her head also under water, used the form of words. Then he departed, and the women took her out of the water, and clothed her again in white garments.‡"

Those who have read the writings of Dr. Featley, and of Messrs. Baxter, Wills, Russen, Burkitt, and

---

* Monthly Review, for Sep. 1784, p. 237.

† Apud. Witsium, Œcon. l iv. c. xvi. § 14.

‡ Hist. Inf. Bap. part ii. chap. ix. § 3. Vid. Vossium, Disputat. de Bap. disput. i. thes. vi. vii. viii., and Mr. Bingham's Origines Ecclesiast. b. xi. chap. xi. § 1, 2, 3.

various others, in vindication of Pædobaptism, cannot be ignorant, that the Baptists have been frequently treated in the most illiberal manner. I will here present the reader with an extract from the famous Mr. Baxter, and leave the impartial to judge, whether it be the language of calm reason, of authenticated fact, and of Christian charity; or the clamour of prejudice, the distortion of misrepresentation, and the raving of a persecuting temper. Thus, then, Mr. Baxter: "My sixth argument shall be against the usual manner of their baptizing, as it is by dipping over head in a river, or other cold water.... That which is a plain breach of the sixth commandment, *Thou shalt not kill,* is no ordinance of God, but a most heinous sin. But the ordinary practice of baptizing over head in cold water, as necessary, is a plain breach of the sixth commandment. Therefore it is no ordinance of God, but an heinous sin. And as Mr. Cradock in his book of *Gospel Liberty* shows, the magistrate *ought to restrain it,* to save the lives of his subjects.... That this is *flat murder,* and no better, being ordinarily and generally used, is undeniable to any understanding man.... And I know not what trick a covetous landlord can find out to get his tenants to die apace, that he may have new fines and heriots, likelier than to encourage such preachers, that he may get them all to turn Anabaptists. I wish that *this device* be not it that countenanceth these men. And covetous physicians, methinks, should not be much against them. Catarrhs and obstructions, which are the two great fountains of most mortal diseases in man's body, could scarce have a more notable means to produce them where they are not, or to increase them where they are. Apoplexies, lethargies, palsies, and all comatous diseases, would be promoted by it. So would cephalalgies, hemicranies, phthises, debility of the stomach, crudities, and almost all fevers, dysenteries, diarrhœas, colics, iliac passions, convulsions, spasms, tremors, and so on. All hepatic, splenetic, pulmoniac persons, and hypocondriacs, would soon have enough of it. In a word, it is good for nothing but to despatch men out of the world that are burdensome, and to ranken churchyards.... I conclude, if murder be a sin, then dipping ordinarily in cold water over head, in England, is a sin: and if those that would make it men's religion to murder themselves, and urge it on their consciences as their duty, are *not to be suffered* in a common wealth, any more than *highway murderers;* then judge how these Anabaptists, that teach the necessity of such dipping, are to be suffered.... My seventh argument is also against another wickedness in their manner of baptizing, which is their dipping persons *naked,* as is *very usual* with many of them; or *next* to naked, as is usual with the modestest that I have heard of.... If the minister must go into the water with the party, it will certainly tend to his *death,* though they may escape that go in but once.... Would not vain young men come to a baptizing to see the nakedness of maids, and make a mere jest and sport of it?"*—Were this representation just, we should have no reason to wonder if his following words expressed a fact: " I am still more confirmed, that a visible judgment of God doth still follow Anabaptistry, wherever it comes.†" Compare Chap. III. No. 4, and No. 60, of this Chapter.—It was not without reason, I perceive, that Mr. Baxter made the following acknowledgment: " I confess my style is naturally keen."‡ I am a little suspicious also, that Dr. Owen had some cause for speaking of his writings as follows. " I verily believe, that if a man who had nothing else to do, should gather into one heap all the expressions which in his late books, Confessions and Apologies, have a *lovely* aspect towards himself, as to ability, diligence, sincerity, on the one hand; with all

---

* Plain Scripture Proof, p. 134—137.
† Ut supra, p. 88.   ‡ Ibid. p. 246.

those which are full of *reproach* and *contempt* towards others, on the other; the view of them could not but a little startle a man of so great modesty, and of such eminency in the mortification of pride, as Mr. Baxter is.*"—Hence we learn, that Baptists are not the only persons who have felt the weight of Mr. Baxter's hand; so that, if a recollection of others having suffered under his keen resentment can afford relief, the poor Baptists may take some comfort: and it is an old saying,

Solamen miseris socios habuisse doloris.

Besides, there is a precept of Horace which occurs to remembrance, and is of use in the present exigence. *Amara lento temperet risu,* is the advice to which I refer; and under the influence of this direction, we are led to say: Poor man! He seems to be afflicted with a violent hydrophobia! for he cannot think of any person being immersed in cold water, but he starts, he is convulsed, he is ready to die with fear. Immersion, you must know, is like Pandora's box, and pregnant with a great part of those diseases which Milton's angel presented to the view of our first father. A compassionate regard, therefore, to the lives of his fellow creatures, compels Mr. Baxter to solicit the aid of magistrates against this destructive plunging, and to cry out in the spirit of an exclamation once heard in the Jewish temtemple: 'Ye men of Israel, help!' or Baptist ministers will depopulate your country. Know you not, that these plunging teachers are shrewdly suspected of being *pensioned* by avaricious landlords, to destroy the lives of your liege subjects? Exert your power; apprehend the delinquents; appoint an *Auto da Fé;* let the venal dippers be baptized in blood, and thus put a salutary stop to their pestiferous practice."—What a pity it is, that the celebrated History of Cold Bathing, by Sir John

---

* Of the Death of Christ, p. 5, subjoined to his **Mystery of the Gospel vindicated.**

Floyer, was not published half a century sooner! It might, perhaps, have preserved this good man from a multitude of painful paroxysms, occasioned by the thought of immersion in cold water.—Were I seriously to put a query on these assertions of Mr. Baxter, it should be, with a little variation, in the words of David: "What shall be given unto thee, or what be done unto thee, thou FALSE pen?" Were the temper which dictated the preceding caricatura to receive its just reproof, it might be in the language of Michael: "The Lord rebuke thee!"

Before I dismiss this extraordinary language of Mr. Baxter, it is proper to be observed, that the charge of shocking indecency, which he lays with such confidence against the Baptists of those times, was not suffered by them to pass without animadversion. No, he was challenged to make it good: it was denied, it was confuted by them. With a view to which Dr. Wall says: "The English Antipædobaptists need not have made *so great an outcry* against Mr. Baxter, for his saying that they baptized *naked;* for if they had, it had been no more than the primitive Christians did."* But surely they had reason to complain of *misrepresentation;* such misrepresentation, as tended to bring the greatest *odium* upon their sentiment and practice. Besides, however ancient the practice charged upon them was, its antiquity could not have justified their conduct; except it had been derived from divine command, or apostolic example, neither of which appears.—Whether Mr. Henry, in the passage already marked, proceeds on the authority of Mr. Baxter, in regard to that outrage on decency with which we are charged, or what induced him to record such things, is not for me to determine; but I cannot forbear wondering that Mr. Robins should *publish* the obnoxious sentence; as it appears from his own declaration,† that he has *very much abridged* the treatise.

---

* Hist. Inf. Bap. part ii. chap. ix. § 3. † Advertisement, p. 7.

He hopes, indeed, that very few expressions will be found in the work, that are " *offensive* to serious and candid readers of any denomination :"* but whether the expressions to which I advert be not *justly offensive;* whether the offence given to many of his brethren, who, I trust, have some degree of candour and seriousness, be not owing to *his* labours, as the editor; and whether both candour and seriousness do not oblige him to imitate the following confession of Mr. Baxter, I leave to my reader's judgment. " Upon the review of my arguments, upon the controversy about infant baptism," says the famous Nonconformist, " I find that I have used too many provoking words, for which I am heartily sorry, and desire pardon of God and him,"† i. e. of Mr. Tombes.

Now, as it appears by the concessions, declarations, and reasonings of so many learned Pædobaptists themselves, that the natural and proper idea of the term baptism, the design of the institution, and the example of the apostles, are all in favour of immersion, and all agree with our practice; we do not, we cannot want any thing more to justify our conduct, either before God or man. This must be the case, except the united testimony of such a cloud of witnesses, and the reasons of it, can be confronted with superior evidence. We have, however, a few more testimonies and concessions to review, relating to this branch of the subject.

---

* Ut supra, p. 8.
† In Mr. Crosby's Hist. Bap. vol. iii. Pref. p. 55.

CHAPTER V.

The present Practice of the Greek and Oriental Churches, in regard to the Mode of Administration.

Hasselquist.—"The Greeks christen their children immediately after their birth, or within a few days at least, dipping them in warm water; and in this respect they are much wiser than their brethren the Russians, who dip them into rivers in the coldest winter." Travels, p. 394.

2. Anonymous.—"The Muscovite priests plunge the child three times over head and ears in water." Encyclopæd. Britan. vol. ix. p. 6910.

3. Venema.—" In pronouncing the baptismal form of words, the Greeks use the third person, saying, ' Let the servant of Christ be baptized, in the name of the Father, and of the Son, and of the Holy Spirit;' and immerse the whole man in water." Hist. Eccles. tom. vi. p. 660.

4. Deylingius.—" The Greeks retain the rite of immersion to this day; as Jeremiah the patriarch of Constantinople declares." De Prudent. Pastoral. pars. iii. c. iii. § 26.

5. Mr. Millar.—" In baptism they [the Muscovites] dip their children in cold water." Propagation of Christ. vol. ii. chap. vi. p. 115.

6. Buddeus.—" That the Greeks defend immersion is manifest, and has been frequently observed by learned men; which Ludolphus informs us is the practice of the Ethiopians." Theolog. Dogmat. l. v. c. i. § 5.

7. Witsius.—" That immersion may be practised in cold countries, without any great danger of health and life, the Muscovites prove by their own example; who

entirely immerse their infants three times in water, not believing that baptism can be otherwise rightly administered. Nor do they ever use warm water, except for those that are weak or sickly." Œcon. Fœd. l. iv. c. xvi. § 13.

8. Sir Paul Ricaut.—"The modern Greek church defines baptism to be, 'A cleansing, or taking away of original sin, by thrice dipping or plunging into the water;' the priest saying at every dipping, 'In the name of the Father, Amen; and of the Son, Amen; and of the Holy Ghost, Amen.' This thrice dipping, or plunging into the water, this church holds to be as necessary to the form of baptism, as water to the matter." Present State of the Greek Church, p. 163.

9. Dr. J. G. King.—"The Greek church uniformly practises the trine immersion, undoubtedly the most primitive manner." Rites and Cerem. of the Greek Church in Russia, p. 192.

10. Dr. Wall.—"All the Christians in Asia, all in Africa, and about one third part of Europe, are of the last sort, [i. e. practise immersion;] in which third part of Europe are comprehended the Christians of Græcia, Thracia, Servia, Bulgaria, Rascia, Walachia, Moldavia, Russia Nigra, and so on; and even the Muscovites, who, if coldness of the country will excuse, might plead for a dispensation with the most reason of any. Hist. of Inf. Bap. part ii. chap. ix. p. 477.

REFLECTIONS.

Reflect. I. As it appears from the preceding chapter, that immersion was the general and almost universal practice for a long course of ages; and, as various of those learned authors assert, for THIRTEEN CENTURIES; so it is manifest from these quotations, that it has been uninterruptedly continued as the general mode of proceeding, in all the Greek and oriental churches. Now these churches, as Dr. Wall informs us, comprehend "very near one half the Christians in the world."* Nay, Dr. King tells us, that they have " a greater extent than the Latin, with all the branches which are sprung from it."† Consequently, though we are far from considering the numbers that adopt a sentiment, or a practice, as the criterion of truth, or of right; yet we may confidently assert, that our practice of immersion, as essential to the ordinance, is neither that novel, not yet that singular thing, which many of our opponents are very desirous of making their neighbours believe it to be. Nor can I forbear to wonder at their inadvertency, when they act in this manner: and as to ministers of the English establishment, it requires an uncommon degree of ignorance, of prejudice, of prevarication, or of assurance, for any of *them* to treat immersion as a novel, an indecent, or an unjustifiable practice; because the rubric of their liturgy, that rubric which they have solemnly professed to believe and approve, even that very rubric which they have engaged to treat as the *law* of their proceedings, in the administration of baptism, as well as in other cases, expressly requires it; except the sponsors inform the priest, that the child cannot well bear to be dipped. To which the catechism of the same establishment plainly adverts, when it instructs the catechumen to say; " Water, *wherein* the person is baptized." For the idea of pouring, or of sprinkling, cannot be applied here without rendering the language absurd. " Upon the review of the Common Prayer-book at the restoration," says Dr. Wall, " the church of England did not think fit (however prevalent the custom of sprinkling was) to forego their maxim; *That it is most fitting to dip children that are well able to bear it.* But they leave it wholly to the judgment of the godfathers and those that

---

* See Vol. II. Chap. V. No 7, of this work.
† Rites and Cerem. of the Greek Church, p. 3.

bring the child, whether the child may well endure dipping or not. The difference is only this: By the rubric, as it stood before, the priest was to dip, unless there were an averment or allegation of weakness: now he is not to dip, unless there be an averment or certifying of strength sufficient to endure it."* Agreeable to this, is the former confession of Helvetia: "Baptism, according to the institution of our Lord, is the font of regeneration; in which holy font we do therefore dip our infants."† The confession of Saxony, thus: "Baptism is an entire action; to wit, a dipping, and the pronouncing of those words, 'I baptize thee in the name,' and so on."†

Reflect. II. In respect of the *trine* immersion, practised by the Greek Church and the eastern Christians, though it be undoubtedly of great antiquity; and though it appear to have originated in a strong but misapplied regard to that capital article of the Christian creed, the doctrine of the Holy Trinity; yet as there is no intimation in the New Testament, that it was either enjoined by Christ, or practised by his apostles, we cannot agree with Dr. King, when he calls it, "the most primitive manner." See No. 9.—An apostle indeed mentions the *doctrine of baptisms;* but, as a Pædobaptist author observes, "That the trine immersion was the occasion of the expression, there is no ground to believe, because so much later than that time."‡ It was, however, practised even here, in the time of Edward the Sixth; for, according to his first Common Prayer-book, "the minister is to dip the child in the water *thrice;* first dipping the right side; secondly, the left; the third time, dipping the face towards the font."§

---

* Hist. Inf. Bap. part. ii. chap. ix. p. 473.
† Harmony of Confessions, p. 397, 404.
‡ Cure of Deism, vol. i. chap. iv. p. 131, 132.
§ Encyclopædia Britan. article, Baptism.

Mr. Henry, when pleading the cause of aspersion, says: " I believe that immersion, yea *trine* immersion, or plunging the person baptized three times, was commonly used in very early ages; and that, *as far as* Popery *prevailed*, a great deal of stress was laid upon it."* Would this ingenious author, then, persuade us that immersion, whether once or thrice, originated in Popery, and that it was peculiar to such professors of Christianity as acknowledged the Papal authority? If so, he labours to possess his readers of a gross mistake. For as to immersion, it appears, I think with sufficient evidence, by quotations already produced from the most eminent Pædobaptists, that it has the sanction of divine authority in the apostolic practice. And as to the *trine* immersion, it is manifest from Tertullian, that it was commonly used, long before the supremacy of the bishop of Rome was either claimed by himself, or acknowledged by others; yet the term *Popery* signifies a system of religious principles and practices, in which an acknowledgment of that supremacy makes a distinguishing and capital figure. " By *Popery*, says that excellent polemical author, Stapferus, we understand that religion which considers the Pope as the visible and principal head of the church;—whence also it has its name."† Besides, it appears that the Greek and oriental churches, which include one half of the Christian world, have always practised immersion; and that, for a long course of ages, the trine immersion has been their general custom: yet they never acknowledged the Papal power; nor, so far as I have observed, was their profession of Christianity ever called *Popery*. How unfair then is the insinuation contained in these words; "As far as *Popery* prevailed!" As if the Papists in former

---

* Treatise on Bap. p. 137.
† Institut. Theolog. Polem. cap. xiv. § 1.

times had been the only persons that pleaded for the baptismal plunging; and as if our practice had been derived from them! That an author of Mr. Henry's learning, reading, and character should insinuate such things, is amazing. We are indeed so far from having derived immersion from Popery, that quite the reverse is a fact; for learned Pædobaptists themselves assure us, that pouring and sprinkling, as a common practice, have an exclusive claim to the honour of such an original. See Chap. VII. No. 21, 23, and Reflect. V.

CHAPTER VI.

The Design of Baptism more fully expressed by Immersion, than by Pouring or Sprinkling.

WITSIUS.—" It must not be dissembled, that there is in immersion a greater fruitfulness of signification, and a more perfect correspondence between the sign and the thing signified; as we shall show, when we come to that part of our subject." Œcon. Fœd. l. iv. c. xvi. § 13.

2. Alstedius.—" The rite of immersion, which is intimated by the very word baptism, certainly bears a greater analogy to the thing signified." Lexicon Theologicum, cap. xii. p. 223.

3. Mr. John Rogers.—" I dare not deny my judgment to teach thus far for dipping, above the other forms of sprinkling or pouring; that were it as orderly in our church, and used, and no offence to weak souls, I would sooner be induced to dip one that was never before baptized, than to sprinkle one; for to me it would be more significant, and full, and pregnant with former practices." In Mr. Crosby's Hist. Bap. vol. iii. Pref. p. 53.

4. Heideggerus.—" Though the rite of immersion be more ancient, and on account of its more fully representing a death and burial, more expressive, (Rom. vi. 4;) yet it appears, from what has been said, that aspersion makes no alteration in the essence and mystery of baptism." Corpus Theolog. loc. xxv. § 35.

5. Estius.—" Though the ceremony of immersion was anciently more common, as appears from the unanimous language of the fathers, as often as they speak about baptism; and in a more expressive manner re-

presents the death, burial, and resurrection of our Lord, and of us;—whence St. Thomas affirms, that the rite of dipping is more commendable; yet there have been many reasons, for which it was sometimes convenient to alter immersion into some other kindred ceremony. Hence, therefore, the ceremony of *pouring*, as a medium between dipping and sprinkling, was much used; which custom, Bonaventure says, was in his time much observed in the French churches and some others; though he confesses that the ceremony of immersion was the more common, the more fit, and the more safe, as S. Thomas teaches." Apud Knatchbul. Animadvers. in Lib. Nov. Test. p. 181.

6. Dr. Clarke.—" In the primitive times, the manner of baptizing was by immersion, or dipping the whole body into the water. And this manner of doing it was a very significant emblem of the dying and rising again, referred to by St. Paul, Rom. vi. 4." Expos. of Church Catechism, p. 294.

7. Mr. W. Perkins.—" A question may be made, whether washing of the body in baptism must be by dipping, or by sprinkling? Answer: In hot countries, and in the baptism of men in years, dipping was used, and that by the apostles; and to this Paul alludes, Rom. vi. 3: and dipping doth more fully represent our spiritual washing than sprinkling." Works, vol. ii. p. 256.

8. Pictetus. — " It was usual in ancient times for the whole body to be immersed in water—and it must be confessed, that such a rite most happily represented that grace by which our sins are, as it were, drowned, and we raised again from the abyss of sin." Theolog. Christ. l. xiv. c. iv. § 17.

9. Mastricht. — " Immersion was used by the apostles and primitive churches, because it is not only more agreeable in the warm eastern countries, but also more significant, (Rom. vi. 3, 4, 5.)" Theologia, l. vii. c. iv. § 9.

10. H. Altingius.—After briefly stating the arguments for plunging, and for sprinkling, he adds: "We confess, first, that immersion was the prior rite; because it was first used by John the Baptist and the apostles. Secondly, it is also more expressive, on account of the distinct acts, (Rom. vi.)" Thelog. Problem. Nov. loc. xiv. prob. xi. p. 657.

11. M. Morus.—"Baptism was formerly celebrated by plunging the whole body in water, and not by casting a few drops of water on the forehead; that representing death and the resurrection much better than this." In Mr. Stennett's Answer to Mr. Russen, p. 149.

12. Vossius.—"All the particulars that we have mentioned, concerning the signification of baptism, will appear with sufficient perspicuity in the rite of immersion; but not equally so if mere sprinkling be used. It should not be supposed, however, that all analogy is destroyed by it." Disputat. de Bap. disp. iii. § 10.

13. Daille, speaking of a twofold effect of baptism, says: "In the primitive church, this double effect of baptism was more clearly represented in the external action of the sacrament [by immersion] than it is at this day." Serm. on Epist. to Coloss. on chap. ii. 12, p. 245.

14. Buddeus.—"Though immersion is to be preferred, yet baptism administered by sprinkling, or pouring, is not therefore to be accounted unlawful.... Immersion, which was used in former times, as we have before declared, was a symbol and an image of the death and burial of Christ: by which we are taught, that the remains of sin, which are called *the old man*, should also be put to death; that is, as Paul elsewhere speaks, our *flesh, with its affections and lusts*, should be *crucified*. For in that way, we, as it were, die and are buried with Christ; which Paul expressly shows, Rom. vi. 4. An emersion out of the water follows, (Matt. iii. 16,) which

exhibits a most beautiful image of the resurrection of Christ; and at the same time it affords matter of instruction concerning that spiritual resurrection, which is effected by daily renovation, (Rom. vi. 4.) Now though all these things are a little more clearly exhibited by immersion, than by pouring or sprinkling; yet, nevertheless, in the latter some likeness of them is beheld: seeing, even by pouring, especially if it be performed by a remarkably large quantity of water, the infant is in a manner covered and buried in water; like as it emerges thence, when the water poured upon it is all run off." Theolog. Dogmat. l. v. c. i. §5, 8.

15. Dr. Cave.—" The party to be baptized was wholly immerged, or put under water; whereby they did more notably and significantly express the three great ends and effects of baptism." Primitive Christianity, part i. chap. x. p. 203.

16. Dr. Wall.—" I had the disadvantage [in defending the common practice] to plead for a way of baptism, of which the best I could say was, That it is sufficient for the essence of baptism; but could not deny the other (except in the case of danger of health) to be the fittest.... The immersion of the person, whether infant or adult, in the posture of one that is buried and raised up again, is much more solemn, and expresses the design of the sacrament and the mystery of the spiritual washing much better, than pouring a small quantity of water on the face. And that pouring of water, is much better than sprinkling, or dropping a drop of water on it. If it be done in the church, in, or at the font, and the congregation do join in the prayers there used; it is much more solemn than in a bedchamber, out of a basin, or pipkin, a tea-cup, or a punch-bowl; and a bed chamber is perhaps not quite so scandalous as a kitchen or stable, to which things look as if they would bring it at last.... We have reason to give God thanks, that the present orders and rubrics of our

church are all calculated for the reforming of these abuses, and preserving the dignity of this holy sacrament; and that there wants nothing but the due execution of them, and our conscientious performing of that which we solemnly promised before God and the bishop, when we had the charge of souls committed to us, that *we would conform to the Liturgy of the church of England, as it is now by law established.* . . . I know that some midwives and nurses do, on the christening day, (which they think is observed, not so much for the sacrament itself, as for their showing their pride, art, and finery,) dress the child's head so, that the face of it being hid deep under the lace and trimming which stands up so high on each side, the minister cannot come at the face to pour water on it, so as that it may run off again; but what water he pours, will run in among the headcloths, which really is likely to do the child more hurt than dipping would have done." Defence of Hist. Inf. Bap. p. 404—408.

REFLECTIONS.

Reflect. I. From these quotations we learn, that immersion, compared with pouring or sprinkling, has the honour of priority, in respect of time, No. 4, 10, 14;—that it is more significant, No. 1—16;—that it is more safe, or certain of being right, No. 5;—and that one of these learned authors, who had well studied the subject, felt by painful experience the disadvantage under which a Pædobaptist labours, and the arduous task he has to perform, when he undertakes to defend any mode of administration short of dipping; because the best he can say of it is, that the essence of baptism is not wanting. No. 16. See Chap. III. Reflect. IV.

Reflect. II. I can hardly forbear supposing that the attentive reader anticipates my reflections here, and is ready to exclaim: What! practise a mode of administering baptism, that is rejected by one half of the world;

while you cannot but acknowledge, that antiquity, significancy, and safety of being right, may be all fairly pleaded against it? As if they professedly imitated the Roman Catholics, in regard to the invocation of saints! For Chemnitius tells us, " Many among the Papists acknowledge, that it is better, more agreeable to rule, more certain, and more safe, to invocate God himself in the name of Christ, than to address prayer to saints."* Strange that there should be such charms in a religious custom, which is a confessed variation from the examples of apostles, of martyrs, of Christians almost universally for the long time of thirteen hundred years, and of so great a part of those who bear the character of Christians at this day! Strange, indeed, that any who are the friends of Christ, should confessedly impoverish the significancy of a sacred rite; and then labour, and strive, and toil, in order to prove that they have not annihilated the essence of it! Very singular conduct this, relating to an ordinance of God, a branch of divine worship, and a mean of human happiness! But is it commendable, is it justifiable, is it rational, that the professed followers of Jesus Christ should study to find out the exact boundaries of *essence*, in a positive institution; that they may be able to determine with precision, how far they may vary from the natural import of our Lord's command, his own example, and the practice of his ambassadors, without intrenching on what is essential to the appointment? Let candour, let common sense determine. Dr. Mayo has well observed, that " all great errors and evils in the Christian church had small beginnings; we are, therefore, not to make light of those things in religion, which yet may not be of the essence thereof."†

How much is the conduct of these authors like that of the Roman Catholics in another case! The latter, we know, administer the Lord's supper to the people in

---

* Exam. Concil. Trident. p. 613. † Apology and Shield, p. 166.

one kind;—even while they cannot but acknowledge that Christ appointed the use of wine, as well as of bread; that the apostles administered both kinds; that the church for many centuries received the sacred supper in both kinds; and that the representation of our Lord's death is more complete, by the administration of both kinds;—after all these concessions pretending, that they do not intrench on the *essence* of the ordinance, by administering the bread only! But, strange as their procedure is, it must be with an ill grace that any of the writers here produced object against that mutilation of the holy supper. For though they do not explicitly avow, they seem entirely to approve the reasoning of Bellarmine, when he speaks in the following manner: "Though more grace and advantage be received by partaking of both kinds, than only of one, it is not therefore necessary that all should communicate of both species; because of two evils, the less ought always to be chosen. Now, it is a less evil that some persons should want a benefit which is not necessary, than that the sacrament should be exposed to the evident danger of being irreverently used."* It is *danger* of irreverence, we see, that is pleaded by Papists for their mutilation of the holy supper: it is also *danger* of indecency, or of health, which urges Pædobaptists to lay aside immersion, as the reader may learn from the following chapter. How lamentable to reflect, that, respecting the administration of positive appointments, there should be such a coalition between the subjects of the triple crown and professed Protestants!

Besides, the best evidence yet produced, that pouring or sprinkling contains the essence of baptism, has always been treated, by a very large part of the Christian world, as extremely doubtful. In proof of this assertion, I appeal to the authorities produced, Chap. IV. and V. and to those which follow in the next.—

---

* Apud Chamierum, Panstrat. tom. iv. l. ix. c. x. § 6.

Being taught, therefore, by so many respectable Pædobaptists, that the radical idea of the term baptism, the chief design of the ordinance, the apostolic example, the present practice of one half of the Christian world, and the emphasis of signification, are all in favour of immersion; we must stand acquitted of blame, and our conduct in regard to dipping deserve imitation. It cannot indeed be otherwise, except it should hereafter appear, that substantial reasons may be assigned for altering the practice of immersion to that of pouring, or of sprinkling: and substantial they must be to answer so important an end, in the face of all these concessions and all this evidence. It would be the height of precipitancy, and little short of religious madness to desert, without the most cogent reasons, a practice thus recommended, for one that appears in such embarrassment. What those reasons are, that have been thought sufficient by many of the most learned Pædobaptists; what their force, and what regard they deserve, must be considered in the following chapter.

CHAPTER VII.

The Reasons, Rise, and Prevalence of Pouring, or Sprinkling, instead of Immersion.

DEYLINGIUS.—" So long as the apostles lived, as many believe, immersion only was used :* to which afterward, perhaps, they added a kind of affusion, such as the Greeks practise at this day, after having performed the trine immersion. At length, after the apostles were dead, the baptism of clinics was known; when disease, or extreme necessity in any other respect, forbade immersion, sprinkling and pouring began to be introduced ; which in a course of time were retained, plunging being neglected. For in following times, when adult persons were very seldom baptized, infants were initiated into the Christian church by pouring and by sprinkling." Observat. Sac. pars. iii. observ. xxvi. § 2.

2. Salmasius:—"The clinics only, because they were confined to their beds, were baptized in a manner of which they were capable; not in the entire laver, as those who plunge the head under water, but the *whole body* had water poured upon it. As Cypr. iv. epist. vii. Thus Novatus, when sick, received baptism; being (περιχυθεις) *besprinkled,* not (βαπτισθεις) *baptized.* Euseb. vi. Hist. cap. xliii." Apud Witsium, Œcon. Fœd. l. iv. c. xvi. § 13.

3. Mr. Formey.—" Putting off their clothes, they were dipped three times in water; but when they administered baptism to the cliniques, i. e. to those who

---

* Of this opinion is Mr. Picart, who says: " Baptism by ablution, or aspersion, was not known in the first century of the church, when immersion was only used; and it is said it continued so till St. Gregory's time." Relig. Cerem. vol. ii. p. 82.

were confined to their beds from illness, they made use only of simple sprinkling." Abridg. Eccles. Hist. vol. i. p. 33.

4. *Turrettinus.*—" Immersion was used in former times and in warm climates, as we are taught by the practice of John the Baptist, (Matt. iii. 6, 16;) of Christ's apostles, (John iii. 22, and iv. 1, 2;) and of Philip, (Acts viii. 38.) But now, especially in cold countries, when the church began to extend itself towards the north, plunging (καταποντισμος) was changed into sprinkling, and aspersion only is used." Institut. Loc. xix. quæst. xi. § 11.

5. *Mr. W. Perkins.*—" The ancient custom of baptizing was to dip; and, as it were, to dive all the body of the baptized in the water, as may appear in Paul, Rom. vi. and the councils of Laodicea and Neocæsarea; but now, especially in cold countries, the church useth only to sprinkle the baptized, by reason of children's weakness; for very few of ripe years are now-a-days baptized. We need not much to marvel at this alteration, seeing charity and necessity may dispense with ceremonies, and mitigate in equity the sharpness of them." Works, vol. i. p. 74, edit. 1608.

6. *Dr. Manton.*—" You will say, If the rite [of immersion] hath this signification, [Christ's death for sin, and our death to sin] why is it not retained? I answer, Christianity lieth not in ceremonies: the principal thing in baptism is the washing away of sin, (Acts xxii. 16;) that may be done by pouring on of water, as well as dipping." Serm. on Rom. vi. 4.

7. *Walæus.*—" In warm countries, the ancients practised an immersion of the whole body; but in colder climates, they generally used aspersion: because, a ceremony that is free ought always to give way to charity." Enchiridium, de Bap. p. 425.

8. *Pamelius.*—" Whereas the sick, by reason of their illness, could not be immersed or plunged (which,

properly speaking, is to be baptized,) they had the salutary water poured upon them, or were sprinkled with it. For the same reason, I think, the custom of sprinkling now used, first began to be observed by the western church; namely, on account of the tenderness of infants, seeing the baptism of adults was now very seldom practised." Apud Forbesium, Instruct. Hist. Theolog. l. x. c. v. § 57.

9. Hoornbeekius.—"In the eastern churches baptism was more anciently administered by immersing the body in water. Afterward, first in the western churches, on account of the coldness of the countries, bathing being less in use than in the east, and the tender age of those that were baptized, dipping or sprinkling was admitted." Miscell. Sac. l. i. c. xvii. sect. iv. § 1.

10. Grotius.—"The custom of pouring or sprinkling seems to have prevailed in favour of those that were dangerously ill, and were desirous of giving up themselves to Christ; whom others called *clinics*. See the Epistle of Cyprian to Magnus." Apud Poli Synopsin, ad Matt. iii. 6.

11. H. Altingius. — "The baptismal washing, in warm countries and ancient times, was performed by immersion; but now, especially in cold countries, it is performed by only sprinkling.... The cause of the alteration is, that immersion, which was used in the warm eastern and southern countries, is less convenient in the cold western and northern climates; where there is danger of health from immersion, especially of infants. And therefore that rule is here in force; 'I will have mercy and not sacrifice.'" Loci Commun. pars i. loc. xii. p. 198, 199. Theolog. Problem. Nov. loc. xiv. prob. xi. p. 657.

12. E. Spanhemius.—"In these northern and colder countries, out of regard to the tender age of infants, we use aspersion in the place of immersion; which, of old, was usually practised, either in open rivers or in private

baptisteries, and vessels filled with water." Disputat. Syntag. Disp. de Bap. § 16.

13. Quenstedius.—"When occasion was but seldom given of baptizing adults, and very frequently of baptizing infants, the church consulted their weakness; whence, by little and little, aspersion was introduced, till at length, immersion being laid aside, it prevailed. Of which change there was a threefold reason; the *tenderness* of infants—*shame*, especially in regard to female catechumens—and because, even in the very act of baptizing, *natura cursum suum tenet;* sicut contigit magnis impp. in oriente Constantino Copronymo cognominato, et in occidente Wenceslao; qui cum immergerentur, *aquam baptismalem macularunt."* Antiq. Bib. c. iv. sect. ii. num. i. § 4. p. 319.

14. Riissenius.—"Though in warm countries immersion was practised in former times, yet now, especially in colder climates, aspersion may be rightly used." Summa Theolog. loc. xvii. § 31.

15. Keckermannus.—"Though the term baptism properly signifies immersion, and though also in the ancient church, through the eastern countries, when baptism was administered, it was, not by sprinkling, but by immersion; yet in the colder parts of Christendom, aspersion is used instead of immersion, on account of infants: because charity and necessity may dispense with ceremonies, and temper them with gentleness, so far as may be done without injuring the analogy." System. Theolog. l. iii. c. viii.

16. Piscator.—"Whether the whole body be dipped, and that thrice, or once; or whether water be only poured

---

* Had any Baptist assigned such a reason for immersion's being laid aside, he would, I suspect, have been charged with *gross indelicacy*, and loaded with censure, by many of our opposers; even though they could not have disproved the fact. This, however, proceeds from an eminent Lutheran, who was no friend to the Baptists. See Hist. of Popery, vol. i. p. 141.

or sprinkled on the party; this ought to be free to the churches, according to the difference of countries." Aphorismi Doct. Christ. loc. xxiv. aph. 9.

17. Mr. Rich. Baxter.—"We grant that baptism then [in the primitive times] was by washing the whole body; and did not the difference of our cold country, as to that hot one, teach us to remember, 'I will have mercy and not sacrifice,' it should be so here." Paraphrase on the New Test. at Matt. iii. 6.

18. Bp. Burnet.—"The danger of dipping in cold climates, may be a very good reason for changing the form of baptism to sprinkling." Exposition of Thirty-nine Articles, p. 436.

19. Venema.—"Sprinkling was used in the last moments of life, on such as were called clinics; and also where there was not a sufficient quantity of water." Hist. Eccles. tom. iv. secul. iv. § 110.

20. Dr. Towerson.—"The first mention we find of aspersion in the baptism of the elder sort, was in the case of the *clinici*, or men who received baptism upon their sick beds; and that baptism is represented by S. Cyprian as legitimate, upon the account of the necessity that compelled it, and the presumption there was of God's gracious acceptation thereof because of it. By which means the lawfulness of any other baptism than by an immersion will be found to lie in the *necessity* there may sometimes be of another manner of administration of it." Of the Sacram. of Bap. part iii. p. 59, 60.

21. Sir John Floyer.—"The church of Rome hath drawn short compendiums of both sacraments. In the eucharist, they use only the wafer, and instead of immersion they introduced aspersion.... I have now given what testimony I could find in our English authors, to prove the practice of immersion from the time the Britons and Saxons were baptized, till king James's days; when the people grew peevish with all ancient ceremonies, and through the love of novelty, and the niceness of

parents, and the pretence of modesty, they laid aside immersion; which never was abrogated by any canon, but is still recommended by the present rubric of our church, which orders the child to be dipped discreetly and warily." Hist. of Cold Bathing, p. 15, 61.

22. Dr. R. Wetham.—" The word baptism signifies a washing, particularly when it is done by immersion, or by dipping, or plunging a thing under water, which was formerly the ordinary way of administrating the sacrament of baptism. But the church, which cannot change the least article of the Christian faith, is not so tied up in matters of discipline and ceremonies. Not only the Catholic church, but also the pretended Reformed churches, have altered this primitive custom in giving the sacrament of baptism, and now allow of baptism by pouring or sprinkling water on the person baptized. Nay, many of their ministers do it now-a-days by filliping a wet finger and thumb over a child's head, or by shaking a wet finger or two over the child, which it is hard enough to call a baptizing in any sense." Annotations on the New Test. at Matt. iii. 6.

23. Dr. Wall.—" In the case of sickness, weakness, haste, want of quantity of water, or such like extraordinary occasions, baptism by affusion of water on the face, was by the ancients counted sufficient baptism. I shall out of the many proofs of it produce two or three of the *most ancient*. Anno Dom. two hundred and fifty one, Novatian was, by one party of the clergy and people of Rome, chosen bishop of that church, in a schismatical way, and in opposition to Cornelius, who had been before chosen by the major part, and was already ordained. Cornelius does in a letter to Fabius, bishop of Antioch, vindicate his right, showing that Novatian came not canonically to his orders of priesthood, much less was capable of being chosen bishop; for that 'all the clergy and a great many of the laity, were against his being ordained presbyter, because it was not lawful (they

said) for any one that had been baptized in his bed in time of sickness, [τον εν κλινη δια νοσον περιχυθεντα] as he had been, to be admitted to any office of the clergy'.... France seems to have been the first country in the world where baptism by affusion was used ordinarily to persons in health, and in the public way of administering it.... It being allowed to weak children [in the reign of queen Elizabeth] to be baptized by aspersion, many fond ladies and gentlewomen first, and then by degrees the common people, would obtain the favour of the priest to have their children pass for weak children, too tender to endure dipping in the water. Especially, as Mr. Walker observes, ' if some instance really were, *or were but* fancied or framed, of some child's taking hurt by it'.... Calvin had not only given his dictate in his Institutions, that 'the difference is of no moment, whether he that is baptized be dipped all over, and if so, whether thrice or once; or whether he be only wetted by the water poured on him:' but he had also drawn up for the use of his church at Geneva, and afterwards published to the world, A Form of administering the Sacraments; where, when he comes to order the act of baptizing, he words it thus: 'Then the minister of baptism POURS water on the infant,' saying, 'I baptize thee,' and so on. There had been—some synods in some dioceses of France, that had spoken of affusion without mentioning immersion at all, that being the common practice; but for an office or liturgy of any church, this is, I believe, the first in the world that prescribes aspersion absolutely ....And for sprinkling, properly called, it seems it was, at sixteen hundred and forty-five, just then beginning, and used by very few. It must have begun in the disorderly times after forty-one.... But then came The Directory, and says: 'Baptism is to be administered, not in private places, or privately; *but* in the place of public worship, and in the face of the congregation,' and so on. 'And not in the places where fonts, in the time of Popery, were unfitly and superstitiously placed.' So, they reformed the font into a basin. This learned Assembly could not remember, that fonts to baptize in, had been always used by the primitive Christians, long before the beginning of Popery, and ever since churches were built; but that sprinkling, for the common use of baptizing, was really introduced (in France first, and then in other Popish countries,) in times of Popery. And that accordingly, ALL THOSE COUNTRIES IN WHICH THE USURPED POWER OF THE POPE IS, OR HAS FORMERLY BEEN OWNED, HAVE LEFT OFF DIPPING OF CHILDREN IN THE FONT: BUT THAT ALL OTHER COUNTRIES IN THE WORLD, WHICH HAD NEVER REGARDED HIS AUTHORITY, DO STILL USE IT; AND THAT BASINS, EXCEPT IN CASE OF NECESSITY, WERE NEVER USED BY PAPISTS, OR ANY OTHER CHRISTIANS WHATSOEVER, TILL BY THEMSELVES... What has been said of this custom of pouring or sprinkling water in the ordinary use of baptism, is to be understood only in reference to these western parts of Europe; for it is used ordinarily no where else. The Greek church, in all the branches of it, does still use immersion; and they hardly count a child, except in case of sickness, well baptized without it: and so do all other Christians in the world, except the Latins. That which I hinted before, is a rule that does not fail in any particular that I know of; viz. All the nations of Christians, that do now, or formerly did submit to the authority of the bishop of Rome, do ordinarily baptize their infants by pouring, or sprinkling. And though the English received not this custom till after the decay of Popery, yet they have since received it from such neighbour nations as had begun it in the time of the Pope's power. *But all other Christians in the world, who never owned the Pope's usurped power,* DO, AND EVER DID,

OF SPRINKLING INSTEAD OF IMMERSION. 261

DIP THEIR INFANTS IN THE ORDINARY USE." Hist. of Inf. Bap. part ii. chap. ix. p. 463, 467, 470, 471, 472, 477.

24. Anonymous.—" The custom of sprinkling children, instead of dipping them in the font, which at first was allowed in case of the weakness or sickness of the infant, has so far prevailed, that immersion is at length quite excluded. What principally tended to confirm the practice of affusion or sprinkling was, that several of our Protestant divines, flying into Germany and Switzerland during the bloody reign of queen Mary, and returning home when queen Elizabeth came to the crown, brought back with them a great zeal for the Protestant churches beyond sea, where they had been sheltered and received; and having observed that, at Geneva, and some other places, baptism was administered by sprinkling, they thought they could not do the church of England a greater piece of service than by introducing a practice dictated by so great an oracle as Calvin. This, together with the coldness of our northern climate, was what contributed to banish entirely the practice of dipping infants in the font." Encyclopæd. Britan. article, Baptism, vol. ii. p. 996.

REFLECTIONS.

Reflect. I. By the quotations here produced from eminent Pædobaptists, we are taught, that the most ancient instance on ecclesiastical record, which is yet adduced, of pouring or sprinkling, is that of Novatian, in the year two hundred and fifty-one, No. 23;—that the reason of it, both then and afterwards, was not any real, nor even pretended command or example, in the New Testament; but a supposed necessity, arising, either from bodily disease, a want of water for immersion, or some other similar circumstance, No. 1, 2, 3, 7, 8, 10, 16, 20;—that even then, the water was applied by pouring upon or sprinkling, not the face, but the whole body,

No. 2;—that it was considered as an imperfect administration of the ordinance; so imperfect, as rendered the subject of it ineligible to the ministerial office, and was denominated *sprinkling*, not *baptizing*, No. 2, 23;— that pouring, or sprinkling, as a common practice, originated in the apostate church of Rome, and that the Protestant churches thence derived it, No. 21, 23;— that this mode of proceeding commenced among the English in the time of Queen Elizabeth, but that immersion was the prevailing practice till the reign of James I., No. 21, 23;—that the reasons of this alteration in England were, the love of novelty, niceness of parents, pretence of modesty, and a high regard for the character of Calvin, No. 21, 23, 24;—that Calvin's form of administering the sacraments was probably the first in the world, that prescribed pouring absolutely, No. 23;—that sprinkling, strictly so called, did not commence in England, till the year sixteen hundred and forty-five, and was then used by very few, ibid.;—that the assembly of divines at Westminster, converted the font into a basin; and that basins, unless in case of necessity, had never been used by Papists, or any other Christians whatever, till by the members of that assembly, ibid.;—that Roman Catholics ridicule some of the Protestant ministers, for using only a few drops of water, No. 22;—that the reasons assigned for this novel mode of proceeding are, coldness of climate, No. 4, 5, 7, 8, 9, 11, 12, 14, 15, 17, 18;—tenderness of infants, No. 5, 8, 13;—Christianity's not consisting in ceremonies, No. 6;—that sacred maxim, "God will have mercy and not sacrifice," No. 11, 12;—the authority of the church to alter ceremonial appointments, No. 22;—and (most delicately to crown the whole) because, in the very act of baptizing, it was observed that *natura cursum suum tenet*, No. 13;—finally, that ALL the Christians in the world, who never owned the Pope's usurped power, now do, and ever did, dip their children in the common course of their practice, No. 23. Such is the information which these learned authors give.

Reflect. II. According to this representation, the practice of pouring and sprinkling makes but a poor figure in the eyes of a consistent Protestant; for, if this be a just account, it had no existence till many corruptions had taken deep root in the church; it originated in dangerous error; was fostered by the mother of abominations; and under the powerful influence of her authority and her example, it became the general custom in all those parts of the world to which her tyranny ever extended; BUT NO WHERE ELSE. It seems to have been under the combined operation of different errors that the practice took its rise. For though, as Mr. Henry justly observes, " Many in the primitive times, upon a mistaken apprehension of the unpardonableness of sin committed after baptism, deferred it long, some even till the dying moment;"* yet they imagined the ordinance necessary to their salvation. When, therefore, they were seized with affliction, confined to their beds, and apprehensive of death, the expedient of pouring, or of sprinkling, was devised in the pressing emergency, as a happy succedaneum for immersion. That laborious and learned enquirer, Dr. Wall, could find no instance, of the kind, prior to the case of Novatian; which case is thus described in Eusebius : " He fell into a grievous distemper, and it being supposed that he would die immediately, he received baptism, being *besprinkled* with water on the bed whereon he lay, if *that* can be termed baptism."† On which passage Valesius observes: " This word, $\pi\epsilon\rho\iota\chi\upsilon\theta\epsilon\iota\varsigma$, Rufinus very well renders *perfusus, besprinkled*. For people which were sick and baptized in their beds, could not be dipped in water by the priest, but were sprinkled with water by him. This baptism was thought imperfect, and not solemn, for several rea-

---
* Treatise on Baptism, p. 27.
† Eccles. Hist. b. vi. chap. xliii. Cambridge, 1683.

sons. Also they who were thus baptized, were called ever afterwards, CLINICI; and, by the twelfth canon of the Council of Neocæsarea, these clinici were prohibited priesthood." Yea, so imperfect was this baptism esteemed, that Bp. Taylor tells us: "It was a formal and solemn question, made by Magnus to Cyprian, Whether they are to be esteemed right Christians who were only sprinkled with water, and not washed or dipped? He [Cyprian] answers, that the baptism was good, when it was done in the case of necessity; God pardoning, and necessity compelling. And this," adds the bishop, " is the sense and law of the church of England: not that it be indifferent, but that all infants be dipped, except in cases of sickness, and then sprinkling is permitted."*— Now, that this clinical baptism had no existence in the apostolic times, we are led to conclude, not only by considering the erroneous foundation on which it rests, and the total silence of the New Testament concerning it, but also by the testimony of some learned Pædobaptists. Witness Altmannus, who says, " It has not yet been proved, that the baptism of clinics was used in the time of the apostles; nor, certainly, can any passages be produced from the apostolic writings, nor from those of the first fathers, from which it may be concluded that it is a rite of such great antiquity."† See Chap. IV. No. 84.

It is worthy to be remarked, that a gross mistake about the necessity of baptism, not only introduced sprinkling instead of immersion; but, in some instances, has operated so far as entirely to exclude water from any concern in the ordinance. The following examples have occurred to observation, in the course of my reading. Nicephorus informs us, that a certain Jew, performing a journey in company with Christians, and being suddenly seized with a dangerous illness, earnestly

---

* Ductor Dubitantium, b. iii. chap. iv. rule 15.

† Meletem. Philolog. Critic. tom. iii. p. 131.

desired baptism at the hands of his fellow travellers. They, not having a priest in their company, and being destitute of water, were at first reluctant; but, he conjuring them not to deny him the favour, they yielded to his request. On which, taking off his clothes, they sprinkled him thrice with sand instead of water; adding, that they "baptized him, in the name of the Father," and so on.*—Deylingius furnishes another example of a singular kind. He tells us, that near the beginning of the Reformation, a certain midwife in Thuringia, under the fair pretext of necessity, baptized some sickly children without water, merely by pronouncing these words; " I baptize thee in the name," and so on. The same learned author, from Seckendorf, mentions others who taught that baptism might be administered without water.†—To BAPTIZE by sprinkling a few drops of water; to BAPTIZE by sprinkling of sand, without any water; to BAPTIZE by merely pronouncing a form of words; what misnomers they are! and what an improvement on the institution of Christ! I will here add the following words of Dr. Willett: " We condemn the foolish and ungodly practices and inventions of heretics, that either exclude water altogether, as the Manichees, with others; or do use any other element, as the Jacobites, that, instead of water, burned them that were to be baptized with an hot iron; or as the Ethiopians, which are called Abissines, that used fire instead of water; misconstruing the words of the gospel, (Matt. iii. 11.)"‡

---

* Apud Centur. Magdeburg, cent. ii. c. vi. p. 82.

† De Prudentia Pastoral. pars. iii. c. iii. § 20.

‡ Synopsis Papismi, p. 562. Our brethren who practise Free Communion frequently plead, that those persons whose claim to the holy supper is under dispute, consider themselves as really baptized, and on that ground should be admitted to the Lord's table. This reminds me of what Vasques, a Popish casuist, says : " If any man *think* that to be a relic of a saint, which indeed is not so, he is not frustrate of the merit of his devotion." Thus that veteran in superstition, as quoted by Mr. Clarkson, Prac. Div. of Papists,

Reflect. III. The reasons assigned by these Pædobaptists for pouring or sprinkling, may be compared with the arguments of Roman Catholics, in defence of withholding the cup from the people; the answers returned by Protestants to their futile reasonings; and these, with the replies that Baptists make to the reasonings in favour of sprinkling. Do the Roman Catholics argue, That the *whole essence* of the Lord's supper is contained in one kind? So do Protestant Pædobaptists, that the entire essence of baptism is retained in pouring or sprinkling.—Do the former maintain, that they who have the thing *signified*, need not contend about the *sign?* So do many of the latter.— Do the votaries of Rome tell us, there is no *spiritual benefit* enjoyed by receiving both bread and wine, which is not possessed by those who partake only of the bread? So do our Protestant brethren argue, in reference to pouring and sprinkling, compared with immersion.—Do the subjects of the triple crown endeavour to persuade the Reformed, that there were various *types* and *figures* of the holy supper, in the Old Testament, which favour the receiving it in one kind? Do they plead for this end the paschal lamb, the manna, the show-bread, and the sacrifices, the flesh of which was to be eaten, but their blood not to be drunk? So Pædobaptists endeavour to persuade us, that some typical rites, and that various allusive expressions in the Old Testament, (such as, *I will* pour *water on him that is thirsty—He shall* sprinkle *many nations*,* with others of a similar kind,) are in

---

p. 189. But would our brethen receive a candidate for communion, who sincerely believes he has been baptized, merely because he was sprinkled with sand, as, in the case of this Jew; or on account of some zealous midwife having pronounced over him a solemn form of words; or because he has been marked with a hot iron? Let them *consider of it, take advice, and speak* their minds, (Judges xix. 30.)

* Mr. Henry's Treatise on Bap. p. 140.

favour of sprinkling.—Have Protestants united in replying to the first of these arguments: It is *not a fact*, that the whole essence of the Lord's supper is contained in the species of bread? So do we assert, that the entire essence of baptism is not retained in pouring or sprinkling; because an immersion of the whole body, is as really a distinct act from applying a few drops of water to the face only, as eating bread is distinct from the drinking of wine.—Do the Reformed answer to the second; This is the ready way to *cast off* all sacraments and ordinances at once? So do we; for if the servants of Christ may administer baptism in either of the different ways, because the candidate is considered as having the blessings to which it refers, they are at liberty, for the same reason, to neglect or use any ordinance just as they please.—Do the opposers of Papal corruptions reply to the third; That supposing an equal degree of benefit to result from each mode of administration, yet there is not, there cannot be the same degree of *humble obedience* to Jesus Christ, who appointed the sacred supper? So do we, in regard to the different ways of administering baptism. Do the friends of the Protestant cause agree, in respect to the fourth argument; That none of the things mentioned were types or figures of the *Lord's supper*, and therefore the analogical reasoning has no force? We also maintain, that none of the purifications practised in the ancient Jewish church, (whether by dipping, washing, or sprinkling,) were types or figures of baptism. Besides, we have the authority of a learned and famous Pædobaptist, when we assert, That among all the various rites of purification prescribed to the chosen tribes, " the sprinkling of *mere* water was not appointed; for it was either mixed with blood or ashes."* Consequently, no allusion to any of those ancient rites, whether it be found in the Old or in the New Testament, can be a proper direction for

---

* Lampe, Comment. in Evang. Joan. ad. cap. iii. 5.

us in the administration of baptism. See Chap. I. No. 4, 8, 10, 11, 12, 13, 16, 20. Reflect. II. III.

Again: When Protestant writers oppose that mutilation of a divine appointment, which is practised by those of the Romish communion at the Lord's table, they do not fail to show, that the *declared will* of God is the rule of duty; and that the institution of the ordinance, the example of the apostles, the end of the appointment, and the practice of the church for thirteen hundred years, are all against that partial administration, and all in favour of the Reformed.* Now, are not these the very principles on which the Baptists proceed, in all their disputes with Pædobaptists about the right manner of performing baptism? Nay, does it not appear from the preceding chapters, and from the pens of our opponents themselves, that these principles are just, and supported by facts, relating to the controversy about baptism, as well as to that concerning the holy supper?

Farther: Do some of the learned Catholics acknowledge, that receiving the Lord's supper in both kinds, is more *complete* and more *expressive;* and that the present practice of their church, is *a departure* from the institution, from apostolic example, and from the general custom of Christians for many ages? Do certain of their learned writers express an ardent wish to have the primitive practice restored among them? † All this, it appears, have some of our learned opposers done, in regard to the administration of baptism. How far the following reflection upon a concession of Cassander, concerning communion in one kind, may be fairly applied to any of the Pædobaptists, I leave my reader to judge. " Behold," says my author, " behold here an

---

* See Morning Exercise against Popery, serm. xxii. Dr. Willet's Synops. Papismi, controv. xiii. q. viii. p. 640—647; and Mr. Leigh's Bod. Div. b. viii. chap. ix.

† Dr. Willet, ut supra, p. 642. Morning Exer. against Popery, p. 772.

acknowledgment so plain and so full, that I wonder with what countenance men can resist so manifest a truth, and withhold it in unrighteousness! And yet here they muster up the best strength they have, and will not yield an inch of what they have once established, be it right or wrong."*

Once more: Do not Protestant Pædobaptists urge the *necessity* of adhering, strictly adhering to the original institution, in administering the holy supper; the *absurdity* and *iniquity* of departing from it, on account of any supposed inconvenience; and the danger of practising any thing in religious worship that is not warranted by the word of God? Hear a specimen of what they say, and see whither the reasoning tends; for it proceeds on principles that are common to every positive institution of true religion.—Thus Dr. Clarke: "In things of external appointment, and mere positive institution, where we cannot, as in matters of natural and moral duty, argue concerning the natural reason and ground of the obligation, and the original necessity of the thing itself, we have nothing to do but to obey the positive command. God is infinitely better able than we to judge of the propriety and usefulness of the things he institutes; and it becomes us to obey with humility and reverence." †—"The command of Christ," says the judicious Turrettin, "ought not to be violated under any pretence whatever; and in what way soever the thing signified may be received, the sign appointed by Christ is always to be retained." ‡—"There is in the church," says Heidegger, "no more power of changing the rites of the sacraments appointed by Christ, than there is power of changing his word and law. For as his word contains a sign audible, so those rites contain a visible sign of his divine will." §—"It

---

* Morning Exercise, p. 772. † Expos. Church Cat. p. 305, 306. ‡ Institut. loc. xix. quæst. xxv. § 22.
§ In Dr. Du Veil, on Acts viii. 38.

is a universal axiom," says the learned and eminent Chamier, "that the sacrament be celebrated according to its first institution."*—"There being, in this whole institution, the greatest simplicity and unity of design that can be," says Bp. Taylor; "the same form of words, a single sacrament, the same address, no difference in the sanction, no variety, or signs of variety, in the appendages, in the parallel places, or in any discourse concerning it; to suppose here a difference will so intricate the whole affair, that either men may imagine and dream of variety when they please, and be or not be obliged as they list; or else if there be a difference intended in it by our Lawgiver, it will be as good as none at all, he having left no mark of the distinction, no shadow of different commandments, under several representations." †—"All reasoning upon this head," says Bp. Burnet, "is an arguing against the institution; as if Christ and his apostles had not well enough considered it, but that twelve hundred years after them, a consequence should be observed, that till then had not been thought of, which made it reasonable to alter the manner of it.... He who instituted it, knew best what was most fitting and most reasonable; and we must choose rather to acquiesce in his commands, than in our own reasonings." ‡—" The institution, with the elements, makes the sacrament; and so the only rule and balance for them [the elements] must needs be their institution. This being the ground of this ordinance, no man or angel may violate it under a fearful curse. And indeed, if men's will or wisdom might alter and change the revelation of God, nothing would abide firm in religion. It is true, the laws of men may be corrected and annulled, because they foresee not their inconveniences; but our Saviour, certainly, when he

---

* Panstrat. tom. iv. l. i. c. xiii. § 1.
† Ductor Dubitant. b. iii. chap. vi. p. 412.
‡ Expos. xxxix Art. p. 436, 437.

appointed this ordinance, well knew what was necessary and useful for his church to the end of the world. And for this reason the apostle Paul, when some disorders were broken into the church of Corinth, in the use of the Lord's supper, recalls them to the institution, and endeavours by that straight rule to rectify their irregularities, (1 Cor. xi. 23.) By which place it is evident, that there is no such way to obviate any mistake, which in after-times creeps upon God's own ordinance, as by going back to the spring, by considering the institution: insomuch as the same apostle, for their violating Christ's institution in their administration of this ordinance, saith, *This is* NOT *to eat the Lord's supper.*"*——Dr. Erskine, when answering an objection against frequently receiving the sacred supper, says: "Whatever danger there is, God foresaw it, but yet did not see meet to guard against it, by enjoining us to communicate seldom. Shall we then pretend to be wiser than God? Have we found out better means for securing the honour of his institutions, than the means prescribed and practised by those who were under the infallible guidance of his Spirit? Have not attempts of this kind proved the source of the worst corruptions in Popery? Reason has no power to dispense with, or to derogate from the positive laws of God, on pretence of doing them a service. It is blasphemous presumption, though it may put on a cloak of humility, to judge that a sufficient reason to hinder thee from frequent communicating, which our Lord did not judge a sufficient reason to hinder him from commanding it. If thou thus judge the law, *thou art not a doer of the law, but a judge.*"†—Once more: The church of England says, " Before all other things this we must be sure of especially, that this supper be in such wise done and ministered as our Lord and Saviour did and commanded to

---

* Morning Exercise against Popery, p. 764, 765.
† Theolog. Dissert. p. 289.

be done, as his holy apostles used it, and the good fathers in the primitive church frequented it. For, as that worthy man S. Ambrose saith, 'He is unworthy of the Lord, that otherwise doth celebrate that mystery, than it was delivered by him.' Neither can he be devout, that otherwise doth presume than it was given by the Author."*—Quotations of this kind might be greatly multiplied; but I forbear, and appeal to the reader, Whether these be not the very principles on which we proceed; nay, whether these be not some of those very arguments, *mutatis mutandis*, that are used by us against pouring and sprinkling? If, then, this way of arguing be valid from the pens of Protestants, against a mutilation of the holy supper; it must be equally so from the pen of a Baptist, in relation to the substitution of pouring, or sprinkling, instead of immersion. For if these arguments have any force, they will equally apply to every positive institution that is not administered according to its original form. We may, therefore, adopt the following observation of Dr. Owen, respecting the cause of Nonconformity: "We find as yet no arrows shot against us, but such as are gathered up in the fields, shot at them that use them, out of the Roman quiver."†

Nor are Roman Catholics insensible of that advantage which Pædobaptist Protestants give them, in regard to this affair; for thus Bossuet reasons: "Though these are incontestable truths, [namely, that baptism is immersion, and that immersion was practised by the apostles;] yet neither we, nor those of the pretended Reformed religion, hearken to the Anabaptists, who hold mersion to be essential and indispensable; nor have either they or we feared to change this dipping, as I may say, of the whole body, into a bare aspersion, or infusion on one part of it. No other reason of this altera-

---

* Homily on the Sacram. part i.
† Enquiry into the Orig. and Institut. of Churches, Pref. p. 52.

OF SPRINKLING INSTEAD OF IMMERSION. 273

tion can be rendered, than that this dipping is not of the *substance* of baptism; and those of the pretended Reformed religion agreeing with us in this, the first principle we have laid down is incontestable. The second principle is, That to distinguish in a sacrament, what does or does not belong to the substance of it, we must consider the *essential efficacy* of the sacrament. Thus, although the word of Jesus Christ, *baptize*, as has been said, signifies dip, it has been thought, that the *efficacy* of the sacrament was not annexed to the *quantity* of water;* so that baptism by infusion and sprinkling, or by mersion, appearing in reality to have the same efficacy, both the one and the other mode are judged good. Now seeing, as we have said, we cannot find in the eucharist any essential efficacy of the body, distinguished from that of the blood; the grace of the one and of the other, as to the sum and substance of it, cannot but be the same. It signifies nothing to say, The representation of the death of our Lord, is *more express* in the two kinds. I grant it; and in like manner the new birth of a believer, is *more express* in immersion, than in bare infusion, or aspersion. For the believer being plunged in the water of baptism, is 'buried with Jesus Christ,' as the apostle expresses it, (Rom. vi. 4; Col. ii. 12;) and coming out of the water, quits the tomb with his Saviour, and more perfectly represents the mystery of Jesus Christ, who regenerates him. Mersion, in which water is applied to the whole body and to all its parts, also more perfectly signifies, that a man is more fully and entirely washed from his

---

* So says Mr. Henry: "In sacraments, it is the truth, and not the quantity of the outward element, that is to be insisted upon." Here he inadvertently coincides with Bossuet. In another place, however, he says: "Strict conformity to the scripture rule, without the superadded inventions of men, is the true beauty of Christian ordinances." This is the language of a sound Protestant, and worthy of himself. See his Treatise on Bap. p. 139, 149.

VOL. I. T

defilements; and yet, baptism performed by immersion, or plunging, is not better than that which is administered by simple infusion, and on one part only. It is sufficient, that the expression of the mystery of Jesus Christ, and of the efficacy of grace, is found in substance in the sacrament, and the utmost exactness of representation is not required in it. Thus, in the eucharist, the expression of the death of our Lord, being in substance found in it, when that body which was delivered up for us is given to us; and the expression of the grace of the sacrament being also found in it, when the image of our spiritual nourishment is given us, under the species of bread; the blood, which only adds to it a more express signification, is not absolutely necessary."*

The same artful defender of Papal superstition, in another of his books, expresses himself thus: " Baptism by immersion, which is as clearly established in the scripture, as communion under the two kinds can possibly be, has nevertheless been changed into pouring, with as much ease and as little dispute, as communion under one kind has been established ; for there is the same reason why one should be preserved as the other. It is a fact most firmly believed by the Reformed, (though some of them at this time wrangle about it,) that baptism was instituted to be administered by plunging the body entirely; that Jesus Christ received it in this manner; that it was thus performed by his apostles ; that the scriptures are acquainted with no other baptism ; that antiquity understood and practised it in this manner; and that to baptize, is to plunge;—these facts, I say, are unanimously acknowledged by all the Reformed teachers; by the Reformers themselves; by those who best understood the Greek language, and the ancient customs of both Jews and Christians; by Luther, by Melancthon, by Calvin, by Casaubon, by Grotius, with all the rest, and since their time by Jurieu, the most ready to

---

* In Mr. Stennett *against* Mr. Russen, p. 176—178.

contradict of all their ministers. Luther has even remarked, that this sacrament is called *Tauf*, in German, on account of the depth; because they plunged *deeply* in the water those whom they baptized. If then there be in the world a fact absolutely certain, it is *this*. Yet it is no less certain, that with all these authors, baptism without immersion is considered as lawful; and that the church properly retains the custom of pouring. . . . There is, then, the same foundation for continuing the communion under one kind, as to continue baptism by pouring; and the church, in supporting these two customs, which tradition proves are equally indifferent, has not done any thing unusual; but maintained, against troublesome persons, that authority upon which the faith of the ignorant rests."*—I am reminded here of a remark made by Mr. James Owen, concerning Episcopacy; which, with a slight alteration, will apply to the case before us. These are his words: "Our English Episcopacy hath scarce one argument for its defence, but what will indifferently serve the Popish prelacy."†

Our English Episcopalians also do not fail to argue on the same topic, when defending their hierarchy, and various rites, against the objections of Pædobaptist Dissenters. Thus, for example, Bp. Burnet, after having mentioned several things which he thought for his purpose, proceeds: " To these instances another may be added, that must needs press all that differ from us, one body only excepted, very much. We know that the first ritual of baptism, was by going into the waters, and being laid as dead all along in them; and then the persons baptized were raised up again, and so they came out of them. This is not only mentioned by St. Paul, but in two different places he gives a mystical signification of this rite, that it signified our being *buried with Christ in baptism*, and our being *raised up with him to a new*

---

* Hist. des Eglises Protest. tom. ii. p. 469, 470.
† Plea for Scrip. Ordinat. p. 17, 171.

life; so that the phrases, of *rising with Christ,* and of *putting on Christ,* as oft as they occur, do plainly relate to this: and yet, partly out of modesty, partly in regard to the tenderness of infants, and the coldness of these climates, since such a manner might endanger their lives, and we know that God 'loves mercy better than sacrifice,' this form of baptizing is as little used by those [Pædobaptists] who separate from us, as by ourselves ....From all these things this inference seems just, That according to the practices of those who divide from us, the church must be supposed to have an authority to adjust the forms of our religion, in those parts of them that are merely ritual, to the taste, to the exigencies, and conveniences of the several ages and climates."*—The right reverend prelate here speaks out. He talks like one who heartily believes, that "the church hath power to decree rites or ceremonies." This will do almost as well, so far as the ritual part of religion is concerned, as the claim of infallibility, of a dispensing power, and the pretence of unwritten apostolic tradition, which are advanced by the partisans of another communion. Such, however, is the bishop's avowal; and such, he insists upon it, is the implicit language of those Dissenters who practise pouring or sprinkling instead of immersion. What a pity but the church, under the ancient Jewish economy, had been acquainted with this doctrine of *taste,* of *exigence,* and of *convenience,* relating to the ceremonial part of divine worship! What a pity but the hoary Abraham had well understood it, when he received an order to circumcise himself and his male posterity! for had he known and approved of it, he would certainly have performed the rite on a different part from that which Jehovah specified. What shall I say? This doctrine of taste, of exigence, and of conve-

---

* Four Discourses to the Clergy, p. 281, 282. Compare this with what he says, Exposit. of Thirty-nine Art. p. 436, 437, as quoted before, p. 301.

nience is of such extensive application, that it would have saved the venerable ancients a world of trouble, and screened them from a thousand reproaches of their Gentile neighbours, had it been duly improved; because, as God is "in one mind," it cannot be doubted, that "he loved mercy better than sacrifice" in those early times as well as now.

But let us hear another learned Episcopalian or two in reference to the same subject. Thus, then, Mr. Evans, when defending a kneeling gesture at the Lord's table. "There is a confessed variation allowed of, and practised by the generality of Dissenters, both Presbyterians and Independents, from the institution and practice of Christ and his apostles, in the other sacrament of baptism; for they have changed immersion or dipping, into aspersion or sprinkling, and pouring water on the face. Baptism by immersion or dipping, is suitable to the institution of our Lord and the practice of his apostles, and was by them ordained and used to represent our burial with Christ, a death unto sin, and a new birth unto righteousness, as St. Paul explains that rite, (Matt. iii. 16, and xxviii. 19; Rom. vi. 4, 6, 11; Col. ii. 12.) Now, it is very strange that kneeling at the Lord's supper (though a different gesture from that which was used at the first institution) should become a stumbling-block in the way of weak and tender consciences, and that it is more unpassable than the Alps; and yet they can with ease and cheerfulness pass by as great or a greater change in the sacrament of baptism, and christen as we do, without the least murmur or complaint. Sitting, kneeling, or standing, were none of them instituted or used to signify and represent any thing essential to the Lord's supper, as dipping all over was: why cannot kneeling then be without any wrong to the conscience, as safely and innocently used as sprinkling? How comes a gnat (to use our Saviour's proverb) to be harder to swallow than a camel? Or why should not the peace and unity of the church, and charity to the public, prevail with them to kneel at the Lord's supper, as much, or rather more, as mercy and tenderness to the infant's body, to sprinkle or pour water on the face, contrary to the first institution?"*——Thus also Dr. Whitby: "If, notwithstanding the evidence produced, that baptism by immersion is suitable both to the institution of our Lord and his apostles; and was by them ordained to represent our burial with Christ, and so our dying unto sin, and our conformity to his resurrection by newness of life, as the apostle doth clearly maintain the meaning of this rite; I say, if, notwithstanding this, all our [Pædobaptist] Dissenters do agree to sprinkle the baptized infant, why may they not as well submit to the significant ceremonies imposed by our church? For, since it is as lawful to add unto Christ's institutions a significant ceremony, as to diminish a significant ceremony which He or his apostles instituted, and use another in its stead, which they never did institute; what reason can they have to do the latter, and yet refuse submission to the former? And why should not the peace and union of the church be as prevailing with them to perform the one, as is their mercy to the infant's body to neglect the other?"†——Hence the reader may plainly perceive, how much the practice of aspersion is calculated to embarrass Protestants, in their disputes with Papists; and Nonconformists, in their controversies with Episcopalians.

Reflect. IV. Admitting the tenderness of infants to be a sufficient reason for not immersing them, what is the natural inference? That they should be sprinkled, or have water poured upon them? By no means; but that our divine Legislator does not require them to be baptized. For, as our opposers themselves have proved,

---

* Cases to Recover Dissenters, vol. iii. p. 105, 106, edit. 3rd.

† Protestant Reconciler, p. 289. See also Bp. Stillingfleet's Irenicum, part ii. p. 345.

OF SPRINKLING INSTEAD OF IMMERSION. 279

we must insist that baptism is immersion. Consequently, were it evinced that infants cannot bear plunging, without the hazard of health and of life, it would only be a presumptive argument against their claim to the ordinance: and the greater the danger the stronger the presumption; for our opponents inform us, that a natural incapacity will always excuse.*—That it is better to omit a positive ordinance than to perform it contrary to divine appointment, Pædobaptists themselves assure us. Thus the famous Buddeus: " Persons who cannot drink wine, had better entirely abstain from the sacred supper than receive it under one species only."†——Deylingius: " It is better entirely to abstain from using the holy supper, than receive it contrary to the appointment of Christ."‡——Mr. Blake: " Omissions seem better to me, than a prohibited, or a disorderly proceeding, expressly against a command, or ordinance of Jesus Christ. The ark had better stayed where it was, than a new cart should have carried it in that disorder to the place appointed for it. Better that Saul and Uzziah had let sacrifice alone, than any to whom it did not appertain should have undertaken it.....I never saw sufficient reason given, that a man should break an express rule, rather than omit a duty of mere positive institution. Jeroboam must rather have no sacrifice, than that Dan and Bethel should be the place for it."§——Mr. Bradbury: " It is better, I think, to leave such a duty [as baptism] undone, than not to have it well done. God never expects it either from you or me, when he has thrown a bar in our way, that we should break it, or leap over it."‖ To which I may add, Better that the Israelites had entirely omitted circumcision while in the

---

* Morning Exercise against Popery, p. 771.
† Theolog. Moral. pars. iii. c. iii. § 77.
‡ De Prudent. Pastoral. pars iii. c. v. § 16.
§ Covenant Sealed, p. 255, 256.
‖ Duty and Doct. of Bap. p. 21.

wilderness, than to have circumcised a finger instead of the foreskin. So in the present case; better omit baptism entirely, than practise pouring or sprinkling.

But whether, in these colder climates, and in common cases, there be any reason to consider health as endangered by the practice of immersion, let Pædobaptists themselves declare. That learned physician, Sir John Floyer, gives his opinion on the subject without reserve, both in a theological and medical point of light. Among many other things, he says: "I do here appeal to you, [the dean and canons, residentiaries of the cathedral church of Litchfield,] as persons well versed in the ancient history, and canons, and ceremonies of the church of England; and therefore are sufficient witnesses of the matter of fact which I design to prove; viz. That immersion continued in the church of England till about the year sixteen hundred. And from hence I shall infer, That if God and the church thought that practice innocent for sixteen hundred years, it must be accounted an unreasonable nicety in this present age, to scruple either immersion or cold bathing, as dangerous practices. Had any prejudice usually happened to infants by the trine immersion, that custom could not have continued so long in this kingdom. We must always acknowledge, that He that made our bodies, would never command any practice prejudicial to our health; but, on the contrary, he best knows what will be most for the preservation of our health, and does frequently take great care both of our bodies and souls, in the same command."*—This eminent physician endeavours to show, as Dr. Wall observes, " by reasons taken from the nature of our bodies, from the rules of medicine, from modern experience, and from ancient history, that washing or dipping infants in cold water, is, generally speaking, not only safe, but very useful; and that though no such rite as baptism had been

---

* Hist of Cold Bathing, p. 11, 51.

instituted, yet reason and experience would have directed people to use cold bathing, both of themselves and their children; and that it has in all former ages so directed them. For—he shows, that all civilized nations, the Egyptians, Greeks, Romans, and so on, made frequent use of it, and gave great commendations of it; and that nature itself has taught this custom to many barbarous nations; the old Germans, Highlanders, Irish, Japanese, Tartars, and even the Samoiedes, who live in the coldest climate that is inhabited.... He prognosticates that the old modes in physic and religion will in time prevail, when people have had more experience in cold baths; and that the approbation of physicians would bring in the old use of immersion in baptism."*——Dr. Cheyne thus: " I cannot forbear recommending cold bathing; and I cannot sufficiently admire how it should ever have come into such disuse, especially among Christians, when commanded by the greatest Lawgiver that ever was, under the direction of God's Holy Spirit, to his chosen people, and perpetuated to us in the immersion at baptism, by the same Spirit; who with infinite wisdom in this, as in every thing else that regards the temporal and eternal felicity of his creatures, combines their duty with their happiness."†—To the decided opinion of these medical authors, relating to the salutary tendency of cold bathing, we may add the suffrage of that great philosopher, Lord Bacon, who speaks as follows: " It is strange that the use of bathing, as a part of diet, is left. With the Roman and Grecians it was as usual as eating or sleeping; and so it is amongst the Turks at this day."‡ ——Thus also Dr. Franklin: " Damp, but not wet linen, may possibly give colds; but no one catches cold by bathing, and no clothes can be wetter than water itself."§

* Hist. of Inf. Bap. part ii. chap. ix. p. 476, 477.
† Essay on Health, p. 100, 101.
‡ In Dr. Stennett's Answer to Dr. Addington, part i. p. 34.
§ Letters and Papers on Various Subjects, p. 460.

—To all which I will subjoin the following attestation of a nameless opponent: " A child may, with as much propriety, and commonly with equal safety to its health, be baptized by immersion as an adult."* See Chap. V. No. 7.

But supposing there were both difficulty and danger attending the performance of our Lord's positive command, Pædopabtists would still assure us, that we must submit without repining, and without hesitation. Thus, for example, Dr. Sherlock: " If an express law may be disobeyed, as often as men fancy they see reason to do what the law forbids, this overthrows the whole authority of making laws, and makes every subject a judge whether the laws of a sovereign prince should be obeyed or not. At this rate, he has the greatest authority who has the best reason; and since every man believes his own reason to be best, every man is the sovereign lord of his own actions. It is to be presumed, that no prince makes a law, but what he apprehends some reason for; and to oppose any man's private reason against a law, is to set up a private man's reason against the public reason of government: and yet it is much worse to oppose our reason against a divine law; which is to oppose the reason of creatures against the reason of God: unless we will say, that God makes laws without reason; and those who can believe that, may as easily imagine, that those laws which he makes without reason, should be obeyed without reason also; and then, to be sure, all their reasons cannot repeal a law, nor justify them in the breach of it. It becomes every creature to believe the will of God to be the highest reason; and therefore, when God has declared his will by an express law, while his law continues in force, it is an *impudent* thing to urge our reasons against the obligations of it; especially, when the matter of the law is such, [as it is in positive institutions] that whatever reasons may be pretended on

---

* Simple Truth, or A Plea for Infants, p. 2.

one side or other, it must be acknowledged to be wholly at the will and pleasure of the lawgiver which side he will choose.... That no reason or arguments can absolve us from our obedience to an express law till it be repealed, appears from this; that our obligation to obedience does not depend merely upon the *reason* of the law, but upon the *authority* of the lawgiver; and therefore, though the reason of the law should cease, yet while it is enforced by the same authority it obliges still."*— Puffendorff shows, and I suppose it is generally agreed, that laws do not oblige because they are *good*, but because the legislator has a *right* to command; and that no objection arises to the express words of a law, on account of the requisition seeming to be hard in some particular instances.†—Mr. Charnock says, " They must be evasions past understanding, that can hold water against a divine order.... God never gave power to any man to change his ordinances, or to dispense with them."‡——" Surely it is enough," says Abp. Secker, " that He is Lord and King of the whole earth, and that all his dealings with the works of his hands are just and reasonable. Our business is to obey, and trust him with the consequences."§——" No circumstances of prudence or conveniency," says Dr. Hunter, " can ever be with propriety urged as a dispensation with a clearly commanded duty.... Observe the delicacy, and the danger of admitting a latitude and a liberty in sacred things. In what concerns the conduct of human life, in our intercourse one with another as the citizens of this world, many things must be left to be governed by occasions and discretion; but in what relates to the immediate worship of God, and where the mind of the Lord has been clearly made known, to 'assume and

---

* Preservative against Popery, title vii. p. 21.
† Law of Nature and Nations, b. i. chap. vi. § 1, 17; b. v. chap. i. § 24.   ‡ Works, vol. ii. p. 763, 773, first edit.
§ Lectures on the Catechism, lect. ii.

exercise a dispensing power is criminal and hazardous. The tabernacle must be constructed, to the minutest pin and loop, according to the pattern delivered in the mount. If Uzzah presume to put forth his hand to support the tottering ark, it is at his peril. A holy and a jealous God will be served only by the persons, and in the maner which he himself has appointed.... When the great Jehovah condescends to become a legislator, the utmost extent of possibility lying open to his view, *provision is made from the beginning for every case that can happen.*"*—A Deistical writer having objected against circumcision, on account of the pain and danger attending it, Dr. Waterland replies: "The presumption which the author goes upon is, that he is wise enough to direct the counsels of heaven, and to pass an unerring judgment upon all the works and ways of God. It is a fact that God did require circumcision: and *who art thou that repliest against God?* Even Mr. Bayle might teach this author, *that when we are certain God does such or such a thing, it is blasphemy to say it is useless.* God has his own reasons. This writer might be certain of the fact, if any historical fact whatever can be made certain."†——"Surely," says Mr. Towgood, "the supreme Bishop and only Head of his church, well knew what institutions were most for its edification, and what ceremonies and rites would best promote the order and decency of its worship; and either by himself, or by his inspired apostles, has left a perfect plan of both. For any weak uninspired men, therefore, to rise up in after ages, and fancy they can improve the scheme of worship which Christ hath left; that they can add greatly to its beauty, its splendour and perfection, by some ceremonies of their own, is, to be sure, a rude invasion of Christ's throne, which every sober Christian ought highly to

---

* Sacred Biography, vol. iii. p. 93, 94, 362, 363, 435.
† Scripture Vindicated, part i. p. 63, 64.

detest."* — Remarkable, and quite in point, is the declaration of Dr. Owen: "That divine revelation is the only foundation, the only law, and the only rule of all religious worship that is pleasing to God, or accepted by him, is a maxim of the last importance in divinity. This maxim teaches, that every thing appointed by God in his worship, however absurd, or difficult, or unprofitable, it may seem to reason, is to be regarded and performed with the deepest reverence and submission, on account of that supreme authority which appointed and required it."† — To these testimonies I will add that of Bernard: "Non attendit verus obediens, QUALE sit quod præcipitur; hoc solo contentus QUIA PRÆCIPITUR."

Mr. Henry has observed, that circumcision was "a painful and bloody rite."‡ So the wife of Moses considered it; but yet Abraham and his posterity were bound to observe it, on the peril of Jehovah's keen displeasure. Concerning that sanguinary ceremony, Pædobaptists have spoken their minds very freely. M. Saurin, for instance, tells us: "The command of circumcision did, without doubt, frighten those who first received it; it was dangerous to grown persons in hot countries: but for an old man to receive the token of circumcision in so advanced an age, was in all appearance to be put out of the condition of seeing himself a father.... The pain which circumcision produced was extremely sensible, especially to grown people; this we may infer from the example of the Shechemites."§——Quenstedius: "Circumcision was a work full of pain, as Philo asserts; which appears by the history of the Shechemites, (Gen. xxxiv. 25.) Hence Zipporah, having circumcised her son, said to Moses, 'A bloody husband art thou to

---

* Dissent. Gent. Letters, lett. iii. p. 10, 11.
† Theologoumena, l. iv. c. iii. digress. iii. p. 326.
‡ Treatise on Bap. p. 12.
§ Dissertat. upon the Old Test. vol. i. p. 141, 143.

me'....As if she had said, This rite of thy nation forces me to shed blood, (Exod. iv. 25.)"*——Bucanus: "Circumcision could not be performed without putting the infant to most exquisite pain."†——Sir John Chardin: "I have heard from divers renegadoes in the East who had been circumcised, some at thirty, some at forty years of age, that the circumcision had occasioned them a great deal of pain, and that they were obliged to keep their bed upon it, at least twenty or twenty-two days."‡ ——Mr. Findlay: " Maimonides having said, *Circumcision was a rite of such a nature, that no person would perform it upon himself or his children, but on account of religion;* gives the reason of his judgment: *For it is not a slight hurt of the leg, or burning of the arm, but a thing* MOST HARSH *and* UNEASY....So likewise Philo speaks of circumcision, as an operation attended with grievous anguish....It may even seem to have been hazardous to life: for Lightfoot, in his Exercitations upon 1 Cor. vii. 19, produces some passages from Rabbinical writings, in which mention is made of a man whose brethren had died of circumcision. Nay, one from the Jerusalem Talmud itself, where R. Nathan says, 'There was a woman in Cesarea of Cappadocia, who had lost three sons successively by it.'"§ Now, can any thing like this be asserted with propriety concerning the baptismal immersion? Yet Abraham, who first received the command, readily obeyed; for he circumcised himself and his son Ishmael, together with all the males that were born in his house, or bought with his money, on the *very day* he received the divine order.‖

---

* Antiq. Bib. pars. i. c. iii. p. 269, 270.

† Theolog. Loc. loc. xlvi. § 31.

‡ In Mr. Harmer's Observations, vol. ii. p. 498, 499.

§ Vindicat. of the Sacred Books, p. 278, Note. Vid. Gussetii Comment. Ebr. sub rad. מול; and Scheuchzeri Physica Sacra, p. 93, 450. Aug. Vindilic. 1731.

‖ Gen. xvii. 23, 24.

In regard to the supposed *indecency* of plunging, about which a hideous outcry is often raised, as if that of itself were a sufficient conviction of our practice proceeding on a gross mistake, we answer with Mr. Baxter, in another case; " It is GOD's way, and then no inconvenience will disgrace it."* Some of the Romish casuists have told us, indeed, that it is no sin to break a divine law, if it be very difficult to keep; if we should be thought fools for observing it; or if the observance of it would be accounted ridiculous:† but we dare not place much dependence on their determination. Besides, whatever of this kind is objected by our brethren, would have applied with incomparably greater force against the ancient rite of circumcision. But let us hear what Pædobaptists themselves have said concerning this particular. Calvin: " This command, 'Ye shall circumcise the flesh of your foreskin,' might at first sight appear extremely absurd and ridiculous."‡——Witsius having described the painful rite, expresses himself thus: " On account of which ceremony, the Jews were contemptuously, and by way of reproach, called *Apellæ*, and *Recutiti*, because they wanted that pellicle or little skin. But it pleased God, to confound all carnal wisdom, and to try the faith and obedience of his people, to appoint a rite for the seal of his covenant, at which they might blush, and be almost ashamed of performing it: like as he founded our whole salvation in a fact, which seems no less shameful to the flesh, namely, the cross of Christ."§——Heideggerus: " God, according to his unsearchable wisdom, appointed a rite so much to be blushed at, to be a type of what was yet more shameful, namely, the cross of Christ."‖——Buddeus: " The

---

* Disputat. of Right to Sacram. p. 32.
† In Mr. Clarkson's Pract. Div. of Papists, p. 385, 386.
‡ In Gen. xvii. 11.
§ Œcon. Fœd. l. iv. c. viii. § 2. Ægyptiaca, l. iii. c. vi. § 4.
‖ Corp. Theolog. loc. xii. § 86.

rite of circumcision, considered in itself, was contemptible, and almost shameful."*—— F. Fabricius: "Circumcision, I confess, considered externally, that is, without a divine institution, and without the design and signification of that institution, might seem to be an exceedingly ridiculous and shameful rite."†—Nay, were not some other appointments of Jehovah, under the Jewish economy, such as the customs of our country, and present prevailing notions of the rational, the decent, and the useful, would lead many persons to consider as puerile, indelicate, and unprofitable? Such, if I mistake not, were several of those laws which related to ceremonial impurity; and yet the posterity of Abraham, of both sexes, were obliged to regard them with strict punctuality. It must, therefore, be at our peril to pronounce that *indecent* which God requires.‡—But why such complaints of indelicacy against the baptismal plunging, as performed in public assemblies? What immodesty is there in the solemn immersion of candidates for baptism, when properly clothed, any more than in the public and promiscuous bathing of both sexes, at Bath, Southampton, or any other place of a similar kind?§ As to the baptizing of persons that are not properly clothed, it has our cordial disapprobation.

Farther: For any of our opposers to imagine that pouring, or sprinkling, is *lawful*, without being *necessary;* or that it is necessary *now* and in *these* countries, though not so in the apostolic times and in the eastern parts, is unbecoming the character of any Protestant. Remarkable are the words, and forcible is the argument of Dr. Willet, when he says: " If it be not *necessary* to receive [the Lord's supper] in one kind, it is not to be done *at all*. For, either it is agreeable to the institution of

---

* Theolog. Dogmat. l. iv. c. i. § 15.
† Christologia, dissert. xi. § 16.
‡ Vid. Pfeifferi Dub. Vexat. p. 310. Lips. 1685.
§ See Dr. Stennett's Ans. to Dr. Addington, part i. p. 31, 32, Note.

Christ, to receive in one kind, or disagreeable. If it be agreeable and prescribed, it is of necessity to be observed: if it be not prescribed, it is of necessity not to be used at all.* This will apply, with all its force, to the subject before us.—The celebrated Montesquieu's reasoning will also apply in the present case. " It is in the nature of human laws, to be subject to all the accidents which can happen, and to vary in proportion as the will of man changes; on the contrary, by the nature of the laws of religion, they are never to vary. Human laws appoint for some good; those of religion for the best: good may have another object, because there are many kinds of good; but the best is but one: it cannot, therefore, change. We may change [human] laws, because they are reputed no more than good; but the institutions of religion are always supposed to be the best."†—Thus Mr. Arch. Hall: " All that concerns the glory of God, [and the honour of his church] is unerringly and unalterably settled in the word of God, which is 'not yea and nay.' It does not accommodate its doctrines to succeeding periods of time, nor to the changing tempers, humours, or fashions of place; like its divine Author, it is ' the same yesterday, and to-day, and for ever.' "‡

Latomus having represented the first Christian churches as in a rude, uncultivated state, while the people received both kinds at the Lord's table, but as omitting the wine in following ages, when they were better taught and more polished—Chamier exclaims, " Shall I be silent? or shall I refute him? For, verily, the absurdity is of such a magnitude, that every one may see it, and guard against its influence, without my assistance."§—One of our Dissenting Brethren also, when

---

* Synopsis Papismi, p. 643.   † Spirit of Laws,
b. xxvi. chap. ii.   ‡ Gospel Church, p. 52.
§ Panstrat. tom. iv. l. viii. c. x. § 24, 25.

engaged in the Popish controversy, says: " Let us consider; Things necessary—at one time, and not at another? Necessary in our days, and not so in the days of the apostles? Necessary to Christians of later ages, and not so to the primitive Christians? Sure, this cannot be true: I always thought that to be the Christian faith, which was once, and *at once* delivered to the saints, by Christ and his apostles."*—Again: For any to practise aspersion, on a presumption that it includes the whole essence of baptism, and to avoid supposed indecency, even while they acknowledge that immersion was appointed by Christ and used by the apostles; is to impeach the wisdom of our divine Lawgiver, by implicitly saying, that he did not well consider to what a pitch the refined and virtuous delicacy of his disciples would arise in our modern times. " As if," says Mr. Bingham, " Christ himself could not have foreseen any dangers that might happen, or given as prudent orders as the Pope concerning his own institution."† It is to proceed on the same foundation with the Council of Constance, when forbidding the use of the sacred cup to the people: for that prohibition was founded on a supposition, that communicants receive the entire body and blood of Christ, under the species of bread; and it was intended to preclude certain dangers and scandals, supposed to arise from the ancient practice.‡ The mem-

---

* Mr. Smyth's Serm. at Salters' Hall, on the Church of Rome's Claim of Infallib. p. 30, 31.

† Origines Eccles. b. xv. chap. iii. § 34.

‡ Vid. Caranzæ Sum. Concil. p. 389. Lovan. 1681. Venem. Hist. Eccles. tom. vi. p. 193. The learned Chemnitius, when exploding the futile reasons of Roman Catholics for withholding the cup from the people, among other things observes: " Their arguments reproach the Author of the sacrament himself, who instituted it so that it cannot be observed in the church without danger of scandal. ... The church is now become *exceedingly delicate.*" Exam. Concil. Trident. p. 308, 309.

bers of that council, it seems, discovered something as *dangerous* and as *offensive*, in administering both species at the holy table, as others do in the baptismal immersion; and they were equally unwilling to acknowledge that the substance of the sacred supper was at all impaired by their innovation. But would any authority on earth bear, without marks of displeasure, to be treated in a similar manner? We will suppose, for example, that a subject, or a servant, neglects the law of a magistrate, or the command of a master; we will farther suppose him called to account for his disobedience, and that in his own vindication he says, " I considered the precise performance of the order as of little importance, provided it were but *substantially* observed. I have, therefore, substituted something in its room, that will do quite as well, without being attended with such inconveniences as would have been inseparable from a punctual compliance." Would this be thought a modest excuse, or a just vindication? It may be answered, in that obsolete phrase of our biblical version, I trow not.

Once more: As the primitive immersion has been laid aside for pouring or sprinkling, upon a supposition of its being dangerous and indecent; so kneeling at the Lord's table has been substituted for a table gesture, and is defended under a fair pretext, that the latter is a bold and saucy posture. Dr. Nichols, when vindicating the practice of his own communion, and when showing that various of our festal customs are improper to be used at the holy table, has the following words. " Now since these customs at other feasts are not admitted here, why may not *sitting*, for the same reason, be changed, as too *bold* and *saucy* a posture, far from a becoming humility and modesty, when we are so immediately in the presence of God?"—To which Mr. Peirce replies: " Say you so? Do you think the posture the apostles used, with our Saviour's approbation, was too bold and saucy, or not sufficiently humble and modest? Do not you see whom you injure by these reproaches? Truly, not so much the Dissenters, as the apostles, and our Lord and Saviour Jesus Christ himself."*—So when Teriphyllius, a Cyprian bishop, having occasion before Spiridion to cite those words of our Lord, "Take up thy bed and walk," used the term σκιμποδα, as being in his opinion more elegant than the word κραββατον; Spiridion, with becoming resentment, replied, "Art thou better than He who said κραββατον, that thou shouldst be ashamed to use his words?"† The reader will apply these particulars to the case before us.

Reflect. V. From the preceding reflections it appears, I think, with superior evidence, that the sacred maxim, "I will have mercy and not sacrifice," must be misapplied when urged against us. For if it will apply so as to justify sprinkling in a cold country, when immersion was intended by our Lord, submitted to by him, commanded by him, and practised by the apostles, it would certainly have applied much more strongly in many cases under the former economy; for the maxim is founded in moral truth, which is the same in all ages and in every nation. That God loves mercy better than sacrifice, was always a fact, since man transgressed and ceremonial obedience was required: nor did our Lord give the least intimation, by his application of that important saying, of any thing contained in it being peculiar to gospel times. The Christian dispensation is indeed much superior to that of the ancient Hebrews: but that superiority is far from consisting in our having more liberty to neglect, alter, or transgress the divine appointments than they had. For as Mr. Reeves ob-

---

* Vindication of Dissenters, part iii. p. 204.
† Sozom. Hist. Eccles. l. i. c. i.

serves, "When God says that he 'will have mercy and not sacrifice,' it is not to be understod as if God would have any of his laws broken; but as our Saviour explains it, 'These ought ye to have done, and not to leave the other undone.'"*—Bellarmine, when vindicating a mutilated administration of the holy supper, argues upon a supposition of the gospel " church having a greater liberty than the church under the law; though she have no power to alter things of a moral, but only such as are of a positive nature."† How lamentable and how shameful, to think of eminent Protestants adopting the principle, and arguing upon it, in favour of pouring and sprinkling! For I am persuaded, that none of them ever considered the Jewish church as authorized by these words, "I will have mercy and not sacrifice," to alter any divine appointment. Shall Christians, then, make more free with divine authority than Jews, because they live under a better dispensation? far be it! That would represent the Holy One of God as the minister of sin—would be contrary to scripture and reason, to conscience and common sense. The disciples of Christ are as much obliged to regard the positive laws of the New Testament with strict punctuality, as the Jews were to observe their divine ritual contained in the books of Moses. Nay, our superior privileges are so many additional motives to perpetual obedience. Whenever any one therefore is inclined to substitute aspersion for plunging, on a supposition of the latter being burdensome or indelicate, upon the foundation of those condescending words, "I will have mercy and not sacrifice;" he should recollect that command of God to Abraham, "Ye shall circumcise the flesh of your foreskin;" and see how far the

---

* See Chap. I. No. 3.
† In Morning Exercise against Popery, p. 777.

gracious declaration would have applied there, before he ventures to alter a positive appointment of Christ on that ground.

Here also the argument used by Protestant Pædobaptists in opposition to immersion, is like that of the Papists against communion in both kinds. For thus we find Salmero argues: "If it had not been lawful from the beginning of the church to communicate under one species, either very many must have been entirely deprived of communion, or obliged to that which they could not perform; as is manifest with regard to those who have not plenty of wine, which is the case with many in the northern parts of the world; in respect of those who are abstemious, and of those also that are not able to drink wine without a nausea being excited.... Seeing, therefore, that the yoke of our Lord is easy, and his burden light, it should not be believed that he requires what is impossible, or that he obliges to communicate under both kinds."*—That Mr. Horsey took the hint from Salmero I dare not assert, nor do I believe; but be that as it may, he has learned to argue against plunging as a grievous hardship, and that from the same text which is pleaded by the Papal veteran for communion in one kind. For he says, "Christ's yoke is easy, and his burden light. His commandments are not grievous:"† and hence, among other things, he infers that immersion is not the proper mode of proceeding.

——This brings to remembrance a good-natured rule which Popish casuists have given for the interpretation of divine laws, with a view to relieve scrupulous consciences. The rule to which I advert, as produced by Mr. Clarkson, is this: Persons "must persuade themselves that they sin not, though they break the law in a

---

* Apud Chamierum, Panstrat. tom. iv. l. ix. c. iv. § 25.
† Inf. Bap. Defend. p. 20.

strict sense, if they observe it according to some *complaisant* interpretation. A benign sense is rather to be put upon any precept, than that which is strict; for the precepts of God and the church are not against that *pleasantness* which a scrupulous interpretation takes away." On which Mr. Clarkson makes the following remark: " That a person may be the better pleased, he may make the interpretation himself, and so make it as benign as he desires, and as favourable as his inclination and interest would have it. For though in other courts the interpretation belongs to him who makes the law, yet, according to their St. Antonius, in the court of conscience it belongs to every one to do it for his own practice."*

Were it allowable to prosecute the hint which some of these learned authors give, (No. 5, 7, 15;) that is for charity and necessity to erect a court of chancery, to sit in judgment on the equity of God's commands, and either mitigate their severity, or dispense with them, as we think proper; something indeed might then be done, that would effectually obviate those shivering apprehensions, and that painful modest feeling, which the word *baptize* might otherwise excite in the breasts of some. Nor would the relief afforded by such a court, be confined to the frighful idea of plunging; for it would extend its benign influence to every other case, in which our sovereign wills happen to clash with positive laws; because the uniform language of its decrees would be that of Peter to Christ, SPARE THYSELF. While however the validity of such a court of equity remains doubtful, it will be our wisdom when the Most High speaks, not to reason and object, but to adore and obey.

How strange it is that Protestant authors should

---

* Pract. Div. of Papists, p. 384, 385.

ever talk of dispensing with divine laws, or of mitigating their severity! Not much more detestable, though a little more blunt, is the well-known saying ascribed to Alphonso, "Si ego adfuissem, melius ordinassem." But let the learned Vossius assert, if he please, "That we are compelled ———" By what? not the appointment of Christ; not the design of the ordinance; nor yet by apostolic practice; but by something which he calls the law of *charity*, and of *necessity*, "to retain sprinkling in our churches:"* we had much rather adhere to that excellent maxim of Turrettin, "The appointment of God is to us the highest law, the supreme necessity."† With sincerity and zeal may we adopt the language of Dr. Cotton Mather, and say, "Let a precept be never so difficult to obey, or never so distasteful to flesh and blood, yet if I see it is God's command, my soul says, *It is good; let me obey it till I die.*" ‡ — Dr. Witherspoon has remarked, that, "when men will not conform their practice to the principles of pure and undefiled religion, they scarce ever fail to endeavour to accommodate religion to their own practice." §—Mr. Henry also has justly observed, that "in sacraments, where there is appointed something of an outward sign, the inventions of men have been too fruitful of additions, [and of alterations too,] for which they have pleaded a great deal of *decency* and significancy; while the ordinance itself hath been thereby miserably obscured and corrupted." ‖ —To which I will add the following remark of Dr. Oswald: "To take advantage of dark surmises, or doubtful reasoning, to elude obligations of any kind, is always looked upon as an indication of a dishonest heart." ¶

---

* Disputat. de Bap. disp. i. § 9.
† Institut. Theolog. loc. xix. quæst. xiv. § 14.
‡ Life, by Dr. Jennings, p. 118. § Treatise on Regeneration, p. 178. ‖ Treatise on Baptism, p. 153.
¶ Appeal to Common Sense, p. 21.

Reflect. VI. Suffer me now to reason and remonstrate in the language of Mr. Charnock; after which I will conclude this part of my subject with the ingenuous confession of a learned foreigner, and the declaration of Dr. Wall. " The wisdom of God is affronted and invaded," says the famous Charnock, " by introducing new rules and modes of worship, different from divine institutions. Is not this a manifest reflection on this perfection of God, as though he had not been wise enough to provide for his own honour, and model his own service; but stood in need of our directions, and the capricios of our brains? Some have observed, that it is a greater sin, in worship, to *do* what we should not, than to *omit* what we should perform. The one seems to be out of *weakness*, because of the high exactness of the law; and the other out of *impudence*, accusing the wisdom of God of imperfection, and controlling it in its institutions.—Whence should this proceed, but from a partial atheism, and a mean conceit of the divine wisdom? As though God had not understanding enough to prescribe the form of his own worship; and not wisdom enough to support it, without the crutches of human prudence.... The laws of God, who is *summa ratio*, are purely founded upon the truest reason, though every one of them may not be so clear to us. Therefore, they that make [any] alteration in his precepts, either dogmatically or practically, control his wisdom and charge him with folly..... Hence it is that sinners are called *fools* in scripture. It is certainly inexcusable folly, to contradict undeniable and infallible wisdom. If infinite prudence hath framed the law, why is not every part of it observed? If it were not made with the best wisdom, why is any thing of it observed?"*

---

* Works, vol. i. p. 401. On Man's Enmity to God, p. 112, 113.

The ingenuous confession to which I refer, is that of M. de la Roque, and it is as follows. " The greatest part of them [the Protestants] hitherto baptize only by sprinkling: but it is certainly an abuse; and this practice which they have retained from the Romish church, without a due examination of it, as well as many other things which they still retain, renders their baptism very defective. It corrupts both the institution and ancient usage of it, and the relation it ought to have to faith, repentance, and regeneration. Monsieur Bossuet's remark, that dipping was in use for thirteen hundred years, deserves our serious consideration, and our acknowledgment thereupon, that we have not sufficiently examined all that we have retained from the Romish church; that seeing her most learned prelates now inform us, that it was SHE who first abolished a usage authorized by so many strong reasons, and by so many ages, that she has done very ill on this occasion, and that we are obliged to return to the ancient practice of the church, and to the institution of Jesus Christ. I do not say, that baptism by aspersion is null; that is not my opinion: but it must be confessed, if sprinkling destroys not the substance of baptism, yet it alters it, and in some sort corrupts it; it is a defect which spoils its lawful form."*

The declaration of Dr. Wall is as follows: " Since the time that dipping of infants has been generally left off, many learned men in several countries have endeavoured to retrieve the use of it; but more in England than any where else in proportion." Then, after having mentioned Sotus, Mr. Mede, Bp. Taylor, Sir Norton Knatchbull, Dr. Towerson, and Dr. Whitby, as being all desirous of having immersion restored to common use, he adds: " These, and possibly many more, have openly declared their thoughts concerning the present

---

* In Mr. Stennett's answer to Mr. Russen, p. 185, 186.

custom. And abundance of others have so largely and industriously proved that a total immersion was, as Dr. Cave says, 'the almost constant and universal custom of the primitive times,' that they have sufficiently intimated their inclinations to be for it now. So that no man in this nation, who is dissatisfied with the other way, or does wish, or is but willing, that his child should be baptized by dipping, need in the least to doubt, but that any minister in this church would, according to the present direction of the rubric, readily comply with his desire, and, as Mr. Walker says, be glad of it."*

---

* Hist. Inf. Bap. part ii. chap. ix. p. 473—476.—The desire of many learned men in the church of England to have immersion restored, reminds me of another particular in that establishment; concerning which Mr. Bingham, who was a true son of the church, speaks as follows:

"The church of England [in her Office for Ash-Wednesday] has for *two hundred years wished* for the restoration of this [primitive] discipline, and yet it is but an ineffective wish: for nothing is done towards introducing it, but rather things are gone backward, and there is less discipline for these last sixty years, since the times of the unhappy confusions, than there was before." Origines Eccles. b. xv. chap. ix. § 8.

Thus Mr. Hervey, when adverting to the subject of discipline, as practised in his own church: "The grosser kind of simony seems to be practised by a certain court, styled *spiritual* or *ecclesiastical;* which thunders out excommunications and curses, debars poor creatures from religious privileges, and causes them to be 'buried with the burial of an ass;' unless they pacify their pious indignation by a little filthy lucre."

Again: "This is the language of that same spiritual judicature: 'If thou wilt lug out a few crowns or guineas from thy purse, all shall be well; heaven shall smile, and the church open her arms. Whereas, if thou art refractory in this particular; and unwilling, or unable, to comply with our pecuniary demands; thou art cut off from the means of grace. Thou shalt no longer hear that word of the gospel, by which the spirit of faith cometh. Nor any more be partaker of that sacramental ordinance, which is a sign and seal of spiritual benefits.'"

Again: "Is not this a most infamous traffic, whereby sacred

things are bought and sold ? In the present state of affairs, what can be a nearer approach to the sin of the mercenary magician? What can be a more indelible blot on the purity and discipline of any church?

> ' Pudet hæc opprobria nobis
> Et dici potuisse, et non potuisse refelli.'"

See Theron and Aspasio.

Mr. Bisset, thus : "I have returned several of my charge, for scandalous immoralities, to the spiritual court; but nothing was done, only some money was squeezed out of them." Plain English, p. 28. Dublin, 1705.

An observation of Dr. Owen, respecting pluralities, will here apply. "An evil this, like that of mathematical prognostications at Rome, always condemned, and always retained." Gospel Church and its Government, p. 107.

PART II.

THE SUBJECTS

OF

BAPTISM.

CHAPTER I.

Neither Express Precept, nor Plain Example, for Pædobaptism, in the New Testament.

Bp. BURNET.—" There is no express precept, or rule, given in the New Testament for baptism of infants." Exposit. of Thirty-nine Articles, art. xxvii.

2. Dr. Wall.—" Among all the persons that are recorded as baptized by the apostles, there is no express mention of any infant.... There is no express mention indeed of any children baptized by him," i. e. John the Baptist. Hist. Inf. Bap. Introduct. p. 1, 55.

3. Mr. Fuller.—" We do freely confess, that there is neither express precept, nor precedent, in the New Testament, for the baptizing of infants.... There were many things which Jesus did, which are not written; among which, for aught appears to the contrary, the baptizing of these infants [Luke xviii. 15, 16, 17,] might be one of them." Infant's Advocate, p. 71, 150.

4. Mr. Marshall.—" I grant, that in so many words it is not found in the New Testament, that they should be baptized; no express example where children were baptized.... Express command there is, that they [the apostles] should teach the heathen, and the Jews, and make them disciples, and then baptize them.... It is said indeed that they taught and baptized, and no express mention of any other.... Both John and Christ's disciples and apostles did teach before they baptized, because then no other were capable of baptism." In Mr. Tombes's Examen, p. 110, 161; and Antipædobaptism, part ii. p. 84.

5. Luther.—" It cannot he proved by the sacred scripture that infant baptism was instituted by Christ,

or begun by the first Christians after the apostles." In A. R.'s Vanity of Inf. Bap. part ii. p. 8.

6. Mr. Baxter.—" If there can be no example given in scripture, of any one that was baptized without the profession of a saving faith, nor any precept for so doing, then must we not baptize any without it. But the antecedent is true; therefore so is the consequent ....In a word, I know of no one word in scripture, that giveth us the least intimation that ever man was baptized without the profession of a saving faith, or that giveth the least encouragement to baptize any upon another's faith." Disputat. of Right to Sac. p. 149, 151.

7. Mr. Obad. Wills.—" Christ did many things that were not recorded, and so did the apostles; whereof this was one, for aught we know, the baptizing infants.... Calvin, in his fourth book of Institutes, chap. xvi. confesseth, that it is no where expressly mentioned by the evangelists, that any one child was by the apostles baptized." To the same purpose are Staphilus, Melancthon, and Zuinglius quoted. Inf. Bap. Asserted and Vindicated, part ii. p. 37, 40, 199, 200.

8. Vitringa.—" That some in the ancient church long ago doubted, and that others now doubt, whether infants ought to be baptized, proceeds principally, I think, from hence; It is not related as a fact, in the Gospels, and in the Acts of the primitive church, that infants were baptized by Christ, or by the apostles." Observat. Sac. l. ii. c. vi. § 2.

9. Mr. Samuel Palmer.—" There is nothing in the words of the institution, nor in any after accounts of the administration of this rite, respecting the baptism of infants; there is not a single precept for, nor example of, this practice through the whole New Testament." Answer to Dr. Priestley's Address on the Lord's Sup. p.7.

10. Stapferus.—" There is not any express command in the holy scripture concerning the baptism of infants." Theolog. Polem. cap. iii. § 1647.

11. Limborch.—" There is no express command for it in scripture; nay, all those passages wherein baptism is commanded, do immediately relate to adult persons, since they are ordered to be instructed, and faith is prerequisite as a necessary qualification, which [things] are peculiar to the adult.... There is no instance that can be produced, from whence it may indisputably be inferred, that any child was baptized by the apostles.... The necessity of Pædobaptism was never asserted by any council before that of Carthage, held in the year four hundred and eighteen.... We own that there is no precept, nor undoubted instance, in scripture, of infant baptism; but this is not enough to render it unlawful." Complete Syst. Div. b. v. chap. xxii. sect. ii.

12. M. De la Roque.—" As to the baptism of infants, I confess there is nothing formal and express in the gospel, to justify the necessity of it; and the passages that are produced, do at most only prove that it is permitted, or rather, that it is not forbidden to baptize them. If all the Anabaptists only held to this, without condemning this practice as criminal and sacrilegious, they would have reason on their side, and would say nothing but what is founded on such principles as are common to all Protestants." In Mr. Stennett's Answer to Mr. Russen, p. 188.

13. Magdeburg Centuriators.—" Examples prove that adults, both Jews and Gentiles, were baptized. Concerning the baptism of infants, there are indeed no examples of which we read." Cent. i. l. ii. c. vi. p. 381.

14. Erasmus.—" Paul does not seem in Rom. v. 14, to treat about infants.... It was not yet the custom for infants to be baptized." Annotat. ad Rom. v. 14. Bas. 1534.

15. Mr. Leigh.—" The baptism of infants may be named a *tradition*, because it is not expressly delivered in scripture that the apostles did baptize infants, nor any express precept there found that they should so do;

yet is not this so received by bare and naked tradition, but that we find the scripture to deliver unto us the ground of it." Body of Div. b. i. chap. viii. p. 93, 94.

16. Dr. Freeman.—" The traditions of the whole Catholic church—confirm us in many of our doctrines; which, though they may be gathered out of scripture, yet are not laid down there in so many words: such as infant baptism, and of episcopal authority above presbyters." Preservative against Popery, title iii. p. 19.

17. Mr. T. Boston.—" It is plain that he [Peter, in Acts ii. 38,] requires their repentance antecedently to baptism, as necessary to qualify them for the right and due reception thereof. And there is no example of baptism recorded in the scriptures, where any were baptized but such as appeared to have a saving interest in Christ." Works, p. 384.

18. Mr. Cawdrey.—" The scriptures are not clear, that infant baptism was an apostolical practice.... We have not in scripture either precept or example of children baptized." In Mr. Crosby's Hist. of Bap. vol. iii. pref. p. 53. Mr. Tombes's Antipædobaptism, part ii. p. 84.

19. Dr. Field.—" The baptism of infants—is therefore named a *tradition,* because it is not expressly delivered in scripture, that the apostles did baptize infants; nor any express precept there found, that they should do so." On the Church, p. 375.

20. Bp. Prideaux.—" Pædobaptism, and the change of the Jewish sabbath into the Lord's day, rest on no other divine right than Episcopacy." Fascicul. Controvers. loc. iv. sect. iii. p. 210.

21. Bp. Sanderson.—" The baptism of infants, and the sprinkling of water in baptism, instead of immersing the whole body, must be exterminated from the church —according to their principle; i.e. that nothing can be lawfully performed, much less required, in the affairs of religion, which is not either commanded by God in the

scripture, or at least recommended by a laudable example." De Obligat. Conscient. prælect. iv. § 17, 18.

22. Bp. Stillingfleet.—"Whether baptism shall be administered to infants, or no, is not set down in express words, but left to be gathered by analogy and consequences." Irenicum, part ii. chap. iv. p. 178.

23. Dr. Towerson.—"That which seems to stick much with the adversaries of infant baptism, and is accordingly urged at all times against the friends or asserters of it, is, the want of an express command, or direction, for the administering of baptism to them. Which objection seems to be the more reasonable, because baptism, as well as other sacraments, receiving all its force from institution, they may seem to have no right to, or benefit by it, who appear not by the institution of that sacrament to be entitled to it; but rather, by the qualifications it requires, to be excluded from it." Of the Sacram. of Bap. part xi. p. 349, 350.

24. Mr. Walker.—"Where authority from the scripture fails, there the custom of the church is to be held as a law.... It doth not follow, that our Saviour gave no precept for the baptizing of infants, because no such precept is particularly expressed in the scripture; for our Saviour spake many things to his disciples concerning the kingdom of God, both before his passion and also after his resurrection, which are not written in the scriptures; and who can say, but that among those many *unwritten* sayings of his, there might be an express precept for infant baptism?"[*] Modest Plea for Inf. Bap. p. 221, 368.

25. Anonymous.—"As to the seed of the church, the children of Christians, at what age, under what circumstances, in what mode, or whether they were baptized at all, are particulars the New Testament does not expressly mention.... We may safely conclude,

---

[*] Just so Andradius, in defence of Popish traditions. Vid. Chemnitii Exam. Concil. Trident. p. 21.

whatever the apostle Paul might do, who baptized households among the Gentiles, yet *the other apostles, and the church at Jerusalem* DID NOT BAPTIZE INFANTS; for this reason, because they still continued to circumcise,—which [circumcision] initiated into the law of Moses; and they could not initiate their infants both into Moses and into Christ. But after the destruction of Jerusalem, which evidently proved the Mosaic economy to be at an end, circumcision subsided by degrees, and infant baptism took place of it. Thus infant baptism came into the church, in the very manner our Lord foretold his kingdom should come, without observation; neither lo here, nor there." Simple Truth, p. 5, 21.

26. Heideggerus.—"Though there be neither express precept, nor example, for infant baptism, yet that it is implicitly contained in the scripture, sufficiently appears from what we have said. Nor was it necessary that it should be expressly enjoined. Nay, it is quite sufficient that it was not forbidden by Christ." Corp. Theolog. loc. xxv. § 55.

27. Witsius.—"We do not indeed deny that there is no express and special command of God, or of Christ, concerning infant baptism; yet there are general commands, from which a particular one is deduced." Œcon. l. iv. c. xvi. § 41.

28. Anonymous.—"I do not remember any passage in the New Testament, which says expressly, that infants should be baptized; and, as I am informed by better judges, the evidences for this practice from antiquity, though very early, do not fully come up to the times of the apostles." In Mr. Richards's Hist. of Antichrist, p. 19.

29. Œcolampadius. —" No passage in the holy scripture has occurred to our observation as yet, which, as far as the slenderness of our capacity can discern, should persuade us to profess Pædobaptism." Apud Schyn Hist. Mennonit. p. 168, 169.

30. Cellarius.—" Infant baptism *is* neither commanded in the sacred scripture, nor is it confirmed by apostolic examples." Apud Schyn, ut supra.

31. Staphilus.—" It is not expressed in holy scripture, that young children should be baptized." In T. Lawson's Baptismalogia, p. 115.—N. B. Mr. Lawson, who was one of the people called Quakers, has produced Zuinglius and Melancthon, as expressing themselves to the same effect. He also tells us the Oxford divines, in a convocation held one thousand six hundred and forty-seven, acknowledged, " that without the consentaneous judgment of the universal church, they should be at a loss, when they are called upon for proof, in the point of infant baptism." Ut supra, p. 113, 115, 116. Vid. Chemnitium, Exam. Concil. Trident. p. 69. Chamierum, Panstrat. tom. i. l. ix. c. x. § 40.

REFLECTIONS.

Reflect. I. As these Pædobaptists unanimously agree that there is neither express precept, nor plain example for infant baptism in the New Testament; so it appears from one or another of them, that the passages usually produced for it only prove that it is permitted, or not forbidden, No. 12;—that all those places where baptism is commanded regard none but adults No. 11; —that Pædobaptism must be supported by analogy and illation, No. 22, 27;—that there is no instance from which it may be incontrovertibly inferred, that any child was baptized by the apostles, No. 11;—that infant baptism rests on the same foundation as diocesan Episcopacy, No. 20;—that Pædobaptism is properly denominated a tradition, No. 15, 16;—that though Paul baptized certain households, it is doubtful whether he ever practised Pædobaptism; and very certain that the other apostles did not baptize infants; because a supposition of their so doing would infer a gross absurdity, No. 14, 25;—that *unwritten* truth (or weak surmise) and tradition, are a succedaneum for express precept and plain example, No. 3, 7, 24, 31; and that persons have need of great penetration to find a warrant in scripture for the avowal of Pædobaptism, No. 29.

Such concessions are our opponents obliged to make, in reference to this affair! With propriety, therefore, I may here demand and remonstrate, in the remarkable words of Mr. Baxter: "What man dare go in a way which hath neither precept nor example to warrant it, from a way that hath a full current of both? .... Who knows what will please God but himself? And hath he not *told* us what he expecteth from us? Can that be *obedience* which hath no *command* for it? Is not this to supererogate, and to be righteous overmuch? Is it not also to accuse God's ordinances of insufficiency, as well as his word, as if they were not sufficient either to please him, or help our own graces? O the pride of man's heart, that instead of being a law-obeyer, will be a law-maker; and instead of being true worshippers, they will be worship-makers!.... For my part, I will not fear that God will be angry with me for doing no more than he hath *commanded* me, and for sticking close to the rule of his word in matter of worship; but I should tremble to add or diminish."*

Let us now see what our impartial friends the Quakers have to say on this part of the subject.

1. Robert Barclay.—" As to the baptism of infants, it is a mere human tradition, for which neither precept nor practice is to be found in all the scripture." Apology, proposition xii.

2. Samuel Fothergill.—" I do not find in any part of the holy scripture, either precept or example for the practice of sprinkling infants.... If any such proof, or plain declaration, could be produced in support of sprinkling infants, it would have been long ere now produced,

---

* Plain Scrip. Proof, p. 24, 303.

by those who have continued the practice of that ceremony. The present advocates for it would not be reduced to the necessity of *presumptive* arguments, and *uncertain consequences;* such as the supposition, that there were children in the household of Lydia, the gaoler of Philppi, and Stephanas....The sprinkling of infants is utterly destitute of any proof of divine institution." Remarks on an Address, p. 5, 6, 30.

3. Joseph Phipps.—" The practice of sprinkling infants under the name of baptism, hath neither precept nor precedent in the New Testament. For want of real instances, *mere suppositions* are offered in support of it. Because it is said, in the case of Lydia, that 'she was baptized and her household;' and by the apostle, 'I baptized also the household of Stephanas;' it is supposed there might be infants, or little children, in those households: from whence it is inferred such were baptized." Dissertations on Bap. and Communion, p. 30.

4. Elizabeth Bathurst.—" Infant baptism, or sprinkling infants, this they [the Quakers] utterly deny, as a thing by men imposed, and never by God or Christ instituted; neither is there any scripture precept or precedent for it. Indeed how should there, since it was not taken up, nor innovated for above two hundred years after Christ died?....Yet we grant the baptism of those that were adult, or come to age, and had faith to entitle them to it. This was the baptism of John." Testimony and Writings, p. 44, 45, edit. 4th.

5. Thomas Lawson.—" Sprinkling of infants is a case unprecedented in the primitive church; an irreptitious custom, sprung up in the night of apostasy, after the falling away from the primitive order....Such as rhantize, or sprinkle infants, have no command from Christ, nor example among the apostles, nor the first primitive Christians for so doing." Baptismalogia, p. 69, 117.

6. Richard Claridge.—"As for the baptism of infants, it ought not to be retained in the church, there being neither precept nor example for it in the scripture." Life and Posthumous Works, p. 179.

7. George Whitehead.—"As to dipping or sprinkling infants, or young children, we find no precept or precedent in holy scripture for the practice thereof.... What great hypocrisy and insincerity are these persons justly chargeable with, in the sight of God, angels, and men, in their not practising that baptism they have pleaded for from the practice of the apostles! but instead thereof rhantism, or sprinkling of infants, to make them thereby members of Christ, and of his church militant, who are neither capable of teaching, nor of confession of faith. If these men believe what they themselves write, argue, and urge on this subject, for the necessity of baptizing only believers when taught, by what authority do they in practice so easily dispense with this, and evade and change it into their rhantizing, or sprinkling and crossing infants on the face; and yet so demurely profess and tell the people, the holy scripture is their *only rule of faith and practice?* when they can, contrary to their own demure pretences, practise unscriptural traditions, both human and Popish." The Rector Examined, p. 23. Truth Prevalent, p. 125, 126.

8. William Penn.—There is "not one text of scripture to prove that sprinkling in the face was the water baptism, or that children were the subjects of water baptism, in the first times." Defence of Gospel Truths, against the Bishop of Cork, p. 82.

Such being the concessions of our learned opposers, and such the harmonious testimony of impartial Friends, I am reminded of the following apostolic declarations, which may be here applied; "We gave no such COMMANDMENT—We have no such CUSTOM."* The apostles, it seems, gave no command for the baptizing of in-

---

* Acts xv. 24; 1 Cor. xi. 16.

fants; and therefore a precept cannot be found. They had no such custom, and therefore an example of it is not recorded in the history of their practice.

Reflect. II. As it is evident by the confession of our opposers, that nothing explicit is contained in the New Testament relating to infant baptism; and as Pædobaptists have taught us, that positive institutions cannot be inferred by remote consequences from general principles, but require an express appointment;* it might have been expected, had consistency prevailed, that Pædobaptism would have made as little appearance in the practice of Protestants, as it does in the writings of the apostles. For it is generally maintained by the Reformed, when contending with Papists; and by Nonconformists, when disputing with English Episcopalians; that it is the safest way to take things as we find them in the records of inspiration, and to perform nothing, as a part of religious worship, which is not commanded or exemplified in the New Testament.—Thus Mr. Alsop, for instance: " I never liked either the addition of officers to those Christ has commanded to govern his church, nor the addition of canons to those by which he has appointed his church to be governed : I always thought it safest, to leave the doctrine, worship, and government of Christ as we found them. We may be chidden for adding, or subtracting, but never for being no wiser than the gospel: and when we have done our best, and chopped and changed, we shall hardly ever make better than those Christ made for us."†——Mr. Polhill: "The pattern of Christ and the apostles is more to me than all the human wisdom in the world."‡ ——Mr. White: "As Protestants, we have only to bear the Bible in our hands; to expatiate on its importance and its truth; to teach what it reveals with sincerity;

---

* See Part I. Chap. I. No. 4, 8, 12, 13, 20, Reflect. II. III.
† Antisozzo, p. 156, 157.   ‡ Discourse on Schism, p. 74.

and to enforce what it commands with earnestness."*
——Dr. Owen: "It is not safe for us to venture on duties not exemplified [in the scripture;] nor *can any instance* of a necessary duty be given, of whose performance we have not an example in the scripture.... It [an enthusiastic affection for Christ] is no way directed, warranted, approved by any command, promise, or rule of the scripture. As it is without precedent, so it is without precept; and hereby, whether we will or no, all our graces and duties must be tried, as unto any acceptation with God. Whatever pretends to exceed the direction of the word, may be safely rejected; cannot safely be admitted."†—Now if these declarations be founded in truth, what becomes of Pædobaptism? It must be consigned over to that obscurity in which it was left by the sacred writers.

Reflect. III. That the testimony of scripture, in favour of any religious tenet or practice, is of great importance, none but Infidels will deny: for even the Papists themselves, notwithstanding their two great resources of confidence, tradition and infallibility, are never willing to waive the advantage of pleading it in their own defence, if it can be done with the least appearance of reason. That the sacred writings are our only rule of doctrine and worship, was the grand principle of the Reformation; and happy would it have been, if each concerned in that excellent work had uniformly acted under its influence. On this foundation, and in many cases, Protestant writers have successfully opposed the Papal system. Nor is any thing more frequent with them, when engaged in that controversy, than a recurrence to this capital principle, and an adoption of Chillingworth's maxim: THE BIBLE ONLY IS THE RELIGION OF PROTESTANTS. Here, that excellent saying of Basil is pleaded: "It is a manifest mistake, in regard

---

* Sermons before the University, p. 472.
† On the Person of Christ, p. 134, 170.

to faith, and a clear evidence of pride, either to reject any of those things which the scripture contains; or to introduce any thing that is not written in the sacred page."*
That of Ambrose also is held in esteem; "Where the scripture is silent, who shall speak?" †—Nor is Tertullian's maxim in less repute: "The scripture forbids what it does not mention." ‡—Here they tell us, that "we ought to respect the silence of the scripture;" § and they lay it down as a general rule, that "no one need be ashamed of not knowing what God has not revealed;" because, "he that would go farther, gives up his wisdom and endangers his safety." ‖ They farther assure us, " that divine revelation is the only foundation, the only rule, and the only law, of all religious worship that is pleasing to God, or accepted by him;" and that, "when once a person maintains it allowable to pass over the limits of the divine command, there is nothing to hinder him from running the most extravagant lengths." ¶ They assure us "that will-worship was always condemned of God, and that it is profane to present to God what he does not require, or to perform worship which he did not appoint." **—They tell us that "we ought not to worship God with any other external worship, than what himself hath commanded and appointed us in his holy word." ††
—" The scripture," say they, "hath set us our bounds for worship, to which we must not add, and from which we ought not to diminish; for whosoever doth either the

---

* In Bp. Taylor's Liberty of Prophesying, sect. v. No. xi. p. 97.
† In Morning Exercise against Popery, p. 214.
‡ De Monog. cap. iv.
§ Mr. Claude's Essay on Comp. of a Serm. vol. i. p. 316.
‖ Dr. Ellis's Knowledge of Divine Things from Revelation, p. 434, edit. 2nd.
¶ Dr. Owen's Theologoumena, l. iv. digress. iii. § 8; l. v. c. xv. § 2. See also his Exposit. of Heb. vol. ii. p. 68, 133.
** Christ. Schotanus, apud Lomeierum, De Vet. Gent. Lust. cap. xiv.   †† Bp. Hopkins's Works, p. 107.

one or the other, must needs accuse the rule either of defect in things necessary, or of superfluity in things unnecessary: which is a high affront to the wisdom of God, who, as he is the object, so is he the prescriber of that worship which he will accept and reward."*—They insist, that he who "shall appoint with what God shall be worshipped, must appoint what that is by which he shall be pleased;" that "by nothing can he be worshipped, but by what himself hath declared that he is well pleased with;" that "to worship God, is an act of obedience and of duty, and therefore must suppose a commandment—and is not of our choice, save only that we must choose to obey;" consequently, that " he that says God is rightly worshipped, by an act or ceremony, concerning which himself hath no way expressed his pleasure, is superstitious, or a will-worshipper." † They "admire that ever mortal man should dare, in God's worship, to meddle any farther than the Lord himself hath commanded." ‡ They tell us, that "nothing is lawful in the worship of God, but what we have precept or precedent for; which, whoso denies, opens a door to all idolatry and superstition, and will-worship in the world." § They say, " From the words of our Saviour, 'In vain do they worship me, teaching for doctrines, (viz. about worship,) the commandments of men,' we clearly demonstrate that it is unlawful to worship God with any rites, however indifferent in themselves, if they are not prescribed by God." ‖ They entreat us "to consider, that what God hath thought needless to appoint, men ought not to make, or pretend to be necessary or important, or even useful. What he commands not in his worship, he virtually forbids." ¶

---

* Bp. Hopkins's Works, p. 107.
† Bp. Taylor's Ductor. Dub. b. ii. chap. iii. p. 347, 348.
‡ Mr. Marshal, in Jerubbaal, p. 484.
§ Mr. Collings, in Jerubbaal, p. 487.
‖ Mr. Peirce's Vindicat. of Dissenters, part i. p. 16.
¶ Dr. Mayo's Apology and Shield, p. 44.

They inform us, that "a practice [in religious worship] not being enjoined, is forbidden;—being disallowed, is reprobated;"* that, "the declared will of God being the most certain and happy rule of man's practice, especially in those duties which have no foundation, save in divine revelation; it is the greatest arrogance and affront to the wisdom and will of our Lawgiver, to contradict him therein;"† that "to prescribe any thing [in religious worship] which God hath not commanded, though he hath not forbidden it, is such an invasion of his prerogative, that he hath punished it by a remarkable judgment, (Lev. x. 1;)"‡ that "in religious matters, and especially in the worship of God, it is not only sinful to go *contra statutum*, but to go *supra statutum*;" or that, "to speak home in the case, in religious matters, acting *supra statutum*, is all one with acting *contra statutum*: therein God's not requiring being equivalent to forbidding; and doing more than he commandeth, to doing contrary to it."§ They insist, that "works not required by the law, are no less an abomination to God, than sins against the law." ‖ "To serve God," they assure us, "is to do every thing under this contemplation, that what we do is the will of God. His will must be not only the rule of what we do, but the very reason why we do it; else our doings are not his servings."¶ They tell us, " that the silence of scripture" is a sufficient ground of rejecting the sign of the cross, exorcism, and similar appendages of baptism in the church of Rome; because those things "not being written in the sacred volume, are there-

---

* Bp. Hurd's Introduct. to Stud. of Proph. p. 393, edit. 1st.
† Morning Exercise against Popery, p. 760.
‡ Mr. Charnock On Man's Enmity to God, p. 97.
§ Vanity of Human Inventions, p. 23, 24.
‖ Dr. Owen on Justification, chap. xiv. p. 494.
¶ Mr. Caryl on Job. xxxvi. 11.

fore condemned."*—Once more: They commend the renowned Waldenses, for declaring and maintaining, some hundreds of years ago, that "nothing is to be admitted in religion but what only is commanded in the word of God." †

Reflect. IV. Such being the grounds of those arguments, and the tenour of that reasoning, which are used against the unscriptural ceremonies of the Romish church; what should hinder a fair application of the same principles and the same arguments to Pædobaptism, if there be neither precept nor precedent for it in the sacred volume? No Protestant, I presume, will question the propriety of Chillingworth's remark, or the justness of that inference to which it leads, when, reasoning against the Papal infallibility, he says: "That our Saviour designed the bishop of Rome to this office, and yet would not say so, nor cause it to be written—*ad Rei memoriam*—by any of the evangelists or apostles, so much as *once*; but leave it to be drawn out of uncertain principles, by thirteen or fourteen more uncertain consequences; he that can believe it, let him." ‡—Is then the infallibility of the Roman pontiff, so strange and so incredible to Protestants, because it is not once mentioned by Christ or his apostles; and shall any of our Brethren charge us with gross ignorance or strong prejudice, for opposing infant baptism, while they themselves allow that it is not so much as once expressly mentioned in all the New Testament? Were the Papal infallibility a fact, it must be considered as a positive grant of our divine Lord, resulting merely from his own sovereign pleasure; and, consequently, it would be impossible for us to know any thing about it farther than revealed in the Bible. And is not Pædobaptism, in this respect, a similar case? May not

---

* Mastricht Theolog. l. vii. c. iv. § 19. Turret. Institut. Theolog. loc. xix. quæst. xviii. § 3, 4. † In Jerubbal, p. 162.

‡ Relig. of Protest. part i. chap. ii. § 22.

we therefore, with a little alteration, adopt the language of Mr. Chillingworth? Yes, we will thus take up his idea: That our Saviour designed infants should be baptized, and yet would not *say so*, nor cause it to be written so much as *once* by evangelists or apostles; though they often mention baptism, as appointed, as practised, as important; but leave the claim of infants on that ordinance to be made out by the long labour of inferential proof—by a consideration of proselyte baptism, Jewish circumcision, the Abrahamic covenant, and such passages of scripture where baptism is either not mentioned at all, or mentioned only in reference to adults; he that can believe it, let him. — Or, shall we renounce this Protestant principle of the famous Chillingworth, and follow the example of Mr. Fisher the Jesuit? who, when vindicating the worship of images, says: "In the scripture there is no express practice, nor precept, of worshipping the image of Christ; yet there be principles which, the light of nature supposed, convince adoration to be lawful."* — The following appeal of Dr. Mayo will also apply, *mutatis mutandis*, in all its force: "Had our Lord and his apostles, who esteemed not their lives dear unto them to promote the good of souls, thought parochial, diocesan, and metropolitan districts necessary, or even important and useful, judge you whether they would not have given at least *one* instruction or command concerning them." †

Reflect. V. Is it not strange, is it not absolutely unaccountable, if our Lord intended infants should be baptized, and if they actually were baptized by the apostles, that it should not be so much as once expressly recorded in all the New Testament? Baptism itself is frequently mentioned—mentioned, as an appointment of Christ, as a duty to be performed, as an ordinance

---

* In Popery confuted by Papists, p. 127. Vid. Chemnitium, Exam. Concil. Trident. p. 562.

† Apology and Shield, p. 21.

often administered, as a motive to holiness, and also by way of allusion; yet, though all these occasions of expressly mentioning infants as entitled to baptism, or as partakers of it, repeatedly occurred, the sacred writers have united in observing a profound silence with regard to both the one and the other. Admitting the baptism of infants to be from heaven, the silence of inspired authors on this head is the more surprising, because they were far from being backward expressly to mention children on other occasions of much less importance to the purity of Christian worship, the conduct of believing parents, and the edification of our Lord's disciples. For instance: Do infants fall a sacrifice to envy and cruelty, by the sanguinary edict of an Egyptian tyrant, or the bloody order of an infamous Herod? they are expressly mentioned.* Do children partake with their parents, once and again, of miraculous food? it is expressly recorded, a first and a second time.† Are little children presented to Christ for his healing touch, or his heavenly blessing? we are expressly informed of it by three evangelists.‡ Did children along with their parents attend Paul, when taking leave of his Christian friends in the city of Tyre? they also are expressly mentioned.§ Now though the particular mention of children in all these cases was pertinent, they being concerned in the several transactions recorded; yet, as none of these instances refers to a positive ordinance of divine worship, of which kind baptism is; we may safely conclude, that if Christ had warranted, and if the apostles had practised infant baptism, it was of much greater importance to the church of God for the sacred writers to have expressly mentioned it, than for them to have been so particular in the cases here adduced. It is observable also, that the explicit mention of children in these passages has little

---

* Acts vii. 19; Matt. ii. 16. † Matt. xiv. 21, and xv. 38.
‡ Matt. xix. 13; Mark x. 13; Luke xviii. 15.
§ Acts xxi. 5.

or no tendency to establish any doctrine, to enforce any duty, or to prevent any dispute among the disciples of Christ; whereas a plain information of our Lord's having commanded children to be baptized, or of the apostles' baptizing infants, might have answered those important purposes. But infants are *not* expressly said to be baptized, our opponents themselves being judges; consequently, we may conclude, that infants were not then concerned in any such transaction.

Again: Remarkable are the words of Luke, with which he introduces his evangelical narrative, and his apostolic history: " Forasmuch as many have taken in hand to set forth in order a declaration of those things which are most surely believed among us — it seemed good to me also, having had perfect understanding in all things from the very first, to write unto thee in order, most excellent Theophilus, that thou mightest know the certainty of those things wherein thou hast been instructed.... The former treatise have I made, O Theophilus, of all that Jesus began both to do and teach." From an exordium of this kind to each of his inspired narratives, the reader may justly suppose, that an article of such importance as Pædobaptism has long been esteemed by millions, would not have been entirely omitted by him, had our Lord enjoined, or had the apostles practised such a rite. Yes, had it been the custom of those times to baptize infants, it might be justly expected the sacred historian would have expressly mentioned it once and again, with some of its leading circumstances. Considering his conduct with regard to other affairs, in which he omits, or mentions children, we certainly had reason to expect it.—To the instances already produced from his writings, I will here add one or two more. Does Luke, for example, inform us, when describing the outrageous conduct of Saul, that he "committed men and women to prison," without mentioning children? Relating the triumphs of divine truth, he also tells us, that when the Samaritans believed, they " were baptized, both men and women ;" but says not a word of infants.* If then we justly infer, that little children, along with their parents, were not the objects of Saul's persecuting rage, because they are not mentioned as such in the history of his cruelty; why may we not for the same reason conclude, that infants, together with their parents, were not the subjects of baptism, as administered by Philip? It was, undoubtedly, as much the business of Luke to relate, with explicit precision, what Philip did in the course of his evangelical ministry, as it was to narrate the persecuting conduct of a blind bigot, who endeavoured to exterminate the Christian cause; and a plain account of the former was of incomparably more importance to succeeding generations, than the most accurate information respecting the latter. For Philip's beneficent labours, in preaching and baptizing, are an example which the ministers of Christ are obliged to imitate; but every one is bound to detest the persecuting conduct of Saul. Must we then consider the historian, when mentioning *men and women* in verse the third, as meaning *adults only;* but, in verse the twelfth, where he uses the very same words, as intending parents and their *infant offspring?* Nothing but the rage of hypothesis can suggest the thought. If, then, common sense and common honesty unite in affixing the same ideas to the same words in each of those places, the consequence is obvious; for, either no infants were baptized in those days, or Philip departed from the usual practice. To prove the latter, will be an arduous task; to grant the former, is giving up the cause.—This reasoning, if I mistake not, is perfectly agreeable to the following rule of bishop Taylor: " If that which is omitted in the discourse be pertinent and material to the enquiry, then it is a very good probability that that is *not true*

---

* Acts viii. 3, 12; compare chap. xxii. 4.

that is not affirmed.... The reason is, every thing is to be suspected false that does not derive from that fountain whence men justly expect it, and from whence it ought to flow. If you speak of any thing that relates to God, you must look for it there where God hath manifested himself; that is, in the scriptures.... We cannot say, because a thing is not in scripture, therefore it is not at all; but therefore it is nothing of divine religion."* Conformable to this rule is the reasoning of that learned author, Vitringa, in opposition to Episcopacy. " Certainly," says he, " if we were disposed to judge impartially, laying aside all prejudices and predilections, we should scarcely be induced to believe, that neither Luke in the Acts, nor Paul, nor yet any of the apostles in their epistles, should not have made the least mention of any bishop superior to presbyters, if there had really been any such pre-eminence, or dignity, or peculiar office, or singular title of one of the presbyters, instituted or known in their time. For they were obliged frequently to speak, and actually did speak about the churches, and concerning the government of the churches. Now seeing they often wrote concerning all other offices, but are entirely silent about what was afterwards called *Episcopacy;* it is to us an evidence, that in their time the name of such an office or dignity was not in use."† Or shall we say with Bellarmine, "Things that are generally known, and daily practised, do not use to be written?"‡ But this would be to insult common sense.

Once more: Supposing the divine authority of infant baptism, it will readily be allowed, that it was of unspeakably more importance for us to have been plainly informed of an apostle *baptizing* some little child, than to be expressly told that Paul *circumcised* Timothy. Of

---

* Ductor Dubitantium, b. ii. chap. iii. p. 383, 384.

† De Vet. Synag. p. 479, 480. ‡ In Preserv. against Popery, title vii. p. 85.

the former, however, Luke says not a word; though of the latter he is most explicit.* Did many Jewish Christians in the apostolic churches *circumcise their children?* of that also we have the most plain information from the pen of our divine historian.† This last particular is very remarkable. For who, on Pædobaptist principles, can possibly account for the perfect silence of Luke, respecting the *baptism* of infants; while he so plainly informs us, that the Jewish believers in general *circumcised* their offspring, even after the obligation of that rite had entirely ceased? If, as our opposers imagine, all the ministers and members of the apostolic churches were Pædobaptists, baptism, for an obvious reason, must have been much oftener administered to infants than circumcision, fond as the Jewish converts were of the latter. Shall an ordinance, then, of the New Testament, which is to continue to the end of time —an ordinance, that was very frequently performed and of great importance, be quite overlooked by an historian, who knew he was writing for the direction of the church in all future ages; while he so expressly mentions children as partakers of a rite which had been antiquated for many years? What! shall he plainly mention a practice which was then the fruit of ignorance, and of bigotry to an obsolete system; while he quite overlooks a still more common practice, that was matter of indispensable duty to every Christian parent on the behalf of his infant offspring? Plainly mention a prevailing *fault* among the primitive Jewish converts, respecting their male children; but omit their *duty* and their *obedience*, in regard to both male and female infants respecting baptism? Not over-kind, surely, would he in this case be to the character of those ancient Christians, nor over-scrupulous in his examples for the use of posterity! This, though not naturally impossible, exceeds the utmost bounds of probability; and, therefore, should be rejected as an absurdity.—The language

---

* Acts xvi. 3. † Acts xxi. 21. See No. 25.

of archbishop Wake, in opposition to an idle opinion concerning the apostles' composing a creed which goes under their name, will here apply, " It is not likely, that had any such thing as this been done by the apostles, St. Luke would have passed it by without taking the least notice of it."*

Our opponents insist, that the writers of the New Testament were all Pædobaptists. But either this is a great mistake, or those venerable authors must have had a very low idea of their own practice—much lower than Cyprian or Austin, or any of our zealous opposers in the present age. For while those infallible writers mention children on various occasions, where baptism is not concerned; they relate the baptizing of great numbers, in different parts of the world, without once mentioning infants as parties in that affair. Nay, they relate the baptizing of believers, in different places, with as little notice of infants, as if no infant had belonged to any whom they did baptize; yet, strange to conceive, the hypothesis of our opposers manifestly implies that infant baptism was then *a very common* practice! For it implies, that the baptism of children always accompanied that of their parents; and that the future offspring of such converted parents were made partakers of the sacred rite. On this principle, what a prodigious number of children must have been baptized, before the canon of scripture was completed! Yet all passed over in profound silence by the sacred writers!—Now as this is an example which no ecclesiastical historian, allowed to have been a Pædopabtist, has chosen to imitate; and as it is an example which could not have been imitated, when recording the transactions of later times, without omitting facts that were essential to a good narrative; so there is ground to believe, that the inspired historians had really *no facts* to relate, concerning the baptism of infants; which is a sufficient reason for their

---

* Apostolical Fathers, Introduct. p. 103, 104, edit. 2d.

saying nothing about it. For, surely, they were not inferior to later historians, either as to spiritual wisdom, or holy zeal, or historic fidelity; nor could they be ignorant that the immortal productions of their pens were to be considered by all the disciples of Christ, not only as a mirror of past facts, but also as *the law* of divine worship, and *the rule* of religious practice, to the end of time.—We may, therefore, confidently say with Mr. Baxter: "I conclude that all examples of baptism in scripture do mention only the administration of it to the professors of saving faith; and the precepts give us no other direction. And I provoke Mr. Blake [and all other Pædobaptists,] as far as is seemly for me to do, to name *one* precept or example for baptizing any other, and make it good if he [or they] can."*—The learned and laborious Dupin tells us, agreeably enough to his own principles; That the apostles did not give themselves the trouble of regulating what related to the ceremonies of Christian worship; but that their successors in the ministry settled those affairs.† This, though inimical to the creed of a consistent Protestant, is in my opinion true, as to infant baptism. For it does not appear that the apostles either did or said any thing relating to that ceremony, but that it was invented in a succeeding period, with a number of other things that were equally foreign to the language of the New Testament, and to the practice of apostolic churches.

The following words of an Episcopalian author, concerning the Congregational Pædobaptists, shall conclude this reflection: "If I had seen it my duty to accede to the church order of the Independents, I know not but their principles would have led me from them again to join with the Baptists. How they who, maintaining infant baptism, press scripture precedent so strongly upon me, answer the Baptists, who, in this

---

* Disput. of Right to Sacram. p. 156.
† Hist. Eccles. Writers, vol. i. p. 181, edit. 2nd.

point, press it as strongly upon themselves, is not my concern."*

---

* Apologia, p. 108. Leaving our Independent brethren to solve the difficulty here suggested as well as they can, I would observe; That as this worthy author informs us he made the subscription required of candidates for orders in the national establishment, "REALLY *ex animo,*" so we may take it for granted, he cordially approves of that article in the national creed, which says; "The church hath power to decree rites or ceremonies." This being the case, it is no wonder that he does not feel himself much embarrassed by the thought of departing from *scriptural precedents;* because, whoever has authority to decree *new* rites or ceremonies in religious worship, must possess a plenitude of power to lay *old* ones aside, by whomsoever they were appointed. "They who may institute new worship," says Mr. Alsop, "may destroy the old worship. For *Cujus est instituere, ejus est destituere;* the same authority that can make a law, can repeal a law." Sober Enquiry, p. 282. I have observed, however, that this author, in his Messiah, talks in a different strain, and treats the language of inspiration with due respect. For, speaking of real converts, he says: "One, *thus saith the Lord,* has the force of a thousand arguments. They desire no farther proof of a doctrine, no other warrant for their practice, no other reason for any dispensation, than *Thus the Lord has said, this he requires,* and *this is his appointment.* Thus their wills are brought into subjection; and they so understand, as to believe and obey," vol i. p. 224, 225. This is the language of Protestantism; this, I will venture to say, is the language of Nonconformity; and exceedingly different from that irreverent manner, in which he has treated "scripture precedents," when defending his own conformity. Yet how he can reconcile these things, "is not my concern."

But, though Mr. Newton, in his Apologia, does not consider himself as obliged by *scriptural precedents;* and though he expressly says, "I thought the example of our Lord pleaded AS MUCH *for circumcision* as for *baptism;*" yet, while he abides by this acknowledgment, "I am BOUND, by my subscription, to the form and rubric of the Common Prayer;" it might be expected that he would never publicly *sprinkle* an infant, and call the ceremony *baptism,* unless the sponsors informed him that the child could not bear immersion. For a Protestant minister to think himself at liberty to desert scriptural precedents, while he confesses himself *bound* to the rubric of a liturgy; and yet notoriously contradict that *very rubric,* by constantly sprinkling infants instead of immersing them; are things that grate upon my understanding. Apologia, p. 108, 109, 124. See Part I. Chap. VI. No. 16.

Reflect. VI. That the argument here employed is neither novel nor inconclusive, will appear by adverting to the conduct of Protestants in general, when disputing with Roman Catholics, and that in a great variety of cases. For instance: Do the Popish writers assert, that Peter was *the bishop of Rome* for a course of years, and mention many particulars of his conduct there? "All these things," replies Mr. Millar, " seem to be false, and without foundation; as appears from the silence of Luke, the inspired writer of the Acts of the Apostles, who recorded many things concerning Peter ....Peter himself speaks not one word of what the Papists allege. If he had founded the Roman church, why does he no where make mention of it?"*—Thus also the learned Buddeus: " If Peter had been at Rome when Paul wrote his epistle to the church there, who can believe that he would have omitted him among others whom he salutes by name? Or, if he had been there before, who can believe that Paul would have made no mention of him in any part of that epistle? especially seeing various occasions offered for him to have done so." †—Is *the supremacy* of Peter, or that of the Pope, the subject in question? Chamier says: " If Christ appointed Peter to obtain both temporal and spiritual power, what is the reason that he does not so much as once carefully, explicitly, and most emphatically express it? Had it been a fact, he would have expressed it. But he has not expressed it; therefore it was not his intention that Peter should have it."‡—Is it the Papal *infallibility?* Abp. Tillotson says: "There is not the least intimation in scripture of this privilege conferred upon the Roman church; nor do the apostles, in all their epistles,

---

* Propagat. of Christianity, vol. i. chap. iii. p. 278. Vid. Turret. Institut. loc. xxviii. q. xviii. § 4; and Dr. Doddridge's Note on Rom. xvi. 15. † Ecclesia Apostolica, p. 714.

‡ Panstrat. tom. ii. l. xv. c. xv. § 2. Vid. Dr. Doddridge's Note on 1 Cor. xiv. 26.

ever so much as give the least directions to Christians, to appeal to the bishop of Rome for a determination of the many differences, which even in those times happened among them. And it is strange they should be so silent in this matter, when there were so many occasions to speak of it, if our Saviour had plainly appointed such an infallible judge of controversies."*—Is it the *invocation of saints?* Dr. Hughes declares: "That the very silence of scripture is enough to condemn the praying to saints."†——Dr. Doddridge: "Dr. Whitby justly observes, that it is very remarkable that Paul, who so often and so earnestly entreats the intercession of his Christian friends, should never speak of the intercession of the Virgin Mary, or of departed saints, if he believed it a duty to seek it."‡—Is it *confession to a priest?* Bp. Stratford says: "We find no such sort of confession required by Christ or his apostles." §—Is it *confirmation?* Chemnitius opposes it by saying: "The Popish sacrament of confirmation was neither appointed nor dispensed, either by Christ or by the apostles; because it is not mentioned in scripture."‖—Is it *extreme unction?* The same author declares against it, by observing: "That there is neither precept nor precedent for it in the scripture, except so far as relates to the miraculous gift of healing." ¶—Is it their *clerical celibacy?* Mr. Wharton considers the silence of scripture, as the "greatest of all" arguments against it.** Thus Protestants, at every turn, against the Papists.

We will now produce an instance or two of similar conduct among Protestant Dissenters, when disputing with Episcopalians about the hierarchy and rites of the

---

* Preserv. against Popery, title iii. p. 231.
† Sermon at Salters' Hall, on Veneration of Saints, p. 37.
‡ Note on Col. iv. 3. See also his Note on chap. ii. 18.
§ Preserv. against Popery, title i. p. 21.
‖ Exam. Concil. Trid. p. 250. ¶ Ibid. p. 205.
** Preserv. against Popery, title i. p. 281.

church of England. Is *diocesan Episcopacy* the subject of debate, or of animadversion? Dr. Doddridge says: "The late learned, moderate, and pious Dr. Edmund Calamy observes, that if the apostles had been used, as some assert, to ordain diocesan bishops in their last visitation, this had been a proper time [when Paul took his leave of the Ephesian elders] to do it; or that, if Timothy had been already ordained bishop of Ephesus, Paul, instead of calling them all *bishops,* would surely have given some hint to enforce Timothy's authority among them.... Ignatius would have talked in a very different style and manner on this head."*——Mr. James Owen, thus: "How comes it to pass, when the apostle (Eph. iv. 11,) reckons up the several sorts of ministers which Christ had appointed in his church, that he makes no mention of superior bishops, if they be so necessary as some would have us believe?.... It is unaccountable that St. Paul should write an epistle to the Ephesians, —and not mention their pretended bishop, Timothy, in the whole epistle.... It is a *certain* evidence he was neither bishop there, nor resident there."†—Is it the *sign of the cross,* as an attendant on baptism? Mr. Arch. Hall says: "The reader will give me leave to quote the words of Mr. Thomas Bradbury on this point: 'If,' says that excellent person, 'Christ had thought that washing with water was not sufficient without the sign of the cross, *he would have told us so.*'"‡—Thus also Nonconformists reason in various other cases; and thus the most eminent writers in all cases, where the silence of sacred, of ecclesiastical, or of profane authors, can be fairly pleaded against any hypothesis; concerning which no person of reading and of observation is ignorant.

---

* Note, on Acts xx. 25. Vid. his Note on Ephes. iv. 11; and Lectures, proposit. cl. p. 494.

† Plea for Scrip. Ordination, p. 16, 17, 22. Vid. Turrett. loc. xxviii. q. xxi. § 9. ‡ Gospel Worship, vol. i. p. 326. Vid. Turrett. Institut. loc. xix. q. xviii. § 3.

Again: That Protestants of different communions unite in considering negative arguments of this kind as conclusive, may still farther appear by the following instances. Turrettinus: "The silence of scripture ought, with us, to have great weight."*——Bp. Porteus: "Our divine Lawgiver showed his wisdom equally in what he enjoined, and what he left unnoticed.... He knew exactly—where to be silent, and where to speak."†—— Dr. Owen: "The scripture is so absolutely the rule, measure, and boundary of our faith and knowledge in spiritual things, as that what it conceals is instructive, as well as what it expresseth."‡——Dr. Doddridge: "To be willing to continue ignorant of what our great Master has thought fit to conceal, is no inconsiderable part of Christian learning."§——Anonymous: "Protestant divines have ever thought this a sufficient convincing argument, against the fooleries of the Papists; *That Christ hath no where commanded them;* therefore they may justly reject them as unlawful."||——Anonymous: "To demand more than—perpetual silence in these cases is unreasonable; because no satisfactory account can be given of it but this, *That the worship we speak of, was indeed no part of their religion.*" ¶

In opposition, however, to this capital principle of Protestantism, Mr. Cleaveland says: "It belongs to them [the Baptists] to produce an *express and positive precept*, or command, for the exclusion of infant-membership under the New Testament administration of the covenant; and till they can produce such a precept, they act without any warrant or authority from the word of God in refusing to baptize the children of covenanting parents."**——Mr. Reeves: "Circumci-

---

* Ut supra, quæst. xxvii. § 19. Vid. q. xxix. § 6, 7; q. xxx. § 6, 7. † Sermons, p. 421, edit. 4th.
‡ On Heb. vii. 1, 2, 3, vol. iii. p. 116.
§ Note on John viii. 6. || Jerubbaal, p. 163.
¶ Discourse concerning the Worship of the blessed Virgin, p. 37, 38.   ** Infant Baptism from Heaven, p. 39.

sion being changed into baptism without any change of time, that must continue upon the old foot, without some *express command* to the contrary; and therefore there was no occasion for any particular express precept in the gospel for baptizing infants."*——Dr. Taylor: "We may not say, The apostles did not [baptize infants;] therefore we may not. But thus, they were not *forbidden* to do it; there is no law against it; therefore it may be done."†——Mr. De Courcy: "Since I find infant baptism not forbidden by any *express prohibition*, I rather think it virtually enjoined by the *very silence* of scripture."‡

Reflecting on these doughty arguments in defence of infant baptism, I am reminded of one that is quite similar, which is used to prove the divine right of tithes; or to "establish," as Mr. Adair expresses it, "the most *delicious* part of the Jewish law."§—"We need," says the author of The Snake in the Grass, no new commandment for [tithes] in the gospel, if they are not *forbidden* and abrogated by Christ."—To which friend Wyeth replies: "If they are not expressly commanded to be continued under the gospel, they are not of force; that law being *temporary*, by which they were commanded, and now expired. It was adapted to the economy of the Jews; made to answer that dispensation....So that an express abrogation of tithes, in the gospel, was no more necessary than an express repeal of an act of parliament which was but temporary, and would expire of course at the end of that term for which it was appointed." ‖

The intelligent reader will easily perceive, that this

---

* Apologies, vol. i. Preface, p. 17, 18.

† In Mr. Leigh's Body of Divinity, b. viii. chap. viii. p. 671.

‡ Rejoinder, p. 88. See also Cases to Recover Dissenters, vol. ii. p. 441. Dr. Lightfoot's Horæ Heb. on Matt. iii. 6, *cum multis aliis.* § History of the American Indians, p. 463.

‖ Switch for the Snake, p. 419, 420.

reasoning applies with all its force to the case before us. For that interest which the infant offspring of Abraham's descendants had in the Jewish church, being part of a temporary and less perfect economy, must in the very nature of the case be temporary; nor could it, without a new divine charter, have an existence under the gospel dispensation, any more than the divine right of tithes. To produce a new charter, however, our Brethren do not pretend. As well, therefore, may persons who are manifestly unregenerate plead their title to full communion with any particular church, on the ground of ancient privilege granted by Jehovah to the carnal Israelites, provided they were not guilty of some flagitious evil, or ceremonially unclean; as any contend that infants must be members of the church now, because they were so under the former economy. With equal reason may the professed members of a national church argue from the want of an express prohibition lying against an ecclesiastical constitution of that kind, as any of our opponents require an explicit declaration that the church-membership of infants is now at an end. Such membership is indeed the very basis of national churches; but quite inconsistent with churches of the congregational form.—An apostle has taught us, that the ancient " priesthood being changed, there is made of necessity a change also of the law."* That is, as Dr. Owen explains it, "the whole 'law of commandments contained in ordinances;' or the whole law of Moses, so far as it was the rule of worship and obedience unto the church; for that law it is that followeth the fates of the priesthood." We may, therefore, adopt the sacred writer's principle of reasoning, and say; The constitution of the visible church being manifestly and essentially altered, the law relating to qualifications for communion in it, must of necessity be changed. Consequently, no valid inference can be

---

* Heb. vii. 12.

drawn from the membership of infants under the former dispensation, to a similarity of external privilege under the new covenant.

I shall take the liberty of once more adverting to the article of tithes. The Snake in the Grass having asserted, that "there are plain intimations in the gospel" of tithes being continued; Mr. Wyeth, having in his hand a convenient *Switch*, gives him the following lash: "*Intimations!*—Is it come to that? Must the world be decimated by *intimations?* Does God's right, God's due, God's tithes, depend upon *intimations* at last?"*— Excuse me, reader, if I should express my suspicions, that the divine right of tithes, and the *jus divinum* of infant baptism, depend upon similar *intimations*. Or, if you please, they are both, in regard to substantial evidence, like the doctrine of purgatory; which, according to Peter *à Soto*, though not demonstrated in scripture, is nevertheless *insinuated* there. † We will venture to assert, however, with Dr. Ridgley: "As for the [positive] ordinances, our attendance on them depends on a divine *command*,"‡ or an apostolic example; and not on intimations, or insinuations.—There is another particular, or two, in which a likeness appears between the divine right of tithes, and that of infant baptism. For as those who earnestly plead the former are compelled to confess, that the apostolic ministers did not *act* upon it; so the most strenuous patrons of the latter are obliged to acknowledge, that the apostles have not plainly told us, either of our Lord *appointing*, or of themselves *performing* it.... As our opposers imagine satisfactory reasons may be given, why the apostles, who are supposed to have baptized vast numbers of children, said nothing expressly about our Lord's command for that purpose, nor concerning their practice of it; so

---

* Switch for the Snake, p. 417.
† Apud Chemnitium, Exam. Concil. Trident. p. 562.
‡ Bod. of Div. quest. cx. p. 509.

those who feel their interest in decimating the property of their neighbours, can easily assign sufficient causes why the primitive ministers waived that lucrative privilege:* while they maintain on solid grounds the antiquity of paying tithes, as prior to the Mosaic system —prior to circumcision †—and, were it not for what some of our learned opposers have said, I should have boldly added, prior to the proselyte baptism. But I am aware that antediluvian, and almost paradisiacal antiquity, is claimed for that rabbinical rite.

That our opponents may see whose weapons they use, when attacking us after the manner of Mr. Cleaveland and others, I will transcribe a few lines from a nameless Roman Catholic author. The writer to whom I advert, when addressing Protestants, defies their opposition in the following words. " You cannot show one positive argument against the invocation of saints, either from scripture or from fathers; not one against the doctrine of the real presence, transubstantiation, veneration of images upon account of their representations; not one against the number of sacraments; not one to prove communion under both kinds to be indispensable; or that children dying without baptism are saved. In a word, you cannot show one positive argument against any one doctrine of our church, if you state it right: all you can say, is, *It does not appear to us out of scripture; it does not appear to us from antiquity.* Show us, you say, *your authentic records, your deeds of gift, your revelation, and we will believe*: as if an uninterrupted possession were not sufficient."‡—I will now present the reader with this Popish objection, as expressed by Mr. West, and with part of the answer which he returns. Thus then my author: Cavil: " We have brought never

---

* See Mr. Bingham's Orig. Eccles. b. v. chap. v. § 2.

† Gen. xiv. 20; Heb. vii. 4, 6, 9.

‡ Vindicat. of Bishop of Condom's Exp. of Doct. of Cath. Church, p. 111, 112.

a positive scripture, that says, *There is no such place as purgatory;* and a huge outcry is on such occasions taken up against our *negative* way of arguing against a doctrine that they positively profess.... Truly, on their part it lies to have given us *positive* and *express* scripture for purgatory, that would impose it on us as a positive article of faith.... It seems absurd to provoke to positive express scripture against every chimera that may come into men's heads a thousand years after the scriptures were writ; for so, if any man should assert, especially if many should agree to it, that Mahomet is a true prophet, or that the moon was a mill-stone, or whatever else can be supposed more unlikely; I am bound to subscribe to it, except I can bring particular, positive, express scripture against it."*—Thus also Mr. Vincent Alsop: " Amongst all the crafty devices of the devil to induce our grand-mother Eve to eat of the tree of knowledge; and of all the weak excuses of Eve for eating of that tree, I wonder this was not thought on; *That it was not contrary to any express law of God.* For (Gen. ii. 16, 17,) 'God commanded the MAN, saying, Of every tree of the garden THOU mayest freely eat; but of the tree of the knowledge of good and evil, thou shalt not eat.' But it seems the devil had not learnt the sophistry to evade the precept, because the express law was given to the *man,* and not to the *woman....* It had been impossible that all negatives should be expressed, *Thou shalt not stand upon thy head; Thou shalt not wear a fool's coat; Thou shalt not play at dice, or cards, in the worship of God:* but thus [by pleading the want of an express prohibition] he [Dr. Goodman] thinks he has made good provision for a safe conformity to the ceremonies; because it is not said, *Thou shalt not use the cross in baptism; Thou shalt not use cream, oil, spittle; Thou shalt not conjure out the devil.* At which back-door came in all the superstitious fopperies of Rome.

---

* Morning Exercise against Popery, p. 830.

And with this passport we may travel all over the world; from Rome to the Porte, from thence amongst the Tartars and Chinese, and conform to all; for perhaps we shall not meet with one constitution that contradicts an *express* law of scripture."*

Reflect. VII. Many were the positive rites ordained by Jehovah, in the ancient Jewish church; some of which were intended for the people at large, and others for particular characters among them. There is not, however, that I remember, a single instance of any ritual service designed for persons of a particular description; and of those persons, whether priests, Levites, or others, being under a necessity of inferring their interest in that service by a chain of reasoning from remote principles. No, the persons whose duty it was to regard the rite, were plainly described, as well as the manner of performing it; so that the most ignorant among them, as far as we can perceive, were at no loss in that respect. Nor have we any reason to think that the positive laws of the New Testament are less easy to be understood, than those of the Jewish economy. Dr. Owen, however, seems to have been of this opinion when he said, " Every thing in scripture is so plain as that the meanest believer may understand all that belongs unto his duty, or is necessary unto his happiness.... There can be no instance given of any obscure place or passage in the scripture, concerning which a man may rationally suppose or conjecture, that there is any doctrinal truth requiring our obedience contained in it, which is not elsewhere explained."†—— Thus also Mr. W. Bennet: " What is the rule of all instituted worship?—The revealed will of God only; who hath given us a *full* discovery thereof, in all things

---

* Sober Enquiry, p. 345, 346.
† Ways and Means of Understand. Mind of God, p. 176, 185.

necessary for our faith and practice, by his written word."*

To imagine, therefore, that the first positive rite of religious worship in the Christian church, is left in so vague a state as Pædobaptism supposes, is not only contrary to the analogy of divine proceedings in similar cases, but renders it morally impossible for the bulk of Christians to discern the real grounds on which the ordinance is administered. For, doubtless, a great majority of those who profess Christianity, are quite incapable of entering into several subjects, the discussion of which is found so necessary by learned men, in order to establish the right of infants to baptism. On this plan of proceeding, a plain unlettered man, with the New Testament only in his hand, though sincerely desirous of learning from his Lord what baptism is, and to whom it belongs, is not furnished with sufficient documents to form a conclusion. No; he must study the records of Moses, and well understand the covenant made with Abraham, as the father of the Jewish nation. Stranger still! he must, according to the opinion of many, become a disciple of those who are the humble pupils of Jewish rabbies—of those learned authors who, being well versed in the writings of Maimonides, and in the volumes of the Talmud, imagine themselves to have imported into the Christian church a great stock of intelligence concerning the mind of Christ, relative to the proper subjects of baptism. For it is thence only he is able to learn, that the children of proselytes were baptized along with their parents, when admitted members of the Jewish church; and thence also he must infer, that our Lord condescended to borrow of his enemies an important ordinance of religious worship for his own disciples.—Nor is this all: He must study the antiquated rite of circumcision; he must know to whom

---

* View of Relig. Worship, quest. viii. See Preface, p. 1—6.

it belonged, and the reasons why: then he must compare it with baptism, in this, that, and the other particular; after which he must draw a genuine inference, respecting the point in hand.—Nor has he yet performed the arduous task. For, as the New Testament says nothing expressly about the object of his enquiry, he must sift the meaning of several passages in sacred writ that say not a word about it, in order to find that infants, of a certain description, are entitled to baptism. For instance: He must consider 1 Cor. vii. 14, in a very particular manner. Here he must settle what is meant by the word *sanctified*, and by the term *holy*. He must accurately distinguish between the holiness attributed to the *child*, and the sanctification ascribed to the *unbelieving parent;* so as to give the infant a right, which the parent has not, in a positive institution of Jesus Christ.—When all this is duly performed, he must fortify his mind against the objections to which this finespun theory is liable. He must enquire, for example, so as to satisfy his own conscience, Why, when our Lord gave commision to teach and baptize; why, when his apostles required a profession of faith from those whom they did baptize, no exception was made in favour of infants: and, by a train of reasoning, he must at last infer, that, so far as appears, they *meant* what they never said, nor ever did.* Such is the roundabout logical labour which the ploughman has to perform, if he would not pin his faith on the sleeve of the learned.

But if, on the other hand, we consider positive precepts and apostolic examples as the *only* rule of administering baptism; if we consider evangelists and apostles as recording, plainly recording, all that our Lord meant us to know concerning this institution; the labour of the

---

* So the Papists are justly charged by Mr. Hurst, with representing Peter as *thinking* one thing, and *writing* another. Morning Exercise against Popery, p. 55.

most illiterate, who can read his own language, is both short and easy. For the New Testament being the only book that he wants to give him a complete idea of baptism, he has nothing to do but to open that sacred volume; consult a few express commands and plain examples; consider the natural and proper sense of the words; and then, without the aid of commentators, or the help of critical acumen, he may safely decide on the question before him: because, our opponents themselves being judges, we have in that code of divine law and history of apostolic practice, both express commands and express examples for baptizing such as profess faith in Jesus Christ, but NONE ELSE.

When these things are duly considered, we shall not wonder that learned and eminent Pædobaptists have expressed themselves as follows. Lord Brooke, for instance, has made the ensuing acknowledgment: "To those that hold we may go no farther than scripture, for doctrine or discipline, it may be very easy to err in this point now in hand [i. e. infant baptism;] since the scripture seems not to have clearly determined this particular."*——Mr. Baxter: "If the very baptism of infants itself, be *so dark* in the scripture, that the controversy is thereby become *so hard* as we find it; then, to prove not only their baptism, but a new distinct end of their baptism, will be a hard task indeed." † N. B. This acknowledgment is contained in his book, entitled, Plain Scripture Proof of Infants' Church-membership and Baptism.——Dr. Wall: "At what age the children of Christians should be baptized, whether in infancy, or to stay till the age of reason, is not so clearly delivered, but that it admits of a dispute that has considerable perplexities in it."‡——Mr. Henry: "There are difficulties in this controversy, which may puzzle the minds of well-

---

* On Episcopacy, sect. ii. chap. vii. p. 97.
† Plain Scrip. Proof, p. 301.
‡ Hist. Inf. Bap. part ii. chap. xi. p. 547.

meaning Christians."*——Dr. Isaac Watts: "Though there be no such express and plain commands or examples of it [infant baptism] written in scripture, as we might have expected; yet there are several inferences to be drawn from what is written, which afford a just and reasonable encouragement to this practice, and guard it from the censure of superstition and will-worship."†——Anonymous: "In the controversy about infant baptism, the enquiry ought not to be, Whether Christ hath commanded infants to be baptized? but, Whether he hath excluded them from baptism?"‡——Thus also the very learned and excellent Vitringa: "He, in my opinion, that would argue prudently against the Anabaptists, should not state the point in controversy thus; Whether infants born of Christian parents, ought necessarily to be baptized? but, Whether it be lawful, according to the Christian discipline, to baptize them? Or, what evil is there in the ceremony of baptizing infants?"§—These extracts remind me of a remarkable interview between Saul and Samuel. The former, when recent from his expedition against Amalek, said; "I have performed the commandment of the Lord." To which the venerable prophet replied, "What meaneth then this bleating of the sheep in mine ears, and the lowing of the oxen which I hear?"‖ So, in the present case, these respectable authors would fain persuade us that they perform the will of the Lord when they sprinkle infants. But if so, we may ask, What mean these *concessions* and *cautions* which we hear? Do they not betray a conviction of some capital defect in the foundation upon which Pædobaptists proceed? Yes, the two last of these learned authors especially, were keenly sensible that Pædobap-

---

* Treatise on Bap. p. 70.
† Berry Street Sermons, vol. ii. p. 180, 185.
‡ Cases to Recover Dissenters, vol. ii. p. 405.
§ Observat. Sac. tom. i. l. ii. c. vii. § 9.
‖ 1 Sam. xv. 13, 14.

tism is tender ground; and that whoever walks upon it had need be careful how he treads.

Reflect. VIII. We are taught by various learned pens, that the practice of John, surnamed the Baptist, and the qualifications required of those persons for whom our Lord intended the ordinance, unite in excluding infants from a participation of it. Riissenius, for instance, in answer to this objection; "John admitted no one to baptism, except he confessed his sins;" replies as follows: "His business was with adults, that were to be baptized and called to the Christian church; but it does not thence follow, that the same thing should have place in respect of infants who are already in the church."*—— Anonymous: "The baptism [of John] belongs not properly to infants: for, first, it is a baptism of repentance, of which infants are not capable; secondly, it is for remission of sins, which therefore imply actual sins, whereas infants are only guilty of original sin, and that is but one."†——Turrettin: "John admitted none to baptism, but those who confessed their sins; because his business was to baptize the adult."‡——Dr. Whitby: "It is not to be wondered at, that infants were not baptized during John's ministry; because the baptism then used by John and Christ's disciples, was only the baptism of repentance, and faith in the Messiah which was for to come, of both which infants were incapable."§ ——Thomas Lawson: "Faith and repentance were the qualifications of such as were admitted to John's baptism."‖ Thus that impartial Friend.

That the *qualifications* required of those for whom our Lord intended the ordinance, do not agree to an infantile state, appears from the declarations of many others. The celebrated Cocceius, for instance, informs us; "That sacraments, properly speaking, were insti-

---

* Sum. Theolog. loc. xvii. p. 719. † Nonconformists' Advocate, p. 48.   ‡ Institut. loc. xix. quæst. xxii. § 14.
§ Annotat. on Matt. xix. 13, 14.   ‖ Baptismalogia, p. 108.

tuted for believers, and given to them, (Rom. iv. 11;) that is, for those 'who hunger and thirst after righteousness.'"*——The language of Limborch is remarkably strong. "The subject of baptism," says that learned Arminian, "to whom it is to be administered, is a believer; one who is endued with a true faith in Jesus Christ, and touched with a serious repentance for his past offences."†——Meierus thus: "None have a title to baptism, but such as profess faith and the true religion."‡ ——Doutrin: "To whom ought baptism to be administered? Only to believers, or those that may be considered as such, (Matt. xxviii. 19; Acts viii. 37.)"§—— Turrettin: "Faith, devotion, and an internal exercise of the mind, are required to the efficacy of a sacrament; because the scripture expressly asserts it, (Mark xvi. 16; 1 Cor. xi. 27; Acts ii. 37, 38;) because without faith it is impossible to please God, (Heb. xi. 6;) and because the promise, as contained in the sacraments, and faith, are correlates."∥——Calvin: "From the sacrament of baptism, as from all others, we obtain nothing except so far as we receive it in faith."¶——Dr. Doddridge: "I think that illumination as well as regeneration, in the most important and scriptural sense of the words, were regularly to precede the administration of that ordinance," i. e. baptism.**—— Mr. Jonathan Edwards: "That baptism, by which the primitive converts were admitted into the church, was used as an exhibition and token of their being visibly regenerated, dead to sin—as is evident by Rom. vi. throughout.... He [the apostle] does not mean only that their baptism laid them under special obligations to these things, and was a mark and token of their engagement to be thus hereafter; but was designed as a mark, token, and exhibition of their being visibly thus already.... There are some du-

---

* Sum. Doct. de Fœd. c. vi. § 209. † Syst. Div. b. v. chap. xxii. § 2. ‡ Biblioth. Brem. class. iv. p. 169.
§ Scheme of Div. Truths, p. 260. ∥ Institut. loc. xix. q. viii. § 12. ¶ Institut. l. iv. c. xv. § 15. ** Note on Heb. vi. 4.

ties of worship that imply *a profession* of God's covenant; whose very nature and design is an exhibition of those vital active principles and inward exercises, wherein the condition of the covenant of grace [consists.] Such are the Christian sacraments; whose very design is to make and confirm a profession of compliance with that covenant, and whose very nature is to exhibit or express those uniting acts of the soul."*———Venema: "Faith and repentance—are pre-required in baptism. He who presents himself as a candidate for baptism, professes, by that very act, to be a Christian; declares himself to have passed into the discipline of Christ. Hence Philip said, 'If thou believest with all thy heart, thou mayest,' (Acts viii. 37.) The command of Peter was, 'Repent and be baptized,' (Acts ii. 38;) the effect of which was, that they who gladly and sincerely believed his gospel were baptized....In baptism, therefore, we have a sign and testimony of *present* regeneration; and in regard to the person baptized, a public demonstration of it."†——Mr. Thomas Boston gives us, not only his own views of the subject, but those also of Mr. Rutherford and of Ursinus, in the following words. "The sacraments are not converting, but confirming ordinances; they are appointed for the use and benefit of God's children, not of others; they are given to believers, *as* believers, as Rutherford expresseth it, so that none other are capable of the same before the Lord....Ursin, upon that question, *Who ought to come to the supper?* tells us, the sacraments are appointed for the faithful and converted ONLY, to seal the promise of the gospel to them, and confirm their faith."‡—— Dr. Goodwin: "Baptism supposeth regeneration sure in itself first. Sacraments are never administered for to begin or work grace; you suppose children to believe before you baptize them. Read all the Acts, still it is

---

* Enquiry into Qualif. for full Commun. p. 20, 114, 115.

† Dissertat. Sac. l. ii. c. xiv. § 4.   ‡ Works, p. 384, 385.

said, They *believed* and were baptized. I could give you a multitude of places for it." *———"There are, or may be, innumerable persons baptized externally with water," says Hoornbeekius, "who yet are not real Christians; neither were they rightly baptized, because they were unbelievers; nor can they be justly said to have baptism, not that which Christ appointed.... Without faith, water baptism cannot by any means be lawful; for the command is, *believe*, first; then also, and not otherwise, *be baptized*. ' He that believeth and is baptized,' (Mark xvi. 16.) ' Then they that gladly received his word were baptized,' (Acts ii. 41.) ' If thou believest with all thy heart, thou mayest be baptized,' (Acts viii. 37; xvi. 31, 33.)"†———" A profession of faith," says Dr. Waterland, " was from the beginning always required of persons before baptism. We have plain examples of, and allusions to, something of that kind, even in scripture itself, (Acts viii. 12, 37; 1 Pet. iii. 21.) Upon these instances the Christian church proceeded." ‡———" Faith and repentance were the great things required," says Dr. Watts, " of those that were admitted to baptism. This was the practice of John, this the practice of the apostles, in the history of their ministry, (Matt. iii.; Acts ii. 38, xix. 4, and viii. 37.)....Those who are baptized, are professed Christians; they are avowed disciples of Christ."§ ——Anonymous: " Sacraments are administered only to those, who either have faith, or pretend to have it." ‖———Once more: Dr. Erskine says, " I have fully shown, that the seals of the covenant are, under the New Testament, peculiar to the inwardly pious." ¶—That these authors had any intention to impeach the propriety of infant baptism, is not pre-

---

* Works, vol. i. part i. p. 200. † Socin. Confut. tom. iii. p. 384, 389. ‡ Eight Serm. p. 317, edit. 2nd.
§ Berry Street Serm. vol. ii. p. 177, 178.
‖ In Mr. Baxter's Disput. of Right to Sac. p. 245.
¶ Theolog. Dissertations, p. 82.

tended; but whether the natural import of their language be quite consistent with it, the reader will judge.

Reflect. IX. Some of these authors imagine that Pædobaptism is lawful, though it be not commanded. But here they seem to forget that baptism is a positive rite, and that when practised it is as an act of divine worship. A precept therefore, or an example, must be necessary to warrant the performance of it; and consequently to authorize its administration to any description of persons whatever. Whether infants only; whether all infants, or only some; and if the latter, whether none but the children of church-members, or of all that appear to be converted; or, finally, whether those persons only who profess faith in Jesus Christ, should be baptized; are things which lie entirely at the sovereign pleasure of the great Institutor. His will, which is always perfectly wise and good, is the sole determiner here. Now as we cannot know his divine pleasure unless it be revealed; as every intimation of his pleasure is attended with divine authority; and as the whole of his revealed will is contained in scripture; if the sacred page exhibit no command for Pædobaptism, nor any example of it, the lawfulness of baptizing infants must be a mere surmise—a conjecture without probability. For, not to urge the common arguments against Popish superstition; and, waiving that excellent maxim of Ambrose before mentioned, "Who shall speak where the scripture is silent?" I would only demand, whether the performance of a religious rite, in the name of JEHOVAH, the Father, the Son, and the Holy Spirit, can be lawful, if the divine Majesty have not appointed it? It is clear, Mr. James Owen thought it was not; because in a similar case he says, "It is a plain profanation of God's holy name, and of a great and holy ordinance, by lying and taking God's name in vain."* So Chemnitius, having informed us that the unction used in the

---

* Validity of Dissenting Ministry, p. 143.

Popish sacrament of confirmation, is performed in the name of the Father, Son, and Holy Spirit, says, "If the divine name be employed without the injunction of God, it is an offence against the second command; which offence is the more aggravated, in proportion as the effects attributed to that which has neither the command nor the promise of God, are supposed to be the more excellent." *— Or is the name of HIM who is *a consuming fire* so cheap, that we may borrow its most venerable sanction to dignify and adorn our own inventions? Surely, if the performance of any thing either does or can require the most explicit divine authority, it must be that which, if performed at all, should be expressly done *in the* NAME of the great Supreme. A requisition to administer baptism in that most holy name, implies the strongest prohibition of performing it in any manner, or on any subject, different from what is required by the law of administration. In this case, *may* and *must* are the same thing; agreeably to the following words of Mr. Baxter: "We enquire whether we either *must*, or *may*, baptize such; and suppose that the *licet* and the *oportet* do here go together: so that what we *may* do, we *must* do, supposing our own call; as, no doubt, what we must do, we may do."†— Thus also Dr. Owen: "What men have a *right* to do in the church by God's institution, that they have a *command* to do." ‡ If then the law of proceeding, in this case made and provided, require that infants should partake of the institution; we undoubtedly must act a condemnable part in withholding it from them. If, on the contrary, that divine rubric, that sacred canon, confine all that is said of it to such as profess faith in the Son of God; our opponents, for the same reason, must be highly culpable: because their practice restrains it al-

---

* Exam. Concil. Trident. p. 248, 253.
† Disputat. on Right to Sacram. p. 42.
‡ On Heb. vii. 4, 5, 6; vol. iii. p. 127.

most entirely to such as lie under a natural incapacity of professing repentance and faith. Nor do we imagine any of them will say, with some of the Popish casuists, That a practice is innocent, because it is customary.*

We are frequently charged with being extremely fond of getting people into the water; but whether it be really so, I leave the impartial to judge. We, however, may say this for ourselves, that we never immerse a person in the sublimest of all names, without his *consent;* no, nor yet without his *explicit request:* whereas, those who lodge the complaint against us are well aware, that it would in general be very absurd for them to ask the consent of those whom they sprinkle in the same glorious name, because they are certain it could not be granted. Besides, they consider the consent of a parent, or of a proxy, as quite sufficient, though the subject of the ordinance be ever so reluctant.

Farther: Positive laws imply their negative. A command from undoubted authority to perform an action in such a manner, and on such a subject, must be considered as prohibiting a different manner, and a different subject. So, for instance, when God commanded Abraham to circumcise his male posterity, on the eighth day; there was no necessity that a prohibition should be annexed, relating to any similar ceremony which might have been performed on females; nor to expressly forbid the circumcision of a finger, instead of the foreskin; nor to say in so many words, It shall not be performed on the seventh day; those positive precepts, "Ye shall circumcise the flesh of your foreskin—he that is eight days old shall be circumcised," plainly implying the forementioned prohibitions. So when Jehovah commanded the Israelites to take a lamb, a male of the first year, for the paschal feast, there was no need to forbid the choice of a ewe lamb, nor yet a ram of the second or third year. So likewise, when

---

* See Mr. Clarkson's Pract. Div. of Papists, p. 377, 378.

Paul, speaking of the sacred supper, says, "Let a man EXAMINE HIMSELF, and so let him eat," there was no necessity of adding, Those who *cannot* examine themselves *ought not to eat.*—Thus in regard to the ordinance before us. Our Lord having given a commission to baptize those that are taught, without saying any thing elsewhere, by way of precept or of example, concerning such being included in that commission as are not instructed; there was no necessity for him to prohibit the baptizing those who are not taught; much less to forbid the baptizing of infants, that cannot be taught, in order to render the baptism of them unlawful. We may safely conclude, therefore, that though negative arguments in various cases have no force; yet, in positive worship and ritual duty, they are, they must be valid. Otherwise, it will be impossible to vindicate the divine conduct in punishing the sons of Aaron, for *offering strange fire;* or Uzzah, for *touching the ark;* seeing neither the one nor the other of these particulars was expressly forbidden.

Remarkably strong to our purpose, are the words of Dr. Owen, on Heb. i. 5: "An argument taken negatively," says he, "from the authority of the scripture, in matters of faith, or what relates to the worship of God, is valid and effectual, and here consecrated for ever to the use of the church by the apostle." And on those words: *Our Lord sprang out of Judah; of which tribe Moses spake nothing concerning the priesthood;* the same excellent author says: "This silence of Moses in this matter, the apostle takes to be a sufficient argument to prove that the legal priesthood did not belong, nor could be transferred unto, the tribe of Judah. And the grounds hereof are resolved into this general maxim: That whatever is not revealed and appointed in the worship of God, by God himself, is to be considered as nothing, yea, as that which is to be rejected. And such he conceived to be the evidence of this maxim, that he chose rather to argue from the silence of Moses in general, than from the particular prohibition, that none, who was not of the posterity of Aaron, should approach unto the priestly office. So God himself comdemneth some instances of false worship on this ground, That he never *appointed* them; that they never *came into his heart;* and thence aggravates the sin of the people, rather than from the *particular prohibition* of them, (Jer. vii. 31.)"

That it may still farther appear we are not led by mere hypothesis thus to reason and thus to conclude, I will present my reader with an extract from another learned Pædobaptist and an able writer, who adopts the principle on which we argue in the present case, and considers it as applicable to laws and duties in general. " Since office, or duty," says Heineccius, " means an action conformable to law, it is plain that duty cannot be conceived without a law; that he does not perform a duty who imposes on himself what no law commands; that an action ceases to be duty, when the law, or the reason of the law ceases; and that when a law extends to certain persons only, of two persons who do the same action, the one performs his duty, and the other acts contrary to his duty."* — To all which I may add, unless the principle of reasoning here adopted be just, the arguments of Protestants against unscriptural ceremonies in the Romish communion, will almost universally fail of proving the several points for which they were produced.

Reflect. X. Mr. Edward Williams, convinced there is no express precept, nor plain example for infant baptism in the New Testament, endeavours to evade the force of our arguments in the following manner: "Whatever there may be in the ordinance of baptism of a *positive* consideration, there is nothing relative to the *subjects* of it so merely positive as to be independent on all

---

* System of Universal Law, b. i. chap. v. § 121.

moral grounds;—nay farther, whatever relates to the qualifications of the subjects, is of a nature *entirely* moral; and to say otherwise must imply a contradiction. Baptism, therefore, is an ordinance of a *mixed* nature, partly positive and partly moral. As far as this, or any such ordinance, partakes of a *moral* nature, the reason and design of the law, or if you please the *spirit* of it, is our rule of duty—and only so far as it partakes of a positive nature is the letter of the law our rule. As what relates to the qualification of the subjects is of *moral* consideration, we are necessitated to seek in them the reason and intention of the command; but infants partaking of the great *primary* qualification, which the evident design of the ordinance requires, ought to be baptized; and it must imply a breach of duty in a minister to decline it. To argue on this principle— *Baptism is a positive rite, and therefore ought to be express, full, and circumstantial*—is, on the principles, concessions, and practice of Antipædobaptists, demonstrably fallacious. For the law of baptism is evidently, in *fact*, not circumstantial and determinate; and therefore is not, cannot be an institution entirely positive."*

Baptism then, according to Mr. Williams, is of a *mixed* nature; an ordinance, partly moral and partly positive. This, to me, is a new idea; for, of all the writers quoted in this work, of all the authors I have perused, not one occurs to remembrance who has thus represented baptism. Nor do I suppose Mr. Maurice's annotator would have adopted the singular notion, if he had not felt himself embarrassed by the want of both precept and precedent for infant baptism. If, however, the evidence produced be valid, the novelty of his notion is not material. His principal reason in favour of the position is; "Whatever belongs to the qualifications of the subjects is entirely moral." But will this prove that baptism is not, strictly speaking, a positive institute?

---

* Notes on Mr. Maurice's Social Religion, p. 68, 69.

Will it not apply with all its force to the Lord's supper? On this principle, we have no ordinance entirely positive under the new economy; because it is plain the qualifications for that appointment are chiefly of the moral kind. Many are those theological writers who have more or less treated on positive institutions; some of whose books I have seen and perused with care: but I do not recollect any author, who so defines or describes a religious appointment merely positive, as to exclude every idea of what is moral from the qualifications of its proper subjects. To constitute any branch of religious duty purely positive, it is enough that the rite itself, the manner of performing it, the qualifications of the subject, the end to be answered by it, and the term of its continuance, depend entirely on the sovereign pleasure of our divine Legislator. The *nature* of the qualifications, whether moral or not, makes no part of those *criteria* by which the definition of a positive rite should be directed. Consequently, baptism is a positive institute; and therefore, by his own acknowledgment, the *letter* of the law must be the rule of its administration, both as to mode and subject.*

Whatever belongs to the qualifications of the subjects is ENTIRELY *moral.* Agreed: it must be allowed, however, that those qualifications are absolutely dependant on the sovereign pleasure of God. But how should an infant, of a few days or of a month old, be a partaker of such qualifications, to render it a proper subject of baptism? Or, supposing such qualifications to exist, by what means are they to be discovered? What is there discernible, that can with propriety be called *moral*, in one that is not capable of moral agency? Morality, in all its branches, is nothing but the discharge of moral obligation; or, a conformity of heart and of life to the rule of duty. Of this, it is manifest, mere infants are naturally incapable. On whatever ground,

---

* See Part I. Chap. I. No. 1—20.

therefore, Mr. Williams fixes the right of infants to baptism, I do not see how it either is or can be of a *moral* nature. Parents may have the requisite moral qualifications for the ordinance; but I cannot conceive how their new-born offspring, for whom our author pleads as proper subjects of the rite, should be so qualified; and yet he maintains, that "whatever belongs to the qualifications of *the subjects* is ENTIRELY moral." This respectable annotator is here guilty, if I may so express it, of logical *felo-de-se;* for his argument subverts the cause it was intended to serve, and proves the reverse of what he designed.

Infants partake of the great primary qualification which the design of the ordinance requires, and therefore should be baptized. Infants—what, in general? Of all mankind? He will not, I presume, assert it. Or if he did, his argument would be equally feeble. I take it for granted, however, that he means the infants of professed believers. But there is no more of a moral temper, or of a moral conduct, in the mere infant of a real Christian, than there is in that of a Jew, or of a Turk. Besides, Mr. Williams himself has opposed the notion of hereditary grace.* If then the infants he means be descended from parents of a certain description, their qualifications must be derived from those parents, whoever they be; consequently, not from any thing moral in themselves. But our author's position requires that the infants themselves possess moral qualifications, to render them the subjects of baptism. What that "great primary qualification" is which infants have, he has not informed us; nor will I indulge conjecture: but I may venture to say, that it is not their being *taught;* that it is not *repentance;* that it is not *faith;* that it is not *a profession* of the one or the other. Consequently, whatever it be, it is not that which John the Baptist required; it is not that which the evangelist Philip required;

---

* See Part II. Chap. IV. Sect. IV. § ii. No. 11.

nor is it that which our Lord in his commission appointed; and if so, it is not the *primitive* qualification, whatever else it may be.

Our annotator speaks with a decisive tone when he adds; *The law of baptism is evidently and in fact not circumstantial and determinate, and therefore cannot be an institution entirely positive.* The LAW *of baptism.* Then some specific action, called *baptism*, is absolutely and in earnest required by it; contrary to what he maintains in another place, on which we have already animadverted. This divine law, however, is *not circumstantial*—is *not determinate.* In one of his notes, to which I have just adverted, he would fain persuade us, that the meaning of our Lord, in his enacting term *baptize*, is not now understood with precision, even by the most eminent authors; and therefore he is of opinion, that persons concerned in the administration should have it performed according to their own mind; which, to be sure, is the way for every one to be *pleased*, whether Jesus Christ be obeyed or not. Now he tells us, with an air of assurance, that this law of the Lord is, " not circumstantial and determinate," with regard to the *subjects* of the institution. According to him, therefore, nothing is plain, determinate, or certain, relating to either the mode or the subject. Aristotle is reported to have said, of some of his works, " That they were *Edita quasi non edita;* so *published as not to be made public*, by reason of their obscurity."* Just such, according to our author, is the promulgation of the heavenly statute under consideration. But what a representation this, of a positive divine law! If Mr. Williams be right, one might almost as well study John viii. 6, 8, to know what our Lord *wrote on the ground*, as endeavour to penetrate his meaning in the law of baptism. When I consider the language of our annotator on another occasion, I do not see how he can steadily believe any thing

---

* History of Popery, vol. ii. p. 468.

at all relating to this positive institute. For he declares, in the passage to which I refer, That "nothing should be considered as an established principle of faith, which is not in some part of scripture delivered with *perspicuity.*"* The baptismal command, therefore, being so indeterminate and so obscure, in regard to both mode and subject, he ought, on his own principle, to be silent about it. How much more agreeable is the language of Mr. Vincent Alsop, when he says; "The law of Christ was as perfect as his discoveries. He has told us as fully and clearly what we should *do,* as what we should *believe.* He that may invade the royal office, upon pretence there are not laws enow, [or not sufficiently clear,] for the government [or worship] of the church; may, with equal appearance of reason, invade the prophetic office too, upon pretence there are not revelations now for its instruction."†—Though I take it for granted that Mr. Williams is not a stranger to the Popish controversy, relating to positive ordinances of holy worship, yet I cannot help thinking that he quite overlooked it, when penning his notes concerning baptism; because that want of perspicuity and of precision, which he charges on a positive law, is much more becoming the creed of a Papist, than that of a Protestant Dissenter.

That the law of baptism is neither *circumstantial,* nor *determinate,* in favour of the present prevailing custom, is cheerfully granted; for it says nothing at all about pouring or sprinkling water upon infants: nor does the history of baptismal practice in the apostolic churches. But is this any proof that the law itself is not explicit, either as to mode or subject? Mr. Maurice's annotator seems to have assumed, as a principle, *That infants are to be baptized:* but applying this principle to the law of baptism, he soon perceives a disagreement between them. Then, instead of renouncing the principle as false, he impeaches the law as obscure. Take but the

---

* Notes on Social Religion, p. 368. † Sober Enquiry, p. 42.

commanding terms* of the heavenly statute in their natural, primary, obvious meaning; and I appeal to impartiality, whether the law of baptism be not as plain as that of the holy supper. If indeed our Lord intended infants to be baptized, and if he designed to publish that intention by his evangelists,† the law of baptism might well be considered as vague and obscure. But this, we contend, is not the case; as it is inconsistent with the nature of a positive institution, impeaches the legislative character of Jesus Christ, and enervates the arguments of Protestants against Papal superstition. See Part I. Chap. I. No. 4, 8, 12, 13, 20. Reflect. II. III.

Farther: That neither infants nor adults have any thing to do with baptism as a religious rite, except in virtue of divine institution, will be acknowledged. If, therefore, infants, *jure divino*, be entitled to baptism, it must be because the institution itself gives them that right, of which it makes an essential part. Now, of what nature the institution is, and to whom it relates, cannot be known, unless by the formula of it, ‡ or by the practice of the apostles. But that neither the right of infants to the ordinance, nor their participation of it, is plainly mentioned, either in the words of the institution, or in the history of apostolic practice, is readily granted by our opposers. Must we then suppose that an essential part, nay, according to modern custom, the *principal* part of the institution was passed over in silence by evangelists and apostles, and left in obscurity for posterity to infer by a train of consequences? Chamier, I remember, when opposing the pretended necessity of mixing the eucharistical wine with water, and when pleading the silence of the New Testament, says: "No one maintains the necessity of mixing wine with water on the ground of divine institution; unless the evangelists and Paul were *traitors*, who passed over in silence a part of

---

* Μαθητευσατε and βαπτιζοντες. † Matt. xxviii. 19;
Mark xvi. 15, 16.   ‡ Ibid.

the institution so useful and so important."* Now is any thing said concerning *infants*, in the baptismal appointment, any more than about *water*, in the institution of the holy supper? Supposing it should be objected, " There was no occasion for children to be mentioned in the divine command, because it was then common for them to partake of the proselyte baptism." It would be easy to answer, There is abundantly more ground to conclude, that it was customary among the ancient Jews, in their convivial entertainments, to mix the wine with water, than any one has to assert, that the proselyte baptism was of so early a date; as will appear in its proper place. If, therefore, the institution of baptism comprehend infants, why may not our Lord's appointment of the sacred supper include that mixture for which the Papists plead? Consequently, supposing infants to have been comprehended by our Lord in his baptismal institution, and admitting the observation of Chamier to be just; the severity of his remark will equally apply to such evangelists as professedly recorded the divine appointment of baptism, as to that particular for which it was designed. That Christ, in his institution, should order infants to be baptized, and the evangelists not be inclined to mention it; or that, with a full intention to inform us of it, they should use such language as they do, in recording the appointment, are to me *alike incredible*.

Mr. Williams farther says: " Should any ask me why, as a Christian minister, I baptize an infant? I can truly answer, that I have the *very same reason* for doing it that John the Baptist had for baptizing penitent sinners, in Jordan and Enon; the *same* reason that Jesus, by the ministry of his apostles, had for baptizing a still greater multitude; and, finally, the *same* reason that our Baptist brethren have, or ought to have, and which they profess to have, in the general tenour of their practice,

---

* Panstrat. tom. iv. l. vi. c. iii. §. 23.

for baptizing adults."* But why distinguish between *penitent* sinners, and those *adults* of whom he speaks? for Mr. Williams either knows, or might have known, that we do not baptize adults because of their *age*, but because they *profess repentance*. Or does he mean to distinguish between penitent *adults* and penitent *infants?* —Again: Why did not the annotator inform us, what that "very same reason" is, of which he speaks? Had he done this, we might, perhaps, have concluded with some degree of precision, whether there be that identity of reason for him to baptize an infant, as there was for John, and for the apostles, to baptize penitent sinners. That reason, however, is not specified, nor is there any thing but mere assertion; on which account we cannot forbear to hesitate. It is indeed extremely singular, that he should speak of "the *very same reason—the same—the same;*" and yet leave us entirely to conjecture what that reason is. It brings to remembrance the following words of an old Nonconformist, when contending with Papists: "*Jure Divino,*" saith the Canonist, "*by divine right;* but the Canonist who saith it, hath the wit to let us seek the text."†—Pleasing it is to think, that, in the judgment of this opponent, we baptize persons on " the very same reason," or ground, as that upon which the harbinger of Christ and all the apostles proceeded, when administering the sacred rite: but we have our suspicions whether Mr. Williams "can truly" say this, with regard to his pouring or sprinkling water upon any infant. John, it appears, received a commission from heaven to baptize those who made a credible profession of repentance; and this we consider as "the reason" of his baptizing penitent sinners. But has our opposer a divine command for baptizing an infant that cannot repent? John, it is plain, frowned upon some who came for his baptism, because they gave no

---

* Notes on Social Relig. p. 68.
† Morning Exercise against Popery, p. 72.

evidence of repentance. Does Mr. Williams reject any infants for that "very reason?"—The apostles received an express order to "teach all nations," by preaching "the gospel to every creature;" and to baptize those that were taught—so taught as to believe in Jesus Christ. This we consider as "the very reason" of their baptismal conduct. But has our Pædobaptist Brother any divine injunction to baptize those who cannot be taught, by either preaching or conversation, and who are equally incapable of believing? The Baptists profess to act on the united ground of divine precept and apostolic example, in baptizing those, and only those, who make a credible declaration of repentance and faith, without regard to age or any other circumstance. But is this "the very reason," or the single ground, on which Mr. Williams proceeds, when he baptizes an infant?

Farther: Why, in the name of consistency, why should this opponent speak with such assurance of having "the very same reason" for *baptizing* an infant, which John and the apostles had for baptizing a multitude of penitent sinners? while it is clear, from his own confession, that he does not know what our Lord meant by his command *to baptize.* Nay, so sensible is he of his own ignorance in this respect, and so suspicious that a want of certainty is now become universal; that he thinks it quite reasonable for the parties concerned, to use the water as they may think proper. See Part I. Chap. II. Reflect. IX.—His reasoning admits, indeed, that the apostles perfectly understood the mind of our Lord, in his commanding term, *baptize;* and as they were fully disposed to perform his will, we may safely conclude that they administered the ordinance to one and another; for "the very same reason." But as every mode of using water cannot be baptism, any more than it can be sprinkling; as that only can be real baptism which our Lord appointed, in distinction from every other action; and as Mr. Williams acknowledges his ignorance of what the Lawgiver intended by the enacting word *baptize;* he must act upon a conjecture extremely shrewd and uncommonly happy, if at any time he really *baptize* an infant for " the *very same* reason" that John or the apostles baptized multitudes of penitent sinners. The very same form of words might, indeed, be used by him; whether, with John, he plunged a penitent in Jordan, or sprinkled a few drops of water on the face of an infant; but surely he could not act upon " the *very same* reason" in both cases. This, I think, must be allowed; except he can prove, that a commission to immerse penitents, is equally an order to sprinkle infants. But, besides the absurdity of any one making such an attempt, it is a task to which this opposer cannot pretend; because, by so doing, he would endeavour to fix the sense of a word which is considered by him as indeterminable: for he insists that the most eminent authors are divided about our Lord's meaning in the term *baptize;* and therefore proposes that people should please themselves, with regard to the mode of administration. If Mr. Williams, however, should at any time write professedly against the Baptists, it may be expected, (unless he give up this point,) that his *grand reason* for sprinkling infants, will be the *very same* which is given by us for immersing penitent sinners; and then the author of a certain *Apology* for clerical conformity will have an humble imitator.*

---

* In the Apologia, to which I refer, the following uncommon and surprising positions are contained. " My first and *principal* reason [for ministerial conformity] is, *The regard I owe to the honour and authority of the Lord Jesus Christ, as Head and Lawgiver of his church....* It seems to me, that I could no more officiate as a minister among any people who insist upon other terms of communion than those which our Lord has appointed, faith and holiness, than I could subscribe to the dogmas of the Council of Trent.... My second reason for not being a Dissenter is, *Because I highly value the right of private judgment, and my liberty as a man and as a Christian....* I cannot become a Dissenter till I am

Reflect. XI. I will present the reader with an extract from a celebrated Roman Catholic author, expressing the opinion that Papists have concerning the mode of reasoning used by Protestants in favour of Pædobaptism. The writer to whom I refer is Bossuet, the bishop of Meaux, and his language is as follows: "As for infants, those of the pretended Reformed religion indeed say, their baptism is founded on the scripture; but they produce no passage express to that purpose, but argue from very remote, not to say very doubtful, and even very false consequences. It is certain, that all the proofs they bring from the scripture on this subject,

---

weary of my liberty." Apologia, p. 61, 116, 119, 121.—If these be solid reasons for clerical conformity, those ministers that were ejected in the year sixteen hundred and sixty-two must be considered as a set of maniacs. Being loth, however, to impeach the intellects of two thousand persons, who suffered so much for the sake of a good conscience, I cannot forbear suspecting, that these positions are an insult upon the understandings of Dissenters, and that sensible Episcopalians themselves must despise them; for it is on these and similar principles Dissenters have always proceeded in justifying their Nonconformity. When our Apologist says, " We [conforming clergy] are not so much at the mercy of our hearers for our subsistence, as the Dissenting ministers are," we perfectly understand him. We have been frequently told of this, by those who have defended civil establishments of religion; and we freely acknowledge, that secular prudence is very apparent in many who act upon the principle thus avowed. But when we find a pious Episcopalian author seizing the grand principles of our Protestant Dissent, in order to found a vindication of his own Conformity upon them, we are surprised, and cannot forbear thinking of those doughty champions for Popery, Jacob. de Graffiis, and Father Mumford the Jesuit: the former of whom found image-worship enjoined in the *second command;* and the latter discovered a convincing proof of clerical celibacy in those words of Paul, *A bishop must be the husband of one wife.* See Preserv. from Popery, title i. p. 341. vol. ii. Gen. Discourses against Popery, p. 140.—Nor can we avoid considering the conduct of this Apologist as unprecedented in the Nonconformist controversy—as betraying an uncommon degree of rage for hypothesis, and of predilection for paradox. See Apologia, p. 136.

have no force at all; and those that might have some strength, are destroyed by themselves.... The proofs that are drawn from the necessity of baptism, to compel men to allow it to infants, are destroyed by our Reformed gentlemen; and these that follow are substituted in their room, as they are noted in their catechism, in their confession of faith, and in their prayers; namely, that the children of believers are born in the covenant, according to this promise, 'I will be thy God, and the God of thy offspring to a thousand generations.' From whence they conclude, that since the virtue and substance of baptism belongs to infants, it would be injurious to them to deny them the sign, which is inferior to it. By a like reason, they will find themselves forced to give the communion together with baptism; for they who are in the covenant, are incorporated with Jesus Christ: the infants of believers are in the covenant; therefore, they are incorporated with Jesus Christ. And having by this means, according to them, the virtue and substance of the communion; they ought to say, as they do of baptism, that the sign of it cannot without injury be refused them."*

Reflect. XII. To the tenour of this reasoning it is often objected; That there is no express command to baptize believers. With an air of confidence, in reference to this affair, Dr. Addington asks and answers; "Is there no express command of Christ to baptize believers? Not *one* in all the New Testament." † If, by an *express* command, he mean these very words, *Baptize believers*, it is allowed; but what is that to the purpose, while the ideas conveyed by those terms, are as plainly and strongly expressed, as if the identical words had been repeatedly used? Nor will Dr. Addington deny this. With equal reason, therefore, does cardinal Bellarmine object the want of these express

---

* In Mr. Stennett *against* Mr. Russen, p. 180, 182, 183.
† Summary of Christian Minister's Reasons, p. 24.

words, *the imputed righteousness of Christ*, against the Protestant doctrine of justification; or Socinus oppose the atonement, because the term *satisfaction* is not syllabically used concerning that capital fact.—But let us reflect on a passage or two. Does not Christ say, "Preach the gospel to every creature: he that BELIEVETH and is baptized shall be saved?" Is it not the language of his evangelist, "If thou BELIEVEST with all thy heart, thou mayest" be baptized? Now can any person thus believe the gospel, without being a *believer?* Or will this opponent aver, that neither of these passages *enjoins* the administration of baptism to *believers?* Let him produce a text from the New Testament, that is equally express for the baptism of infants, and we will immediately give up the argument.—Besides, Dr. Addington well knows that we connect the want of a *plain example*, with the want of an express command for infant baptism. To have done our objection justice, he ought, therefore, to have put the question thus: Is there no *express command* of Christ, nor any *plain apostolic example*, for baptizing believers? and then he would have been far from teaching his catechumen to answer; "Not *one* in all the New Testament." Such a negative, to such a question, would have been an outrage on the common faith of the whole Christian world; and yet, if you substitute the term *infants*, for the word *believers*, Pædobaptists themselves must answer in the negative.

It is farther objected; That there is neither precept nor example for baptizing the *children of Christian parents* when they are grown up; and that on the same principles, applied in similar arguments, we must neither observe the *Lord's day*, nor admit *women* to the holy table. Thus, Dr. Mayo, for instance: "They [the Baptists] have not a single precedent in scripture—of their subjects of baptism, the children of Christian parents, whose baptism was delayed till they were of adult years, to make a profession of their faith."* But if this objection have any weight, it must lie with equal force against the continuance of baptism among Christians, or the administration of it to any description of subjects; except in reference to such persons as are converted from Judaism, Mohammedanism, or Paganism: and it was, if I mistake not, first employed by Socinus for that purpose.† To which the learned Hoornbeek replies; "That such as were educated in the Christian religion, and were never alienated from it, are not expressly mentioned in the New Testament as baptized; does not arise from hence, That such never were baptized, nor ought so to have been: but because the apostolic writings contain the history of the *first* times, when Christianity was recent." ‡ This answer applies to the case before us. Our opposers, therefore, should be cautious how they urge such an objection against us, lest inadvertently they give up to the arguments of Socinus, of Emlyn, and of others, the continuance of baptism, except in extraordinary cases.—But is it not enough, that we have both an express command, and plain examples, for baptizing those who are *taught*, who are *made disciples*, and *profess faith* in the Son of God? Nay, I appeal to Dr. Mayo himself, who on another occasion declares; "It is sufficient for my purpose, that our practice *can be found* in the New Testament."§ It is but grateful to acknowledge, how much we are obliged to this author for presenting us with such a *shield*, to prevent the dart of his own objection from piercing our cause.—It seems, indeed, hard to conceive why our Brethren should lay such a stress upon this particular, as if it were decisively against us, unless it be the want of more cogent objections. For it is manifest, that the idea of *carnal descent*, from parents of any de-

---

* Apology and Shield, p. 82.   † De Baptismo, cap. x.
‡ Socin. Confut. tom. iii. p. 279.   See Dr. Doddridge's Lectures, p. 510, 511.   § Ut supra, p. 78, 79.

scription, makes no part of the institution, or law of baptism; and consequently should have no influence upon our practice. No; whether the candidate be descended from real, or from barely nominal Christians; whether his parents be Jews, Turks, or Pagans; nay, whether he be old or young; it is, properly speaking, a mere *circumstance;* provided he make a credible profession of faith—equally a circumstance, with learning or illiteracy, riches or poverty. The character of parents, and family relations, have nothing to do in the new economy, which is entirely spiritual—are of no avail in that kingdom which " is not of this world;" the subjects of which " are born, not of blood, nor of the will of the flesh, nor of the will of man, but of God." If the candidate give evidence of his being a disciple of Christ, it is all the institution demands, and all that apostolic practice required. Such being the true state of the case, why should our opposers insist on a scriptural precedent for baptizing the adult offspring of Christians? Why call for an example of that which makes no part of the institution, but is merely circumstantial? We sometimes baptize persons of sixty or seventy years of age. As well, therefore, might it be objected, that there is no instance in sacred writ of any person so far advanced in years being baptized by the apostles. How far the following observation of Dr. Owen will here apply, is left with my reader. " It is merely from a spirit of contention that some call on us, or others, to produce express testimony, or institution, for every circumstance in the practice of religious duties in the church; and on a supposed failure herein, to conclude, that they have power themselves to institute and ordain such ceremonies as they think meet, under a pretence of their being circumstances of worship."*

As to the *Lord's day,* our opponents themselves allow, that we have not only apostolical examples of as-

---

* Enquiry into the Orig. and Nat. of Churches, p. 14.

sembling on the first day of the week for the solemnities of public devotion, but plain intimations that this was the common practice of the primitive churches;* and therefore, the objector himself being judge, there is no force in what is alleged. Besides, there is something of a *moral* nature in the observation of a sabbath; but not so in the administration of baptism. In regard to the supposed want of an explicit warrant for admitting *women* to the holy table, we reply by demanding; Does not Paul, when he says, " Let a man examine himself, and so let him eat," enjoin a reception of the sacred supper? Does not the term ανθρωπος, there used, often stand as a name of our species, without regard to sex? Have we not the authority of lexicographers, † and, which is incomparably more, the sanction of common sense, for understanding it thus in that passage? When the sexes are distinguished and opposed, the word for a *man* is not ανθρωπος, but ανηρ.‡ This distinction is very strongly marked in that celebrated saying of Thales, as given in his Life, by Diogenes Laertius. § The Grecian sage was thankful to Fortune, " that he was ανθρωπος,

---

* Acts xx. 7; 1 Cor. xvi. 1, 2.

† Mr. Parkhurst says : " Ανϑρωπος is a name of the species, without respect to sex."——Mintert: " Homo, in genere, sive mas sit, sive fœmina."——Schwarzius : " Homo, i. e. humanâ naturâ præditus, habens ea quæ hominis natura postulat."——" Sæpissimè," says the learned Schaubius, "in scripturâ sacrâ *filii* pro utroque sexu occurrunt, ut 1 Joh. ii. 1; iii. 7, 18; v. 12. 28. Imo pro totâ posteritate et prole, vid. Ps. ciii. 17; Prov. xiii. 22 .... Etenim, tam a Græcis, quam in jure Romano, *pronunciatio sermonis in masculino sexu, ad utrumque sexum plerumque porrigit;* et semper sexus masculinus fœmininum continet." Bib. Bremens. class iv. p. 722, 723. Vid. Bezam, in 1 Cor. xiii. 11. Stockium, Interpres Græcus, cap. ii. § 28. So the words, אדם, *Homo*, and *Man*, are frequently used for one of the human species, without regard to sex.

‡ See, amongst a multitude of instances, 1 Cor. xi. 3—12.

§ Lib. i. cap. i. § 7. Lips. 1759. Thus Mr. Blackwall : " Ανθρωπος—is generally, in the best writers, used to include both sexes, all the human race. Herodotus uses it for γυνη." Sacred Classics, vol. i. part i. chap. ii. § 9.

one of the *human* species, and not a beast; that he was ανηρ, a *man*, and not a woman; that he was born a Greek, and not a barbarian. Besides, when the apostle delivered to the church at Corinth what he had *received of the Lord*, did he not deliver a command—a command to the whole church, consisting of *women* as well as men? When he farther says, "We, being many, are one bread, and one body; for we all are partakers of that one bread;" does he not speak of *women*, as well as of men?* Again: Are there any prerequisites for the holy supper, of which women are not equally capable as men? And are not male and female *one in Christ?* When we oppose the baptism of infants, it is not because of their tender age; but because they neither do nor can profess faith in the Son of God. Whenever we meet with such as are denominated by the apostle, τεκνα πιστα, *faithful,* or believing *children,*† whoever may be their parents, or whatever may be their age, we have no objection to baptize them. A credible profession of repentance and faith being all we desire, in reference to this affair, either of old or young.

---

* 1 Cor. x. 17, and xi. 28. Compare Acts i. 13, 14, with Acts ii. 42, 47. † Tit. i, 6.

CHAPTER II.

No Evidence of Pædobaptism, before the latter End of the Second, or the Beginning of the Third Century.

SALMASIUS and Suicerus.—" In the two first centuries no one was baptized, except, being instructed in the faith, and acquainted with the doctrine of Christ, he was able to profess himself a believer; because of those words, ' He that believeth and is baptized.' First, therefore, he was to believe. Thence the order of catechumens in the church. Then, also, it was the constant custom to give the Lord's supper to those catechumens, immediately after their baptism." Epist. ad Justum Pacium, apud Van Dale Hist. Baptism. Suiceri Thesaur. Eccles. sub voce Συναξις, tom. ii. p. 1136.

2. Ludovicus Vives.—" No one in former times was admitted to the sacred baptistery, except he was of age, understood what the mystical water meant, desired to be washed in it, and expressed that desire more than once. Of which practice we have yet a resemblance in our baptism of infants; for an infant of only a day or two old, is yet asked, ' Whether he will be baptized?' and this question is asked three times. In whose name the sponsors answer, ' He does desire it.'" Annot. in Aug. de Civ. Dei, l. i. c. xxvii.

3. M. Formey.—" They baptized from this time, [the latter end of the second century,] infants as well as adults." Abridg. Eccles. Hist. vol. i. p. 33.

4. Curcellæus.—" The baptism of infants, in the two first centuries after Christ, was altogether unknown; but in the third and fourth was allowed by some few. In the fifth, and following ages, it was generally received ....The custom of baptizing infants did not begin before the third age after Christ was born. In the former

ages no trace of it appears—and it was introduced without the command of Christ." Institut. Relig. Christ. l. i. c. xii. Dissert. Secund. de Pecc. Orig. § 56.

5. M. De la Roque.—" The primitive church did not baptize infants; and the learned Grotius proves it in his Annotations on the Gospel. Even the practice of the Romish church is an evident token of it; for with them baptism must be desired before they enter into the church, and it is the godfather that asks it in the name of the child. A formal and express profession of faith must be made, which the godfather also makes in the child's name; a promise must be made, to renounce the world and the pomps of it, the flesh, and the devil; all which is done by the godfather in the name of the child. Is not this a visible sign, that formerly it was the persons themselves, who in their own name desired baptism, made a profession of their faith, and renounced their past life, to consecrate themselves to the Lord Jesus Christ for the time to come?" In Mr. Stennett's Answer to Mr. Russen, p. 188, 189.

6. Mr. Chambers.—" It appears, that in the primitive times none were baptized but adults." Cyclopædia, article Baptism.

7. Johannes Bohemius.—" Baptism of old was administered to none (unless upon urgent necessity) but to such as were before instructed in the faith and catechized. But when it came to be judged necessary to everlasting life, it was ordained that infants should be baptized, and that they should have godfathers and godmothers, who should be sureties for infants, and should renounce the devil in their behalf." In Thomas Lawson's Baptismalogia, p. 88.

8. Rigaltius.—" In the Acts of the Apostles we read, that *both men and women* were baptized, when they believed the gospel preached by Philip, without any mention being made of infants. From the apostolic age, therefore, to the time of Tertullian, the matter is

doubtful. Some there were, from that saying of our Lord, 'Suffer little children to come to me,' (to whom, nevertheless, our Lord did not command water to be ministered,) who took occasion to baptize new born infants. And as if they had been transacting some secular affair with God, they offered sponsors or sureties to Christ, who engaged that they should not depart from the Christian faith when adult; which practice displeased Tertullian." In Mr. Stennett's Answer to Mr. Russen, p. 74, 75.

9. Dr. Holland.—" In the first plantation of Christianity amongst the Gentiles, such only as were of full age, after they were instructed in the principles of the Christian religion, were admitted to baptism." In Dr. Wall's Hist. Inf. Bap. part ii. chap. ii. p. 281.

10. Cattenburgh.—" Though it cannot be unanswerably proved, that infant baptism was practised from the beginning of Christianity; yet its original is to be derived much higher than those learned men, Episcopius and Limborch, have admitted."* Spicileg. Theol. Christ. p. 1059.

11. Wolfgangus Capito.—" In the first times of the church no one was baptized, nor received into the holy communion of Christians, till after he had given himself up entirely to the word and authority of Christ." Apud Schyn Hist. Mennonit. p. 170.

12. Venema.—" It is indeed certain, that Pædobaptism was practised in the second century; yet so, that it was not the custom of the church, nor the general practice; much less was it generally esteemed necessary that infants should be baptized.... Tertullian has no where mentioned Pædobaptism among the tradi-

---

* Episcopius denies that any tradition can be produced for Pædobaptism, till a little before the Milevitan Council, A.D. 418; and maintains, that it was not practised in Asia till near the time of that council. Institut. l. iv. c. xiv.—Mr. Brandt speaks to the same effect. Hist. Reform. Annotat. on b. ii. vol. i. p. 9.

tions of the church, nor even among the customs of the church that were publicly received and usually observed; nay, he plainly intimates, that in his time it was yet a doubtful affair. For in his book, De Baptismo, (cap. xviii.) he dissuades from baptizing infants, and proves by certain reasons, that the delay of it to a more mature age is to be preferred; which he certainly would not have done, if it had been a tradition and a public custom of the church, seeing he was very tenacious of traditions; nor, had it been a tradition, would he have failed to mention it. It is manifest, therefore, that nothing was then determined concerning the time of baptism; nay, he judged it safer that unmarried persons should defer their baptism.... Nothing can be affirmed with certainty, concerning the custom of the church before Tertullian; seeing there is not any where in more ancient writers, that I know of, undoubted mention of infant baptism. Justin Martyr, in his Second Apology, when describing baptism, mentions only that of adults. Irenæus alone (Contra Hæres. l. ii. c. xxii.) may be considered as referring to Pædobaptism, when he says; ' Christ passed through all the ages of man, that he might save all by himself; all I say,' thus he proceeds, ' who by him are regenerated to God, infants, and little ones, and children, and youths, and persons advanced in age.' For the word, *regenerated,* is wont to be used concerning baptism; and in that sense I freely admit it may be here understood. Yet I do not consider it as undoubtedly so, seeing it is not always used in that sense, especially if no mention of baptism precede or follow; which is the case here: and here, to be *regenerated* by Christ, may be explained by *sanctified,* that is, saved by Christ. The sense, therefore, may be; That Christ's passing through all the ages of man, intended to signify, by his own example, that he came to save men of every age, and also to sanctify or save infants. I conclude, therefore, that Pædobaptism cannot be certainly proved to have been practised before the times of Tertullian; and that there were persons in his age who desired their infants might be baptized, especially when they were afraid of their dying without baptism: which opinion Tertullian opposed, and by so doing, he intimates that Pædobaptism began to prevail. These are the things that may be affirmed with apparent certainty, concerning the antiquity of infant baptism, after the times of the apostles; for more are maintained without solid foundation." Hist. Eccles. tom. iii. secul. ii. § 108, 109.

REFLECTIONS.

Reflect. I. It is well observed by Limborch, "That many, when they enquire after the opinions of ancient writers, ascribe to them, not what they really taught, but what they wish them to have taught. Hence different opinions are attributed to them, according to the various prejudices that are entertained by the enquirers."* This, there is reason to think, is a fact; and therefore it is to the honour of our cause, that the writers produced have made such declarations. For though, as Dr. Bishop remarks, " the scriptures are the only rule of faith,—we are apt to enquire how the earliest authors understood and explained them; what opinions they held and professed, as the true and necessary doctrines [and practices] of Christianity; and what they denied and condemned."† We farther observe, with the celebrated Mr. Claude; "That the scripture is the only rule of our faith; that we do not acknowledge any other authority able to decide the disputed points in religion, than that of the word of God; and that if we sometimes dispute by the fathers, it is but by way of condescension to [our opposers,] to act upon their own principle, and not to submit our consciences to the word of men."‡

---

* Liber Sentent. Inquisit. Tholos. Præf. p. 3.
† Eight Sermons, Serm. iv. p. 132.
‡ Defence of the Reformation, part iii. p. 81, 82.

That most of these authors were well versed in the ancient monuments of the Christian church, few of my readers acquainted with their characters will deny; and being Pædobaptists, they were under no influence, from their avowed hypothesis, to make such declarations as these before us. Consequently, we must consider these learned men, as led by plain historical evidence, and by a commendable regard for truth, to express their views of the case in this remarkable manner. Now such concessions, from writers whose literary abilities cannot be questioned, and who are entirely free from suspicion of intending to sink the reputation of Pædobaptism, afford a strong presumption in our favour, so far as ecclesiastical antiquity is concerned in the dispute. Nay, I may venture to add, concessions of this kind from the pens of such men as Salmasius and Suicerus, of Rigaltius and Venema, must rebuke that haughty confidence with which we are sometimes treated, even by juvenile opponents; as if the highest and purest ecclesiastical antiquity were quite against us, and as if no man of learning and of impartiality would risk a denial of it. But whether our opposers be hoary with learned age, or bloom with precipitate youth, it must, I think, be confessed, that these authorities have sufficient force to acquit us from the charge of ignorance, and of partiality to a favourite opinion, because we maintain, That the first two centuries knew either nothing at all, or very little, of infant baptism.

To the foregoing quotations I would here subjoin the attestation of Mr. Lawson, and of an ecclesiastical writer in the ninth century.—Thus Thomas Lawson, an impartial Friend: "See the author of rhantism, that is, sprinkling; not Christ, nor the apostles, but Cyprian; not in the days of Christ, but some two hundred and thirty years after.... Augustine, the son of the virtuous Monica, being instructed in the faith, was not baptized till about the thirtieth year of his age.—Ambrose, born of

Christian parents, remained instructed in Christian principles, and was unbaptized till he was chosen bishop of Milan.—Jerome, born of Christian parents, was baptized when about thirty years old.—Nectarius was made bishop of Constantinople before he was baptized.... It seems the doctrine of Fidus, concerning dipping, or sprinkling of children, was new, and seemed strange to Cyprian; seeing he could not ratify, nor confirm the same, without the sentence and advice of sixty-six bishops. Had it been commanded by Christ, practised by the apostles, and continued in matter and manner to Cyprian's days, there had not been a necessity for the concourse of so many bishops concerning the same."*——The ecclesiastical writer to whom I refer, is Walafridus Strabo, who speaks as follows: "It should be observed, that, in the primitive times, the grace of baptism was usually given to those *only* who were arrived at such maturity of body and mind, that they could understand what were the benefits of baptism; what was to be confessed and believed; and, finally, what was to be observed by those that are regenerated in Christ." †——On this passage the remark of Colomesius, as quoted by a nameless writer, is as follows: " Hence with reason you may infer, that adults only are the proper subjects of baptism." ‡ Perfectly conformable to which is a canon of the Council of Paris, in the year eight hundred and twenty-nine, as produced by the same anonymous author. Thus it reads: " In the beginning of the holy church of God, no one was admitted to baptism, unless he had before been instructed in the sacrament of faith and of baptism; which is proved by the words of Paul, Rom. vi. 3, 4."§

Reflect. II. One of these learned men supposes, indeed, that a passage in Irenæus *may* be understood,

---

* Baptismalogia, p. 75, 80, 81, 86, 87. † Apud Vossium, Thes. Theolog. p. 429. ‡ En Le Baptême Retabli, part ii. p. 3. § Ibid. p 166, 167.

as referring to infant baptism; yet candidly confesses it admits of a doubt, whether the ancient father had any such practice in view: nay, he asserts, that there is no certainty of Pædobaptism being practised before the time of Tertullian. See No. 12.—Le Clerc, however, seems confident that the quotation from Irenæus, to which we advert, has no relation to baptism. "We see nothing here," says he, "concerning baptism; nor is there any thing relating to it in the immediately preceding or following words."*—A writer in one of our periodical publications, when reviewing a pamphlet of Mr. John Carter's, in defence of infant baptism, says; "The authorities produced [by Mr. Carter] are J. Martyr and Irenæus, in the second century; called by the author the *first* century *after* the apostles, in order, we suppose, to give it a more ancient *look*.... With respect to the testimony of Justin, it requires very considerable ingenuity to make it, in any view, an argument in favour of infant baptism. There is a passage in Irenæus more to the purpose: but the passage is equivocal; and nothing can with certainty be decided from it, in favour of that species of infant baptism which is generally contended for by the Pædobaptists of modern times."† Besides, if these expressions, "Who by him are *regenerated* to God," signify the same as being baptized, they convey the idea of our Lord's baptizing persons of different ages. But this was far from being a fact; for "Jesus himself baptized not." Of this the ancient writer could not be ignorant; and therefore it is not likely that he should in such a connection, substitute the term *regenerated* for the word *baptized*. It is also worthy of observation, that the supposition against which we contend, represents our Lord as coming into the world to save those only who are baptized; an ima-

---

* Hist. Eccles. secul. ii. ann. 180, § 33, p. 778.
† Monthly Review for May 1784, p. 394, 395.

gination which is abhorrent from truth, and ought not, without the clearest evidence, to be charged on the venerable ancient.

Perfectly agreeable to this is the language of Mr. Hebden, who, having produced the words of Irenæus, proceeds thus: "This has been often cited against the Antipædobaptists.... It is one of the passages usually quoted to support the practice of baptizing infants from ancient testimonies; baptism being, say these learned Pædobaptists, often called *regeneration* by the ancients, and Irenæus here speaking of *infants* and *little* ones as, together with persons of other ages, *regenerated* or baptized. But, though baptism may be here alluded to, it does not seem to be directly intended. The *all* whom Christ came to save, are said to be *regenerated to God*. Can this be meant of baptism? Are none saved but such as are baptized? Or, are all who are baptized saved by Christ? That must be the case, according to Irenæus, if regeneration was here put for baptism; for he evidently intimates, that all whom Christ came to save are regenerated; and that all who are regenerated to God are saved. A plain proof this, supposing the passage to be *genuine*, that Irenæus did not believe universal redemption, in the modern Arminian sense, and that he had no notion of the baptismal regeneration since devised.... I cannot help questioning whether the passage of Irenæus is so clear and full in favour of Pædobaptism as learned men suppose."*

Incompetent, however, as the testimony of Irenæus is in favour of Pædobaptism, Dr. Wall will have it speak directly in point, saying: "This is the first express mention we have met with of infants baptized."†
Express mention! Then the terms *baptized* and *regenerated*, must be perfectly equivalent, in the works of Irenæus, and the ecclesiastical authors of those times.

---

* Baptismal Regeneration disproved, Appendix, p. 55.
† Hist. Inf. Bap. part i. chap. iii. p. 16.

But this cannot be proved, as the learned and impartial Venema acknowledges. See No. 12.—Yet, while we insist that this is far from being an express testimony, or indeed any testimony at all in favour of infant baptism; we may venture to conclude, that it is the first passage in ecclesiastical antiquity, which Dr. Wall considered as having any appearance of being directly to his purpose, and the very best he could find to support his hypothesis. But if it had been a divine appointment, and customary in the church from the apostolic age, is it not strange, is it not quite unaccountable, that such ambiguous words as those of Irenæus should be considered by our opponents, as the most explicit of any on record, in proof that Pædobaptism was practised so early as the year one hundred and eighty? What! is there nothing in those monuments of Christian antiquity, which go under the name of Barnabas, of Clemens Romanus, of Hermas, of Ignatius, and of Polycarp, as much to the purpose as this passage of the celebrated bishop of Lyons? Is there nothing in the writings of Justin Martyr, of Athenagoras, or of Theophilus Antiochenus, (which are all considered by learned men as prior to those of Irenæus) that is equally plain, and equally favourable to the antiquity of Pædobaptism? Strange, indeed, supposing infant baptism to have been derived from the apostles, and to have been generally practised in the times of those authors, that none of them should speak of it with as much clearness and precision as the venerable Irenæus in those equivocal words before us! That confidence with which the passage under consideration has been often produced against us, reminds me of another, that is quoted from the same father by the Papists, in favour of invocating the virgin Mary. Thus, then, the ancient author, as translated by Dr. Clagett: " As Eve was seduced and forsook God, so Mary was induced to obey God, that the virgin Mary might be a comforter of the virgin Eve; and that as mankind was, through a virgin, bound over to death, so they should be released through a virgin: one thing being thus rightly balanced against another, the disobedience of a virgin by the obedience of a virgin." Dr. Clagett observes, that "Fevardentius triumphs in this testimony, as if he had found here the primitive church, and all antiquity, for the invocation of the blessed virgin."*

Dr. Wall has produced a passage from Clemens Alexandrinus, who wrote a little before Tertullian, by which he seems to think it apparent, that the Alexandrian catechist considered the apostles as having baptized infants. The words of that ancient author, as quoted and rendered by Dr. Wall, are these: "If any one be by trade a fisherman, he would do well to think of an apostle, and the *children* taken out of the water."† —If, however, we would not be led by the sound of these words, rather than their sense, it seems necessary we should advert to the title and scope of the work, in which the passage is found; concerning which, let us hear a learned Pædobaptist. Dupin, when describing the works of Clement, and speaking of that book from which the quotation is made, says: "The second book, entitled the Pedagogue, is a discourse entirely of morality. It is divided into three books.` In the first, he shows what it is to be a *pedagogue*, that is to say, a conductor, pastor, or director of men. He proves that this quality chiefly and properly belongs only to the Word incarnate. He says, that it is the part of the pedagogue to regulate the manners, conduct the actions, and cure the passions.... That he equally informs men and women, the learned and the ignorant, because all men stand in need of instruction, being all *children* in one sense. Yet, however, that we must not think that the doctrine of the Christians is childish and contempti-

---

* Preservative against Popery, title vi. p. 194.

† Defence of Hist. Inf. Bap. Appendix, p. 8, 9.

ble; but that, on the contrary, the quality of *children*, which they receive in baptism, renders them perfect in the knowledge of divine things."*

From this account of the work, we are naturally led to suppose that Clement, when addressing, or speaking of Christian converts, would frequently call them *children;* and, that this is a fact, appears by those extracts which Mr. Barker has made from the book, which he seems to have carefully read with a view to this particular. The design of this ancient book, as concisely represented by him, and part of his quotations from it, are as follow: "The catechist of Alexandria here describes the persons he was to teach, what they were to be taught, and how they were to be admitted into the church. Pæd. i. 5. 'Παιδαγωγια, instruction, is *guiding of children,* (παιδων αγωγη) as the name shows: it remains to see whom the scripture calls *children,* and then to set a master (παιδαγωγος) over them. We then are the *children*—who are in the state of *disciples.—Unless ye be converted, and become as these children, ye shall not enter into the kingdom of heaven;* not figuring a new birth, (αναγεννησις,) but commending the innocence of children'.... Representing the innocence of the mind by childhood, he calls us *children,* (παιδας,) *young, little ones,* (νηπιους,) sons,—and a new people.... He figuratively calls us *young ones,* who are not enslaved to sin, —pure, leaping to the Father only,—running to the truth, and swift to salvation ;—such—our divine Guide of the young (πωλοδαμνης) takes care of.... The Lord plainly shows who are meant by *children:* when a question arose among the apostles, *which of them should be the greatest,* Jesus set a child among them, saying: *Whoever shall humble himself as this* [little] *child, the same is greatest in the kingdom of heaven.*... Those are truly children, *who know God only* as their father, are pure, meek, (νηπιοι,) and sincere.... He commands us to

---

* Hist. Eccles. Writers, vol. i. p. 62, 63.

be without care of things here,—and cleave only to the Father:—he who fulfils this command, is truly a *little one*, (νηπιος,) and a child (παις) of God.... The Lord is called a *perfect man*, as being perfect in righteousness;—but we are *little ones* (νηπιοι) perfected (τελειουμεθα) when we become of the church, and receive Christ as our head*....A person is not called νηπιος, because foolish,—but as meek and mild (νηπιος, ηπιος)—a little one is meek,—without guile,—which is the foundation of truth:—the new minds of little ones were once foolish, now newly wise.... He calls the Lord himself a *child*,—'Shall not the instruction of this child be perfect,—who guides us *children* (παιδας) who are his (νηπιους) *little ones?*'

"Far from confining the words, παιδες and νηπιοι, to infants, he [Clement] calls all *children*, whom he, as a teacher (παιδαγωγος), is to instruct; as having before been ignorant, now become sensible, yet still meek, teachable, and unprejudiced; judging it the perfection of a man to imitate the innocence and teachableness of children. But those who are in a course of instruction for baptism, are what he especially calls *children* (παιδες and νηπιοι;) for when baptized they become *perfect*, τελειοι.—Pæd. iii. 10. 'The Lord taught his disciples to catch men, as fishes out of the water.—Pæd. iii. 11. If any be a fisher, let him remember the apostle, and the *children* (παιδιων) drawn out of the water.'—Those are baptized, who believe and seek Christ. The *children* (νηπιοι and παιδια) here said to be baptized, whom Wall supposes to be infants, are, as appears above, *all*, of whatever age, who being meek and teachable, seek Christ the true teacher (ὁ παιδαγωγος), and submit to him."†

It is worthy of remark, that the frequent use of these familiar terms, *children* and *little children*, here applied

---

* Just so Paul opposes παιδια to τελειοι, (1 Cor. xiv. 20.)

† Duty and Benefits of Bap. p. 73, 74, 75. Note: The edition of Clement's works, from which the quotations are made, is that of Dr. Potter, p. 104, 106, 107, 108, 109, 112, 285, 289.

by Clement to such as were under a course of instruction, of whatever age they might be, seems to have been derived from the example of Paul, and of John, in their epistles. For the words, νηπιοι and παιδια, so frequently used by the Alexandrian catechist, are applied by those apostles in various places, to young or feeble converts.* The term τεκνια, *little children*, is also abundantly used in the same acceptation.† So the word παιδαγωγους, *pedagogues, instructors of children*, is used by Paul for such as succeeded him in preaching the gospel among the Corinthians.‡—To which I may add an observation of the learned Mr. Bingham: " The Christians were wont to please themselves with the artificial name *pisciculi, fishes;* to denote, as Tertullian [who was cotemporary with Clement] words it, that they were regenerate, or born again into Christ's religion by water, and could not be saved but by continuing therein. And this name was the rather chosen by them, because the initial letters of our Saviour's names and titles in Greek, Ιησους Χριστος, Θεου Υιος, Σωτηρ, JESUS CHRIST, THE SON OF GOD, OUR SAVIOUR, technically put together, make up the name ΙΧΘΥΣ; which signifies a *fish*, and is alluded to both by Tertullian and Optatus."§—While it appears, therefore, that the title, the phraseology, and the design of Clement's performance, unite in leading us to consider the term παιδιων, as expressive of *young converts* to Christianity, and not of *infants;* there cannot be the least ground for concluding, that the celebrated catechist had any thought of infant baptism, when he spake of " παιδιων, *children*, drawn out of the water;" but of solemnly immersing such as had been instructed in the doctrine of Christ. And, indeed, as Dr. Wall is the only one of our learned opponents, whom I have ob-

---

* See 1 Cor. iii. 1; Ephes. iv. 14; Heb. v. 13, 14; 1 John ii. 13, 18.
† See Matt. xi. 25; Luke x. 21; 1 John ii. 1; xii. 28; iii. 7, 18; iv. 4; v. 21; and Dr. Doddridge's Note on 1 Pet. ii. 2.
‡ 1 Cor. iv. 15. § Origines Eccles. b. i. chap. i. § 2.

served, that has produced the passage against us in the course of this controversy, there is reason to think, that few of them ever considered it as proving any thing at all in their favour.

Reflect. III. As I humbly conceive it must be allowed by all competent and impartial judges, that Tertullian is the first author who speaks expressly of infant baptism; and as it is equally clear that he opposes it; so, we may justly presume, it was then a novel practice, was just commencing, and approved by very few. Had it been otherwise, there is no reason to imagine that the celebrated African father would have treated it as he did; not only because he was very tenacious of ecclesiastical traditions, as Venema has well observed, No. 12; but also because he mentions with approbation various religious rites as practised by the church, which in his own view had no pretence to scripture authority. His opposition to infant baptism is expressed in the following manner, as the passage is translated by Dupin: "What necessity is there to expose godfathers to the hazard of answering for those whom they hold at the fonts? since they may be prevented by death, from being able to perform those promises which they have made for the children, or else may be disappointed by their evil inclinations. Jesus Christ says, indeed, 'Hinder not little children from coming to me;' but that they should come to him as soon as they are advanced in years, as soon as they have learned their religion, when they may be taught whither they are going, when they are become Christians, when they begin to be able to know Jesus Christ. What is there that should compel this innocent age to receive baptism? And since they are not yet allowed the disposal of temporal goods, is it reasonable that they should be entrusted with the concerns of heaven? For the same reason it is proper to make those who are not married wait for some time, by reason of the temptations they have to undergo till they are married, or have attained to the gift of continency. Those who shall duly consider the great weight and moment of this divine sacrament, will rather be afraid of making too much haste to receive it, than to defer it for some time, that so they may be the better capable of receiving it more worthily."* The treatise of Tertullian, (De Baptismo,) from which this is extracted, is supposed by learned men to have been written about the year two hundred and four.† Again he says; "Baptism is the seal of faith; which faith is begun and adorned by the faith of repentance. We are not, therefore, washed that we may leave off sinning, but because we have already done it, and are already purified in heart."‡ Sentiments and assertions these, that cannot be reconciled with the baptism of infants.—On the former of these passages Rigaltius makes the following remark : " Tertullian thought that one who has no understanding of the Christian faith, should not be admitted to baptism; and that he does not want the remission of sins, who is not yet capable of deceit, or of any fault."§ Vossius, when adverting to the same passage, says, " Some reply, *The discourse of Tertullian regards the infants of infidels.* To us it seems more probable, that he treats concerning the children of believers." ‖ To this we readily agree, and here subjoin the following acknowledgment of Mr. Baxter: " Again I will confess, that the words of Tertullian and Nazianzen show, that it was long before all were agreed of the very time, or of the necessity, of baptizing infants before any use of reason, in case they were like to live to maturity."¶

---

* Hist. Eccles. Writers, cent. iii. p. 80.

† Vid. J. Fabricium, Hist. Biblioth. Fabrician. tom. i. p. 157.

‡ Opera, De Pœnitentiâ, p. 144. § Observat. de Tertull. p. 72. Lutet. 1634. ‖ Disputat. de Bap. disput. xiv. § 12. See Dr. Whitby's Note on Matt. xix. 13, 14.

¶ In Dr. Wall's Hist. Inf. Bap. part. i. p. 23. See Dr. Doddridge's Lectures, p. 522.

That Tertullian had a high regard for traditional rites in the affairs of religion, is plain beyond a doubt, from what he says when professedly handling that subject. His words, as given us by an eminent Pædobaptist, are as follow: "Let us try, then, whether no tradition ought to be allowed that is not written; and I shall freely grant that this need not to be allowed, if the contrary be not evinced by the examples of several other customs, which without the authority of any scripture are approved, only on the account that they were first delivered, and have ever since been used. Now, to begin with baptism—When we are taken up out of the water, we taste a mixture of milk and honey; and from that day we abstain a whole week from bathing ourselves, which otherwise we use every day. The sacrament of the eucharist, which our Lord celebrated at meal-time, and ordered all to take, we receive in our assemblies before day; and never but from the hands of the pastor. We give oblations every year for (or in commemoration of) the dead, on the day of their martyrdom.... At every setting out, or entry on business; whenever we come in, or go out from any place; when we dress for a journey; when we go into a bath; when we go to meat; when the candles are brought in; when we lie down, or sit down; and whatever business we have, we make on our foreheads the sign of the cross. If you search in the scriptures for any command for these and such like usages, you shall find none. Tradition will be urged to you, as the ground of them; custom, as the confirmer of them; and our religion teaches to observe them."* Hence it appears, with superior evidence, that this ancient author considered infant baptism as a novel invention—as a practice that was neither enjoined by divine command, nor warranted by apostolic example, nor yet recommended by the poor pretence of tradition, nor even countenanced by prevailing custom.

---

* In Dr. Wall's Hist. Inf. Bap. part ii. chap. ix. p. 480, 481.

BEFORE THE SECOND OR THIRD CENTURY. 385

While, it is very observable, tradition and custom are actually pleaded by him, in favour of certain rites (and one of them an appendage of baptism) which Protestants have generally agreed to reject, as manifestly superstitious.

It seems apparent also, from Tertullian, that the use of sponsors is of as high antiquity as the practice of infant baptism. For as this famous African father is the first that expressly mentions the former, so Deylingius tells us, that he is the first who says any thing about the latter;* with whom Mr. Towgood agrees.† Of these sponsors, Deylingius informs us, there were three sorts; namely, for infants who could not answer for themselves, by reason of their tender age; for such adults as were incapable of answering, on account of great affliction; and for all adults in general.‡ Nor have we sufficient reason to suppose, that sponsors were first used at the administration of Pædobaptism: no, the learned Mosheim is express to the contrary. His words are these: " Adult persons were prepared for baptism by abstinence, prayer, and other pious exercises. It was to answer for them that sponsors, or godfathers, were first instituted, though they were afterwards admitted also in the baptism of infants."§ Sponsors were used for adults in the following ages also, as learned writers inform us: || nay, the church of England still requires godfathers and godmothers in the administration of baptism to those who are able to answer for themselves. For thus the rubric: " When any such persons as are of riper years are to be baptized.... if they shall be found fit, then the *godfathers*

---

* De Pastoral. Prudentiâ, pars iii. c. iii. § 29.
† Dissent. Gent. Letters, let. ii. p. 6.
‡ Ut supra. See Bingham's Orig. Eccles. b. xi. chap. viii.
§ Ecclesiastical Hist. vol. i. p. 171, 172. || Magdeb. Centur. cent. vii. c. vi. p. 73. Fox's Acts and Mon. vol. i. A. D. 636, p. 123. Forbesii Instruct. Hist. Theolog. l. x. c. v. § 22.

VOL. I. 2 C

and *godmothers* (the people being assembled upon the Sunday or holy day appointed) shall be ready to present them at the font.... Then shall the priest take each person to be baptized by the right hand, and placing him conveniently by the font, according to his direction, shall ask the godfathers and godmothers the name; and then shall dip him in the water, or pour water upon him."*—As to infants, Dr. Wall assures us; "There is no time, or age, of the church, in which there is any appearance that infants were ordinarily baptized without sponsors, or godfathers."†—Bucanus tells us, when writing in favour of sponsors, that "as a midwife is used to facilitate the birth in carnal generation; so in the spiritual generation of baptism some one is employed who acts in the place of a midwife, and of a pedagogue in those things which pertain to the end of baptism and to the Christian life." ‡ What an admirable proof is this of the utility of sponsors! Few, I suppose, however, have had the honour conferred on a girl mentioned by Moschus, for whom two angels were sureties at her baptism.§

The Baptists have often been charged with Anabaptism; a sentiment and practice which they detest, as much as any of their opposers. It may be observed, however, that, were they inclined to vindicate Anabaptism, Tertullian might be challenged as an evidence of its high antiquity. For though he says there is but one baptism, and that it should not be repeated, yet he excepts the baptism of heretics; "who," he adds, "are not able to give it, because they have it not; and therefore it is, that we have a rule among us to rebaptize them." ‖

---

* Baptism of such as are of Riper Years.
† Hist. Inf. Bap. part ii. chap. ix. p. 477.
‡ Institut. Theolog. loc. xlvii. § 47.
§ In Dupin's Eccles Hist. cent. vii. p. 20.
‖ In Dupin's Hist. Eccles. Writers, cent. iii. p. 80.

Reflect. IV. It is common for our opponents, when defending the antiquity of infant baptism, to produce various passages from Origen, who flourished in the former part of the third century; some of which passages, it must be allowed, are plain and express to the point. It ought, however, to be observed, that those quotations are made, not from the Greek of that celebrated father, but from such Latin versions of his works as are very corrupt, and consequently render it quite uncertain what was his opinion in reference to that affair. That the works of Origen have been greatly injured by his translators, the most learned Pædobaptists declare.—Grotius, for instance, when speaking of that celebrated ancient with regard to infant baptism, says: "Some things ascribed to him, were penned by an uncertain author; and some things are interpolated.... What Origen thought about the final punishment of the wicked, is difficult from his writings to be asserted; all things are so interpolated by Rufinus."*——The Magdeburg Centuriators inform us, that Origen's Homilies on Paul's Epistle to the Romans, "were translated by Rufinus; who rather altered and corrupted than faithfully translated, as Erasmus intimates in the censure he passed upon them."†——Scultetus asserts, "That Rufinus, the translator of many of Origen's books, used so great a liberty, that he retrenched, added, and altered such things as appeared to him necessary to be cashiered, added, or changed. So that the reader is often uncertain, whether he peruses Origen or Rufinus; seeing the Greek works of Origen are not now extant, by which the Latin version might be corrected and amended."‡ ——Vossius, having produced a passage from Origen's Homilies upon the Romans, in favour of infant bap-

---

* Apud Poli. Synops. ad Matt. xix. 14; xxv. 46.
† Cent. iii. c. x. p. 180.   ‡ Medull. Theolog. Patrum, p. 124. Francf. 1634.

tism, adds: "But concerning Origen we say the less, because the things which might be quoted are not extant in the Greek."*——The learned Vitringa, when handling the same subject, makes a similar acknowledgment, and blames Rufinus.†——M. Daillé is very explicit on this point; his language is; "Certainly, Rufinus—hath so filthily mangled, and so licentiously confounded the writings of Origen, Eusebius, and others, which he hath translated into Latin, that you will hardly find a page in his translations where he hath not either cut off, or added, or at least altered something." ‡——Dupin says, "We have none of the Scholia [written by Origen] remaining, nor have we hardly any of the Homilies in Greek; and those which we have in Latin, are translated by Rufinus and others with so much liberty, that it is a difficult matter to discern what is Origen's own, from what has been foisted in by the interpreter.... The liberty which Rufinus has given himself is still more evident, by what he has written in the prologue to his version of the Commentary upon the Epistle to the Romans; which, he says, he has abridged by above the half. St. Hierom's versions are not more exact; and the most faulty of all is that of an ancient translator, who has interpreted the Commentaries upon St. Matthew.... Having only the version of the greatest part of the Homilies, we cannot be certain whether that which relates to doctrine and discipline be Origen's own, or Rufinus's." §——Mr. Western, speaking of Rufinus as a translator of Eusebius, passes the following severe censure upon him. He "hath ventured on downright forgery, and pretended to

---

* Thes. Theolog. de Pædobap. pars ii. thes. viii. p. 433.

† Obs. Sac. l. ii. c. vi. § 9.

‡ Right Use of the Fathers, book i. chap. iv. p. 40, 41. Vid. ejusdem Disputat. de Cult. Relig. Objecto, l. i. c. viii. p. 49.

§ Hist. Eccles. Writ. cent. iii. p. 100; see cent. iv. p. 4; cent. v. p. 108.

translate from Eusebius what Eusebius never wrote." *
——Mr. Twells: "We are not sure that Origen ever really spake of Hermas's Pastor, as of a writing inspired by God. For this saying is extant only in his Commentary on the Romans, the Greek of which is lost, and the Latin a miserable version, in which the original is interpolated as well as contracted by Rufinus the interpreter." †——Mr. Peirce: "As for what our author [Dr. Nichols] refers to in Origen, we cannot tell whether it be Origen's or Rufinus's testimony."‡——Quenstedius: " Rufinus translated many of Origen's books, but in translating (as he himself acknowledges in his prefaces, and for which Jerome reproves him,) he has used so great a liberty, that he retrenched, added, and altered whatever he considered as deserving to be cashiered, added, or changed: so that the reader is frequently uncertain whether he read Origen or Rufinus."§—— Huetius, when speaking of Origen's remains in general, has the following remark: "They are very imperfect and much abused, or else changed and deformed by abominable translations."‖——Rivetus, when speaking of a certain work that goes under the name of Origen, says: "Concerning the Homilies on various passages in the Gospel according to Matthew, it appears to Erasmus, that they are not Origen's; but were penned by some Latin author, the remains of which have been impudently corrupted by Rufinus." ¶ ——Once more: Chamier says, "All the learned know, that Rufinus used but little integrity in translating authors."**

---

* Enquiry into Reject. Christ. Miracles, p. 209.
† Critical Exam. of New Text and Version, part iii. p. 81.
‡ Vindicat. of Dissent. part iii. p. 240.
§ Dialog. de Patriis Illust. Doct. Script. Virorum, p. 632.
‖ In Dr. Gale's Reflect. p. 522. ¶ Critici Sacri, l. ii. c. xiii. p. 205. ** Panstrat. t. iv. l. vii. c. ix. § 30. Vid. tom. i. l. iv c. viii. § 2; tom. ii. l. xx. c. v. § 14. See also Mr. Clarkson on Liturgies, p. 141. J. Fabricii Hist. Biblioth. Fabrician. tom. i. p. 85, 86. Venemæ Hist. Eccles. secul. iii. § 3. Bp. Bull's Def. Fid.

Such, in the opinion of the best judges, being the character of Origen's translators, we have sufficient reason to except against all testimonies produced from the ancient versions of his writings, in favour of Pædobaptism. And, indeed, were there not a great poverty of evidence in support of that practice, for about two hundred and fifty years, it is hardly to be supposed that our Brethren would ever subpœna witnesses, whose veracity is thus impeached, in order to prove any part of their hypothesis. We have reason also to wonder at the inadvertency of Dr. Addington, who, speaking of Rufinus, tells us that he "lived in the THIRD century;" and that his "*knowledge* or INTEGRITY HAVE NEVER BEEN DOUBTED."* Palpable, gross mistakes!

There is, however, one passage in the Greek of Origen, sometimes quoted by our opponents; and it is this, as produced and rendered by Dr. Wall. "One may enquire, When it is that the angels here spoken of are set over those little ones, showed, or signified, by our Saviour? Whether they take the care and management of them from the time when they, by the washing of regeneration, whereby they were new born, do 'as new born babes DESIRE THE SINCERE MILK OF THE WORD,' and are no longer subject to any evil power? Or from their birth, according to the foreknowledge of God, and his predestinating of them?" and so on.† That the persons here intended by Origen, were not infants in a literal sense, but such as were *newly born again*, is plain from his describing them in the language of inspiration, as "desiring the sincere milk of the word." Dr. Wall, therefore, might well acknowledge, that the

---

Nic. sect. ii. cap. ix. Chemnitii Exam. Concil. Trident. p. 629, 630. Mr. Altham, Preserv. against Popery, title i. p. 190. Abp. Wake, Preservative against Popery, title iv. p. 197. Dr. Doddridge's Lectures, p. 519. Mr. Jones's Catholic Doct. of Trinity, chap. i. § xiv. p. 9. Hist. of Popery, vol. ii. p. 147.

* Christian Min. Reasons, p. 163. † Hist. Inf Bap. part i. p. 33.

latter part of the passage does "very much puzzle the cause," for which Pædobaptists produce the quotation; "and make it doubtful whether Origen be to be there understood, of infants in age, or of such Christian men as are endued with the innocence and simplicity of infants."* If, indeed, the language of this learned ancient had been, as it is partially represented by Sir Peter King, of which Dr. Wall intimates his disapprobation;† or if the representation of it which Dr. Addington has lately given, had been candid and fair, ‡ it would have been clearly in favour of Pædobaptism. But as neither of these is the case, we may venture to affirm, that no substantial evidence for infant baptism from the works of Origen has been yet produced; and that there is no proof of its being a common practice, for two centuries and a half after the Christian æra commenced. To indulge conjectures of its being far more ancient, is to imitate the conduct of Bellarmine, who says, concerning another affair; "Although there is no express testimony amongst the ancients, to prove, that they at any time offered sacrifice without some one or more communicating with the priests; yet it may be gathered by *conjecture.*"§

I will conclude this reflection with some remarks on the following extract from Dr. Doddridge. "Tertullian is known to have declared against infant baptism, except in case of danger. Gregory Nazianzen advises to defer it till three years old. Basil blames his auditors for delaying it, which implies, there were then many unbaptized persons among them; but these might not, perhaps, have been the children of Christian parents.... It is indeed *surprising*, that nothing more express is to be met with in antiquity upon this subject; but it is to be remembered, that when infant baptism is first apparently mentioned, we read of no remonstrance made

---

* Hist. Inf. Bap. part i. p. 32, 33.   † Enquiry into Constitut. of Prim. Church, part ii. p. 46.   ‡ Christ. Min. Reas. p. 162.
§ In Popery Confuted by Papists, p. 81.

against it as an innovation."* Surprising indeed! had it been the appointment of Christ, the practice of the apostles, and a constant custom in the Christian church; all which the doctrine of Pædobaptism now supposes. On this occasion our opposers may well wonder, and have reason to be disgusted with their own hypothesis. Dr. Doddridge, however, wishes to persuade us, that Pædobaptism was an apostolic practice; because " we read of no remonstrance made against it as an innovation," when it is first plainly mentioned. But is not Tertullian the first author who apparently mentions infant baptism? and was not he, by the doctor's own confession, against it? But supposiug we had not read of the least remonstrance against Pædobaptism, when it was first mentioned, what then; That it was practised from the beginning? by no means. For if so, infant communion must be received as of divine appointment; because we read of no remonstrance being made against it as an innovation, when first apparently mentioned by Cyprian. See Chap. V.—Nay, were there not many innovations in the second and third centuries, against which we read of no remonstrance being made at their first appearance? Were the reason assigned by this respectable author for the primitive antiquity of infant baptism, to be admitted by Protestants, the Papists would ask no more to justify a great number of their superstitions. It is indeed one of their arguments in favour of antiscriptural customs; for thus they reason, in defence of communion in one kind. "Seeing men, tenacious of religion, are easily disturbed by an alteration of things pertaining to it; if through a course of twelve hundred years the holy supper had been administered in the church under both kinds, without its being declared lawful to communicate under one only; immediately, upon this custom being changed, the greatest disturbances and disputes would have arisen in the church about the alteration. Con-

---

* Lectures, p. 522.

cerning which, whereas in history there is no mention, we receive it as an undoubted conjecture, that the practice was never considered as *new*, but always used from the beginning, and fixed in the minds of believers as lawful."*—To which the learned Chamier answers: " Disturbances are excited about such alterations, either when they are made, or afterwards. That all changes in religious affairs excite commotions when they are made, may be safely denied. For long before the advent of Christ many changes were made in the Jewish religion—and yet without any tumult."†—The argument of Dr. Doddridge is also used by our English Conformists in favour of Episcopacy. Thus, for instance, Mr. Reeves: " I would ask a conscientious Dissenter, whether in his heart he can believe that the primitive saints and martyrs would invade the Episcopal power of their own heads?.... And if they did, whether it was possible for the invaders to prevail in so short a time over Christendom, and *without opposition,* or *one word of complaint* from the degraded presbyters against the usurping prelates? For usurpations of this sacred kind, we know with a witness, never come in without remarkable clamours and convulsions; are seldom perfectly forgotten, and the revolution skinned over without a scar. That bishops, therefore, should obtain wherever the gospel did, so soon and with such *universal silence,* cannot be accounted for any other way, than that the gospel and the episcopate came in upon the same divine title."‡—I will here add the following short quotation from Chillingworth: " If any man ask, How could it [corruption in the church of Rome] become universal in so short a time? Let him tell me how the—communicating of infants became so universal; and then he shall acknowledge, what was done in some, was possible in others."§

---

* Salmero, apud Chamierum, Panstrat, tom. iv. l. ix. c. iv. § 18.
† Ibid. § 20. ‡ Apologies, vol. i. Preface, p. 31, 32.
§ Relig. of Protestants, part i. chap. v. § 91.

So happily have these Pædobaptists answered Dr. Doddridge, and secured our inference against the exceptions of Protestant opposers, whether they be Episcopalians or Nonconformists!

Reflect. V. As it appears, from this and the preceding chapter, that the New Testament contains neither express precept for, nor plain example of infant baptism, and that no substantial evidence can be produced from ecclesiastical authors, of its being a prevailing custom, till about the middle of the third century; we may with great propriety (*mutatis mutandis*) adopt and apply to Pædobaptism, the reasonings of Protestants against the peculiarities of Popery. The following may serve as a specimen. Turrettin, when opposing the superstitious appendages of baptism, as practised in the Papal communion, argues not only from the silence of scripture, but also from that " of the most ancient Christian writers. Because, in the genuine books of undoubted and pure antiquity, nothing occurs relating to those things.... Whence," he adds, "there is no reason for us to imagine that they were used in those first times. Nay, a solid argument is thence drawn, that no such things were then practised: because it cannot be doubted, had they been then in use, but the fathers would have mentioned them; like as, in the following ages, they were not silent about things that were frequently added to the legitimate and apostolic rite of baptism."*—Mr. Neal, when opposing the supremacy of the Roman pontiff, says; " Had our Lord appointed a vicar-general on earth, we might expect to meet, not only with his name in scripture, but with the time and manner of his instalment, and with the deed of conveyance to his successors, in the most plain and significant words; or, at least, that it should be read in every page of antiquity. But if the most ancient fathers of the church consent in any thing, it is in a general silence about this matter. The whole stress of the evidence is,

---

* Institut. loc. xix. q. xviii. § 6.

therefore, laid upon—obscure and metaphorical passages of scripture.... If we lay these things together, and consider the silence of the scripture records and genuine remains of antiquity, about a supreme visible head,—it will amount to a demonstration, that the hierarchy of the church of Rome is built upon the sand."*——Dr. Harris: "There is scarce any thing in which the church of Rome puts in a stronger claim, or makes a louder boast, than the sense of antiquity and the judgment of the ancient fathers; though in points peculiar to Popery, and in which they differ from the Protestants, scarce any thing is less fair, or more unjust."†——Dr. Hughes: " If antiquity be of any consequence in determining matters of religion, the earliest must be the best; and this is clearly against the church of Rome, in the affair now before us."‡——Bp. Burnet: " The silence of the first and purest ages, about these things which are controverted among us, is evidence enough that they were not known to them; especially, since in their Apologies, which they wrote to the heathens for their religion and worship, wherein they give an abstract of their doctrines, and a rubric of their worship, they never once mention these great evils for which we now accuse that [Romish] church."§——Mr. Bingham: " The silence of all ancient authors is good evidence in this case; [that is, the religious use of images.].... Of images or pictures there is not a syllable; which is at least a good negative argument, that there was no such thing in their churches."‖—— Dr. Owen: " No instance can be given, or hath been, for the space of two hundred years, or until the end of the second century, of any one person who had the care of more churches than one committed unto him, or did

---

* Serm. at Salters' Hall, on Suprem. of Bishop of Rome, p. 9, 30.
† Do. at   Do. on Transubstan. p. 31.
‡ Do. at   Do. on Venerat. of Saints, p. 30, 31.
§ Preserv. against Popery, title i. p. 125.
‖ Orig. Eccles. b. viii. chap. viii. § 6.

take the charge of them upon himself."*—— Dr. Goodman: "For about two hundred years we find not one word of this kind of confession which we enquire for.... If this business had been of such consequence as is pretended, it is strange that those holy men, Ignatius, Clemens, and Justin Martyr, should not have any mention of it."†

——Ottius: "As they [the primitive Christians] had no temples, no altars, so neither had they any incense; which is inferred from the silence of those times. I do not mean a kind of uncertain silence, on which no argument can be formed; but such as, in cases to be disputed, may serve for a substantial reason."‡

Again: Our learned opposers have taught us to consider ecclesiastical terms and religious rites, which are not found in scripture, as coming into use about the time when they are first mentioned by one or another of the ancient writers. Is our enquiry, for example, In what age baptism obtained the name of *a sacrament?* Gomarus replies, Tertullian is the first who gives it that appellation.§—Is it the consecration of *baptismal water?* Tertullian is the most ancient author produced that mentions it.‖—Is it concerning the time when, in reference to baptism, the use of *sponsors* commenced? Deylingius and others assure us, Tertullian is the first who says any thing of it.¶—Is it *the imposition of hands*, as an attendant on the administration of baptism? Mr. Peirce tells us, Tertullian is "the most ancient author who mentions that rite.... We make no doubt it began about the time of Tertullian, and was at first annexed to baptism."**—Is it that *unction* which was used in the

---

* Enquiry into Orig. Nat. of Churches, Preface, p. 24.
† Preserv. against Popery, title viii. p. 10.
‡ Biblioth. Bremens. class. ii. p. 539.
§ Opera, disputat. xxxi. § 3.
‖ Bingham's Orig. Eccles. b. xi. chap. x. § 1.
¶ De Prudent. Pastoral. par. iii. c. iii. § 29. Dissent. Gent. Letters, lett. ii.
** Vindication of Dissenters, part iii. p. 172, 175.

ancient rite of confirmation? Mr. Bingham answers, "There being no author before Tertullian who mentions the material unction, as used in confirmation, it is most probable it was a ceremony first begun about his time, to represent the unction of the Holy Ghost."* Thus also Quenstedius: "That before the time of Tertullian this rite was not used in the church appears from hence, neither Justin Martyr, nor any other author of a former age, makes mention of it. Tertullian first of all, therefore, speaks of the unction."† — Is it the custom of making *prayers and oblations* for the dead? Chemnitius replies, "Tertullian is the first of the fathers who mentions it."‡ — Is it the *white garment* usually worn for a few days, while recent from the baptismal font? Quenstedius tells us, "that none of the fathers who flourished in the three first centuries make mention of it. . . . The custom, therefore, seems to have been introduced in the fourth century."§ — Is it the custom of those that were newly baptized carrying *lighted tapers* in their hands, when going to public worship? Quenstedius informs us, that "Justin Martyr, in his Second Apology, and Tertullian, De Baptismo, make no mention of any such thing, though they very accurately describe the baptismal rites;"‖ and therefore it must be considered as of a later date. — Once more: Is it that prostitution of a sacred rite, *the baptizing of bells?* Mr. Bingham replies, "The first notice we have of this is in the capitulars of Charles the Great, where it is only mentioned to be censured."¶

The substance of this reasoning may be thus expressed, and applied to our present purpose. Infant

---

* Orig. Eccles. b. xii. chap. iii. § 2.
† Antiq. Bib. p. 338. ‡ Exam. Concil. Trident. p. 536.
§ Ut supra, p. 343. ‖ Ibid. p. 344.
¶ Orig. Eccles. b. xi. chap. iv. § 2. Vid. Vander Waeyen, (Varia Sacra, p. 616,) who considers some of these rites as having an earlier date, and as being derived from the Pagans.

baptism, for which our Brethren contend, is not mentioned in scripture. They are obliged, therefore, to lay the whole stress of their argument on obscure passages of sacred writ. But had the matter in dispute been appointed by Jesus Christ, and practised by the apostles, there is reason to think the writers of the New Testament would have recorded it in a clear and explicit manner; consequently, it is unreasonable to believe and practise any such thing. — Again: The earliest Christian antiquity must be the best. But Pædobaptism does not occur in the genuine writings of the highest and purest antiquity. It cannot be doubted, however, that if it had been practised in those times, the fathers would have mentioned it, as well as other things of much less importance. We have, therefore, abundant reason to conclude, that those ancient authors knew nothing of it. — Once more: Learned men in general conclude, that the commencement of any practice in the Christian church is to be fixed about the time of its being first mentioned by ancient writers. But the practice of infant baptism is not mentioned by any ecclesiastical author before Tertullian; and even by him, like the baptism of bells, in the capitulars of Charles the Great, it is mentioned with a mark of censure; though he informs us of several unscriptural rites annexed to baptism, without the least sign of disapprobation.

That we are able to plead something more than the *mere* silence of primitive fathers, will appear, I think, from the following paragraphs. The learned Basnage, when proving against Baronius, that unction and the imposition of hands were not connected with baptism in primitive times, produces a passage from Justin Martyr, which I will here give a little more at large, in the translation of Mr. Reeves: " I shall now lay before you, (says Justin to the Roman emperor) the manner of dedicating ourselves to God, through Christ, upon our conversion; for should I omit this I might seem not to deal sincerely in this account of the Christian religion. As many, therefore, as are persuaded and believe that the things taught and said by us are true, and moreover take upon them to live accordingly, are taught to pray, and ask of God with fasting the forgiveness of their former sins; we praying together, and fasting for and with them; and then, and not till then, they are brought to a place of water, and there regenerated, after the same manner with ourselves; for they are washed in the name of God the Father and Lord of all, and of our Saviour Jesus Christ.... The reason of this we have from the apostles; for having nothing to do in our first birth, but being begotten by necessity, or without our own consent, and trained up also in vicious customs and company, to the end therefore we might continue no longer the children of necessity and ignorance, but of freedom and knowledge, and obtain remission of our past sins by virtue of this water, the penitent, who now makes his second birth an act of his *own choice*, has called over him the name of God the Father, and Lord of all things.... And moreover the person baptized and illuminated, is baptized in the name of Jesus Christ, and in the name of the Holy Ghost."*—Upon this passage Basnage, among other things, observes: "That the apologist plainly mentions the ceremonies of the church, without circumlocution or ambiguity. Dissimulation was not then used by Christians. Unless, therefore, we would represent Justin as telling the emperor a falsehood, it must be confessed, that unction and the imposition of hands were not yet annexed to baptism, nor used upon baptized persons. For it was the custom to unite without delay the baptismal water and the chrism, from the time of the latter being brought into the church .... Either, therefore, having cast off all sincerity, he concealed in silence confirmation, or confirmation was not at all used; the latter of which, as more probable,

---

* Apologies, vol. i. p. 104—108.

we prefer, lest the holy martyr should lie under a charge of perfidy. This argument is of so much force with me, that I think the patrons of confirmation cannot possibly answer it."* He proceeds on the same principle, in order to prove, that various orders of ecclesiastics in the Papal communion had no existence among the primitive Christians. For having produced a passage from Clemens Romanus, who speaks of the apostles as "preaching through countries and cities, and appointing bishops and deacons;" he adds, "If, in the age of Clement, subdeacons, chanters, door-keepers, and exorcists had been appointed to those offices which their names import; what was the reason of Clement's mentioning none but bishops and deacons?" †—Again, with reference to the office of a subdeacon, he says: "It was not known before the third century. Cyprian honoured that confessor of Christ, Optatus, with the new title of a subdeacon.... Let us hear Tertullian in his book, De Baptismo. *The high-priest has the right of administering baptism; then the elder, and also the deacon.* Why does the ancient author stop here? Does not authority to administer baptism belong to the subdeacon, when the elder and the deacon are absent? Seeing, therefore, the name of a subdeacon first came into use after the death of Tertullian, we justly infer that the office of subdeacon was unknown to the church for upwards of two hundred years." ‡ — Now, if these principles and this course of arguing be pertinent and conclusive, in opposition to such particulars in the church of Rome as are not mentioned in the scripture, nor in primitive antiquity; what reason can be assigned why they should not have equal force against infant baptism? For it is manifest, that all their force arises, not from an application of them to the religious customs of a particular people; but from those religious customs not being

---

* Exercitat. Hist. Crit. p. 76, 77.   † Ibid. p. 608.
‡ Ibid. p. 642.

mentioned in the divine word, nor in the genuine writings of the most ancient ecclesiastical authors.

With regard to the passage produced from Justin, Dr. Wall acknowledges, that it is not directly in favour of infant baptism; though he is of opinion the famous apologist says nothing inconsistent with the practice of it in those times.* But if the silence of our venerable martyr, concerning unction and the imposition of hands, would have impeached his integrity, had those rites been then used, as Mr. Basnage justly pleads; much more would his entire omission of infants, as partakers of baptism, have inferred the same reflection upon him, had Pædobaptism been then practised. " If," as Dr. Gale observes, " he was so cautious not to seem unfair, in hiding any thing from the powers before whom he pleaded; it is strange he should entirely omit, without the least intimation, so important an article as the custom of baptizing infants, if it had been practised at that time. The heathens were apt enough to charge the Christians with using infants very barbarously; it concerned St. Justin, therefore, not to give any umbrage by seeming to avoid the mentioning of them. So careful an apologist would certainly have taken occasion to mention them, and describe the Christians' treatment of them very exactly, in order to remove all suspicions from the emperor's mind. When they were reported to murder infants, or make some impious use of their blood, what could possibly fortify the suspicion more, than that so great a man as Justin should, in a public and formal apology, decline saying any thing at all of what they did to them? It was altogether necessary, therefore, for St. Justin, at least to have taken *some* notice of infants, if they had used any ceremony about them.... But, supposing he had not, must he therefore describe baptism in such a manner as cannot be at all applicable to the case of infants, as he has done? This

---

* Hist. Inf. Bap. part i. chap. ii. § 5.

would have been directly deceiving the emperor, who certainly understood St. Justin's account to be full and true of baptism in general, and never imagined the Christians baptized otherwise. Had there been such a thing as infant baptism at that time, how easy had it been for St. Justin, and how necessary, to have said, Not only *they who are persuaded and do believe*, and so on; but also to have added, *together with their infant children, are baptized*..... Nothing can be plainer than that the new birth [of which Justin speaks,] together with the remission of sins to be obtained by water, is here said to depend, not upon any *necessity*, or the will of *another*, as our being born into this world did; but, on the contrary, on our *own* wills, or free choice and knowledge. For the opposition lies here: We were at first generated *without* our knowledge, or choice; but we must be regenerated, and obtain the remission of our sins by water, *with* our knowledge and choice. And this shows that infants, who are not capable of that knowledge and choice, are consequently not capable of this baptism: if they are to be baptized, it must be without their choice, as much as their first generation was; which destroys St. Justin's opposition, and therefore must be thought inconsistent with his notion of the matter."*

Should any be disposed to answer with Bellarmine, in a similar case; "Things that are generally known, and daily practised, do not use to be written:" we reply with Dr. Clagett, " But if this will do, it is impossible these men should ever be convinced. For when we charge them with innovation in any matters of doctrine and practice, if they can show that those things are written in the ancients, we are certainly gone that way; for this proves that to be well known, and commonly practised in the primitive times, which we pretend was but of yesterday. But if we can show that they were

---

* Reflections on Dr. Wall's Hist. Inf. Bap. lett. xii. p. 454—457.

not written, we get nothing by it at all; for it seems the reason they were not written is, because they were generally known and daily practised."*

I will conclude this reflection with the following quotation from Dr. Clagett: "The profound silence of the first three ages—as to the worship of the blessed Virgin and the saints—should be enough to determine the point in question. And this silence is not only directly confessed by some of our adversaries, but as effectually confessed by the rest, that labour to find some hints of these practices in these primitive fathers; but by such interpretations and consequences, that it is almost as great a shame to confute, as to make them. Now the silence of these fathers ought not be rejected, as an incompetent proof, because it is but a negative. For since we pretend that these practices are innovations, and were never heard of in the ancient church; it is not reasonable to demand a better proof of it, than that in their books, some of which give large and particular accounts of their worship, and of their doctrines concerning worship, we can no where meet with the least intimation or footstep of them. Would our adversaries have us bring express testimonies out of the fathers against these things, as if they wrote and disputed by the Spirit of prophecy, against those corruptions that should arise several ages after they were dead?.... To demand more than their perpetual silence in these cases, is unreasonable; because no satisfactory account can be given of it, but this, *That the worship we speak of was indeed no part of their religion.* Had it been some indifferent rite or ceremony that we contend about, this argument, from the silence of the fathers, against its antiquity, might with some colour be rejected; because it were unreasonable to expect, that they should take notice in their writings of every custom, of how little moment soever: and yet we find, that in matters even of

---

* Preservative against Popery, title vii. p. 85.

this slight nature, in comparison, they have not been wanting to give us very much information. But it is altogether incredible, that so notable and famous a part of the worship of Christians, as that which is now given to the blessed virgin, and to the saints, should not be mentioned by any one of them, if it had been the custom of those times.... We have seen that in these latter ages the doctrine of her [the virgin Mary's] worship, is grown to be no mean part of the body of divinity with the doctors of the Roman church. There is no end of writing books in her honour, and to excite and direct devotion to her.... One would, therefore, expect to find all things full of veneration and addresses to the blessed virgin, in the writings of the primitive fathers; that is, to meet with it at every turn—but if you look for any such thing, I will be bold to say you will lose your labour.... I know not how the fathers can be excused, but that the scriptures speak as sparingly of her as they."*—The intelligent reader will easily perceive that this will apply with peculiar force, *mutatis mutandis*, to the case before us.

Reflect. VI. Though the practice of infant baptism did prevail in the latter part of the third century, yet learned Pædobaptists themselves inform us, that many eminent persons descended from Christian parents, in following times, were not baptized till they arrived at the age of maturity. Bp. Taylor says: "The wisest of our fathers in Christ did not come unto baptism, until they were come to a strong and confirmed wit and age .... There is no pretence of tradition, that the church in all ages did baptize all the infants of Christian parents. It is more certain that they did not do it always, than that they did it in the first age. St. Ambrose, St. Hierom, and St. Austin, were born of Christian parents, and yet not baptized until the full age of a man, and

---

* Preserv. against Popery, title vi. p. 192, 193, 194.

more."*——Daillé bears the following testimony: "In ancient times they often deferred the baptizing both of infants and of other people, as appears by the history of the emperors, Constantine the Great, of Constantius, of Theodosius, of Valentinian, and of Gratian, in St. Ambrose; and also by the orations and homilies of Gregory Nazianzen, and of St. Basil, upon this subject. And some of the fathers too have been of opinion, that it is fit it should be deferred; as, namely, Tertullian, as we have formerly noted of him."†——The famous Austin, in his Confessions, having said; " I was then signed with the sign of his [Christ's] cross, and was seasoned with his salt, so soon as I came out of my mother's womb, who greatly trusted in thee;" his translator, Dr. W. Watts, has the following note upon it: " This was the practice of the primitive times; by which religious parents devoted their children unto Christ, long before their baptism, which in *those days was deferred till they were able to answer for themselves.*"‡—Gregory Nazianzen, born in the year three hundred and eighteen, whose parents were Christians, and his father a bishop, was not baptized till about thirty years of age:§ and Chrysostom also, born of Christian parents in the year three hundred and forty seven, was not baptized till near twenty-one years of age.‖ See the immediately following chapter, No. 1.—Now, if the parents of these Christian fathers and Cæsars, though professing themselves the disciples of Christ, did not baptize their infant offspring, we may justly presume, whatever might be the reasons of their conduct, that many others in those times were influenced by the same reasons, and acted a similar part.

---

* In Dr. Wall's Hist. Inf. Bap. part ii. chap. ii. § 10.
† Right Use of the Fathers, book ii. chap. vi. p. 149.
‡ Austin's Confessions, book i. chap. xi. p. 17. 1650.
§ Dupin, cent. iv. p. 159. Gen. Biog. Dict. art. Greg. Naz.
‖ Grotius, apud Poli Synops. ad Mat. xix. 14. Dupin's Eccles. Hist. cent. v. p. 6, 7.

The language of Boniface, bishop of Thessalonica, in a letter to Austin, is far from expressing a warm regard, either for infant baptism, or the business of sponsors. "Suppose I set before you an infant," says he to Austin, "and ask you, *Whether, when he grows up, he will be a chaste person?* or, *Whether he will be a thief?* You doubtless will answer, *I do not know.* And, *Whether he, in that infant age, have any thought, good, or evil?* You will still say, *I do not know.* If then you dare not assert any thing concerning his future conduct, or his present thoughts, what is the reason that, when they are presented for baptism, their parents, as sponsors for them, answer and say; They *do* that, of which their infant age is not able to *think;* or, if it can, it is a profound secret? For we ask those by whom they are presented, and say; *Does he believe in God?* (which question concerns that age which is ignorant whether there be a God.) They answer, *He does believe.* And so likewise an answer is returned to all the rest. Whence I wonder that parents in these affairs answer so confidently for the child, that he does so many good things, which at the time of his baptism the administrator demands! And yet, were I at that very time to ask; *Will this baptized child*, when grown to maturity, *be chaste?* or, *Will he not be a thief?* I know not whether any one would venture to answer, *He will*, or, *He will not*, be the one or the other; as they answer without hesitation, *He believes in God—He turns to God.*"*—Hence it appears, that in the time of Austin a profession of faith was always required, prior to the administration of baptism, agreeably to the primitive pattern;† that when an infant was presented for baptism, this profession was made by proxy, as it is now in the church of Rome, and in the church of England; that Boniface considered this vicarious profession, as a bold, unwarrantable, absurd procedure, as it undoubtedly is; and, consequently,

---

* Augustini Epistola ad Bonifacium, epist. xxiii. † Acts viii. 37.

that he was far from being, like Austin, a sanguine admirer of Pædobaptism; there being, as Dr. Wall observes, " no time or age of the church, in which there is any appearance that infants were ordinarily baptized, without sponsors or godfathers,"* to make that vicarious profession, against which Boniface with so much reason and force objects.

To these difficulties the celebrated bishop of Hippo, among other trifling and impertinent things, replies: " As the sacrament of Christ's body is, after a certain fashion, Christ's body; and the sacrament of Christ's blood, is his blood; so the sacrament of faith, is faith; and to believe, is nothing else but to have faith. And so when an infant, that has not yet the faculty of faith, is said to believe, he is said to have faith, because of the sacrament of faith; and to turn to God, because of the sacrament of conversion; because that answer belongs to the celebration of the sacrament. . . . An infant, though he be not yet constituted a believer, by that faith which consists in the will of believers, yet he is by the sacrament of that faith: for, as he is said to believe, so he is called a believer; not from his having the thing itself in his mind, but from his receiving the sacrament of it. And when a person begins to have a sense of things, he does not repeat that sacrament, but he understands the force of it, and by consent of will squares himself to the true meaning of it. And till he can do this, the sacrament will avail to his preservation against all contrary powers; and so far it will avail, that, if he depart this life before the use of reason, he will, by this Christian remedy of the sacrament itself, (the charity of the church recommending him) be made free from that condemnation which, by one man, entered into the world. He that does not believe this, and thinks it cannot be done, is indeed an infidel, though he have the sacrament of faith; and that infant is much better, who,

---

* Hist. Inf. Bap. p. 477.

though he have not faith in his mind, yet puts no bar of a contrary mind against it, and so receives the sacrament to his soul's health."*—Such is the solution given by Austin, which the celebrated Chamier justly pronounces *frigid*.† How far any of those who now administer baptism on the creed of a proxy, whether latent in the parent, or avowed by the sponsor, may approve of his reasoning, I cannot pretend to say; but I think it is plain, that the New Testament is equally silent about a vicarious faith, and a vicarious baptism. He, therefore, who admits the former, could not consistently oppose the latter, were any to plead for it.

The very learned and famous Daillé, when animadverting on this passage of Austin, says; "Whether these things satisfied Boniface, I know not. To me, I confess, they seem strange. How can the infant offered to baptism, be truly said, therefore, to have faith, because he has the sacrament of faith, i. e. baptism, at the time when he has not yet received baptism? nay, who is for no other reason asked the question, than that he may obtain baptism, which as yet he wants? As though none ought to be baptized who does not believe. An infant is presented to the minister to be baptized: the minister, as though he thought it unlawful to baptize even an infant, except he believes, demands, and, which aggravates the absurdity, he demands of the *infant himself*, whether he believes? tacitly implying, he may not baptize him unless he does so. Here the godfather, that the infant may be capable of baptism, answers as his surety, that he believes. When Boniface was in doubt, how the godfather could truly and certainly affirm this; Austin answers, he could, though the infant had not yet faith; because, when he says *he believes*, he only means, he has the sacrament of faith. Is not this a brave solution of the difficulty? But I say the infant

---

* In Dr. Wall, ut supra, p. 115.
† Panstrat. tom. iv. l. v. c. xv. § 22.

has not what you call the sacrament of faith; nor, if he had, would there be any occasion to offer him to you to be baptized: and therefore, in that very sense Austin puts upon the answer, the godfather lies when he says, the infant believes, i. e. has the sacrament of faith."*

Whether the form of proceeding in the administration of baptism to infants, according to the English Liturgy, do not deserve a similar censure, let my reader judge by the following extract from Mr. Peirce. "The priest thus speaks unto the godfathers and godmothers: 'Wherefore *this infant must also faithfully for his part*, promise by you that are his sureties, (until he come of age to take it upon himself) that he will renounce the devil and all his works, and constantly believe God's holy word, and obediently keep his commandments. I demand, therefore; Dost thou, in the name of this child, renounce the devil and all his works, the vain pomp and glory of the world?' and so on. 'I renounce them all.' 'Dost thou believe in God the Father almighty?' and so on. 'All this I steadfastly believe.' '*Wilt thou be baptized* in this faith?' 'So is my desire.' '*Wilt thou* then obediently keep God's holy will and commandments, and walk in the same all the days of thy life?' 'I will.' Who now is so blind as not to see, the minister all along asks the infants themselves these questions? Of whom else can he ask, whether *he will be baptized?* or who else can answer, *I will?* For the godfathers and godmothers have been baptized themselves long before. It is plain then the godfathers are not properly asked these questions, and that they answer them for no other reason, but because the infants are not able to speak for themselves. Which to many seems absurd and childish, and unworthy of the gravity of a Christian assembly, and the solemnity of the ordinance of baptism. Hereto we may add the words of the

---

* In Mr. Peirce's Vindicat. of Dissenters, part iii. p. 169, 170.

Catechism : 'Why then are infants baptized, when, by reason of their tender age, they cannot perform [repentance and faith?] Because they promise them both by their sureties,' and so on." He adds; "And truly they seem by this method to betray the cause of infants to the Anabaptists. For if an express and actual profession of repentance and faith is necessarily to be required of every one before he is baptized, infant baptism can never be defended; since a vicarious profession is not founded upon any text in the whole Bible."*—To the latter part of this quotation a Conformist might reply: "We acknowledge, Sir, that there is an air of puerility attending those questions and answers which you have recited; but notwithstanding this we insist, that there is a more plain reference to primitive practice than can be perceived in your mode of proceeding.† In the administration of baptism according to our Liturgy, a profession of repentance and faith makes a signal appearance; not so in your procedure. We baptize on the professed faith of sponsors; you, on the presumed faith of parents. Show us your warrant for baptizing a child on the latter, and you shall not wait long for ours on behalf of the former. Produce your text from the Bible for baptizing one or another, without a personal profession made by the subject; and you shall soon have ours for administering baptism upon the declared creed of proxy.

Once more: Cattenburgh informs us, that in the former part of the sixth century many opposed infant baptism.‡—The Petrobrussians in the twelfth century maintained, as Venema shows, "That Pædobaptism cannot save infants, nor the faith of another be profitable to them:"§ and Mosheim assures us, that "Peter

---

* Vindicat. of Dissent. part iii. p. 166, 167.
† Matt. iii. 6—10; Acts viii. 36, 37; 1 Pet. iii. 21.
‡ Spicileg. Theol. Christ. l. iv. c. lxiv. sect. ii. § 4.
§ Hist. Eccles. tom. vi. p. 129.

de Bruys, who made the most laudable attempts to reform the abuses and to remove the superstitions that disfigured the beautiful simplicity of the gospel,"—insisted, "That no persons whatever were to be baptized before they came to the full use of their reason."*——Hence J. A. Fabricius calls the Petrobrussians, "the Anabaptists of that age."†—In the same century, according to Venema, there was another sect of professing Christians, denominated *Publicans,* who asserted, "That infants are not to be baptized, till they arrive at years of understanding." The same historian mentions another denomination of Christians in that age, called *Arnoldists;* who, he says, "considered Pædobaptism in a different light from that of the Romish church—Concerning which sect, Bernard exclaims, *Utinam tam sanæ esset doctrinæ, quam districtæ vitæ!"*‡—I will conclude this chapter with the following concession of a Roman Catholic writer, the principle of which will here apply. "No true believer now doubts of purgatory; whereof, notwithstanding, among the ancients there is very little or no mention at all." §

---

* Eccles. Hist. cent. xii. part. ii. chap. v. § 7.
† Bibliographia Antiq. p. 388. Hamb. 1716.
‡ Ut supra, p. 130, 131, 132. See Dupin, cent. xii. p. 88. 89.
§ In Morning Exercise against Popery, p. 251.

CHAPTER III.

The high Opinion of the Fathers, concerning the Utility of Baptism, and the Grounds on which they proceeded in administering that Ordinance to Infants, when Pædobaptism became a prevailing Practice.

VITRINGA.—" The ancient Christian church, from the highest antiquity after the apostolic times, appears generally to have thought, that baptism is absolutely necessary for all that would be saved by the grace of Jesus Christ. It was therefore customary in the ancient church, if infants were greatly afflicted and in danger of death; or if parents were affected with a singular concern about the salvation of their children, to present their infants, or children in their minority, to the bishop to be baptized. But if these reasons did not urge them, they thought it better, and more for the interest of minors, that their baptism should be deferred till they arrived at a more advanced age; which custom was not yet abolished in the time of Austin, though he vehemently urged the necessity of baptism, while with all his might he defended the doctrines of grace against Pelagius." Observat. Sac. tom. i. l. ii. c. vi. § 9.

2. Venema.—" The ancients connected a regenerating power, and a communication of the Spirit, with baptism. Justin Martyr (Apol. ii. 79,) asserts it in express words; and to baptism he applies that saying of our Lord, 'Except a man be born of water and of the Spirit, he cannot enter into the kingdom of God.' Besides, (Contra Tryph. p. 231,) he asserts, ' that baptism only can cleanse and purify a penitent;' where it is also called, 'the water of life'.... Irenæus (Advers. Hæres. iii. 17,) says, ' *That Christ gave to his disciples the power of regenerating to God,* when he sent them to baptize.'

And Clemens Alexandrinus (Pædag. i. 6,) says; 'Being dipped, or baptized, we are illuminated; being illuminated, we are adopted for sons; being adopted, we are perfected; being perfected, we are rendered immortal: whence baptism is called grace, illumination, and the perfect laver,' which words he there explains.—The doctrine of Tertullian is of a similar kind. Thus he speaks, (De Pænit. c. vi.) 'A divine benefit, that is, the abolition of offences, is ascertained to those that are about to enter the water;' yet only in respect of such as repent. In his book concerning baptism, he explains his opinion more at large, and there attributes to the water, by an union with the divine virtue, a sanctifying power.... That baptism is connected with the remission of antecedent sins, and confers a sanctifying power on the person baptized, is the undoubted opinion of Cyprian, which he every where inculcates, so that there is hardly any need to produce the particular passages. In his first epistle to Donatus he declares, that before his conversion it seemed impossible to him, 'that a person should all on a sudden put off sin, in the laver of the salutary water,' which he himself had experienced; saying, 'Afterward, by the help of the generating water, the spots of the former time are cleansed away; a serene and a pure light from above, infuses itself into the peaceful breast; afterward a second birth, the Spirit being drawn from heaven, restored me into a new man.'—In his lxiii[d] epistle, to Cæcilius, he expressly says, 'By baptism the Holy Spirit is received.' In his lxx[th] epistle, to Januarius, he says, 'It is necessary, therefore, that the water should be first purified and sanctified by the priest, that he may be able, by the baptism which he administers, to wash away the sins of a man who is baptized;' where also many other things of a similar kind occur. In his lxxi[st] epistle, to Quintus, he says; 'There is one water in the holy church, which maketh sheep.' In his lxxii[d] epistle, to Stephanus, he applies what our Lord says (John iii.) concerning the necessity of regeneration, to baptism. In his lxxiii^d epistle, to Jubaianus, these remarkable words occur: 'Thence begins the origin of all faith, the saving entrance to a hope of eternal life, and a divine grant to purify and quicken the servants of God:' soon after he also attributes the remission of sin, and sanctification, to baptism, and applies to it John iii. 5. In his lxxivth epistle, to Pompeius, he says, 'We are born, in Christ, by the laver of generation. Water only cannot purge away sins and sanctify a man, unless it have also the Holy Spirit. It is baptism, in which the old man dies and the new man is born.' Firmilianus also, in the lxxvth epistle, to Cyprian, among the effects of baptism, particularly mentions, 'washing away the filth of the old man, forgiving of old sins, that were deserving of death; making persons, by a heavenly regeneration, the sons of God; and a restoration to life eternal, by the sanctification of the divine laver'.... Gregory Nazianzen declares, (Orat. xl. p. 653,) That they who die unbaptized, without their own fault, go neither to heaven nor hell; but, if they have lived piously, to a middle place." Hist. Eccles. tom. iii. secul. ii. § 124; sec. iii. § 61; tom. iv. sec. iv. § 115.

3. Salmasius.—" An opinion prevailed, that no one could be saved without being baptized; and for that reason the custom arose of baptizing infants." Epist. ad Justum Pacium, apud Van Dale Hist. Baptism.

4. Hospinianus.—" Austin, when writing against the Pelagians, too inconsiderately consigns over the infants of Christians to damnation that died without baptism. There is nothing that he more zealously urges, nor any thing on which he more firmly depends, than those words of Christ, 'Except a man be born of water and of the Spirit, he cannot enter into the kingdom of God.'" Hist. Sacram. l. ii. c. ii. p. 52.

5. Suicerus.—" We cannot deny, that many of the ancients maintained the absolute necessity of baptism.

Chrysostom says, 'It is impossible, without baptism, to obtain the kingdom:' and soon after, 'It is impossible to be saved without it'.... This opinion concerning the absolute necessity of baptism, arose from a wrong understanding of our Lord's words; 'Except a man be born of water and of the Spirit, he cannot enter into the kingdom of heaven'.... Chrysostom again says, 'If an infant die without baptism, through the negligence of the presbyter, wo to that presbyter! but if, through the negligence of the parents, wo to the parents of that infant!'" Thesaur. Eccles. tom. i. p. 3, 650.

6. Episcopius.—" Pædobaptism was not accounted a necessary rite, till it was determined so to be in the Milevitan Council, held in the year four hundred and eighteen." Institut. Theol. l. iv. c. xiv.

7. Dr. Owen.—" Most of the ancients concluded, that it [baptism] was no less necessary unto salvation than faith or repentance itself." On Justification, chap. ii. p. 173.

8. Dr. Wall.—" If we except Tertullian—Vincentius [A. D. 419] is the first man upon record that ever said, that children might be saved without baptism; if by being saved, we mean going to heaven; for that many before him thought they would be in a state without punishment, I have showed before.... All the ancient Christians, without the exception of one man, do understand the rule of our Saviour, (John iii. 5,) 'Verily, verily, I say unto you, Except a man be born of water and of the Spirit, he cannot enter into the kingdom of God,' of baptism. I had occasion in the first Part to bring a great many instances of their sayings, where all that mention that text, from Justin Martyr down to St. Austin, do so apply it; and many more might be brought. Neither did I ever see it otherwise applied in any ancient writer. I believe Calvin was the first that ever denied this place to mean baptism." Hist. of Inf. Bap. part i. chap. xx. p. 232, 233; part ii. chap. vi. p. 354.

REFLECTIONS.

Reflect. I. Though it is manifest from the concessions and assertions of learned Pædobaptists in the preceding chapter, that there is no evidence of infant baptism before the time of Tertullian, by whom it was opposed; yet from these quotations it plainly appears, that both he and others before him spake of baptism in such a manner, as had a natural tendency to introduce and promote Pædobaptism. When Justin, for instance, had learned to call baptism *the water of life,* and to interpret John iii. 5, as relating to that institution; when Clement of Alexandria had ascribed to it an *illuminating power,* and connected *adoption, perfection,* and *immortality* with it; and when Tertullian had pronounced it *a divine blessing,* which ascertains the *abolition of sin,* and is attended with a *sanctifying energy;* it is no wonder, that in the time of Cyprian it should be thought necessary for infants to be baptized, and that Pædobaptism should become a prevailing practice. The language of this venerable African is like that of Rupert, in the twelfth century, who says: "Baptism is therefore called *tinctio,* in Latin, because a man when baptized is, by the Spirit of grace, altered for the better, and is rendered very different from what he was before. He was a son of death and of perdition; he is made a child of life and of acquisition. He was a son of hell; he is made an heir of God's kingdom. He was an enemy of God; he is reconciled and made a child of God."* A pernicious opinion this, by whomsoever espoused! The language of Cyprian, and of others in following times, concerning the energy of baptismal water, administered occasion for the apostate Julian to reproach the Christians, with reference to the solemn rite.†

It is worthy of observation, that while Cyprian stands

---

* Apud Magdeburg. Centur. cent. xii. p 252.
† Vid. Biblioth Bremens. class. i. fascic. iii. p. 243.

forth as the first patron of infant sprinkling, he appears also as giving the sanction of his authority in favour of *holy water;* asserting the necessity of having the baptismal element consecrated by a priest, in order to render it more effectual for the washing away of sin. See No. 2.*—Austin and others, we find, in the following times, proceeded a step farther than Cyprian; and, not contented with asserting at an extravagant rate the utility of baptism, boldly maintained its absolute necessity: consigning over to eternal ruin all such infants as died without it. See No. 4, 5.—Now as both Cyprian and Austin were African bishops, there is reason to conclude with Grotius, "That anciently the baptism of infants was much more common in Africa than in Asia, or elsewhere; and with a greater opinion of its necessity."† So fond of baptism were the superstitious Africans, that, as Deylingius informs us, they frequently baptized the dead.‡

Reflect. II. From the quotations before us it plainly appears, that the baptism of infants was introduced and prevailed, on the supposition of its being a necessary mean of human happiness; and that this weak surmise was founded on a mistake of our Lord's meaning, in John iii. 5. See No. 2, 5, 6, 7, 8.—In like manner a misunderstanding of John vi. 53, produced infant communion; as we shall see in its proper place.—It is worthy of remark, as Mr. Richards observes, that "those words of our Lord were the principal texts that could be thought of for some time, as proper to urge in their

---

* Vid. Quenstedium, Antiq. Bib. pars. i. cap. iv. sect. ii. num. i. § 12. The present form of consecrating baptismal water in the Church of England is as follows: "Almighty everliving God.... regard, we beseech thee, the supplications of thy congregation; *sanctify* this water to the mystical washing away of sin; and grant that this child, now to be baptized therein, may receive the fulness of thy grace,"—and so on. Public Baptism of Infants.

† Apud Poli Synops. ad Mat. xix. 14.

‡ De Prudent. Pastoral. pars iii. c. iii. § 16.

favour. How vastly are the times altered since! What heaps of texts the modern advocates for these customs are able to quote in support of them, which the ancients could never think of; while those which the latter thought the most favourable to their cause, are now deemed little, or nothing at all to the purpose! Whatever others may think of this circumstance, I must confess that I cannot help looking upon it as rather unfavourable to the cause of the usages in question; for had they been really commanded in scripture, one cannot conceive why the ancients should not have been as well acquainted with those commands as the moderns; especially, as they must have been equally interested, and in all probability took no less pains to find them out. But by viewing both the customs as *corruptions* of Christianity, the circumstance at once ceases to be mysterious; as it is well known that the ordinances of [men] are capable of *improvement;* which is by no means the case with those of Jesus Christ." *

In regard to John iii. 5, it may be observed, that had our divine Teacher, when he declared it absolutely necessary to be "born of water and of the Spirit," intended the ordinance of baptism by the term *water;* then indeed the necessity of that institution would have unavoidably followed, as being placed on a level with the renewing agency of the Holy Spirit. But were that the sense of our Lord, it would inevitably follow, that a positive rite is of equal necessity with the renovating influence of the Holy Spirit; that the salvation of infants, in many cases, is rendered impossible, because numbers of them are no sooner born than they expire; that the eternal happiness of all who die in their infancy must depend, not only on the devout care of their parents, but also on the presence and pious benevolence of administrators; that all the dying infants of Jews, of Mohammedans, and of Pagans, are involved in final ruin; and, that multitudes of adults

---

* **History of Antichrist, p. 81.**

must also perish, merely for the want of baptism. But who can imagine that the Lord should place our immortal interests on such a footing, as neither tends to illustrate the grace of God, nor to promote the comfort of man,—on such a footing as is quite inimical to the spirit of that maxim, BY GRACE YE ARE SAVED; and has no aptitude to excite virtuous tempers in the human heart? A sentiment of this kind is chiefly adapted to enhance the importance of the clerical character, and to make mankind consider themselves as under infinite obligations to a professional order of their fellow mortals, for an interest in everlasting blessedness. — Remarkably strong is the following language of Mr. Arch. Hall respecting this particular: "We might well say, *Wo to the earth!* if it were in the power of a selfish and peevish order of men, to dispose of happiness and damnation according to their humour."* We may, therefore, safely conclude, that the term *water*, in our Lord's converse with Nicodemus, does not signify baptism; and consequently whatever its meaning be, the emphatical passage neither enjoins nor encourages the administration of baptism to infants. Hence it appears, that the main foundation of Pædobaptism among the ancients was a great mistake; and as such it has long been deserted by the generality of Calvinistic Pædobaptists.

Reflect. III. That my reader may see in what an important point of light baptism is considered by the generality of modern Pædobaptists, and to convince him that it is with an ill grace any of them charge us with laying an unwarrantable stress upon it, the following extracts are produced, partly from public formulas of doctrine and worship, and partly from the writings of individuals. Thus then the church of Rome, when speaking by the *Council of Trent*. "If any one shall say that baptism

---

* Gospel Worship, vol. i. p. 288. See Mr. Bradbury's Duty and Doct. of Bap. p. 19, 20.

is—not necessary to salvation, let him be accursed.... Sin, whether contracted by birth from our first parents, or committed of ourselves,—by the admirable virtue of this sacrament, is remitted and pardoned.... In baptism, not only sins are remitted, but also all the punishments of sins and wickedness are graciously pardoned of God.... By virtue of this sacrament, we are not only delivered from those evils which are truly said to be the greatest of all, but also we are enriched with the best and most excellent endowments; for our souls are filled with divine grace, whereby being made just and the children of God, we are trained up to be heirs of eternal salvation also.... To this is added a most noble train of all virtues, which, together with grace, is poured of God into the soul.... By baptism we are joined and knit to Christ, as members to the head.... By baptism we are signed with a character which can never be blotted out of our soul.... Besides the other things which we obtain by baptism, it opens to every one of us the gate of heaven, which before, through sin, was shut."*

Cyril, the patriarch of Constantinople, expresses his own faith, and that of the *Greek church*, respecting baptism, in the follwing manner. "We believe that baptism is a sacrament appointed by the Lord, which except a person receive, he has no communion with Christ; from whose death, burial, and resurrection, proceed all the virtue and efficacy of baptism. We are certain, therefore, that both original and actual sin is forgiven, to those who are baptized in the manner which our Lord requires in the gospel; so that whoever is washed 'in the name of the Father, and of the Son, and of the Holy Spirit,' is regenerated, cleansed, and justified."†—Stapferus, when speaking of the Greek church, says: "The

---

* Concil. Trident. sess. vii. can. v. Catechism of Council of Trent, p. 166—175.

† Confess. Christ. Fidei, cap. xvi. A. D. 1631, ad calcem Syntag. Confess. Fid. Genev. 1654.

Oriental Christians attributing too much efficacy to rites and ceremonies, it is no wonder if they teach the absolute necessity of baptism; that without it no one can become a real Christian; and that it cannot be omitted in respect of infants without endangering their salvation: so that, a priest being absent, and in case of necessity, baptism may be administered by a layman, or by a woman. For the same reason they also teach, that there is an equal necessity of the Lord's supper; which, therefore, they administer under both species to baptized infants."*

Let us now examine the Protestant confessions, respecting this affair. Thus, then, the Confession of Helvetia: " To be baptized in the name of Christ, is to be enrolled, entered, and received into the covenant and family, and so into the inheritance of the sons of God; yea, and in this life, to be called after the name of God, that is to say, to be called the sons of God, to be purged also from the filthiness of sins, and to be endued with the manifold grace of God, for to lead a new and innocent life."——Confession of Bohemia: " We believe, that whatsoever by baptism—is in the outward ceremony signified and witnessed, all that doth the Lord God perform inwardly; that is, that he washeth away sin, begetteth a man again, and bestoweth salvation upon him .... For the bestowing of these excellent fruits was holy baptism given and granted to the church."——Confession of Augsburg: " Concerning baptism they teach, that it is necessary to salvation, as a ceremony ordained of Christ; also, that by baptism the grace of God is offered."——Confession of Saxony: " *I baptize thee;* that is, I do witness that, by this dipping, thy sins be washed away, and that thou art now received of the true God."——Confession of Wittenburg: " We believe and confess, that baptism is that sea, into the bottom whereof, as the prophet saith, God doth *cast all our sins.*"——

---
* Theolog. Polem. tom. v. p. 82.

Confession of Sueveland: "As touching baptism, we confess, that it is the font of regeneration, washeth away sins, and saveth us. But all these things we do so understand, as St. Peter doth interpret them, (1 Pet. iii. 21.)"*——Church of England: "Baptism, wherein I was made a member of Christ, the child of God, and an inheritor of the kingdom of heaven.... How many sacraments hath Christ ordained in his church? Two only, as generally necessary to salvation; that is to say, baptism and the supper of the Lord."†——Westminster Assembly: "Before baptism, the minister is to use some words of instruction,—showing, that it is instituted by our Lord Jesus Christ; that it is a seal of the covenant of grace, of our ingrafting into Christ, and of our union with him, of remission of sins, regeneration, adoption, and life eternal."‡—Such is the language of modern Pædobaptists in their public formulas.

The following extracts are from the writings of individuals of different communions. Thus that famous reformer, Luther: "There is in the baptism of infants, the beginning of faith and of a divine operation, in a manner peculiar to themselves."§——Gerhardus: "The sacrament of baptism does not profit without faith; nevertheless it is the efficacious mean by which God of his grace works faith, regeneration, and salvation in the hearts of infants."‖—— Buddeus: "All men should be baptized, who are to be brought to eternal salvation .... No one can be saved except by faith, as our Saviour expressly declares. Now seeing infants cannot be brought to faith by the preaching of God's word; it follows, that it must be effected in another way, namely, by baptism: by which men are born again, and so receive faith, as our Saviour declares.... The

---

* Harmony of Confessions, sect. xiii. p. 395—410.
† Catechism.   ‡ Directory, article Baptism.
§ Apud Venem. Hist. Eccles. tom. vii. p. 107.
‖ Loci Theolog. tom. iv. De Bap. § 195.

effect of baptism, which has the nature of an end, is, in respect of infants, regeneration.... That effect, therefore, which immediately results from baptism, consists in regeneration, by which faith is produced in infants ....In baptism a divine virtue is connected with the water, and with the action conversant about it; which is in a particular manner to be regarded.... Baptism is not a mere sign and symbol, by which a reception into the covenant of grace is denoted: but by regeneration, which baptism effects, we are *really received* into that covenant; and so are made partakers of all the blessings peculiar to it. To which blessings (besides remission of sins, or justification, renovation, adoption into the number of God's children, a right to the heavenly inheritance, and a certain hope of eternal life) pertains communion with Christ, and with his mystical body.... Concerning the highest necessity of baptism, the thing itself will not suffer us to doubt; seeing it is expressly asserted, that without it no one shall enter the kingdom of heaven, (John iii. 5.)"*—— Deylingius: "Baptism is the sacrament of initiation, and, as it were, the gate of heaven; in which a man is regenerated by the washing of water and the word of God, purged from the guilt of sin, and declared to be an heir of all celestial blessings.... If Christian parents defer the baptism of their infants; or, seized by the spirit of Anabaptism, or of fanaticism, will not have them baptized at all,—then, by the authority of the consistory, or of the magistrate of the place, the infant must be taken from the parents, and when initiated by baptism returned to them." †——Vossius: "In infants, upon whom the word has no efficacy, there is room for the sacraments to generate faith in them; without which no one shall see eternal life.... It is manifest, that in baptism we are born again, adopted,

---

* Theolog. Dogmat. l. v. c. i. § 5, 6, 7, 8, 10.
† De Prudent. Pastoral. pars. iii. c. iii. § 2, 15.

received into the covenant of grace; and upon that receive remission of sins, are renewed by the Holy Spirit, and made heirs of the heavenly kingdom."*——— Mr. Isaac Ambrose: "By baptism we are washed, we are sanctified, we are justified, in the name of the Lord Jesus, and by the Spirit of our God."†———Dr. Fiddes: There is no "reason for excluding infants from baptism, as it is a means of reinstating them in the favour of God, or of conveying, in virtue of God's appointment, inward and spiritual grace.... Baptism is a means of conveying both pardoning and sanctifying grace, to those who are qualified to receive it as they ought."‡ ———Mr. Gee: "This sacrament of baptism doth confer on the person baptized the grace of remission, of adoption, and sanctification.... It is granted, that baptism is ordinarily necessary to salvation; that God hath made it the instrument of remission, of regeneration, and of salvation to us."§———Anonymous: "It [baptism] was ordained, that the baptized person might by that solemnity pass from a state of nature, wherein he was a child of wrath, into a state of adoption and grace, wherein he becomes a child of God.... Baptism was instituted for a sign to seal unto baptized persons the pardon of their sins, and to confer upon them a right of inheritance unto everlasting life: but baptism hath this effect upon infants, as well as upon adult persons; for it washes them clean from original, as it doth men and women both from actual and original sin. I say, it washes them clean from original sin, and seals the pardon of it, and the assurance of God's favour unto them."||———Dr. Waterland: "Baptism alone is sufficient to make one a Christian, yea, and to keep him

---

* Disputat. de Bap. Disp. de Sac. Efficac. § 46, 47; disput. iv. § 9.
† Works, p. 196.
‡ Theolog. Pract. b. ii. part ii. chap. i. p. 178, 181.
§ Preservative against Popery, title vii. p. 20, 33.
|| Cases to Recover Dissenters, vol. ii. p. 444, 445.

such, even to his life's end; since it imprints an indelible character in such a sense as never to need repeating."*
——Dr. Whitby: "The end of baptism [is] the remission of sins, and the effect of it justification, or the absolution of the baptized person from his past sins."†
——Bp. Wilson: "I believe that Jesus Christ is the Son of God. It was upon this declaration of the eunuch, that he was baptized by Philip; and if he was sincere, (which Philip could not tell, nor pretend to know his heart,) his sins were forgiven by that act of Philip, (Acts xxii. 16.)....It would be wicked to say, that the eunuch, by believing in Jesus Christ, would have had his sins forgiven, though he had not been baptized."‡——Dr. Featley: "Βαπτω, from whence *baptize* is derived, signifieth as well to *dye*, as to dip; and it may be, the Holy Ghost in the word baptism, hath some reference to that signification, because by baptism *we change our* HUE. For as Varrow reporteth of a river in Bœotia, that the water thereof turneth sheep of a dark or dun colour into *white;* so the sheep of Christ which are washed in the font of baptism, by virtue of Christ's promise, though before they were of never so dark, sad, or dirty colour, yet in their souls become white and pure, and, as it were, *new dyed.*§—— The reader will here excuse a remark, by way of query. Would then the doctor have treated the Baptists in such an illiberal manner as he has done, if he had, either by dipping or sprinkling, thoroughly imbibed that excellent *dye* of which he speaks? Or would his calumniating pen have recorded the following sentence? "The resort of great multitudes of men and women together in the evening, and going *naked* into rivers there to be dipped and plunged, cannot be done without scandal."|| What a pity it is, but the doctor had been soundly

---

* Discourse of Fundamentals, p. 48.
† Note on Acts viii. 37.   ‡ Ibid. Acts viii. 41.
§ Dippers Dipt, p. 41, edit. 7. || Ibid. p. 39.

plunged in Varro's Bœotian river! It might have rendered his mind more white, and his language more fair, and then the Baptists would not have been so dirtily handled by him. Mr. Obadiah Wills expresses himself thus: "Baptism is God's *sheep-mark*, as Mr. Ford calls it, to distinguish those that are of his fold, from such as graze in the wild common of the world."* It is rather dubious, however, whether the excellent mark will prove permanent; for this writer assures us, that "the covenant of grace is not absolute and saving to all that are once within it."†—Mr. Burkitt also, speaking of infants under the notion of lambs, calls baptism "Christ's *ear-mark*, by which Christ's sheep are distinguished from the devil's goats."‡ Thus happily have these authors provided for the honour of baptism, when the disciples of Christ are considered under the notion of sheep; for it *washes* their fleeces and *marks* their ears.§ What Pædobaptists may think of such language, from such pens, I cannot pretend to say; but there is reason to conclude, that were any of the Baptists to talk at this rate, their conduct would be exploded with the keenest ridicule.

Remarkable is the language of Dr. Scott, when showing the import of Matt. xxviii. 19. Among other things of a similar kind, he says: "By this commission, Christ's ministers are authorized and constituted the legal proxies of the Holy Trinity, in the stead of those blessed persons, to seal the new covenant with the

---

* Inf. Bap. Asserted and Vindicated, p. 273.
† Ibid. p. 199.   ‡ In Mr. Keach's Rector Rectified, p. 98.
§ Mr. Bingham tells us, from Clemens Alexandrinus, that some of the ancient heretics, "when they had baptized men in water, also made a mark upon their *ears* with fire; so joining water baptism and, as they imagined, baptism by fire together." Orig. Eccles. b. x. chap. ii. § 3.—The Jacobites and others of the Oriental Christians make, with a hot iron, the figure of a cross on the foreheads of persons baptized. Vid. Hoornbeekii Miscel. Sac. l. i. c. xvii. § 16. Now *these* are marks indeed.

baptismal sign to those whom they baptize; and thereby legally to oblige the Father, Son, and Holy Ghost, to perform the promises of it to all those baptized persons who perform the conditions of it.... When once we have struck covenant with him [God] in baptism, we have him fast obliged to us to perform his part of the covenant, whenever we perform ours."* *Proxies* of the Holy Trinity—*Legally oblige* the Father, Son, and Holy Spirit—God *fast obliged* to us. Peter tells us of some who spake "great swelling words of vanity;" and it seems as if the doctor had copied after them.—Mr. George Whitefield, remarking on John iii. 5, asks and answers in the following manner: "Does not this verse urge the absolute necessity of **water** baptism? YES, where it may be had; but how God will deal with persons unbaptized we cannot tell."†—Mr. John Wesley, among various other things of a similar kind, says: "If infants are guilty of original sin, in the ordinary way they CANNOT be saved, unless this be washed away by baptism."‡ These extracts bring to remembrance an observation of Buxtorf, relating to the opinion of Jewish rabbies about the efficacy of circumcision. "It is almost incredible," says he, "how highly they extol circumcision; how arrogantly and impiously they are frequently boasting of it; while they despise and condemn us, and all that are uncircumcised. Among innumerable other things they say, 'That circumcision is the cause why God hears their prayers, but overlooks and neglects ours, we being uncircumcised.'"§ A pernicious opinion, doubtless deserving the keenest censure. Nor was it without reason that Mr. Walter Marshall gave the following caution: "Beware of making an idol of baptism, and putting it in the place of Christ."||

---

* Christian Life, vol. iii. p. 236, 238. Edinb. 1754.
† Works, vol. iv. p. 355, 356.   ‡ Preservative, p. 160.
§ Apud Basnagium, Exercit. Hist. Crit. p. 591.
|| Myst. of Sanctificat. direct. xiii.

The necessity of this caution will farther appear, by the following extracts from Mr. Matthew Henry's Treatise on Baptism, lately published. When speaking about the ordinance itself, its obligation, and the privileges of baptized persons, he has the following remarkable words: " Such are the privileges which attend the ordinance, that if our Master had bid us do some great thing, would we not have done it, rather than come short of them? much more when he only saith unto us, *wash and be clean;* wash and be Christians.... The gospel contains, not only a doctrine but a covenant, and by baptism we are brought into that covenant.... Baptism wrests the keys of the heart out of the hands of the strong man armed, that the possession may be surrendered to him whose right it is.... The water of baptism is DESIGNED for our cleansing from the spots and defilements of the flesh.*.... In baptism our names are engraved upon the breast-plate of this great High Priest.... This then is the efficacy of baptism; it is putting the child's name into the gospel grant.... We are baptized into Christ's death; i. e. God doth in that ordinance, seal, confirm, and make over to us, ALL the benefits of the death of Christ.... Infant baptism speaks an hereditary relation to God, that comes to us by descent.... Baptism seals the promise of God's being to ME a God, and that is greatly encouraging; but *infant* baptism increases the encouragement, as it assures me of God being the God of my fathers, and the God of my infancy."†

---

* Whether Mr. Henry confines the cleansing efficacy of baptismal water to the pollution of actual sin, or whether he considers its admirably purifying virtue as extending to innate depravity also, is not very clear. If he includes both ideas, he attributes more to baptism than Ambrose did; who represents actual sin as taken away by baptism, but hereditary depravity, by *washing of the feet.* Apud Venem. Hist. Eccles. tom. iv. p. 122.

† Treatise on Bap. p. 12, 40, 42, 43, 59, 130, 170, 193, 201. Mr. Bradbury says, That your children shall be sanctified " from their mother's womb, upon their being received in this ordinance, is

Such are the language and sentiments of Mr. Henry, respecting the utility of baptism! Upon which I would here observe, that we should not have been much surprised, if after all this he had asserted, with the Council of Trent, that baptism "opens to every one of us the gate of heaven, which before, through sin, was shut;* or if he had maintained, with many of the ancient fathers, and with Mr. Dodwell of late, that it is by baptism the soul is rendered immortal.† But as our Brethren often refer us to the ancient rite of circumcision, and to the writings of the Talmud, for instruction about the proper subjects of baptism; so, who can tell, but the opinion of Jewish rabbies, concerning the utility of circumcision, may be of use to direct our enquiries in regard to that of baptism? and then, perhaps, we may have all Mr. Henry says confirmed in a few words. Well, you have their opinion, as expressed by one of them, in the following extract: "So great is the virtue of the precept concerning circumcision, that no circumcised person goes down to hell or to purgatory."‡—But what would our opposers have said, had a posthumous work of the late Dr. Gill, for instance, appeared, if it had been fraught with such high-flown expressions as those of Mr. Henry, concerning the vast importance and various utility of baptism? They would have spoken, there is reason to think, in some such manner as this: "The doctor might well plead for his beloved immersion with all his learning and zeal, while he imagined that such were its

---

making the blessing of the new covenant come by the will of men, and of the will of the flesh, and not of God. But 'be not deceived; God is not mocked.' Do not think so idly of those favours that come by his Spirit." Duty and Doctrine of Baptism, p. 19.

* Catechism of the Council of Trent, p. 175.

† "Many of the primitive fathers in the church explicitly maintained the natural mortality of the soul, which, according to them, was only exempt from dissolution by baptism." Dr. Blacklock's Paraclesis, p. 298.

‡ Apud Witsium, Miscel. Sac. tom. ii. exercit. xxi. § 9.

blessed effects; for, surely, he never could suppose that a *little* water was equal to these advantages. It appears, however, that while he bends his force to maintain a darling practice, he grossly intrenches on the honour of divine grace, for which he affected to be thought an able, and a warm defender; that same favourite plunging of his being represented by him, as little short of a substitute for electing love, atoning blood, and sanctifying influence. For, after having written many a long page against the Arminians, it now appears, that he considered the solemn dipping of a person in water, as putting his name into the gospel grant—as wresting the key of his heart out of the hands of Satan—as putting him into the covenant—as writing his name on the breast-plate of our great High Priest—as cleansing him from the defilements of the flesh—as making him a Christian—as sealing, confirming, and making over to him, all the benefits of our Lord's death—and, finally, as sealing the promise to him of God being to him a God. Admirable plunging, truly! Who, on such grounds, would not be dipped, aye, and dipped again? Had but the doctor soundly proved all these *ipse dixits*, we should no longer have objected against immersion, as being either dangerous or indecent; but have cheerfully submitted to it, though in the cold of Russia and in the presence of ten thousand spectators." —Such, I presume, would have been the remarks of our opponents upon it. The reader perceives, however, that it is not Dr. Gill, that it is not any *Baptist*, but Mr. Henry, who talks at this wonderful rate. So far, indeed, are the Baptists in general from attributing more efficacy to the divine appointment than their opposers do, that it is manifest, from the preceding quotations, their expectations from it are abundantly less. Nay, the very learned Buddeus, who was a person of immense reading, and well acquainted with their sentiments upon the subject, charges them with greatly depreciating the ordinance, in point of utility. His language is, "Their principal error consists in considering baptism as a *mere sign*, or symbol, and not as an *efficacious mean*, of obtaining grace."*

Though I am far from considering Mr. Henry as avowing the natural consequences of his own positions, and equally far from charging them upon him; yet I cannot but view the positions themselves as unwarrantable, extravagant, and of a dangerous tendency. They remind me of the virtues attributed, both by ancients and moderns, to the sign of the cross. Thus, for example, Cyprian: "In this sign of the cross, there is salvation to all who have this mark in their foreheads."†——Ambrose: "All prosperity is in one sign of Christ. He that sows in it, shall have a crop of eternal life; he that journies in it, shall arrive at heaven at last."‡—Once more: A Roman Catholic author teaches how the most ignorant persons may become true believers, by making the sign of the cross."§—Now I feel myself no more disposed to believe that baptism is the mean of conveying to infants, or to adults, all those capital blessings of which, among a thousand others, Mr. Henry speaks, than I do to receive this doctrine concerning the sign of the cross; or to adopt the notion of ancient Pagans, when they teach, that the use of salt and water purifies the heart; ‖ or to imagine, with some of the Roman Catholics, that baptized bells have a mighty efficacy to frighten away devils from their vicinity. ¶ Yet, calculated as the language and sentiments of Mr. Henry are, to excite in the breasts of ignorant persons a deceitful dependence on the baptismal rite, it is manifest from ecclesiastical records, that things of a similar kind, and often, if pos-

---

* Theolog. Dogmat. l. v. c. i. § 21.
† In Mr. Polhill's Discourse on Schism, p. 62.   ‡ Ibid.
§ In Mr. Clarkson's Pract. Div. of Papists, p. 118
‖ See Mr. Weston's Reject. of Christ. Miracles, p. 357.
¶ In Hist. of Popery, vol. i. p. 255.

sible, more grossly erroneous, have been asserted by Pædobaptists in every age, from the time of Cyprian to the present day. And, indeed, when it is considered, that an unwarrantable opinion about the necessity of baptism, seems to have laid the foundation for baptizing infants, it is no wonder that Pædobaptists, both ancient and modern, should frequently represent that practice as vastly important. To a dangerous mistake of this kind, the espousers of infant baptism are apparently more liable, than such as baptize those only who make a profession of repentance and faith; for no Baptist minister, without notoriously confronting the grand principle on which he proceeds in administering the solemn rite, can ever teach that baptism is a mean of producing those great effects which Mr. Henry and a thousand others have mentioned. To maintain, with a resolute perseverance, that the laws of Christ relating to a positive institution should be strictly observed, is one thing; to insist upon it, or to insinuate that baptism, to whomsoever administered, is the medium of procuring those blessings to which we advert, is another. The former is our indispensable duty; the latter is pregnant with dangerous consequences.

Reflect. IV. That baptism is of real importance to the church of Christ, and that believers, in a cheerful submission to it, have reason to expect a blessing, we firmly maintain; but that infant baptism is big with *much greater* advantages than adult baptism, as Mr. Henry insists, we cannot admit. His words are as follow: "That which shakes many in the doctrine of infant baptism, is the uselessness (as they apprehend) of the administration, and the mighty advantages which they fancy in adult baptism. But before they conclude thus, they would do well to answer Dr. Ford's proof of this truth, That there is *much more* advantage to be made, in order to sanctification, consolation, and several other ways, of the doctrine and practice of infant baptism, than of that doctrine and practice, which limits baptism to personal profession at years of discretion."*— Though there are few assertions in this respectable author's treatise, that have less pretence to evidence from scripture than the passage here produced, yet he speaks with an uncommon degree of assurance. This reminds me of what I have somewhere seen remarked concerning Bellarmine. That zealous cardinal, it has been observed, when he had the least appearance of reason, or of scripture, for what he was going to say, commonly assumed the most confident airs, and was pretty sure to introduce it with a *proculdubio.*† Now, though we cannot accept of Mr. Henry's challenge to answer Dr. Ford's arguments in defence of this bold position, because we do not know what they were; yet we will suggest a few thoughts against the position itself, and leave the reader to judge.

What then can be the reason of infant baptism being much more advantageous than adult baptism? Mr. Baxter himself shall answer for us, by giving a general negative to the bold assertion. "Upon my first serious study," says he, "I presently discerned, that infants were not capable of every benefit by baptism, as are the aged."‡—To be more particular. Is infant baptism of greater advantage than that of adults, because it is *more solemn?* If we appeal to Dr. Wall, his answer will be; "The baptism of an infant cannot have all the solemnity, which that of an adult person may have. The previous fasting and prayer, the penitential confessions, the zeal and humility and deep affection of the receiver, may be visible there, which cannot be in the case of an infant."§ — Is it because infants are *better capable* of reflecting on the nature, the design, the obligation of baptism, than adults; or because they are more proper

---

* Treatise on Baptism, p. 179.
† Antisozzo, p. 545.   ‡ Plain Scrip. Proof, Pref. p. 2.
§ Defence of Hist. Inf. Bap. p. 404.

subjects of ministerial exhortation? None will pretend the one or the other.—Peter speaks of baptized persons having *the answer of a good conscience towards God;* and Mr. T. Bradbury tells us, " that the benefit which arises from this ordinance is owing to the answer of a good conscience."* Is it, then, because infants have a *better conscience*, and make a *better answer,* than believing adults? That cannot be; for as the minds of mere infants are not capable of comparing their own conduct with the rule of duty, they have, properly speaking, no conscience at all. Our Brethren, indeed, frequently speak of *covenanting* with God in baptism: but mere infants are totally ignorant; and Mr. Baxter tells us, " It is a known rule in law, that *consensus non est ignorantis.*"† The language of common sense, as well as of casuists, is; " That infants are not capable of contracting,"‡ either with God or man.—Is it because the conscience of a person is more tenderly affected, by considering what was done for him, while *incapable* of moral agency; than by reflecting on what was done by him and upon him, with the full consent of his will? To suppose any such thing insults the understanding and feelings of mankind. For, as Bp. Sanderson observes, " In personal obligations, no man is bound without his own consent;—and a spiritual obligation, which is in the conscience, must necessarily be personal, as every one's conscience is his own; and such an obligation cannot pass into another person."§ Children, when arrived at years of discretion, may be told, that they covenanted

---

* Duty and Doct. of Bap. p. 9.

† Disputat. of Right to Sac. p. 9.

‡ Dr. Ames, De Conscientia, l. v. c. xlii. § 2. Limborch informs us, that Peter Auterius, an eminent minister among the Albigenses, was accused and condemned by the Court of Inquisition, for saying, among other things, "That water baptism performed by the church is of no use to children, because they do not *consent;* nay, they *weep.*" Hist. Inquisit. l. i. c. viii. p. 31.

§ De Juramenti Obligatione, prælect. iv. § 9.

with God when baptized in their infancy; but as engaging to be the Lord's is a personal thing, and as they could have no idea of such transaction at the time of their baptism, so they cannot have any recollection of it: consequently, their consciences cannot feel an obligation in that respect, as those of baptized believers may and ought.—The writer of these pages takes it for granted, that the register of a certain parish bears testimony to his having had something done for him in his infancy, called baptism, attended with all the formalities of proxies, of thanksgivings for his being then regenerated, and so on; but he knows nothing about it, except by report. Nay, though he had no doubts concerning the validity of his infant sprinkling till he was grown up; and, through divine goodness, he had abiding impressions upon his mind, relating to his best interests, from the earliest period of his present remembrance; yet he does not recollect a single instance of his conscience feeling itself under any obligation, in virtue of those transactions. He considers it as very strange, and quite unprecedented in the sacred volume, that any one should have a positive rite administered to him according to divine appointment —a rite which must not be repeated; and that the recipient, through the whole of his life, should entirely depend upon testimony for all that he knows about the fact. This, it is plain, was not the case of those infants that were circumcised. They had no occasion to enquire of a parent, of any senior, or of a register, whether the sign of circumcision had passed upon them; because, from the earliest dawn of reason, to the latest period of life, the unequivocal mark was retained in their own persons.

Farther: It is of importance here to observe, what our opposers themselves, I think, will allow, That the proper standard of usefulness, in regard to any positive rite, is, not our own fancies, or feelings, or reason, but divine revelation; and that even an unscriptural cere-

mony may, through the kindness of Providence, become the occasion of spiritual advantage to one or another. For, without intending an invidious comparison, and merely for the sake of argument, it may be asked; Whether it can be asserted with prudence, that none of the Papal superstitions were ever improved by Providence, as occasions of lasting spiritual benefit to any one? But yet, as Mr. Stoddart observes, " If men act according to their own humours and fancies, and do not keep in the way of obedience, it is presumption to expect God's blessing. ' In vain do they worship me, teaching for doctrines the commandments of men.'"* I will add, in the words of that great man, Mr. Jonath. Edwards; " Though we are to eye the providence of God, and not disregard his works, yet to interpret them to a sense, or apply them to a use, inconsistent with the scope of the word of God, is a misconstruction and misapplication of them. God has not given us his providence, but his word, to be our governing rule. God is sovereign in his dispensations of providence. He bestowed the blessing on Jacob, even when he had a lie in his mouth: he was pleased to meet with Solomon, and make known himself to him, and bless him in an extraordinary manner, while he was worshipping in a high place: he met with Saul, when in a course of violent opposition to him, and out of the way of his duty to the highest degree, going to Damascus to persecute Christ; and even then bestowed the greatest blessing upon him, that perhaps ever was bestowed on a mere man. The conduct of divine Providence, with its reasons, is too little understood by us, to be improved as our rule."†
Candid and cautious is the following declaration of Dr. Owen: " I do not know how far God may accept of churches in a very corrupt state, and of worship much

---

* In Mr. Jonath. Edward's Enquiry into Qualif. for Communion, p. 117.

† Ut supra, p. 131.

depraved, until they have new means for their reformation. Nor will I make any judgment of persons, as unto their eternal condition, who walk in churches so corrupted, and in the performance of worship so depraved."* Farther: Were the dupes of Papal superstition, or our Brethren of the English Establishment asked, what advantage they have, in comparison with us Dissenters; they, very likely, would answer with Paul in another case, " Much, every way." They would also, no doubt, mention a variety of particulars, to prove that their forms and rites are far better adapted to exercise devotional dispositions; and so to promote sanctification, consolation, and so on, than those of Dissenters. But would Mr. Henry have considered such pretences as any kind of proof, that those forms and ceremonies are warranted of God? No, he would have been ready to say, " Show us your authority for them in our only rule of religious worship, and then tell us how useful they are."

These things being observed, we add; If infant baptism be so very useful, the apostles must have known it as well, and have esteemed it as highly, as our author himself. But have they *acted* as if they thus knew and esteemed it? Their immortal writings make a considerable volume; and in that heavenly volume they have recorded their own faith and their own practice. Conscious of being amanuenses to the Spirit of wisdom, they intended that sacred book should be considered as a body of doctrine and a complete code of law for the church in every succeeding age. This being the case, it is quite natural to think, that infant baptism should make a capital figure in such a system of theological doctrine, of spiritual privilege, and of religious duty, if they had known and viewed it in that very advantageous point of light which Mr. Henry did. That they expressly mention the baptism of adults, is allowed by all; and that their baptism is represented in the New Testament as

* Enquiry into the Orig. of Churches, p. 168.

instructive and useful, is denied by few: consequently, if the baptism of infants be *much more* adapted to promote sanctification and consolation than the baptism of those who profess faith, it is but reasonable to suppose, that the apostles would insist upon it in a degree proportional to its greater importance. But is it a fact, that Pædobaptism itself, and the benefits resulting from it, make such a conspicuous figure in the apostolic writings? That the apostles mention baptism, and inform us of great numbers who were baptized, are facts; but where do they mention infant baptism? That they mention the ordinance as containing matter of instruction, motives to holiness, and grounds of exhortation, in reference to baptized believers, is a fact;* but where is Pædobaptism represented by them, as containing any of these things, with regard to children when they grow up? That they mention baptism as affording grounds of reproof to disorderly professors, is a fact;† but where do they mention Pædobaptism as ministering reproof to Christian parents for neglecting the education of their children? That they exhort and caution believing parents respecting their children, is a fact; but where do they fetch their motives from infant baptism? That they exhort and charge children to be dutiful to their parents, is also a fact; but where do they remind children of their filial obligations being enforced by having been baptized in their infancy, or exhort them on that ground? Yet, had Pædobaptism been then practised, and had it been attended with such vast advantages as our author pretends, it might, perhaps, have been as pertinently urged as the latter part of the fifth command, on account of its being more precisely agreeable to the gospel dispensation.‡ Mr. Henry, it is plain, did not fail to exhort both parents and children on the ground

---

* Rom. vi. 1—5; 1 Cor. i. 12—16, and xv. 29; Col. ii. 12; 1 Pet. iii. 21.

† 1 Cor. i. 12—16.   ‡ See Eph. vi. 1, 2, 3.

of infant baptism. No, he treats it as a capital source of motives, by which to enforce the performance of both parental and filial duty, though the apostles have not said a word about it in any of their exhortations. Candour forbids my supposing, that he thought himself, either more wise in the choice of his arguments, or more zealous in the application of them to practical purposes, than those ambassadors of Christ: but yet every one may see a remarkable difference between their conduct and his, in this respect; which difference must have had an adequate cause. I cannot help thinking, therefore, that either the inspired writers knew nothing at all of Pædobaptism, or had a very mean opinion of it; for it seems unaccountably strange, that they should all have approved the practice, and yet all agree, on such a variety of occasions, in saying nothing about it. But supposing it was practised by them, and that they considered it as *much more* advantageous than the baptism of believers, their conduct is yet more amazingly strange; because they expressly apply the latter to practical purposes, though entirely silent about the former:—an example this, which our opponents are not inclined to imitate. Peruse the writings of modern Pædobaptists, and you plainly perceive the advantages resulting from baptism, almost entirely confined to that of infants. Consult the apostolic records, and you find them all connected with the baptism of adults. We may now venture an appeal to the reader, whether he would not suspect any unknown author of being a Baptist, were he to find him treating on all the various topics lately enumerated, and yet perceive that he is quite silent about infant baptism?

The following passages from learned Pædobaptists, *mutatis mutandis*, will here apply in all their force. Anonymous: "The signing one's self with the cross hath neither command nor example in scripture, nor any promise of any special grace or benefit, to be thereupon conferred; therefore, there is no reason to expect any such extraordinary virtues or assistance from using the same."*——Mr. Chillingworth: "Give me leave to wonder—that so great a part of the New Testament should be employed about antichrist, and so little, and indeed none at all, about the vicar of Christ."†—— Dr. Cave: "The places [of scripture] usually alleged to make good their claim [of Papal supremacy,] are so far-fetched, and so little to their purpose, that they contain alone a strong presumption against them; and their own authors sometimes speak of them with great distrust. Here, if any where, sure, we may safely argue, without daring to prescribe rules to the most High, That in a matter of so great moment, had it been designed, it would have been most explicitly delivered, and solemnly inculcated." ‡—— Bishop Stratford: "Were it so good and profitable to invoke the saints, as the Council of Trent teaches, it is strange that so great a lover of mankind as St. Paul, when he so frequently commands us to pray, and hath left us so many directions concerning prayer, should wholly forget to teach us this lesson. Can it be supposed a worship so pleasing to God, when God hath not given us the least intimation in his word that it is so? For that it hath no foundation in scripture we may be assured, when so great a man as cardinal Perron acknowledges, that neither precept nor example is there to be found for it; and when other learned doctors of that church, not only confess the same, but also give us several reasons why no mention is made of it, either in the Old or New Testament."§——Turrettinus: "The invocation of saints has neither precept, nor promise,

---

* History of Popery, vol. i. p. 110.
† Relig. of Protest. p. 450.
‡ Preservative against Popery, title i. p. 137.
§ Preserv. against Popery, title i. p. 28.

nor example in scripture on which it rests; and, therefore, it is no other than vicious and condemnable will-worship. The invocation of God is abundantly urged; but the invocation of creatures is no where mentioned."*——— Chemnitius: "There is not in all the holy scripture any passage which teaches the invocation of saints; no command is found that requires departed saints to be invoked; there is no promise that such invocation shall be acceptable to God, and efficacious; that is, heard, so as to obtain grace and assistance; there is no example in scripture of departed saints being invoked by godly persons; there is no threatening in scripture, nor any example of punishment, against them who do not invocate the saints."†———Once more: Archbishop Tillotson says: "Does either our Saviour, or his apostles, in all their particular directions concerning prayer—give the least intimation of praying to the virgin Mary, or making use of her mediation? And can any man believe, that if this had been the practice of the church from the beginning, our Saviour and his apostles would have been so silent about so considerable a part of religion? insomuch that, in all the epistles of the apostles, I do not remember that her name is so much as once mentioned. And yet the worship of her is at this day, in the church of Rome, and hath been so for several ages, a main part of their public worship;—in which it is usual with them to say ten *Ave Maries* for one *Pater Noster;* that is, for one prayer they make to almighty God, they make ten addresses to the blessed virgin . . . . He that considers this, and had never seen the Bible, would be apt to think, that there had been more said concerning her in scripture, than either concerning God or our blessed Saviour; and that the New Testament were full from one end to the other of precepts and exhortations to the

---

* Institut. loc. xi. quæst. vii. § 12.
† Exam. Concil Trident, p. 611.

worshipping of her: and yet, when all is done, I challenge any man to show me so much as one sentence in the whole Bible that sounds that way; and there is as little in the Christian writers of the first three hundred years."*—*Ten* addresses to the virgin Mary for *one* to the divine Majesty, says our learned author. So we may say, *ten*, or rather a *hundred* infants are sprinkled in these kingdoms, for *one* person that is immersed on a profession of faith; and, to our great discouragement, Mr. Henry tells us, that when an adult is baptized on such profession, it is far from being so advantageous to him, as pouring or sprinkling is to an infant. Now, "he that considers this, and had never seen the Bible, would be apt to think, that there had been more said concerning [Pædobaptism] in scripture, than [about the baptism of adults;] and that the New Testament was full, from one end to the other, of precepts and exhortations to the [practice of infant sprinkling:] and yet when all is done, I challenge any man to show me one sentence in the whole Bible," by which it is either enjoined or exemplified. How much, alas, is our complaint like that of Tillotson, "Ten Ave Maries for one Pater Noster!"

Once more: Mr. Peirce and Dr. Priestley tell us, that various and great advantages would probably attend the revival of infant communion among us, and labour to restore the practice in this country from that consideration. Were Mr. Henry now living, we might, therefore, venture to return his challenge, by saying; Let him answer the arguments produced by Mr. Peirce in favour of that hypothesis, without subverting his own for the utility of infant baptism: for it is plain to us, that most of the principles on which he proceeds to prove the benefits of Pædobaptism, would equally apply to infant communion.—In a word; either the baptism of infants has been sadly misrepresented by the generality

---

* Preservative against Popery, title iii. p. 233.

of those who have pleaded for it, since the time of Cyprian; or it is calculated to do immense mischief to the souls of men, by leading persons to imagine, that they were born again, cleansed from sin, interested in all the benefits of our Lord's death, and made heirs of heaven, by what was done for them while destitute of reason—done for them, in many cases, by ungodly priests and profligate sponsors. For, as Dr. Owen has well observed, the father of lies himself could not easily have invented a more deadly poison for the souls of sinners; as they are taught, by these unscriptural dogmas, to rest satisfied with a supposed regeneration by their baptism.*

---

* Theologoumena, l. vi. c. v. § 3. Brem.

END OF VOL. I.

A Biographical Sketch of Abraham Booth
(1734-1806)

by

John Franklin Jones

A BIOGRAPHICAL SKETCH OF ABRAHAM BOOTH (1734-1806)

Abraham Booth — General-turned-Particular Baptist, teacher, pastor, author — was born May 20, 1734 at Blackwell, in Derbyshire, England. In the first year of his life, his parents removed from Blackwell to Annesley Woodhouse, Nottinghamshire. The oldest of a family of numerous children, Abraham assisted his father in his agricultural concerns well into his teenage years. Though his circumstances prevented a formal education, his father taught the boy to read, and a robust mind early appeared in him. He was almost entirely self-taught in writing and arithmetic and pursued his studies avidly during his leisure hours ("Memoir"). Brought up with a reverence for the national establishment of the Church of England, at about ten years of age he became acquainted with the dissenters via the preaching of some plain and illiterate General (or Arminian) Baptists teachers who occasionally visited his neighborhood. Their influence first awakened Booth to a concern about salvation, and he applied for admission to the General Baptists. He was baptized by Francis Smith at Barton in 1755 at about age twenty-one ("Memoir").

He pursued stocking-making from age sixteen to twenty-four. At twenty-four, he married Miss Elizabeth Bowmar, the daughter of a neighboring farmer; they were married more than forty years. Assisted by Mrs. Booth, he opened a school at Sutton Ashfield to instruct youth. Mrs. Booth taught needle-work to the female pupils ("Memoir").

John Franklin Jones

The General Baptists recognized his abilities and occasionally invited him to preach. He soon became a leader among them and in their neighboring districts. Upon their organizing their churches and appointing pastors over them in 1760, Booth became superintendent of the church at Kirby-Woodhouse. He labored among them successfully for several years but declined to accept the office of pastor ("Memoir").

Booth strenuously advocated the General Baptist-Armenian doctrine of the universality of divine grace and published same in a poem, "Absolute Predestination," in his twentieth year. In the poem, he reviled election and particular redemption ("Memoir"). Later, he wrote of the poem:

I thought it my duty in a particular manner to bear a public testimony to that important part of revealed truth, having in my younger years greatly opposed it, in a poem on "Absolute predestination" which poem if considered in a critical light is despicable, if in a theological view, detestable, as it is an impotent attack on the honor of divine grace in regard to its glorious freeness, and a bold opposition to the sovereignty of God. So I now consider it and as such I here renounce it (Matrunola, 2).

His convictions underwent such a change, though, that he could no longer maintain his relationship with the General Baptists. Regarding the deep convictions he came to hold, he later wrote:

The doctrine of sovereign, distinguishing grace, as commonly and justly stated by Calvinists, it must be acknowledged, is too generally exploded. This the writer knows by experience, to his grief and shame. Through the ignorance of his mind, the pride of his heart, and the prejudice of his education, he, in his younger years, often opposed it with much warmth, though with no small weakness; but after an impartial inquiry, and many prayers, he found reason to alter his judgment; he found it to be the doctrine of the Bible, and a dictate of the unerring Spirit. Thus patronized, he received

A Biographical Sketch of Abraham Booth

the once obnoxious sentiment, under a full conviction of its being a divine truth ("Memoir").

After many cordial and lengthy discussions with them upon his now-firm convictions, he withdrew from the General Baptist ranks ("Memoir") in 1765 (Armitage). His departing remarks upon the occasion were from the parable of the unjust steward. He said: "Fraud and concealment of various kinds may obtain the favor of men, but, when favor is gained by these means, he who gains it and those who grant it, are chargeable with injustice peculiarly censurable" (Matrunola).

Booth would not obtain favor by such fraud and concealment.

Shortly after his withdrawal from the Arminians, Booth procured Bore's Hall, at Sutton Ashfield, and gathered a small group of Calvinistic or Particular Baptists. At Sutton Ashfield, and afterwards, at Nottingham and Chesterfield, where he preached alternate Sundays, he delivered a series of discourses from which came his excellent work, *The Reign of Grace* (1768). That work indicated both the bent of his thoughts at the time and the subjects of his preaching--the reign of divine grace in its nature and properties in election, effectual calling, pardon of sin, justification, adoption, sanctification, perseverance, and eternal glory ("Memoir").

He showed the manuscript to some friends. One of them showed it to Henry Venn, an evangelical clergyman well known for his popular work, *The Complete Duty of Man*. Venn recommended that Booth publish the work and Venn himself wrote a recommendatory preface to it. Booth published the work in April 1768 ("Memoir").

The Particular Baptist Church in Little Prescot Street, Goodman's Fields, London, needed a pastor and contacted Booth. He accepted their call October 1, 1768 and was ordained to that position February 16, 1769. Thereupon he publicly delivered a detailed confession of his faith, which confession was afterwards printed ("Memoir").

Booth moved to London to begin a new era in one of the most respectable among the churches of the English dissenters, and he well-discharged his pastoral duties. Taking full advantage of the opportunities to satisfy his insatiable thirst after learning, he acquired the assistance of a former Roman Catholic priest, an eminent classical scholar, and studied Latin and Greek ("Memoir").

His study of Latin provided the ability to examine the erudite professors of the foreign universities--Witsius, Turretine, Stapferus, Vitringa, and Venema. He examined the ecclesiastical historians--Dupin, Cave, Bingham, Venema, Spanheim. He studied the Magdeburg Centuriators, Lewis, Jennings, Reland, Spencer, Ikenius, Carpzovius, Fabricius of Hamburgh, and others on Jewish Antiquities. He studied English writers, especially John Owen. To Owen he acknowledged great obligation. Excepting Scripture, he quoted Owen more often than any ("Memoir").

In 1770, only a year after his ordination, Booth published *The Death of Legal Hope, the Life of Evangelical Obedience, in an Essay on Gal. 2:19*. The essay demonstrated that grace relaxes no obligations to holiness but produces godliness. That grace denies the moral law as a rule of life to believers--a pernicious sentiment--was rampant in England at the period, and Booth continually opposed the idea both in his writings and his pastoral ministry ("Memoir").

A challenge to the deity of Christ delivering many respectable, established church clergy to the Socinians and their anti-Trinitarian theology occurred about the time Booth came to London. In 1777, Booth presented an improved, revised, corrected, and fortified new edition of *The Deity of Jesus Christ, essential to the Christian Religion*, originally penned in French by James Abaddie, dean of Killaloe in Ireland ("Memoir").

In 1778, he published *An Apology for the Baptists, in Which They Are Vindicated from the Imputation of Laying an Unwarrantable Stress on the Ordinance of Baptism*. This work opposed the more or less prevalent principle of mixed communion introduced to the English churches about the middle of the seventeenth century. Into this book Booth incorporated a series of letters he had written at the request from a fellow minister whose own convictions also opposed the practice ("Memoir").

In 1784, he defended the practice of baptism in his *Pœdobaptism Examined, on the Principles, Concessions, and Reasonings of the Most Learned Pœdobaptists*. Booth took up the Pædobaptists' principles, facts, interpretations of Scripture, and concessions, met them upon their own grounds, and thoroughly refuted them. In 1787, he published a second edition, which he enlarged with additional material ("Memoir"). His *Pœdobaptism Examined* was "never fairly answered" (Armitage, 570).

The *Essay on the Kingdom of Christ*, published in 1788, showed how the kingdom of Christ in its nature so differed from the kingdom of David as to disallow using events occurring under the Mosaic economy being applied to the Christian church. The Christian church differs in its nature, origin, subjects, means of establishment and support, laws by which it is governed, immunities, riches, and honors from the kingdom. Those differences explain and necessitate its dissent from the national establishment and all political efforts to impeach Christ's dominion in His own kingdom ("Memoir").

First appearing in 1796 and followed by a second edition in 1800, *Glad Tidings to Perishing Sinners; or, The Genuine Gospel, a Complete Warrant for the Ungodly to Believe in Jesus Christ* addressed the issue of the persons to whom the Gospel is to be preached and their obligation thereto ("Memoir").

The Amen to Social Prayer, Illustrated and Improved (1800) was a sermon previously delivered at a monthly meeting of Particular Baptist ministers belonging to the Particular Baptist denomination. A series by different ministers addressed the Lord's prayer, and Booth treated the concluding word of the prayer, "Amen." The sermon demanded some extrication from Booth. In *Essay on the Kingdom of Christ*, Booth had solemnly protested the practice of taking a single word or phrase of a text for preaching. Despite his condemnation that the practice disgraced the pulpit and profaned the sacred ministry, on this occasion he admirably met his challenge ("Memoir").

Approaching seventy years of age but with undiminished mental powers, Booth discoursed at one of the monthly meetings of his Baptist brethren on the subject of divine justice. Soon afterwards in 1803, he published the sermon as *Divine Justice Essential to the Divine Character* ("Memoir").

In the last year of his life--1805--he published *Pastoral Cautions*. This work summarized the substance of twenty years of pulpit ministry. He delivered it as a charge at the ordination of Thomas Hopkins as pastor of the Baptist Church in Eagle Street, Red Lion Square, London. Booth had now completed fifty years of ministry, more than thirty-five as pastor of the church in Prescot Street. He cautioned the ministers' behavior in the house of God, in their families, and in the world. He exhorted them to exemplify the character of the Christian pastor and adorn the high, honorable office in which they are placed. Booth's sermon expressed the profitable experience of his maturing years ("Memoir").

Several "Funeral Sermons" and "Addresses" reflect Booth's occupation with the great truths of the Bible--the uncertainty of life, the certainty of death, the necessity of being prepared for death, the folly of taking lightly the interests of the immortal soul and neglecting everlasting peace, and the Gospel as alone giving effectual relief to a sinner under the dread of death and the judgment. The messages contain little regarding the decedents' character. Nor do they contain compliments to surviving relatives ("Memoir").

Though generally blessed with good health, Booth became increasingly afflicted with asthma, especially during the

A Biographical Sketch of Abraham Booth

winter months. Some months before his death and en route home from a meeting of his ministering brethren in the city, he suddenly took ill. Henceforth he largely retired from public labors and demonstrated to his oft-calling friends that his mind retained all its clarity, calmness, and serenity. His uniform answer to their inquiries was "I have no fears about my state. The gospel bears my spirit up. A faithful and unchanging God lays the foundation of my hope in oaths, and promises, and blood" ("Memoir").

The several months preceding his death were occupied with revising and completing *An Essay on the Love of God to His Chosen People and A Conduct Formed under the Influence of Evangelical Truth*. He committed them to a friend for publication ("Memoir").

A few days prior to his death, he gave the same friend the manuscript for *Thoughts on Dr. Edward Williams's Hypothesis Relative to the Origin of Moral Evil*. Notwithstanding the difficulty of the metaphysical topic, Booth's treatment of it demonstrated his mental competence to grapple with the subject at such a late stage in his life. He carefully examined William's theory and exposed its fallaciousness. Regarding his position upon the subject, Booth wrote:

> I have no opinion upon the subject; nor dare I form conjectures about it. . . Of this, however, I have no doubt, that the existence and prevalence of moral evil in the rational creation, are completely consistent with all the perfections of God, and with all his eternal decrees; and that under the management of Supreme Wisdom, when the great system of Providence respecting both angels and men is finished, the conduct of God in reference to evil, both moral and natural, will be to the praise of his glory, in the eyes of all holy creatures ("Memoir").

This declining period left many testimonies to the steadfastness of his faith and hope and the importance he attached to the doctrines he had published throughout his life. Among those testimonies: "I now live," said he, "upon what I have been teaching others" ("Memoir").

To an esteemed friend on the Saturday preceding his death, he communicated his last instructions with a testimony, "I am peaceful but not elevated." To the son of the same gentleman the following day, he replied to the inquiry regarding his health and added:

> Young man, think of your soul; if you lose that, you lose all. Be not half a Christian. Some people have just religion enough to make them miserable; not enough to make them happy. The ways of religion are good ways. I have found them such these sixty years ("Memoir").

On the Lord's day prior to his death, he affectionately spoke to one and then to another of his friends who visited him. To one he said, "But a little while and I shall be with your dear father and mother." To another, "I have often borne you on my heart before the Lord; now you need to pray for me, and you must pray for yourself." To a third, referring to a well-known Socinian minister, he solemnly remarked, "Beware of _____'s sentiments" ("Memoir").

He spent the evening with his endeared family. Two of his daughters and their husbands continued with him. One of the latter led a time of family worship prior to their departure, and the dying Booth joined the time. Without struggle or sigh, he died the next day at age seventy-one ("Memoir").

The Little Prescot Street church records contain many references to its loving regard for the pastor of thirty-seven years. A marble tablet displays its public appreciation for Booth ("Memoir").

A Biographical Sketch of Abraham Booth

Booth and William Newman of Bow attempted to revive a Baptist education society organized earlier. Posthumously, the actions were bolstered by wealthy members of his church to become Stepney Academy in 1810 and later, Regent's Park College. From the outset, he was a supporter, though lesser known than others, of the Particular Baptist Society for Propagating the Gospel among the Heathen, formed at Kettering in 1792. In the 1790s, Booth and his church joined the protest of the African slave trade (Matrunola, 10).

Bibliography

ARMITAGE, THOMAS. —*A History of the Baptists; Traced by their Vital Principles and Practices, from the Time of Our Lord and Saviour Jesus Christ to the Year 1886*. With an introduction by J. L. M. Curry. New York: Bryan, Taylor, & Co., 1887, 569-70.

MATRUNOLA, K.F.T. —*A Brief Account of the Life and Labours of Abraham Booth 1734-1806*. Rushden Northamptonshire, England: Fauconberg, 1981.

"Memoir." In *The Reign of Grace, from the Rise to its Consummation*, by ABRAHAM BOOTH. With an introductory essay by Thomas Chalmers. Corrected ed. Grand Rapids: Eerdmans, 1949.

BY JOHN FRANKLIN JONES
CORDOVA, TENNESSEE
JULY 2004

THE BAPTIST STANDARD BEARER, INC.

a non-profit, tax-exempt corporation
committed to the Publication & Preservation
of the Baptist Heritage.

CURRENT TITLES AVAILABLE IN
THE BAPTIST *DISTINCTIVES* SERIES

KIFFIN, WILLIAM	A Sober Discourse of Right to Church-Communion. Wherein is proved by Scripture, the Example of the Primitive Times, and the Practice of All that have Professed the Christian Religion: That no Unbaptized person may be Regularly admitted to the Lord's Supper. (London: George Larkin, 1681).
KINGHORN, JOSEPH	Baptism, A Term of Communion. (Norwich: Bacon, Kinnebrook, and Co., 1816)
KINGHORN, JOSEPH	A Defense of "Baptism, A Term of Communion". In Answer To Robert Hall's Reply. (Norwich: Wilkin and Youngman, 1820).
GILL, JOHN	Gospel Baptism. A Collection of Sermons, Tracts, etc., on Scriptural Authority, the Nature of the New Testament Church and the Ordinance of Baptism by John Gill. (Paris, AR: The Baptist Standard Bearer, Inc., 2006).

CARSON, ALEXANDER	Ecclesiastical Polity of the New Testament. (Dublin: William Carson, 1856).
BOOTH, ABRAHAM	A Defense of the Baptists. A Declaration and Vindication of Three Historically Distinctive Baptist Principles. Compiled and Set Forth in the Republication of Three Books. Revised edition. (Paris, AR: The Baptist Standard Bearer, Inc., 2006).
BOOTH, ABRAHAM	Paedobaptism Examined on the Principles, Concessions, and Reasonings of the Most Learned Paedobaptists. With Replies to the Arguments and Objections of Dr. Williams and Mr. Peter Edwards. 3 volumes. (London: Ebenezer Palmer, 1829).
CARROLL, B. H.	*Ecclesia* - The Church. With an Appendix. (Louisville: Baptist Book Concern, 1903).
CHRISTIAN, JOHN T.	Immersion, The Act of Christian Baptism. (Louisville: Baptist Book Concern, 1891).
FROST, J. M.	Pedobaptism: Is It From Heaven Or Of Men? (Philadelphia: American Baptist Publication Society, 1875).
FULLER, RICHARD	Baptism, and the Terms of Communion; An Argument. (Charleston, SC: Southern Baptist Publication Society, 1854).
GRAVES, J. R.	Tri-Lemma: or, Death By Three Horns. The Presbyterian General Assembly Not Able To Decide This Question: "Is Baptism In The Romish Church Valid?" 1st Edition.

	(Nashville: Southwestern Publishing House, 1861).
MELL, P.H.	Baptism In Its Mode and Subjects. (Charleston, SC: Southern Baptist Publications Society, 1853).
JETER, JEREMIAH B.	Baptist Principles Reset. Consisting of Articles on Distinctive Baptist Principles by Various Authors. With an Appendix. (Richmond: The Religious Herald Co., 1902).
PENDLETON, J.M.	Distinctive Principles of Baptists. (Philadelphia: American Baptist Publication Society, 1882).
THOMAS, JESSE B.	The Church and the Kingdom. A New Testament Study. (Louisville: Baptist Book Concern, 1914).
WALLER, JOHN L.	Open Communion Shown to be Unscriptural & Deleterious. With an introductory essay by Dr. D. R. Campbell and an Appendix. (Louisville: Baptist Book Concern, 1859).

For a complete list of current authors/titles, visit our internet site at:
www.standardbearer.org
or write us at:

he Baptist Standard Bearer, Inc.

NUMBER ONE IRON OAKS DRIVE • PARIS, ARKANSAS 72855

TEL # 479-963-3831   *FAX # 479-963-8083*
EMAIL: Baptist@centurytel.net   *http://www.standardbearer.org*

Thou hast given a standard to them that fear thee; that it may be displayed because of the truth. — Psalm 60:4

www.ingramcontent.com/pod-product-compliance
Lightning Source LLC
Chambersburg PA
CBHW022006300426
44117CB00005B/51